THE OFFICIAL
Formula 1™
SEASON REVIEW 2006
FOREWORD BY BERNIE ECCLESTONE

F1 Formula 1 (and device), F1, Formula One, FIA Formula One
World Championship (and device) and Grand Prix are
trademarks of Formula One Licensing B.V. a Formula One
Group Company and are used under licence from Formula
One Administration Limited, a Formula One Group Company.

Published in November 2006

A catalogue record for this book is available
from the British Library

ISBN 1 84425 345 7

Library of Congress control no. 2006924150

Editor Bruce Jones
Managing Editor Steve Rendle

Design Lee Parsons, Richard Parsons

Contributors Adam Cooper, Tony Dodgins

Photographs All by LAT (Steven Tee, Lorenzo Bellanca,
Charles Coates, Michael Cooper, Glenn Dunbar,
Steve Etherington, Andrew Ferraro, Thomas Butler
and Tom Russo)
Operations Manager LAT Tim Wright
Director LAT Peter Higham

Technical illustrations Paul Laguette
www.studiopdesign.com
Illustrations Alan Eldridge

Editorial Director Matt Bishop
Publisher Jonathan Haines
Publishing Directors Andrew Golby, Mark Hughes

**Published by Haynes Publishing
in association with Haymarket Magazines Limited
(a division of the Haymarket Publishing Group Limited)**

Haynes Publishing, Sparkford, Yeovil,
Somerset BA22 7JJ, UK
Tel: +44 (0) 1963 442030
Fax: +44 (0) 1963 440001
E-mail: sales@haynes.co.uk
Website: www.haynes.co.uk

Haymarket Magazines Limited, Teddington Studios, Broom
Road, Teddington, Middlesex TW11 9BE, UK
Tel: +44 (0) 208 267 5000
Fax: +44 (0) 208 267 5022
E-mail: F1Review@haynet.com
Website: www.haymarketgroup.com

Printed and bound by J. H. Haynes & Co. Ltd,
Sparkford, Yeovil, Somerset BA22 7JJ, UK

CONTENTS

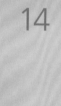

FOREWORD 5

Bernie Ecclestone looks back at
a World Championship packed
with action and intrigue as
Michael Schumacher fought
Fernando Alonso for the title
then brought his astonishing
racing career to a close

THE MAN 6

Having shattered every Formula One
record in the book and gathered
seven world titles, Michael
Schumacher has brought his driving
career to an end. Here is a tribute to
the most illustrious career of all

THE YEAR 10

It was a battle royal between Ferrari
and Renault and Michael Schumacher
and Fernando Alonso, but we look
too at how Super Aguri Racing started
from scratch and yet didn't disgrace
themselves, as well as how the 2006
rule changes affected the way the
teams went racing

THE DRIVERS 14

A specially chosen panel of former
Formula One World Champions,
race winners and stars rank the
drivers, who then tell us how the
2006 season really was for them

THE TEAMS 32

How each of the 11 teams fared through 2006, analysing how their campaigns shaped up or fell apart, and how their cars evolved in their quest to be competitive, with insight from the technical directors – and world-class technical graphics

THE RACES 70

The in-depth story of every one of the World Championship's 18 grands prix, augmented by the inside line from the drivers and the team personnel at the heart of the action along with the news of the day

THE STATISTICS 252

The World Championship table, showing on a race-by-race basis who finished where, along with three pages packed with facts and stats, and how the current drivers compare with the stars of yesteryear in the all-time rankings for every factor including wins, pole positions, race starts, fastest laps and points scored

51 GRAN PREMIO DE ESPAÑA TELEFONICA

CIRCUIT DE CATALUNYA
11-12-13 MAY 2007*

Barcelona

INTERNATIONAL HOTLINE +34 93 571 97 71 www.circuitcat.com

2003 BEST ORGANIZATION FOM
GRAN PREMIO DE ESPAÑA DE F1

Circuit de Catalunya

FOREWORD

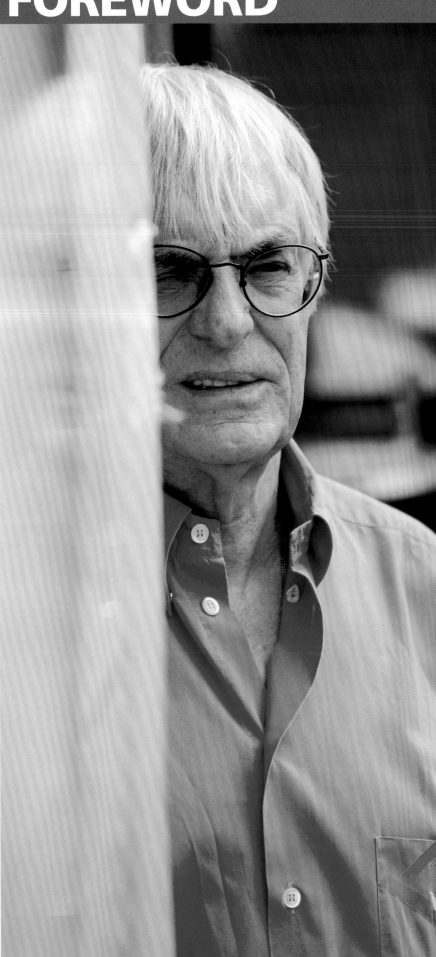

This season started off a little bit quietly, and it looked like maybe it was going to be a terrible year, with Alonso running away with everything. But then everybody got fired up and it was all a bit different. There were so many incidents that happened, and I'm happy with the way the year finished.

Michael really wanted to win the World Championship. I think this year he's been a lot more relaxed. He's been thinking: 'If I win the championship, great, but if I don't, that's how it is. I've won seven.' As for Monaco, when you're like he is, so competitive, and want to win, that's what's going to happen. He's going to do all the things he can to win – whatever it takes. I suppose all of us in a funny way try to cut some corners, and get an advantage wherever it's possible to get one.

I think the important thing for Michael was to finish the way he did in Brazil. It was better than being on pole and getting in the lead. Nobody would have taken any notice, and they would have all just been waiting for Alonso to stop! This way he went off on a super high. He did an awful lot of good for himself in his last race.

Fernando reminds me of Alain Prost. He does exactly what he has to do to get the job done. He doesn't overdo things. If he has to be second, he'll be second. If he has to win, he'll win. Kimi was well let down. He did a good job – McLaren did a bad job! The Polish kid, Robert Kubica, has also done very well. It's a pity that one or two of the other new stars weren't in better machinery, so we could really see their potential.

I was very happy with the new qualifying system, although it was a bit of a fight to get people to agree with it. In the end, it worked out well. We had lots of political stuff earlier in the year, but it wasn't really a worry because I knew what the result was going to be! It was a case of just having to go through the ball play to get there. Everybody's happy, they've all said what they've wanted to say. It's all settled down now.

Next year should be good. Somebody is going to have to put a marker down, and I think in the end you're going to find that there are going to be some new superstars coming out of the woodwork. I can't wait!

Meanwhile, I hope you enjoy this book as the perfect souvenir of a great season.

BERNIE ECCLESTONE

Michael Schumacher's announcement at the Italian Grand Prix in September that he was to retire at the end of the year was, without a doubt, the most dramatic moment of the 2006 season.

The news hardly came as a surprise to the sport's insiders, since in the days and weeks leading up to the meeting at Monza retirement seemed to be the only logical outcome. How else to explain where McLaren's Kimi Räikkönen was going in 2007, or why Michael's team-mate Felipe Massa was so confident that his future was bright? Three into two did not go.

And yet when an emotional Michael faced the live TV cameras for the unilateral interviews, right after stepping off the podium, his carefully chosen words still had a huge impact. We finally had to accept that the man who has been the driver to beat since the death of Ayrton Senna in 1994 was finally going, leaving behind him a series of records that will surely never be approached, never mind broken.

The sheer length of Michael's career goes some way to explaining his remarkable assault on the record books, although the man himself remains bemused by the world's ongoing interest in his statistics. When he finally stopped after Brazil, he was just six races shy of

Riccardo Patrese's mark for all-time starts – the one record that he didn't quite claim as his own. The irony is that when he was injured in 1999, Michael missed precisely six races. But then some analysts don't actually credit him with being present at the 1996 French GP, when he retired on the warm-up lap…

With due respect to Patrese, his 1993 Benetton team-mate, Michael made rather better use of a career that was spread across 16 seasons. He has won more championships, scored more victories, taken more pole positions, set more fastest laps and accumulated more points than any other driver in history.

The hoary old question of how he compares with the greats of the past long ago became irrelevant. Of course, it's impossible to compare eras, and some of the biggest names were cut down in their prime and thus never fulfilled their true potential. That said, Michael's numbers mean that he now stands head and shoulders above the rest in terms of his overall impact on the sport, and even former World Champions are happy to acknowledge that he is the best ever.

Without a doubt, Michael is the most complete package the sport has ever seen. His natural pace, fitness, work ethic, leadership qualities and

CLOCKWISE FROM RIGHT

Michael Schumacher was an instant hit with the tifosi, as shown at Imola in 1996, and they will miss him sorely; 1994 was shaping up to be a mighty battle with Ayrton Senna before the Brazilian died at Imola; Ross Brawn helped Michael to two titles with Benetton before they joined forces at Ferrari; Michael raced to eight wins in 1994…; …but he claimed the title only after clashing with Damon Hill at Adelaide; Michael's Grand Prix debut with Jordan wowed onlookers at Spa in 1991; and it wasn't just for his fresh-faced looks; amazingly, he scored his first win for Benetton at Spa a year later

'It's a good decision, because life is not only F1. Life is family. I think it's his decision and, in my view, it's a good one because he can finish an excellent, tremendous career in style. I think it will be different in F1, because a star will leave, and new ones will come. I think the global F1 circus will miss him, and the media will really feel that. I brought both Felipe and Kimi into F1, and I'm very proud to have both now with Ferrari. I'm sure that Ferrari will have a great time with these drivers, and a fun time.'

Peter Sauber – Team Principal Sauber 1993–2005

> 'It came as a shock. Only he can really understand what's right or wrong. He's on the top of his game. Pele was on the top of his game and stopped. So I think it's the right option. I told him that the same way I thought Senna would never die, because he was so invincible, he died. I had the vision that Schumacher would never stop, because he was such a good racer, and wanted to carry on. But, as he said, the time comes, and it will come to everyone.'

Rubens Barrichello – Ferrari team-mate 2000–2005

THE MAN

It had been widely predicted, but it was still a shock when Michael Schumacher announced his retirement after winning the Italian GP. We look back here at his truly remarkable career

'Obviously, he's one of the greatest drivers of all time. He's also a highly intelligent, sensible person. It's a very rational decision to leave while the going is good. Over the years, I've worked with Michael as he has been a member of the F1 Research Commission. His contributions have always been intelligent and sensible. The media in general have not really understood what a generous person he is, because he keeps himself a little remote. He's given a lot of money to charity. He's been very helpful with other problems. When we lost a marshal at Monza he was the first driver to say 'find out the name and address of the widow', because he wanted to make sure she's financially OK. I think he's a great person. When I got to his crash at Silverstone in 1999, he had taken his helmet off and he said 'call my wife and tell her it's just a broken leg'. He gave me her number while he was on the stretcher...'

Sid Watkins – Former Formula One Medical Delegate

intelligence combined to ensure that he was able to stay at the top for so long.

Michael was not without flaws, though. On more than one occasion the pressure of the climax of a title campaign appeared to get to him. His infamous clashes with Damon Hill at Adelaide in 1994 and Jacques Villeneuve at Jerez three years later proved hard for critics to forget. Those who felt he had put that sort of controversy behind him were disappointed when in Monaco this year he was found guilty of sabotaging the final qualifying attempts of his rivals with that clumsy parking manoeuvre at Rascasse.

That incident did much to undo the good work he had done since the earlier clashes, but he put it behind him and got on with the job of taking the title battle to Fernando Alonso, something he did with great style.

We all knew that Michael would have to stop at some time, and it was just a question of whether it would be sooner rather than later. As he struggled through most of 2005 with an uncompetitive car, many were quick to say that Michael should have retired at the end of the previous year, and gone out as World Champion. Instead, he had committed to two more years, and now we were seeing age catching up

with him. But events were to prove that his 2005 campaign was an unfortunate blip, as for this season Michael was back to his best.

There were times in 2006 when team-mate Massa appeared to have the upper hand, but the real story was perhaps evident in Hungary, where the Bridgestone tyres were hopeless in the wet. Michael's astonishing first lap was every bit as impressive as Senna's in the Grand Prix of Europe at Donington in 1993, and he left Massa splashing around in his wake.

However, perhaps the most impressive thing he's ever done was to find the right time to quit, and to do it with some dignity. As the old adage goes, it's far better to leave people asking why you retired, rather than when you'll retire.

That was neatly summed up at Monza by Schumacher's ultimate boss. "Through 10 years in which we have shared not only fantastic moments, but also difficult moments, Michael has been crucial," said Luca di Montezemolo, "not only as a driver, but also as a man, as a member of the team.

"So, I'm very happy that Michael can announce his retirement after a fantastic victory, in which he has proved once again that he is the best driver in the world, and I think that it's something good for him and good for the team. Having said that, I always told him that the decision to retire was his decision, and he showed once again to be intelligent. Because when you retire at the top, it means that you are intelligent."

So, what next for Ferrari? He may be a great talent in his own right, but Kimi Räikkönen has a difficult job to do in filling Michael's shoes. He also has a tough team-mate in Massa, now well established in the camp, while we have yet to see how a management reshuffle will play out.

Nigel Stepney, one of Ferrari's unsung heroes of the past decade, admits that things will change. "You can't continue forever with the same thing," says the team's Race Technical Manager. "For sure, it will change the team, the family, but we've got to go through that. It's going to be a character-building winter! Ten years is a long time, especially with the results we've had. Very few people have been able to do what we've all been through together. It's something that you can't forget. Kimi is a fantastic driver, but you can't compare him with Michael, and it will be a different ambience."

'On the one hand, it's sad that Michael is retiring. He's a fantastic driver, the most complete driver I know in F1, and it's really sad to see that. But, on the other hand, every driver would love to be in his position, to announce his retirement, winning the race, on the top, fighting for the championship – and with seven championships in the pocket. For sure, Michael realised that maybe it's the right moment to stop. We saw that in the past with Jackie Stewart, with Nelson Piquet, with many, many other drivers who retired. It's sad for F1, but that's life.'

Felipe Massa – Ferrari team-mate 2006

There's no question that 2006 was a classic season for the FIA Formula One World Championship. Not only did it have the extra significance of being Michael Schumacher's final fling, with the added spectacle of watching to see whether he would be able to extend his record tally of world titles to eight, but we saw a truly magnificent, full-blooded confrontation between the Ferrari and Renault camps that went all the way to the final round in Brazil.

While final round deciders have not been uncommon over the years, what was great about the 2006 campaign was that more than in the recent past we saw the two title contenders fighting regularly on the track. Given their superb year-long form, both Schumacher and Fernando Alonso, and indeed both their teams, Ferrari and Renault, deserved to win the respective titles.

There was also much going on off-track. The FIA's decision to force Renault to remove its mass-damper system from the German GP onwards caused something of a controversy, and Renault complained that the championship was being manipulated. Many folk conveniently forgot that at the start of the year the FIA had targeted Ferrari on the thorny issue of

flexible wings. What goes around, comes around...

Then there was a series of high-profile penalties. Michael Schumacher's Monaco qualifying exploits, which led to him blocking the track in the dying moments, led to him being sent to the back of the grid, while later both he and Alonso were docked places in Hungary for indiscretions in qualifying. Then Alonso was hit with a further penalty at the Italian GP. It was all good stuff for the headline writers.

In the end, it came down to a great contest between two superb drivers who were absolutely at the top of their game, and even Schumacher's critics acknowledged that it was good to see him go out on a high after his disastrous 2005 season.

Behind Renault and Ferrari, the other nine teams had to scrabble for the scraps. After pushing Alonso so hard in 2005, McLaren and Kimi Räikkönen could have been forgiven for thinking that they would go into this season as favourites. That was certainly on the mind of Fernando himself, who signed up for McLaren from 2007 in November 2005, having decided that the momentum was with the Woking team. As we saw, things didn't work out that way.

In general, the McLaren was able to use softer tyres

CLOCKWISE FROM TOP RIGHT **The story of the year was the battling between Fernando Alonso and Michael Schumacher; Alonso leads the way at Monaco; Jenson Button was a popular new winner; Minardi metamorphosed into Scuderia Toro Rosso; Nico Rosberg battles with Juan Pablo Montoya; which tyres to chose was one of the many questions of 2006**

THE SEASON

Any championship that isn't settled until the final round is a good one, but 2006 was much more than that with some classic encounters and even some controversy too

than the opposition, a reflection of the good form the team showed in 2005 when tyres had to last all race, and a car that was kind to them obviously benefited. This year, that was a less useful characteristic, especially when very often the tyres Michelin came up with were not soft enough to really suit the MP4-21. Räikkönen claimed several pole positions – one that was misleading when he was underfuelled at Hockenheim – but when there was a sniff of victory, something would go wrong, most notably at Monaco.

The tensions in the camp contributed to a spectacular falling out with Juan Pablo Montoya, who was not seen after his first corner tangle with Kimi in the United States GP at Indianapolis. Test driver Pedro de la Rosa proved a worthy replacement, taking a sensational second place in Hungary.

Alas, de la Rosa's performance that day was largely overshadowed by that of Jenson Button, who finally scored his first win at his 114th attempt. This was also the first for the modern Honda team since its birth as BAR back in 1999. It was a brilliant effort by driver and team, although it took the retirement of Alonso when a wheel fell off his Renault to serve up the victory.

Honda had come into the season with high hopes,

but they were never fulfilled, as the team failed to match its testing form. Button qualified well early on, but didn't have enough race pace. Towards the end of the year, he was often 'best of the rest' behind the title challengers, logging points on a consistent basis. Rubens Barrichello struggled to come to terms with the car in the early races, but improved once brakes and traction control were more to his liking. For the most part, though, he was edged out by Jenson.

Like McLaren, Toyota lost out in the switch back to tyre changes in races, having shown so well in 2005. The problem was compounded – pardon the pun – by a change from Michelin to Bridgestone tyres, which proved to be far more complex than expected. The TF106 was not a great car out of the box, and the confusing tyre situation left the team struggling to know which direction to take. Technical Director Mike Gascoyne carried the can and disappeared after the third race in Australia.

The TF106B that Gascoyne had instigated led to some improvement, but the cars were rarely fast enough to challenge for podium finishes, with the exception of the fortunate one that Ralf Schumacher collected with the TF106 in Melbourne. Once again, the German and team-mate Jarno Trulli were evenly matched over the year.

Many people thought that BMW was ill-advised to dump Williams and take over Sauber, but Mario Theissen had the last laugh as the re-badged team proved to be far more competitive than expected, despite the inevitable headaches of a transition year. The backbone of the Sauber team was always good, but now they had considerable resources to exploit, and the staff expanded rapidly as the year went on.

Jacques Villeneuve did much to redeem himself in the eyes of the paddock, and compared favourably with Nick Heidfeld. However, the team felt that both

men were just a little too comfortable with each other's pace and wanted to throw third driver Robert Kubica into the mix. Villeneuve's furious reaction was to walk away, so Kubica had the drive from the Hungarian GP on. He proved to be a sensational find, adding a deserved third place in Monza to the one Heidfeld had earned in the Hungarian rain.

Red Bull Racing expected an improvement in form after switching from Cosworth to Ferrari power for 2006. And while new technical guru Adrian Newey was focused on his 2007 design, he did have some influence on this year's campaign. In general, though, the package was uncompetitive, and both Red Bull teams were ostracised by their fellow Michelin runners after their crucial votes brought back tyre changes in the races, much to the delight of Bridgestone.

David Coulthard was on great form in Monaco and took a popular third place finish, while Christian Klien was usually as competitive but had appalling luck with reliability. Red Bull's team bosses lost patience, and the unfortunate Austrian was replaced by Robert Doornbos for the final three races.

Meanwhile, at sister team Scuderia Toro Rosso, Tonio Liuzzi and Scott Speed did their best to impress with the 2005 RBR chassis and a restricted Cosworth V10, but even they struggled to understand how they really fared against the V8-powered opposition.

Williams and Cosworth was a marriage of convenience that ended in divorce after a very short honeymoon. There was very little wrong with the V8, and most of the retirements were due to car rather than engine problems, but Frank Williams was keen to get back into bed with a manufacturer. Nico Rosberg was sensational in the first race in Bahrain, but thereafter found out how hard F1 can be. As with Toyota, the switch to Bridgestone was far from straightforward. A frustrated Mark Webber wanted

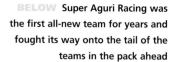

BELOW Super Aguri Racing was the first all-new team for years and fought its way onto the tail of the teams in the pack ahead

THE RULES

A package of technical and sporting regulation changes gave race engineers and strategists plenty to think about for the 2006 FIA Formula One World Championship.

First and foremost was of course the switch from V10 engines to V8s, with a cubic capacity drop from 3.0-litres to 2.4. That had a huge impact on how teams approached their weekends, because even more than before the emphasis was on restricting track mileage and thus extending engine life. It gave a useful advantage to the seven teams with the right to run third drivers on Fridays, that's to say those who ranked fifth or lower in 2005. Indeed, the whole approach of Cosworth and Williams was built around the fact that Williams' third driver Alexander Wurz could do the dirty work on Fridays, and the race drivers could therefore run a lot less over the weekends.

The other side-effect was that the engine men gave the drivers a limited number of high-rev laps for use in qualifying and at crucial periods of the race, usually for the laps immediately before and after pit stops, or when chasing down a rival. How the drivers were able to manage their engines had a crucial effect on reliability.

The return to tyre changes during the grands prix was encouraged by the FIA on the basis that the reduced power of the V8s made cutting back on grip less relevant, although as the season went on that argument proved to be a little shaky as cornering speeds rose. The change was voted through in effect by the two Red Bull teams, much to the chagrin of the other Michelin runners. The immediate effect was to put Ferrari and Bridgestone back in the ballpark as once again the tyre companies were able to fully explore the limits.

The new qualifying system was a major challenge for all concerned, but it proved to be a good compromise, with few drawbacks. The first session eliminated only six of the 22 cars, but it soon became apparent that even the top runners would have to sacrifice a set of tyres to get through. The same went for the second session, when another six were eliminated. Drivers certainly enjoyed the opportunity to run flat-out in these two sessions, something that had been missing under one-lap systems.

The third session proved to be less popular, and it was hard for fans to understand why the cars were running around a little off the pace as they logged their fuel-burning laps. Indeed, it was cut from 20 to 15 minutes mid-season in an attempt to increase the spectacle. To start with, most drivers did one hot lap at the end of the session, but it soon became standard practice to use up two new sets of tyres.

Making the most of the new system was far from easy, and from time to time some big names failed to make the top 10, or sometimes couldn't even make it out of the first session. There was much entertainment to be had as the drivers fought to get out of the pitlane first for Q3, and more than once when the likes of Alonso and Michael Schumacher ended up on the track together there was a little gamesmanship in the fuel-burning period. The system also made for a variety of race strategies, as those outside the top 10 invariably took the option of running with, and thus racing with, a higher fuel load.

out quick, and landed a Red Bull drive for 2007.

Finally, we witnessed a tussle for the minor placings between MF1 Racing and Super Aguri Racing at most of the grands prix. Indeed, the cars made contact on several occasions, so fraught was the battle. MF1 ended the season with new owners in Spyker, plus Ferrari engines and Mike Gascoyne for 2007. By contrast, it was a miracle that Super Aguri was present at all. After a scrappy start, car and team improved thanks to a big push from Honda, but there's still a long way to go for Aguri Suzuki's team in 2007.

ABOVE **Michael Schumacher was as fast as ever in his final year in F1, scoring yet more wins for Ferrari**

BELOW **Poland's Robert Kubica was given a chance by the BMW Sauber team and took it with both hands**

THE DRIVERS

You will have your own ideas on the merits of the 2006 crop of Formula One drivers, but we asked a panel of experts to judge them, with every driver who raced describing his season

As grand prix racing clocked up its century, we selected a panel of judges with the broadest view possible to rank the drivers of 2006, from Roy Salvadori who made his grand-prix debut in 1952 to Damon Hill, World Champion 44 years later. They have been there, done that, won races and pocketed World Championship titles, but what binds them together is that they all still love Formula One, watching its every twist and turn.

There was one thing that was very clear when the votes came in and this was that our octet thought that Michael Schumacher had outperformed Fernando Alonso, for all but one put him top of their list. It's a case of no names, no pack drill, so we won't reveal which juror thought Alonso the better, but the panel were clearly not of the mind that Michael was backing off as he considered his retirement from the big stage.

The only other pattern was that Kimi Räikkönen was considered third best. The rest of the drivers had to fight over fourth. One juror was drawn to the flashes of brilliance from BMW's Robert Kubica, although another put him 18th... Nico Rosberg, Jarno Trulli, Jenson Button and Felipe Massa were all similarly placed fourth by some of the jurors, while even a win failed to convince any to put Giancarlo Fisichella higher than sixth.

"I would have preferred to have been on the podium in Brazil, no doubt, but seeing the circumstances, I guess I have reasons to be happy. At Ferrari, we finished the season on a high. We had a fantastic car, and Felipe transformed it into a victory.

Felipe did a great race, becoming the first Brazilian since Senna to win on home ground, which was fantastic for him. It was also a great result for Fernando, congratulations again.

In all these years, when we have had such a huge amount of success, winning five drivers' titles and six constructors' titles, a tremendous friendship has built up within Ferrari. This was proved even more in the years that were difficult, like last year, when things didn't work out so well, and even more so the years before our first constructors' title in 1999.

In these moments, it's even more important to stick together, work together and to find a way out to come back in a fighting position. I was happy to be back in this position to contest my final season, and my last round of races.

We understood during the winter in particular what would make us go forward, and we obviously worked very closely together and developed it to the point where we had a very competitive package, car and tyres together, and this year we were back on the road of winning races.

We had points to recover from the beginning where things didn't work out for us very well, but if you look since Canada how many points we took in comparison to our opponents, we were very strong.

Monza was just unbelievable. It always has been very special, particularly after the race when all the fans are allowed to celebrate this moment so close to us and with us. Due to the nature of the circumstances, it was obviously an unbelievable feeling.

It was obviously pretty emotional to drive back to the pits after the race at Monza. I was talking to my team, and informed everybody of my decision. This was the most emotional moment, along with being on the podium to celebrate, especially knowing that it was the last opportunity I would have to finish so well with such a crowd, with so much they gave to me in terms of their feelings, it just overwhelmed me.

It has obviously, naturally, been difficult in a way, but at one moment I simply knew that all the effort, all the energy, all the motivation you need in order to be competitive – and that's the only reason I want to be there – I can't see I'm going to have that for future years. You need all the energy and motivation and strength, and getting older does not make it easier. It has been such a good time for all this time and there is absolutely no point just to hang in there and maybe take away the future of a very young talented driver like Felipe.

The team left me every opportunity, and every door open. Obviously, I have a lot of friends there, and naturally we discussed the up and the down sides and so on, but at the end of the day it was down to [my wife] Corinna and myself.

It is natural with the relationship I have with Corinna that we discuss every little thing and the good thing as I mentioned before is that without the support of my family and in particular Corinna all these years I don't think I could have done it. So naturally she supported me in my decision as well. She gave me her point-of-view and we discussed it.

Ferrari existed before I joined the team, and Ferrari will exist after me, and I think Ferrari has taken a very good decision with their driver line-up to make sure that the success can continue.

I always said that the day I will retire, I will just do nothing for a while and then I will see what I'm doing, what is my mood and what's going to happen, but I will always be part of that Ferrari family, I will have to find out how, but I will always stick with my friends there.

The things I will miss are probably the fans. At every moment they have been behind me and always supported me. That support helped me perform, especially in moments when it was difficult. Over the years, that was immensely important. I can only say thank you to all our fans."

NATIONALITY German
DATE OF BIRTH 3/1/69
PLACE OF BIRTH Kerpen, Germany
GRANDS PRIX 250
WINS 91
POLES 68
FASTEST LAPS 75
POINTS 1369
HONOURS F1 World Champion 1994, 1995, 2000, 2001, 2002, 2003, 2004; German F3 Champion 1990, German Formula Konig Champion 1988

2 FERNANDO ALONSO

↓-1 RENAULT WORLD CHAMPION 2006

NATIONALITY Spanish
DATE OF BIRTH 29/7/81
PLACE OF BIRTH Oviedo, Spain
GRANDS PRIX 88
WINS 15
POLES 14
FASTEST LAPS 8
POINTS 381
HONOURS F1 World Champion 2005, 2006, Formula Nissan Champion 1999, Italian & Spanish Kart Champion 1997, World Kart Champion 1996

"Brazil was a fantastic weekend and I probably need some time to believe that I'm World Champion again. I'm 25-years old, two championships now, and two constructors' titles as well. It was my last race for Renault after five years, and it was a fantastic way to finish with this success. I will have these memories with them all my life, and to finish the last race like this is something that you never even try to dream of, because it's always more than what you expected.

My best memory was winning my home grand prix in Barcelona, but also it was great to win for the first time at Monaco, at Silverstone and Suzuka, all big places in Formula One. And the worst memory is all the things that happened with the penalties I had this year.

We also lost too many points, more than we expected because of the problems we had. We had one problem in Hungary with a rear tyre, and we didn't finish, and then at Monza we had the engine failure, and so with these two races the advantage went very quickly.

I was convinced we were able to win, though. I knew that Ferrari was quick, but we were also quick and I think sooner or later everyone would be put in his place. We deserved this championship, and unfortunately we had very bad moments with some decisions, and I think we deserved it and this is just the best.

For sure, those 10 points in Japan were a little present that God gave to us. When I saw Michael's problem, I was at that point leading the race and I just didn't believe what I was seeing, because it's not often that you see a mechanical problem from a Ferrari car.

This season was completely different from 2005. I think this year we had the same advantage in the first part of the season, around 20 to 25 points, and we kept it last year a little bit thanks to the mechanical problems that McLaren had. When normal races happened, the McLaren was quicker than us and it was impossible to fight with them. Sometimes they had problems and we took the advantage back again. This year, with Ferrari, sometimes we could fight with them and we could win or lose, but I had a much better feeling last year about the championship, the sport and about everything.

Maybe the experience you have in one important year, like you have with your first championship, you never forget and you use in the rest of your career.

I knew that 2006 would be a good season for us, and Renault should be on top, fighting for the championship, and I knew that this year there would be the possibility to become champion and we were ready to take it, but nevertheless I feel that for the next three years at McLaren I will also have the opportunity to have a good car. Renault, for sure, will have a good car, but hopefully I will find new motivation with McLaren, new challenge, new people, a new way to work.

We need to see what will happen next year. Every year is different. We saw in 2004 that McLaren finished fifth overall, but in 2005 they were the best on the track. In 2006, they also had some problems, so I hope that in 2007 they come back with the best car

We'll see how everyone adapts to the Bridgestone tyres. I know McLaren will give all effort to be champions again, and I know I will put in all my effort as well, so hopefully together we can have a good championship.

To all the people in the [Renault] team, who did a fantastic job, I want to say thanks again to all of them. They were completely my family in Formula One and I want to say thanks to them and to the test team, to Enstone, to Viry, to Michelin, to Heikki Kovalainen, as well, who did a lot of work for us this year.

The best memories will be both championships, what we felt last year, the emotion and the atmosphere in the team. We grew up together and now we have won in two consecutive years both championships and I will never forget the years I had with Renault.

We all wish Michael the best for his new life with his family. He has been a great champion, with all the records in Formula One. For me to race with him and to win the 2005 and 2006 championships with him on the track for the last two years give my championships more value, and I am really proud to have raced with him."

Va Va Voom x F1=197

The new Clio Renaultsport 197. Like our F1 car, it has a rear diffuser that reduces rear-end lift. Because less lift equals more control. And now, when you're not glued to the road, you can be glued to your mobile. Text 'Game' to 85101 to download your free mobile driving game. For details, or to see more of the Renaultsport range, visit www.renaultsport.co.uk

3 KIMI RÄIKKÖNEN

↓-1 McLAREN

NATIONALITY Finnish
DATE OF BIRTH 17/10/79
PLACE OF BIRTH Espoo, Finland
GRANDS PRIX 105
WINS 9
POLES 11
FASTEST LAPS 19
POINTS 346
HONOURS British Formula Renault Champion 2000, Finnish & Nordic Kart Champion 1998

"We were expecting much more than we got this season, especially after our 2005 season.

Something went wrong somehow over the winter! Of course it's not nice if you know from the beginning of the season that you are not where you should be, or where you are hoping to be. It was quite disappointing.

We knew basically that it was going to be harder, with the change to V8s, and stuff like that. For sure, you notice straight away in the testing when something isn't right. It didn't help that we had a lot of problems with the engine over the winter, and then suddenly before the season started we got rid of the problems. It was good, but we lost a lot of time in terms of pushing it forward, and not just fixing the problems. At that point, you still don't know exactly what the others are doing, and you don't know if they are quick or not.

Early on, the car wasn't quick enough in qualifying, but in the races we seemed to be stronger. The car improved, but the middle of the season was the most difficult part. We were still not as quick as the Ferraris or the Renaults.

We didn't expect to have the suspension problem we had in first qualifying in Bahrain, but the race itself was quite good. In Australia, we were quite quick in the race again, but a lot of things happened.

It would have been nice to win at Monaco. It was one of the races where we were really able to fight for a win, so we were hoping for better. The safety car really decided things for us... I felt that I had a problem with the car a lap and a half before but, in the end, after the safety car it would have been really difficult to overtake. I didn't go back to the pits – I didn't really have anything to say, so it didn't change anything. I wasn't angry about it, I was just really disappointed. But it wasn't the first time, it wasn't anything new.

In Canada, we had a problem with the clutch. We were quite quick in the race until we had a problem, and we could have been a bit closer to the front. After the crash at Indianapolis, I didn't say anything to Juan Pablo. He said that I pushed him on the grass and that it was my fault!

Germany worked out OK. We were fuel-light in qualifying, but the tyres went quite early, so for us it was quite good to stop early. Then we had a problem with the car in the middle of the race. The Ferraris were simply too quick for us, so third was OK there.

In Hungary, we had a problem with the second set of tyres. In fact, the front tyres didn't work at all, so the car just went straight on. The car was good in the first stint, but for some reason when we put on the second set the fronts didn't warm up at all, so I was losing time. Even with that, though, if you look at what happened in the race we were still in a good position. I was going to let Pedro by when suddenly Liuzzi slowed down on the exit of the final corner, which was unfortunate...

We were quite good at Monza. We were a couple of laps lighter than Michael, but I think the car was overall pretty quick there. It was a bit similar to Canada, where we were quite quick. At Monza, if the car is good over the kerbs and under braking, you can usually have a good race there. I don't think I've been on the podium there before, and it was a bit different because it's more for the public. It was nice to be up there, but I would rather win the race than come second!

China could have been another good race, and it started well and we made the right decision with tyres, and then something broke.

The whole season has been quite difficult. There were some races where we've been quick, and something has always gone wrong. In the end, you always try to do the best. If you know the championship is gone, then you try to win some races. Of course, some grand prix weekends are more difficult when you know the car is simply not quick enough to go for a podium finish, and you just need to do your best."

"This has been a really good year for me, especially winning in front of my home crowd. I did very well, I was driving very fast, and in the last few races I was always doing similar lap times to Michael, sometimes quicker, and that's really good for me.

It was definitely a fantastic feeling for me to claim the first grand prix win of my career in F1 in Turkey. It definitely gave me a lot more motivation, and I was really improving a lot at the beginning of the year, and especially from the middle of the championship to the end. So I'm really happy, and much more mature, more experienced, and more motivated.

It was really good to get the first win, especially on a very difficult track. It was a fantastic victory, starting from pole, in front of these two special drivers, Michael and Fernando, and finishing in front of these two drivers. Really, it was the best I could expect for the first victory, but you always need to look forward and try to achieve the next one, because you always want more!

At Indy and Hockenheim, I was very competitive. I was very strong at Monza as well, but I was not lucky. In China, I was very strong from the first practice, and in the race I was very quick with the fuel I had, but I was just not lucky there. But, for example, Australia was a horrible weekend, especially with the first corner crash!

I was strong in many, many races. Especially after the first five races of the championship I was very, very competitive all the time. Sometimes I was not lucky, sometimes something happened, but I had some good results along the way.

I think my role was very important as far as the championships were concerned, like Giancarlo's for Renault. It was very important to have both cars at the front. A single point could make a lot of difference, so everyone in the team was playing an important part. We were looking for the best harmony we could inside the team, between the drivers, but in the end the most important thing is what you do on the track.

You can always show that you are there, that you are competitive, that you are doing what the team expects from you, so the harmony becomes even better inside the team, and you become even more recognised by everybody outside as well.

I have enjoyed working with Michael. We had a good relationship together, and he was always really, really good with me, not just on the professional side, but also on the private side. He was always pushing hard to have me in the team, he was always very, very positive about everything I was doing. When I heard the nice things he said about me at Monza it was something really special, which I will never forget.

You have many different kinds of drivers who are quick, who are consistent, who are good in qualifying, maybe good in the race. But I think Michael can put everything together and become Michael Schumacher. So, in the end, I think he's very complete. If you look at the numbers, you really don't need to say a lot. Just knowing him from the team, working together, I can only say I would love to be as close as possible and to achieve half or maybe a quarter of what Michael has done in his career.

It was really amazing to see that he was able to retire on the top, fighting for his eighth championship. For

sure, he realised that maybe it's the right moment to stop. We saw that in the past with Jackie Stewart, with Nelson Piquet, with many, many other drivers who retired. It's sad for F1, but that's life. He's a very nice guy, very special. I want to see him around, definitely, sharing some experience with us, even playing football together.

For sure, it will be a big loss for Ferrari, that's clear. A driver like him retiring is a big loss for the team, but on the other hand I think Ferrari is a very strong team. We have two good drivers inside the team, and hopefully we can carry on winning races and hopefully titles.

Next year is a big challenge for me. Kimi is definitely another very, very good driver, and it will be a great experience for me. He's another young driver like me, and for sure we will both try to prove everything we can to be in the top."

4 FELIPE MASSA

⬆ +9 FERRARI

NATIONALITY Brazilian
DATE OF BIRTH 25/4/81
PLACE OF BIRTH São Paulo, Brazil
GRANDS PRIX 71
WINS 2
POLES 3
FASTEST LAPS 2
POINTS 107
HONOURS Euro F3000 Champion 2001, European Formula Renault Champion 2000

5 JENSON BUTTON

HONDA

NATIONALITY British
DATE OF BIRTH 19/1/80
PLACE OF BIRTH Frome, England
GRANDS PRIX 119
WINS 1
POLES 3
FASTEST LAPS 0
POINTS 223
HONOURS Formula Ford Festival winner 1998, European Super A Kart Champion 1997

"When we came into the season we expected to be challenging for the championship. Over testing we were amazed at how quick we were, compared to other people, so when we arrived in Bahrain we expected to walk it, really! But we struggled in that race because we had a problem at the start.

In the first four or five races, I was qualifying in the top three, but our race pace wasn't quite where we wanted it to be. Bahrain was a good result considering that I was way back after the start because of the clutch, and I worked my way up to fourth, which was good with the strategy we had. Malaysia was a perfect race, nothing really went wrong, but we just weren't quick enough to beat the Renaults. So we did have some very good races, but the race pace was what we needed to work on.

Still, the first four races weren't too bad, and we were reasonably competitive. Then it sort of dropped off a little bit when other people started improving aerodynamically, and I think also with the engines. So it was a little bit downhill from then for the next four or five races, and we weren't getting the results that we expected. It was pretty tough on everyone. When you come into a season and you think you've got a chance of the championship and you're not even scoring points, it's really tough.

At Imola, I started near the front, and we were looking good for a third or fourth position and some nice points, but then in the pit stop we had a misunderstanding in the team and I ended up getting whacked on the head with a big lollipop! So that wasn't a great result...

At Silverstone, I started back in 19th because of qualifying when I was pulled into the weighbridge and didn't get out on new tyres. That was so painful going to bed on Saturday night. Then I came through the field up to 11th or 12th after six laps, and the oil tank exploded. That was a massive disappointment, but the crowd was very supportive. Hopefully, I won't have another British GP like that!

We realised the areas that we were not strong in, and we worked on them very hard. We sort of got into a position before Hockenheim where the race pace was good but the outright one-lap pace was not good. The car was reasonably competitive, though, and I almost got a podium there. And the weekend after that I got my first win in Hungary. The good thing is that we turned it around when we needed to, but the bad thing is that we didn't have it right at the start of the year.

I love the wet, and the car worked well in the wet in the winter, but we hadn't had so many wet tests, so we didn't know how other people would be in those conditions. But it was a spectacular race in Hungary, coming through the field, picking people off. The pace of the car when I was catching up to Alonso after the safety car was just a phenomenal feeling, having a good car under me and pushing it to the limit. It felt in every corner as though you were going to end up in the gravel, because you were pushing so hard! It was fantastic.

When I won the race it was a dream come true, because as a child you dream about reaching F1, and you dream about your first victory, and obviously winning the World Championship. It was one of those occasions that will always be with me, and I will never forget. I will wake up in 50 years' time and think I won my first race in Hungary, and remember how it was done, also. It wasn't straightforward pole-to-victory, it was a tough fight throughout the race with a lot of drivers.

You can see how close we all are, because the emotions within the team were just unbelievable. We've been through some pretty tough times – some good times as well – but a lot of tough times. We proved that day we were the best team in the pitlane. We probably didn't have the best car, but as a team we were definitely the best. It really did help everyone's confidence for the later races, and I think it also helped us for the future."

6 GIANCARLO FISICHELLA

↑+1 RENAULT

"I'm a little bit disappointed about my season. It wasn't bad, but it wasn't what I expected. First of all, I had a problem straight away with the engine in Bahrain. Then I won in Malaysia, and in Australia I was on the front row, but the engine stalled on the grid!

After that, there were possibilities to score a lot more points than I did. I had a few problems during the season and maybe I made some mistakes. I jumped the start in Canada, and for sure that was my mistake. In Hungary, I spun off. There was a good possibility to score a lot of points there, and for sure a podium, so I lost an opportunity.

Fernando drove very well, and he was always there. For me, it was sometimes difficult to do a good qualifying session. Sometimes I was heavier than Fernando. I had some problems, like at the Nürburgring, with Jacques, and I had a penalty in Monaco. Many times I was in a good position, and then in the race I was at the back. It wasn't easy.

The team has been good all season, and they pushed for both cars. But obviously you understand when there is a big gap between you and your team-mate sometimes the team is more with the other driver. However, that's normal. There is obviously more concentration on one car.

Fernando's style of driving is very aggressive, very different to mine and maybe I was not so comfortable with the tyres or the car.

The car was born with the mass damper, so we ran from January until it was banned with the mass damper, we did a lot of testing mileage with it. To race without it was different in terms of the handling of the car. But that was the rule, and we had to accept what the FIA said.

I scored points in nearly every race. I did my best, and again I had some bad luck, but I'm really confident for next year. It's going to be Bridgestone, so it will be a different story, and it will be my third year with the team, so I think it's going to be alright."

NATIONALITY Italian
DATE OF BIRTH 14/1/73
PLACE OF BIRTH Rome, Italy
GRANDS PRIX 179
WINS 3
POLES 3
FASTEST LAPS 2
POINTS 246
HONOURS Italian F3 Champion & Monaco F3 GP winner 1994

7 RUBENS BARRICHELLO

↑+1 **HONDA**

"I had a lot of expectations before the season, because when we were testing we were doing very well. But if people now look at our mid-season, when we weren't doing very well, when we went for testing we were still leading. So it means that either we had different sorts of fuel loads or our car worked on tracks that had less rubber, or we just went well with new tyres.

So, at the beginning of the year we looked like we were winners big time. The problem was that when we got to Bahrain it was terrible. I had a faulty brake part, something inside the disc. We had been there testing and I should have performed well, but the car was pulling to the right because of it. Malaysia and Australia were still a struggle, and after that we changed the material of the brakes, and then things calmed down. Those three races were good in a way, in that they killed my expectation, but even Jenson felt like we could win and didn't match that. He was mild in his comments, though.

After Ferrari, it was a big drop in performance for me, and I just had to start all over again, and that was what I did.

I think from Imola onwards my performance was a lot better. This is not being critical, but it was not an easy car to drive. It was a very, very good car in so many conditions, but it was just not easy to get in and drive compared to the Ferrari. The main problems were that I had a new traction control system and a new type of brakes to learn. With the V8 and the amount of downforce we had, I didn't know which track would be best for this or for that.

I've been developing and getting better, but every time I hit a new track it was like catching up a little bit. You have to drive and you have to feel the car, and sometimes it doesn't feel good. At least when you've been with a team for six years, sometimes you would come and you would know where the starting point was. With a new team, I can only say that the second year has to be better."

NATIONALITY Brazilian
DATE OF BIRTH 23/5/72
PLACE OF BIRTH São Paulo, Brazil
GRANDS PRIX 235
WINS 9
POLES 13
FASTEST LAPS 15
POINTS 519
HONOURS British F3 Champion 1991, European Formula Opel Champion 1990

8 NICK HEIDFELD
↑+4 BMW SAUBER

NATIONALITY Germany
DATE OF BIRTH 10/5/77
PLACE OF BIRTH Moenchengladbach, Germany
GRANDS PRIX 117
WINS 0
POLES 1
FASTEST LAPS 0
POINTS 79
HONOURS Formula 3000 Champion 1999,
German F3 Champion 1997

"I've been in the points quite a few times this year, and I think we can't expect any more for BMW's first season.

Now of course the most important thing is that we make another step next year. I expect and hope for a bigger step with the new car. It definitely takes time to progress.

I hoped that improvements would come more quickly this year, but it's just not that easy with so many new people coming on board, as everything needs to fit together. More importantly, though, when we did get some new parts, they worked.

After the fourth race, the San Marino GP, there were two or three races when we didn't get any new parts on the aero side, and I hoped that each race we would be getting some parts.

Reliability was a problem at the beginning of the year, and it was a bit disappointing, especially for me in Malaysia, stopping just a few laps before the end of the race. I would probably have finished fifth. It would have been easier to take if it was halfway through the race that the car failed, but not so close to the end!

Third place in Hungary was fantastic… Of course Jenson did a great race and it was a great victory. I was very happy for him, because he really deserved it. But for our team it was really special, because it's the first season for us, and we didn't expect to have a podium this year. We did hope that we would get a podium in the second year, so having it early was really good. It was also important for the team, because of the low points that we had at Hockenheim and Magny-Cours.

For a new team, I think it's important to come out strongly at the other end of the tunnel after such a period, and see that we have to stick together and not start blaming other people and blah, blah, blah.

I was quite happy that we worked pretty well together. And also, for me, the Hungarian GP was my fifth podium. Not so many yet, but it's always nice to be up there, and I didn't expect it."

9 DAVID COULTHARD
⬅=➡ RED BULL RACING

NATIONALITY British
DATE OF BIRTH 27/3/71
PLACE OF BIRTH Twynholm, Scotland
GRANDS PRIX 212
WINS 13
POLES 12
FASTEST LAPS 18
POINTS 513
HONOURS Macau F3 winner 1991, British Junior
Formula Ford Champion 1989, Scottish Kart
Champion 1988

"The reality is that things went wrong effectively when we first ran the car and we had a cooling issue. That was in December 2005, and we didn't appear to solve that before we started running again in January, and then it took us a lot of time to get on top of that.

Annoyingly, all the time that you are trying to solve a fundamental issue you are not manufacturing development parts.

Like pretty much everyone else, we were switching from V10 to V8, so there was always going to be a bit of recalculating. Inevitably, too, when you work with new people you have to find how that relationship is. We had identified that it would be better for us to move, in the same way that Williams have spent a year with Cosworth and then they decided that it was better for them to move to another engine supplier. It is what it is, you've got to try and pick what you believe is the best power plant that you can afford to buy and put in the car.

Monaco was the big result of the year, and obviously I was delighted to be back on the podium. It was my 61st podium, and it had been a long time since I'd been on any podium. It was the dream scenario for Red Bull, and it was very important after all the hard work from the guys on the race team, the test team and the departments back at the factory that are working at 100%. It was a reward for them. But, inevitably, we are still going through the growing pains of how we can strengthen the team, how we can get more out of each other.

I can't recall a really competitive race other than Monaco. Obviously, we had a little bit of good fortune there with other people having reliability issues, but that's racing, and I don't think any of us can feel particularly happy with how we performed, and that has made it difficult for me to really feel like I'm top of my form as well, because it's very difficult to read the car variation from circuit to circuit.

We have to believe that next year we can make a significant step."

10 JARNO TRULLI

↓-4 TOYOTA

"I think everybody was disappointed with our season, because we expected more. But since our start was so slow, I would say we managed pretty well to recover from there. We have to say that the bad start affected our season quite a lot, but on the other hand I have to praise the team for the reaction they had, because we managed to bounce back, and in some races we were extremely competitive.

We've shown that sometimes you are there, sometimes you are not quite there. Our main target for 2007 is to definitely improve the car and not have any more this kind of differing performance through the year.

For us, changing tyre companies was definitely a big shock. It took several months before we really understood it. We suffered a lot with weather conditions during the winter, so it was very difficult to figure out the real performance of the car, the tyres, the set-up. We really lost a lot of time there. The concept of the tyres was the opposite to what we had been used to [with Michelin], so the set-up, the numbers were completely different.

Bahrain was a shock for everyone. We were completely away from the window, tyre-wise and chassis-wise, and when you are there you struggle to point out where the problem is, and what to do. That was our main problem at the beginning of the season.

The B-spec changed our car performance. We were looking more competitive and stronger, and we were handling the tyres better. It was definitely a good step forward. Feedback-wise, in terms of driving style and driving feeling, especially at the front end of the car, it was very different. Monaco was the first bounce back from the start of the season – I was third when I retired with a hydraulic problem. That was really an unfortunate race.

I must say that this year I've had some bad times and bad luck, because everything came at the wrong moment! And even when everything seemed to be looking good, there was something wrong, like in Monaco or Magny-Cours, where I could have achieved two nice podiums. It was, in the end, a very difficult season."

NATIONALITY Italian
DATE OF BIRTH 13/7/74
PLACE OF BIRTH Pescara, Italy
GRANDS PRIX 167
WINS 1
POLES 3
FASTEST LAPS 0
POINTS 175
HONOURS German F3 Champion 1996, World Kart Champion 1994

11 MARK WEBBER

◄=► WILLIAMS

"There's no point in looking at it through rose-tinted glasses: the season has been nothing short of a disaster. There's no beating around the bush. We had just a few points finishes, which was incredibly hard for everyone to swallow, and hard personally of course for me to swallow. It knocks your motivation around, it knocks a lot of things around. You can only take so much, and anyone would go through that.

So, I am looking forward to next year, because I need something fresh, and I need a new environment to recharge my career, hopefully. I see very good potential at Red Bull. Williams will have a better season than they've had this year, I'm sure of that – it can't be any worse – but it was time for me to try something different.

My biggest worry coming into this season was Bridgestone, to be honest. Cosworth didn't worry me at all. And we had the best engine for the first part of the season. It was maybe a little bit fragile, but no more fragile than anybody else's back then. After five or

six races, we had a little bit of a reliability problem, and that affected us with a 10-place penalty at the Nürburgring otherwise I think we should have finished fifth there.

However, we couldn't capitalise on our form early in the season. Even up until Hockenheim we had spells of going reasonably well, although there were a few tracks where it didn't happen for us because we just didn't have the pace. Cosworth haven't held us back at all, but there's no question that we haven't performed with the engine we had.

The Monaco GP was a high and a low. There are so many things that can catch you out over the course of the weekend in terms of keeping the thing off the fence, qualifying with traffic, qualifying with guys stopping on the track. We started on the front row and we were racing quite strongly. Then we had the hydraulic failure. Given the season that we'd had, a podium was going to be a very strong result for us. There are lots of ifs and buts…"

NATIONALITY Australian
DATE OF BIRTH 27/8/76
PLACE OF BIRTH Queanbeyan, Australia
GRANDS PRIX 87
WINS 0
POLES 0
FASTEST LAPS 0
POINTS 69
HONOURS Formula Ford Festival winner 1996

12 PEDRO DE LA ROSA

↑ +6   McLAREN

"It's been an extremely interesting season for me and, at the end of the day, the hard work you put in pays off.

You have to be prepared as a test driver that these things can happen and that you will get the call up to fill one of the team's race seats, and I'm happy that it happened to me because I was prepared. I never lost faith, I was pushing in testing, I was fit, I was doing a lot of training. It came at a good time. You always hope that there's a possibility that you might be called up.

We've had races where the McLaren has been very competitive and others where it has been rather less so. But, all in all, it's been good and it's been the best car I've ever raced by a country mile.

At the French GP, we were already pretty quick, but in fact we've been quick in nearly all the races. If you look at the lap times in all the races I contested, I set the third-fastest lap at Magny-Cours, and I was also the first Michelin-shod car on the list. In the Chinese GP, I had the third fastest lap, and at the Hungaroring I set the second fastest.

The Hungarian GP was my first podium finish, and the race itself was certainly pretty interesting. I was very happy to be up on the podium as it had been a long time since I was last on one in Formula Nippon in 1997, so it was a great feeling to be back up there.

Actually, we could have won that race, but we took some decisions in the pit stop that were wrong. However, if I had to do it again, I would. I was happy that it was also Jenson's first win.

When you cross the start/finish line and you see on your pit board that you are in the top three it's an extra adrenaline flow in your body. It felt very good to be competitive.

You always want as a race driver to be competitive, to be up the front, and when you're starting a race and you have very few cars in front of you on the grid it's so much easier. There's nothing better for a race driver than to see no one in front! You're much more relaxed, and it's much easier to drive at the front than the back."

NATIONALITY Spanish
DATE OF BIRTH 24/2/71
PLACE OF BIRTH Barcelona, Spain
GRANDS PRIX 71
WINS 0
POLES 0
FASTEST LAPS 1
POINTS 29
HONOURS Formula Nippon Champion 1997, Japanese GT Champion 1997, Japanese F3 Champion 1995, British & European Formula Renault Champion 1992, Spanish Formula Ford Champion 1990

JUAN PABLO MONTOYA

↓ -9   McLAREN

"At the Monaco GP, we were competitive all weekend. I lost a bit of ground in the first stint of the race as I passed a backmarker into the chicane and got completely sideways and lost a bit of time.

From there, though, it was just a matter of trying to keep up and, when Renault and Fernando [Alonso] upped the pace, my car was pretty good so I managed to close the gap pretty easily.

We were looking after the car and waiting to see what happens. If you have an opportunity, you take it and just everything fell into our hands. Monaco is a race where you've just got to be there to be good and we were. We had the pace, we probably even had the pace to win the race, but second place was a great result.

In race trim, my car was very good at the Canadian GP as well and it was a bit annoying not to be able to show the pace. I think Kimi had a better qualifying car and I thought I could have had a better race car, so it was a bit frustrating from that point-of-view, but that's the way racing goes.

We had a quick car and I collided with [Nico] Rosberg, and it was one of those racing things that happens. I had a quick car and I needed to make sure that before Fernando escaped off into the distance I moved forward and I was trying to do precisely that.

To be honest, I wasn't enjoying the races. I had done everything I had to do and I had achieved almost all the goals that I had. I only needed to win a title and I realised my chances were very small.

Leaving F1 and McLaren was the best decision that I could have made.

The car drove me to boredom. My team-mate [Kimi Räikkönen] was finishing fifth or sixth too. We were finishing in the same place all the time. It wasn't me, it was the car. Fighting for fifth place is no fun.

I wanted a new challenge, and NASCAR is just that, different, fresh. I could be racing for another 10–15 years. It's a different world, it's more relaxed."

NATIONALITY Colombian
DATE OF BIRTH 20/9/75
PLACE OF BIRTH Bogota, Colombia
GRANDS PRIX 95
WINS 7
POLES 13
FASTEST LAPS 12
POINTS 307
HONOURS Indy 500 winner, Champ Car Champion 1999, Formula 3000 Champion 1998

14 NICO ROSBERG
WILLIAMS

"At the first race of the season, in Bahrain, I was very happy with the car. However, from then on, it dropped away a little bit.

I actually had a better race at Silverstone than I had at Bahrain. From my point-of-view, I really got the maximum out of the car at the British GP, which I didn't in Bahrain, where I should have finished in around fourth place.

The trouble is, nobody sees it because the car isn't as competitive any more, and that's also something I have to get used to in F1. It annoys me a bit because everybody says first race, first race!

It's never easy when you're in your first year and you're picking up and learning everything. No one said it was going to be easy, really!

On the whole, though, I'm pretty pleased with the way it's gone for me personally.

The goal was to establish myself in F1, the first goal, and I've managed to do that. That was important, and I'm very happy about it.

It was quite a big jump for sure, not so much from the driving side of things, because if you're quick you'll be there in every car. It's more difficult to get the car to your liking, though, because it's become so technical, and there's so much you can do to help yourself and get the car right. That becomes very difficult and very challenging. And then also getting used to everything around it.

There's so much more you have to do on the job side of things. You need to get used to that also, and not let it drain your energy. I understand that it helps me a lot, the better I cope with all this, so I make sure I'm strong in every area that I can be.

For example, the German GP was not a good weekend from my point-of-view. The crash on the first lap was my mistake. I just lost the rear of the car, and that was it. A few things just came together, and that was the result of it. The best I can do is learn again and pick up a few things from a weekend like that, and get better for my second season of F1."

NATIONALITY German
DATE OF BIRTH 27/6/85
PLACE OF BIRTH Wiesbaden, Germany
GRANDS PRIX 18
WINS 0
POLES 0
FASTEST LAPS 1
POINTS 4
HONOURS GP2 Champion 2005, Formula BMW Champion 2002

15 ROBERT KUBICA
BMW SAUBER

"Everything went really very quickly indeed for me this year!

I was already very happy when I got the chance to be test driver and Friday driver for BMW Sauber, and I was not really expecting anything beyond that.

I was just trying to do the best that I could, and trying to help the team to make the car quicker and quicker, and to deliver good feedback for them.

I think, especially at the beginning of the year when I was a rookie, no one really knew how I would perform, how the feedback would be, or if I could drive at the same pace all the time – I think it's very important when you are testing tyres and some new stuff.

I did a lot of days of testing, which was good for me, because I got closer to the team, and it gave me the feeling that the feedback that I was giving them could not be so bad if they let me drive so much. So that was really good.

Then everything changed a bit when I got the drive for the Hungarian GP. Especially from the point-of-view of Friday, and changing the 'rules', but in the end it's the same: you have to drive the car, and drive it as fast as possible!

It's much easier just to do Fridays than when you are a regular driver, especially when you are coming to new tracks as one of the team's racers and you don't have a lot of running time, and you always have to save the engine and the tyres.

You also have to be quite quick to understand where you have to put the wheels, and what set-up you have to use, and this is not easy.

I think we did a really good job on aerodynamics for the Italian GP, because we were really quick on the straight and not too bad in the second sector.

Of course, my first podium, after only three races in Formula One, was a really brilliant feeling! It was a really good result, but it's already gone, part of history, and we have to push and we have to do the best that we can in the future."

NATIONALITY Polish
DATE OF BIRTH 7/12/84
PLACE OF BIRTH Krakow, Poland
GRANDS PRIX 6
WINS 0
POLES 0
FASTEST LAPS 0
POINTS 6
HONOURS World Series by Renault Champion 2005, Italian Junior Kart Champion 1998, German & Italian Junior Kart Champion 2000

16 RALF SCHUMACHER
↓-6 TOYOTA

"My overall feeling is that the season was OK. Certainly there are things that we aren't happy about, but the important thing is that we try to address them and learn from them to make the situation better. From where we were at the start of March we fought our way through the year. The potential was there, but it's just that we couldn't show it due to reliability issues and sometimes little mistakes, which is again on our side, and something we have to learn from.

The thing is we should never forget we are an incredibly young team. When Jarno and I joined last year I think the first year was more successful than we thought, due to the rule changes which might have favoured us better than other teams to start with. So I think the expectations were a little too high, from outside as well, due to the season we had before. But things are moving the right way, and there's a consistent approach, the very technical approach that we are heading for at the moment, and therefore things seem to be a little slow from the outside. But

it will work eventually, I'm 100% sure.

It was a combination of things at the start of the year. When you have a new tyre, that involves a learning period. We may have underestimated things a little bit, and we had a particularly cold winter too, so there were temperatures that we never faced before. We thought that when we went to the first few races we would have decent temperatures and it shouldn't be a problem. We learned otherwise, and we made some high-speed action and changed a few things. I must say they proved to be right.

Still, from where we started it was a very tough task to get close to the top teams. It meant developing quicker and better than them, so it wasn't very easy.

Talking about the mechanical design of the car, the TF106B was a necessary step in the right direction, especially the front end. It was certainly not something that allowed us to go a second quicker, but we learned from it. The biggest benefit from all of this you will see next year."

NATIONALITY German
DATE OF BIRTH 30/6/75
PLACE OF BIRTH Kerpen, Germany
GRANDS PRIX 164
WINS 6
POLES 6
FASTEST LAPS 8
POINTS 324
HONOURS Formula Nippon Champion 1996, Macau F3 GP winner 1995

17 JACQUES VILLENEUVE
↓-1 BMW SAUBER

"There wasn't really a huge high point, because we still had some mechanical failures, like the one at Indy – which was very annoying, because we were extremely competitive there.

The Australian GP was good, starting last and getting in the points. The season was just going well and we were going forward, apart from some races like the last one I did – in Germany – when the car just was not competitive, because both Nick [Heidfeld] and I were at the back.

The atmosphere in the team and all that was actually quite good. In the end, Nick scored more points, but on average I think I was ahead, which was good. We were working well, basically.

I'm glad I quit because I didn't wait another three months to see if maybe I'd be wanted or not, I just took a decision on the spot. The second I wasn't going to be in Hungary, the second I heard it, I made the decision on the spot. I didn't think about it for two days. It was 'I can't allow that to

happen to me, I can't allow people to just do stuff like that to me, I'll just take the decision and I'm done'.

After having been in Formula One for 10 years and having won the world championship and so on, even though it's quite a few years ago, I wasn't ready to stay home some weekends just to see how the other guy would go and then be compared to him. Not because I was worried that he would go faster or slower, it could happen both ways and that would be life.

By the time it happened I'd cleansed my image, within the paddock anyway, compared to how it was leaving BAR. Nobody thought any more that I was difficult to work with, that I wasn't driving well. Everything had turned positive again. I'm quite happy to leave F1 like that. The way it was done in 2003, that wasn't good, because it festers. It's like when you have a bad mushroom and it just gets worse and worse! Now you leave clean and happy with what you've achieved."

NATIONALITY Canadian
DATE OF BIRTH 9/4/71
PLACE OF BIRTH St Jean Sur Richelieu, Canada
GRANDS PRIX 165
WINS 11
POLES 13
FASTEST LAPS 9
POINTS 235
HONOURS F1 World Champion 1997, Champ Car Champion & Indy 500 winner 1995

18 CHRISTIAN KLIEN

↓ -3 RED BULL RACING

"It proved to be an extremely disappointing year for me.

Before the season started, we all thought as a team that Red Bull Racing would be able to get on the podium this year, which became hard to achieve because of a lot of problems at the beginning of the season.

These were reliability problems. So it was very difficult for us to get points. That was for sure disappointing for the team, for myself, and we tried to push really hard to improve the car.

In the end, I had only two points to my name, but it could have been a lot more. For example, I could have been on the podium in Monaco. Then I could have had points in Canada. It could have been a lot better if the reliability issues hadn't been there.

Monaco was very disappointing. I was in P5, and in front of David, when I had a gearbox problem. It could have been a podium. In the end, David achieved it, which was good for the team, but it hurts when you see that I could have been on the

podium and it could have looked a lot different. Twenty-three, already on the podium in Monaco, I think that would have been a great achievement.

In Canada, I was running in eighth place and then second gear broke and I lost a couple of positions.

We had so many reliability problems in the first half of the season. Out of the first 12 races, I had six technical problems, and it was just too much. Obviously, we had the cooling issues in winter testing, and we didn't do a lot of miles. That's why when the season started we weren't actually ready.

After Hungary, they told me I would not be racing with Red Bull again in 2007. It was already quite late in the season, and after that I had to look for another direction, another team, for next year. Then after Monza the team told me that I was not going to race the last three races, and obviously that was very disappointing, because for sure I wanted to finish the season with Red Bull Racing."

NATIONALITY Austrian
DATE OF BIRTH 7/2/83
PLACE OF BIRTH Hohenems, Austria
GRANDS PRIX 48
WINS 0
POLES 0
FASTEST LAPS 0
POINTS 14
HONOURS Marlboro Masters winner 2003, German Formula Renault Champion 2002

19 VITANTONIO LIUZZI

↑ +1 TORO ROSSO

"I'm disappointed, because we could have scored some more points this year. I think in Australia, Monaco and Montréal we had a really good chance, and maybe we didn't do things as we should, and also we had a bit of bad luck, but that's part of the game. That's the really disappointing point of the year.

As to the rest, we are all pretty happy in the team. Our aim was to grow all together, me with the team, and I think I made the right step forward. I gave the right support to the team to go ahead. In the second part of the season, things got slightly worse for me, because we had some issues with the chassis that we struggled to find a reason for. For a few races, we were struggling, but then we found the right way again.

At the start of the season, a lot of rumours said that our engine would be massively good, but they were completely wrong. We said from when we tried it the first time that the restriction was too high. Also, the V10 may have more torque at the bottom, but every time you go out, you've got traction-

control activities. So the places where it could have been better, you don't use it, because it's stopped by the traction control.

Overall, it's been a big handicap for the entire season, but Cosworth did a good job for us, and we just had to live with the fact that we had a different engine.

For sure, it was really difficult to accept, because at the beginning everyone was thinking that we would fly, especially at Monaco or Hungary, but in the slow circuits it was even worse for us, because of more traction-control activities.

For me, the highlights were the Australian GP, where unfortunately I had a meeting with Jacques Villeneuve, and Hungary in the wet, where Kimi didn't see me when he was lapping me. We could have finished both races in the points.

Like I said, the most important thing was for the team to grow and establish a really good base for 2007. We are working really hard on the new car, and that's when we have to be ready."

NATIONALITY Italian
DATE OF BIRTH 6/8/81
PLACE OF BIRTH Locorotondo, Italy
GRANDS PRIX 22
WINS 0
POLES 0
FASTEST LAPS 0
POINTS 2
HONOURS Formula 3000 Champion 2004, World Kart Champion 2001, Italian Kart Champion 1996

20 TAKUMA SATO
↓-6 SUPER AGURI

NATIONALITY Japanese DATE OF BIRTH 28/1/77 PLACE OF BIRTH Tokyo, Japan GRANDS PRIX 70 WINS 0 POLES 0 FASTEST LAPS 0 POINTS 40 HONOURS British F3 Champion 2001

"It was a great feeling to go to Bahrain. Nobody could believe it initially, but now they saw us for themselves. It was great to get through scrutineering without any bad moments, get through qualifying and go to the grid. That was our job done, and it was a perfect start. Of course, we had so many problems in the race and were lapped five or six times, but at least we finished our very first race, so that was a great moment. Malaysia was a good one – I never expected I could actually challenge anyone in my second grand prix with this team, but

circumstances allowed me to do so, and again we finished. Then in Melbourne we had a great battle with bigger teams, including Coulthard and Barrichello! But we were still off the pace massively in clean air, and I was always scared that when the honeymoon period ended everyone would be negative about us. But it was great to see everybody still supporting us, and we still believed in ourselves. Although we were still tailenders, I think slowly and gradually we closed the gap. If you see the data, we were always catching up, which was very important."

21 SCOTT SPEED
TORO ROSSO

NATIONALITY American DATE OF BIRTH 24/1/83 PLACE OF BIRTH Manteca, USA GRANDS PRIX 18 WINS 0 POLES 0 FASTEST LAPS 0 POINTS 0 HONOURS European & German Formula Renault Champion, US Formula Russell Champion 2001

"It was more difficult than I expected, and I know I have now raised myself to a different level. And that was unbelievable for me. You assume that there's only so much you can do as a driver, then you go to the next level and you realise that there's more you can do. I definitely learned a lot with the team, and growing with a team like this, who are so much better at the end of the year than they were at the beginning, it's been a good position to be entering F1. Rather than going right into a team that's already so established

and knows exactly what's going on, when you can grow with the team, it's very good. The whole Bahrain race weekend was very difficult. In the race itself, it was my first time in a real pit stop, and to be on the limit for a whole F1 race is really, really difficult. You look at the guys like Alonso and Schumacher, and to be able to do so many grands prix without making any big mistakes is impressive. It's certainly something you get better at as you go through the years, but the first race in Bahrain was a big eye-opener."

22 CHRISTIJAN ALBERS
↑+1 SPYKER MF1

NATIONALITY Dutch DATE OF BIRTH 16/4/79 PLACE OF BIRTH Eindhoven, Netherlands GRANDS PRIX 37 WINS 0 POLES 0 FASTEST LAPS 0 POINTS 4 HONOURS German F3 Champion 1999, Benelux & Dutch Formula Ford Champion 1997

"The team worked really hard this year. Of course I give them quite a lot of push. Sometimes they like it, but sometimes they don't like it! But I think it's also my job to push everybody. I have to say I'm quite happy with the way we are working. We do a good job for the amount of testing we do. We work really hard, and we're making progress all the time. Bridgestone is also pushing us in the right direction and helping us with the right information. Working together gets easier and easier. We can still improve everywhere, but I think

everyone is doing the maximum they can do. That's the most important thing in life sometimes, atmosphere. The team has got a good atmosphere, and with that, you can work to the top. That's what you see with the big teams. Some of them have it, some of them don't have it, and then you see the performance is not there. We know we're not like the top teams, but I am satisfied if you see what we all did with the car to come so far. We're making progress every day, and everyone knows that we're not testing very much."

23 TIAGO MONTEIRO
↓-4 SPYKER MF1

NATIONALITY Portuguese DATE OF BIRTH 24/7/76 PLACE OF BIRTH Oporto, Portugal GRANDS PRIX 37 WINS 0 POLES 0 FASTEST LAPS 0 POINTS 7 HONOURS None

"We didn't have so many opportunities to score points this time, but we've been a lot more competitive. It's a bit of a mixed feeling. It was good to be closer in qualifying, being able to go into the second group sometimes, fighting for positions on track with other drivers, which didn't happen much in 2005. So that was very good and very motivating. On the other side, there's been a lot of reliability from the other teams, not many people going off, not many people stopping on the track, and therefore not many chances for us to score points! It was

a totally different car, balance-wise especially. That's where we made a huge gain, in terms of balance and downforce. We have a lot of things to work on, but it was a different car, a different world. It's looking good for next year – a new engine, Mike Gascoyne coming in with his shopping list, so things are going to be very different. Spyker is a constructor, even if it's a small one. For them it's the perfect sport to be in, so that's how they're going to sell more cars. They're going to make their brand known. So they're motivated, and that's what we need."

FRANCK MONTAGNY

NATIONALITY French **DATE OF BIRTH** 5/1/78 **PLACE OF BIRTH** Feurs, France **GRANDS PRIX** 7 **WINS** 0 **POLES** 0 **FASTEST LAPS** 0 **POINTS** 0 **HONOURS** Formula Nissan World Series Champion 2003, French Formula Campus Champion 1994

"For a few years, I was a test driver, but this year I was back in F1 for racing and I was pleased to do that. Sure, I would like to go with a better team or a better car. You always want more. You know how it is, it's normal for a driver! Monaco was my first finish. Unfortunately we had a lot of little problems with the car, and the set-up was very, very understeering. I had a big problem with the very, very low power steering, which gave me a lot of kickback on my hands. At the end of the race, I could not hold the steering wheel any more! The race at Magny-Cours was a strange feeling for sure, because it was my home grand prix, and it was my last one with Super Aguri. It was the end of a story, but the beginning of a new one. Anyway, I'm very happy about that race, we had a fairly good pace, not too slow compared to the others. I think it was my best race. It's very hard to get a race drive for sure, but you never know – look at Pedro de la Rosa. He never thought that he would have another chance to get out there and race."

25 ROBERT DOORNBOS

↑+1 RED BULL

NATIONALITY Dutch **DATE OF BIRTH** 23/9/81 **PLACE OF BIRTH** Rotterdam, Netherlands **GRANDS PRIX** 11 **WINS** 0 **POLES** 0 **FASTEST LAPS** 0 **POINTS** 0 **HONOURS** None

"It was obviously a big difference coming to a team with 500 people from a team like Minardi that had 80! My first factory tour took a bit longer than expected, but it was great to see some familiar faces: I knew Christian Horner from my F3000 season in 2004. As test driver, I expected a bit more from the team. I was at most of the tests, but just standing around in the pits a lot because of problems on the car. So I didn't get the mileage that a third driver at BMW or McLaren got. That was quite disappointing, but Fridays were the cherry on the cake for me, and it was good to see my name in the top three on a consistent basis. It was really good to finish the season with a race seat for three races, and a chance to prove myself. David Coulthard is a very experienced and quick team-mate, and to outqualify him straight away in China was good. I started in the top 10, but had a bit of a coming together with Kubica, and lost the nose. So I had to start from the back, but if you see the lap times, I was always quicker than David."

26 SAKON YAMAMOTO

SUPER AGURI

NATIONALITY Japanese **DATE OF BIRTH** 9/7/82 **PLACE OF BIRTH** Toyohashi City, Japan **GRANDS PRIX** 7 **WINS** 0 **POLES** 0 **FASTEST LAPS** 0 **POINTS** 0 **HONOURS** Japanese Kart Champion 1999

"I would have liked to have had a whole season with Super Aguri Racing, but I did what I could do in a very short time, only seven grands prix. Before that, I was the team's third driver at four grands prix, but you just have two hours on a Friday, and everybody is watching you – it's not like a normal testing day when you can drive in a relaxed mood and there's no pressure. When I moved up to race for Super Aguri, I didn't really have a satisfying race until the Chinese GP. I finally finished there but, looking at the race time, I knew I still had to improve in lots of areas, like how to use the tyres, or deciding when to pit. Everything was good experience for me. I tried to do my best in every race, but of course Suzuka was very important for me! It was definitely a fantastic feeling to come back to Suzuka as an F1 driver. When I was seven or eight years old, I went to watch a grand prix at Suzuka and I knew at that time that I wanted to become a Formula One driver. I hope this is not the end of my F1 career, as I plan to carry on in the future."

27 YUJI IDE

SUPER AGURI

NATIONALITY Japanese **DATE OF BIRTH** 21/1/75 **PLACE OF BIRTH** Saitama, Japan **GRANDS PRIX** 4 **WINS** 0 **POLES** 0 **FASTEST LAPS** 0 **POINTS** 0 **HONOURS** None

"When I think back to my four grands prix at the start of the season, I feel rather bitter. I knew that Super Aguri Racing was completely new to Formula One, that they didn't have enough equipment or anything like enough time to test properly before the season got underway. In fact, all I did before my first grand prix at Bahrain was a run-out at an airfield near the Super Aguri factory in England. Because of this lack of time with the car, neither my engineer nor I were properly ready to start racing. It was so difficult to drive even on the straights at Sepang and I had to really concentrate just to keep my car on the track in Australia... At the San Marino Grand Prix, things were rather better. I thought that my collision with [Christijan] Albers early in the race was just a racing accident and he said the same thing, but... It all went by so quickly, but I really enjoyed my short time in F1. It was so totally different from all the other forms of racing that I have done up to now in my racing career and I really want to try again some day."

THE TEAMS

Eleven teams, all very different, some successful from the outset, others having to work at it. We talk to the technical directors about how they developed their cars

RENAULT

THE TEAM

PERSONNEL

PRESIDENT Alain Dassas
MANAGING DIRECTOR Flavio Briatore
TECHNICAL DIRECTOR (CHASSIS) Bob Bell
TECHNICAL DIRECTOR (ENGINE) Rob White
DEPUTY MANAGING DIRECTOR (SUPPORT OPERATIONS) André Laine
EXEC DIRECTOR OF ENGINEERING Pat Symonds (above)
HEAD OF ENGINE OPERATIONS Denis Chevrier
VEHICLE TECHNOLOGY DIRECTOR Tad Czapski
CHIEF DESIGNER Tim Densham
R26 PROJECT MANAGER Leon Taillieu
HEAD OF AERODYNAMICS Dino Toso
TEAM MANAGER Steve Nielsen
DRIVERS Fernando Alonso, Giancarlo Fisichella
RACE ENGINEER (Alonso) Rod Nelson
RACE ENGINEER (Fisichella) Alan Permane
TEST TEAM MANAGER Carlos Nunes
TEST/THIRD DRIVER Heikki Kovalainen
CHIEF MECHANIC Gavin Hudson
TOTAL NUMBER OF EMPLOYEES 790
NUMBER IN RACE TEAM 70
TEAM BASE Enstone, England
TELEPHONE +44 (0)1608 678000
WEBSITE www.renaultf1.com

TEAM STATS

IN F1 SINCE 1977–1985 then from 2002 **FIRST GRAND PRIX** Britain 1977 then Australia 2002 **STARTS** 211 **WINS** 33 **POLE POSITIONS** 49 **FASTEST LAPS** 27 **PODIUMS** 88 **POINTS** 925 **CONSTRUCTORS' TITLES** 2 **DRIVERS' TITLES** 2

SPONSORS

Mild Seven, Elf, Hanjin, Telefonica, ChronoTech, i-mode

1 **FERNANDO ALONSO**   2 **GIANCARLO FISICHELLA**

By Pat Symonds (Executive Director of Engineering)
"The R26 had no fundamental changes over the R25 and was largely a tune-up of the 2005 car but, saying that, the switch to V8 engines certainly changed things quite a lot.

In terms of installation, it was not bad at all. You've worked with the people, you know all your heat rejection figures and there was nothing difficult, and the vibration problems that we'd been a bit worried about weren't significant. The hydraulic pump mounting was one issue we had, but there were very few.

The V8 hit the ground running and was quite impressive. We'd got the V10s very smooth to drive with the variable trumpets. There were a couple of occasions when the trumpets hadn't worked properly and the thing became a bit lumpy and hard to drive. I thought that was going to be a characteristic of the V8s without the variable trumpets, even more so because you didn't have the torque, but in fact they did a very good job of smoothing the power curve.

One thing we did realise was that we absolutely could not run the six-speed gearbox with a V8. We'd been the last to hang onto six-speeds with the V10 because we felt it was quicker – and I'm still convinced – but we needed a seven-speed with the V8, and that helped to smooth it out to some extent. It meant our average rpm was up massively, coupled with the fact that you've got less power and are at full throttle a lot more, so the duty cycle of the V8 was staggeringly harder than the V10, even though you had the same bore and basic geometry.

Monza was our only real engine failure, whereas we had a stupid situation with Giancarlo in Bahrain where we had a throttle problem in practice and fixed it without realising that it had damaged the actuator seal and we lost the hydraulic fluid.

We went to the Italian GP aware that there was a potential problem. We do two types of endurance work – the basic endurance cycle to sign off a new part, and that's always been two races at Spa qualifying speed, and then before each pair of races we do a very specific endurance test which simulates the two circuits we are going to. After we lost an engine at the Monza test, we ran some more Monza simulations and realised that for this particular failure it was made more severe by Monza than Spa. We therefore limited the performance for the Monza race, but unfortunately not quite enough. Fernando's engine failed and when Giancarlo's came out it was within a lap or two of doing the same.

We were a bit surprised at the way the V8s used the tyres – it really is very, very different. I think everyone just blindly thought that we'd all go softer, but it didn't quite work like that. It's true that the rear tyres don't get such a hard time at circuits where you are limited by rear tyre usage. What I didn't appreciate until we picked up a bit more experience is that on circuits where you are front-limited, the sliding speed of the cars is such that we were on tyres that were as hard as 2005, give or take a little, despite the fact that they were only doing a third of a race. It took us until Imola to figure that out – we were getting a lot more graining and a few things happening that we weren't sure about."

A GAME OF TWO HALVES

"Obviously, we made a great start to the 2006 World Championship, winning the first three races and, up to the Canadian GP, the halfway point of the season, we took seven of the first nine. But forgetting Indianapolis, where Michelin took a conservative tyre, we'd had plenty of alarm bells pre-Canada that it was not going to be easy, although I hadn't expected it to swing quite so much after North America.

The German GP was a disaster. The mass-damper ban, I guarantee, cost us 0.3s per lap and it's extremely hard work trying to get that back. My appeal documents ran to 116 pages and the FIA's was (Technical Document) TD35 with a cover page on it… We had models, we showed everything, and I was absolutely convinced it was an open-and-shut case. I absolutely know that we were right and what's sad is that it is the sort of thing we should be doing in F1 – simple, passive, easy devices.

If nothing else, I hope it's woken the motor industry up to the use of tuned mass dampers.

The ban in time for Hockenheim coincided with us making our worst tyre choice and having our worst balance on the car. Maybe it wasn't so coincidental because we hadn't been able to go testing. We had run a couple of days at Jerez without the mass damper, but hadn't really optimised the car. Fernando struggled more than Fisi, I think because he uses his tyres rather harder.

But, in Hungary, under any conditions, Fernando was just stunningly quick. He was going to win by miles until car failure let him down. In Turkey, we weren't as bad as in 2005, but I admit we were quite lucky. We had re-optimised the car by the final races and if you had put the mass dampers back on, maybe they wouldn't be worth quite 0.3s but certainly more than 0.2s. If they had been kept on the car, it would have been a different championship.

Fernando drove superbly all year. Last year he made a mistake in Canada and we said there was nothing wrong with making one mistake. But he hasn't made one at all this time, except for signing for McLaren! That didn't actually make a difference. We tease him a bit, obviously, but everyone gets teased at Renault. You have to live for today in this game and just get on with it.

Giancarlo had a bit of a mixed season. He hasn't had the consistency we hoped for and just as Fernando made no mistakes, Fisi made rather too many. It's psychological. Fernando has just got the winning mentality and Fisi hasn't. Yes, he can win and has won, but there are just times when he doesn't quite get there. I'm really hoping that next year he'll rise to the challenge.

Fisi has never been slower than a team-mate until he met Fernando. That's a hard thing to live with and to reconcile, and I think it's got to him a little bit. I really hope that next year we see Fisi back as we know him. It's there. He hasn't lost it, but I think he's just lost that little bit of confidence this year and he really it needs to get back. "

The Mégane Renaultsport 225 Cup.
Feel it for yourself.

Lap up the F1 experience in the Mégane Renaultsport 225 Cup. With its 18" spoked alloys, sharper steering and racing car-inspired chassis as standard, it's more than just another road car. To get in a few practice laps, text 'GAME' to 85101 for your free Renaultsport phone game. Or visit www.renaultsport.co.uk for more details.

Fuel consumption figures for the Mégane Renaultsport 225 Cup in mpg (l/100km): Urban: 24.6 (11.5), Extra Urban: 40.4 (7.0), Combined 32.1 (8.8). CO₂ emissions (g/km): 209.

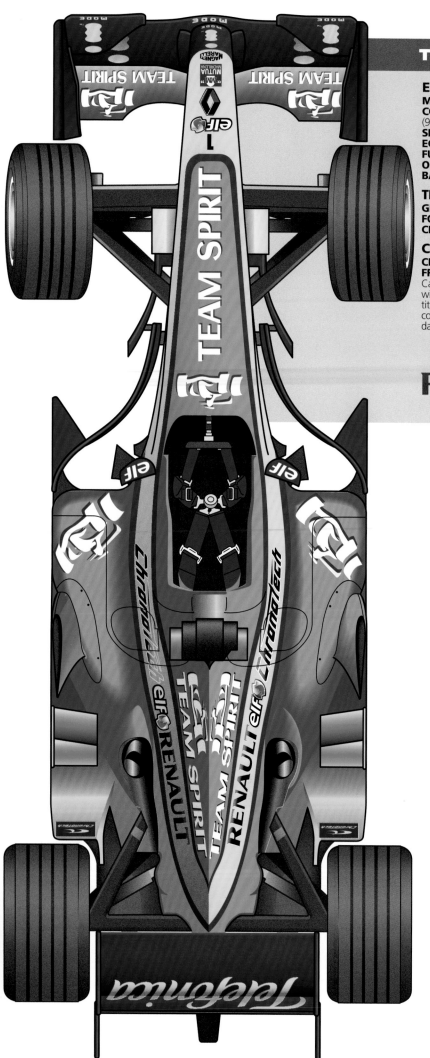

TECHNICAL SPECIFICATIONS

ENGINE
MAKE/MODEL Renault RS26
CONFIGURATION 2400cc V8
(90 degree)
SPARK PLUGS Champion
ECU Magneti Marelli
FUEL Elf
OIL Elf
BATTERY Renault F1

TRANSMISSION
GEARBOX Renault F1
FORWARD GEARS Seven
CLUTCH AP Racing

CHASSIS
CHASSIS MODEL Renault R26
FRONT SUSPENSION LAYOUT
Carbon-fibre top and bottom
wishbones operating an inboard
titanium rocker via a pushrod system
connected to a torsion bar and
damper units

REAR SUSPENSION LAYOUT
Carbon-fibre top and bottom
wishbones operating vertically
mounted torsion bars and
horizontally mounted damper units
DAMPERS Penske
TYRES Michelin
WHEELS OZ Racing
BRAKE DISCS Hitco
BRAKE PADS Hitco
BRAKE CALIPERS AP Racing
RADIATORS Undisclosed
FUEL TANK ATL
INSTRUMENTS Renault

DIMENSIONS
LENGTH 4800mm
WIDTH 1800mm
HEIGHT 950mm
WHEELBASE 3100mm
TRACK front 1450mm
rear 1400mm
WEIGHT 605kg (including driver
and camera)

RENAULT Team

1 New sidepod deflectors and longer flow conditioners on the side of the nose
were a development for the Canadian GP to channel air towards the rear wing
2 The mass damper's presence caused the FIA to ban it, something that annoyed
Pat Symonds, as he stands by the fact that it was passive rather than movable

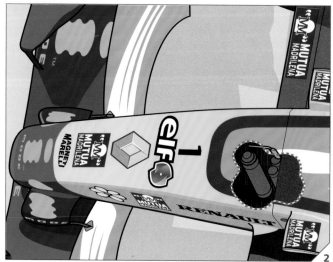

Join the winning team

FERRARI

THE TEAM

PERSONNEL
PRESIDENT Luca di Montezemolo
GENERAL DIRECTOR Jean Todt
TECHNICAL DIRECTOR Ross Brawn (above)
ENGINE DIRECTOR Paolo Martinelli
DIRECTOR OF FORMULA 1 RACING ACTIVITIES
Stefano Domenicali
TECHNICAL CONSULTANT Rory Byrne
CHIEF DESIGNER Nicolas Tombazis
SENIOR AERODYNAMICIST John Iley
HEAD OF DESIGN & DEVELOPMENT Aldo Costa
ENGINE DESIGN & DEVELOPMENT Gilles Simon
RACE & TEST TECHNICAL MANAGER Nigel Stepney
RACE ENGINE MANAGER Mattia Binotto
DRIVERS Felipe Massa, Michael Schumacher
CHIEF RACE ENGINEER Luca Baldisserri
RACE ENGINEER (Massa) Rob Smedley
RACE ENGINEER (Schumacher) Chris Dyer
TEST DRIVERS Luca Badoer, Marc Gené
TEST TEAM MANAGER Luigi Mazzola
CHIEF MECHANICS (Massa) Salvatore Vargetto
(Schumacher) Michele Giuntoli
TOTAL NUMBER OF EMPLOYEES 900
NUMBER IN RACE TEAM 90
TEAM BASE Maranello, Italy
TELEPHONE +39 0536 949450
WEBSITE www.ferrariworld.com

TEAM STATS
IN F1 SINCE 1950 **FIRST GRAND PRIX** Britain 1950
STARTS 741 **WINS** 192 **POLE POSITIONS** 186
FASTEST LAPS 192 **PODIUMS** 581 **POINTS** 3645.5
CONSTRUCTORS' TITLES 14 **DRIVERS' TITLES** 14

SPONSORS
Vodafone, FIAT, Shell, AMD, Bridgestone, Martini, Acer

5 MICHAEL SCHUMACHER　　**6 FELIPE MASSA**

By Ross Brawn (Technical Director)

"As with everyone, we had the change to the 2.4-litre V8 to consider, and there was a packaging issue, which was quite different. We were coming off a bad year in 2005, but a number of good years with the same group of people, so we didn't look towards making radical changes within the team. We just looked at where we felt we hadn't made enough progress, set higher targets and gave the people more resource to achieve them.

The other thing is that it's a fact that the one-race tyre did not suit either our philosophy or Bridgestone's philosophy, so the change back to multi-tyre races was a major help for us.

It's hard to compare with last year because of the one-tyre rule, but compared to 2004 we're running softer this year. It has not made a dramatic difference in the approach to the car, but obviously the V8 has a bit less fuel consumption, although the driver is on the throttle for longer, so it's not as much as you might think.

Tyre wars have pluses and minuses but it has been a very exciting programme in its own right. There was a huge commitment from Ferrari and Bridgestone to being competitive, and it's been great to try to understand how the tyre works, what the variables are and build the department at Ferrari that has worked with Bridgestone. Most of that's going to disappear, which is a shame, but it can also be a bit of an unfair variable in that if you haven't got the right tyre you're really wasting your time.

It's actually quite hard to judge respective car performance levels because the tyres were such a variable and I don't know what Renault were doing. We can only look at our references and we've been gaining 0.1s or 0.2s every couple of races. I'd say that over the season we've gone forward by 0.75s–1.00s per lap.

I said at the start of the season that I thought we had a very good car, but we didn't make good use of it. We had a bit of a tardy pit stop at the opening grand prix in Bahrain and lost the race to Fernando by a very small margin. We also had some engine problems at the beginning of the season and had to drop the revs. That had quite a knock-on effect for two or three races because of the sequencing. We had some 10-place penalties at the beginning of the season and, as is the nature of the regulations now, it tends to impact on you for two or three races before you get yourself sorted out.

In Australia, we made a bad tyre choice, but when they did actually start to work, Michael was very quick. You could see that the car performance was excellent from the start, and I think the team has done a great job of improving and progressing it. The rate of progress has been the highest I've seen while I've been at Ferrari. The failings in 2005 certainly wounded pride and I think the effort made this year was quite exceptional.

The engine performance progressed through the year too and the amount of revs you can use extends. When you increase the rpm it's initially just for qualifying and the odd lap, and then you try and consolidate that and use it for more and more of the race. If you don't do many laps in practice, it gives you a few more laps at higher revs in the race and you do that sort of trade all over the weekend. A lot of rpm management goes on across the two races.

After the Canadian GP, we were 25 points down and I think it was a great effort to go to Japan with Michael and Fernando level. There were obviously a couple of occasions when people questioned our judgement, but hindsight is perfect vision. Undoubtedly, I wish I had told Michael to back off in Hungary and take it easy on those last three laps.

I really don't believe that anyone gets it right all of the time and while you are fortunate if you are running at the front, it also means that you are under close scrutiny all the time, so perhaps our howlers show up a little bit more."

MAKING UP FOR A POOR START

"Overall, I'm pretty happy with the season, and the fact that we went to the final race 10 points behind was not just a reflection on Suzuka but on other things we didn't quite get right through the year. We didn't make a strong enough start, but I think for a large part of the season we had had the upper hand.

The Japanese GP, of course, was bitterly disappointing, but it was a one-off. It was a failure of the top end of a valve where it connects to the collets around the pneumatic piston. It was nothing that we'd seen before and we didn't have a complete explanation.

Despite Michael making his retirement decision, I don't think emotions affected the year too strongly. Not for me personally and I don't think for the team. There was a period when Michael was wrestling his decision, but his performance in China, right after he announced it, was classic Michael. When he dived down the inside of Fisichella to take the lead, we'd spoken before about Michelin having a warm-up problem. We were trying to get a lap difference between ourselves and Giancarlo to take advantage, and Michael knew that he had that one lap to do it. But I didn't expect him to do it in the first corner! It was exciting stuff.

Felipe, too, has had a very good first year at Ferrari. There was his first victory, in Istanbul, pole position at the same race and then again in his home grand prix at Interlagos. He fought tooth and nail to take third place in the drivers' championship behind Michael and Fernando.

Looking back, though, people will remember 2006 as Michael's final year. The thing that's quite outstanding is that he has never had a bad period. He might have a bad race – every driver has a bad race – but he's never had a period when you think he is not performing terribly well. He's always performed at the top level all the time.

Sometimes the races go well for him, sometimes they don't, but you get a footballer or a golfer and they go through a bad spell. But Michael never has. The fact that he's been so consistent at the top, featuring in and challenging for virtually every World Championship throughout his career is outstanding. That's the measure of him. I'm sorry to see him go, but delighted that he went out demonstrating the strength and competitiveness he has this season."

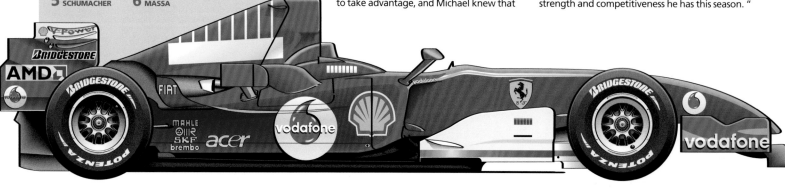

LIVE FOR TODAY.

AND TOMORROW.

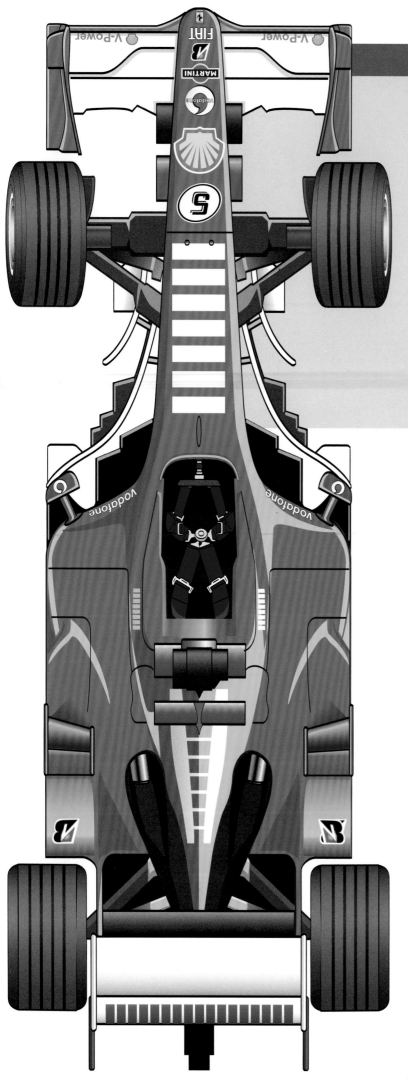

TECHNICAL SPECIFICATIONS

ENGINE
MAKE/MODEL Ferrari 056
CONFIGURATION 2398cc V8 (90 degree)
SPARK PLUGS NGK
ECU Magneti Marelli
FUEL Shell
OIL Shell
BATTERY Magneti Marelli

TRANSMISSION
GEARBOX Ferrari
FORWARD GEARS Seven
CLUTCH ZF Sachs

CHASSIS
CHASSIS MODEL Ferrari 248
FRONT SUSPENSION LAYOUT
Double wishbones with pushrod-activated torsion springs
REAR SUSPENSION LAYOUT
Double wishbones with pushrod-activated torsion springs
DAMPERS ZF Sachs
TYRES Bridgestone
WHEELS BBS
BRAKE DISCS Carbone Industrie
BRAKE PADS Carbone Industrie
BRAKE CALIPERS Brembo
RADIATORS Secan/Marston

FUEL TANK ATL
INSTRUMENTS Ferrari/Magneti Marelli

DIMENSIONS
LENGTH 4545mm
WIDTH 1800mm
HEIGHT 959mm
WHEELBASE 3050mm
TRACK front 1470mm
rear 1405mm
WEIGHT 605kg (including driver and camera)

1 Constant revisions, such as these new bargeboards introduced at the San Marino GP, led to a gain of 0.75–1.00s per lap from the start of the year to the end
2 Among the myriad developments introduced during the season in their quest to catch up with Renault, Ferrari brought in revised brake ducts at the French GP

McLAREN

By Martin Whitmarsh (Chief Operating Officer)

"The 2.4 V8s had the predicted effects in terms of scale and packaging, but I think we underestimated the heat rejection possible. Mercedes pursued revs, clearly the right strategy but, in so doing, the heat rejection is non-linear, and that became an issue. The technical team at Mercedes responded well and did a very good job during the year. We are not looking at the engine as a point of excuse, though, as our overall package was not as good as we wanted.

The changes to the aerodynamic regulations were quite significant, but the change to the tyre rules overrode that. It dominated the technical landscape. Tyres suddenly not having to last through qualifying and a race distance opened up a lot of performance potential despite the reduction in power. Cornering speeds increased, and that brought other challenges. With hindsight, we could have done a better job of anticipating that, although aspects of the car were well defined when the change occurred.

Higher cornering speeds generated higher loads at the contact patch and higher temperatures. With grooved tyres you get this moving tread sensation and, while softer tyres should generate more grip, it was sometimes hard for the driver to understand the limits of the tyre.

Tyres, to a large extent, overshadowed the year. We started off behind Renault but happy with our tyre situation. As the season progressed, things changed. At Indy, we were hoping it was either a conservative Michelin or something we hadn't quite got right, as there was a pendulum in performance between Michelin and Bridgestone.

We hoped it was a one-off, but it proved not to be, and that was quite a pivotal point, although I'm not wishing to excuse ourselves on the performance of our tyre partner. Over time with Michelin, being fair, we can't complain.

We struggled a little getting tyre temperature if we benchmark ourselves against Renault. From halfway through 2005 we had a package that was kinder on the tyres and, in that circumstance, it was an advantage. This year, you had to be able to generate enough heat, and there were times when we could not. At other times, when our car could carry a softer tyre, we overheated it.

I think we had several races that slipped by us, which was frustrating. In Monaco and China, there were opportunities to win. But, overall, our chassis was not good enough to be winning consistently."

THE TEAM

PERSONNEL

TEAM PRINCIPAL, CHAIRMAN AND GROUP CEO
Ron Dennis
VICE-PRESIDENT MERCEDES-BENZ MOTORSPORT
Norbert Haug
CHIEF OPERATING OFFICER, McLAREN GROUP
Martin Whitmarsh (above)
MANAGING DIRECTOR Jonathan Neale
DESIGN & DEVELOPMENT DIRECTOR Neil Oatley
ENGINEERING DIRECTOR Paddy Lowe
CHIEF DESIGNER Mike Coughlan
CHIEF AERODYNAMICIST Simon Lacey
HEAD OF RACE ENGINEERING Steve Hallam
HEAD OF SIMULATION Dick Glover
CHIEF ENGINEER MP4-21 Tim Goss
TEAM MANAGER Dave Ryan
DRIVERS Pedro de la Rosa, Juan Pablo Montoya, Kimi Räikkönen
RACE ENGINEER (de la Rosa/Montoya) Phil Prew
RACE ENGINEER (Räikkönen) Mark Slade
TEST TEAM MANAGER Indy Lall
TEST DRIVERS Pedro de la Rosa, Gary Paffett
CHIEF MECHANIC Stephen Giles
TEAM BASE Woking, England
TELEPHONE +44 (0)1483 261000
WEBSITE www.mclaren.com

TEAM STATS

IN F1 SINCE 1966 **FIRST GRAND PRIX** Monaco 1966
STARTS 613 **WINS** 148 **POLE POSITIONS** 125
FASTEST LAPS 129 **PODIUMS** 394 **POINTS** 3150.5
CONSTRUCTORS' TITLES 8 **DRIVERS' TITLES** 11

SPONSORS

Johnnie Walker, Siemens, Emirates, Mobil, Henkel, Schuco

3 KIMI RAIKKÖNEN **4 JUAN PABLO MONTOYA** **4 PEDRO DE LA ROSA**

A BACKGROUND OF INSTABILITY

"Losing a driver halfway through the year, as we did with Montoya, did not help. And, if you put world-class drivers like Kimi in with a chance of winning races consistently, they tend to find something extra. Having said that, there were plenty of occasions when Kimi did a fantastic job, even if he didn't find it as stimulating as fighting for the championship in 2005. We had some stunning qualifying performances and poles.

The reality was that until days before the Ferrari announcement, you could stare into the eyes of Kimi's management and be told he may well stay. All of our normal F1 antennae and judgement told us to the contrary, but you have to accept it on face value, and we did.

People could criticise and ask if we were really that gullible, but we sensed something awry a year ago and decided to move for Fernando. We had opened a discussion with Kimi and said we'd like to extend. We gave them the chance to sign, but we sensed market activity at play, so we told them that if we didn't have an answer by a given date, we would go into the market.

We approached Fernando and asked if he would like to drive for us. He said yes and we asked who we should speak to. We spoke to the people he nominated and, quickly and simply, did a deal. People characterised it as some clandestine unreasonable act, but it's difficult to approach someone who is the current Team Principal to talk about it, where there's just a little hint of potential conflict of interest, so I think we acted reasonably.

Did it destabilise Juan Pablo? Yes. He was in a difficult situation because we were straightforward and honest, but he recognised that to some extent his future was awaiting the outcome of another driver. I think Juan Pablo is a very brave, very likeable, very skilled individual, but our partnership did not achieve its potential. Silverstone 2005 was fantastic and he had moments of greatness. But having Kimi as a team-mate is a challenge.

The year started with Juan Pablo aiming at keeping his drive, but the pressure builds and it was difficult. We were in no hurry, but he and his management were saying 'Well, we've heard Kimi has definitely gone, ask anyone and it's a done deal, you're not being told the truth'. We just said: 'It may or may not be true, but this is what we are told'. I think we were straightforward and honest, not manipulative. It gradually built up and it wasn't a single incident, although Indianapolis (where Montoya collided with Räikkönen) was a testy point. Undeniably that was the catalyst.

Obviously, people talk about the departure of Adrian [Newey] and [aero chief] Peter [Prodromou], who both joined Red Bull. I was instrumental in recruiting them and worked with Peter for maybe 15 years. They are both very talented individuals and so, yes, something walks out of the door with them. The reality, though, is that our engineering team is 160 strong.

Adrian was very creatively involved, but had stepped back from management of the engineering programme. We have the likes of Paddy Lowe, Neil Oatley, Tim Goss, Pat Fry and Mike Coughlan – tremendous strength in depth.

Aerodynamics, unsurprisingly, has undergone the biggest change. We have a team of 80 aerodynamicists with some pretty good guys, and what tends to happen when people leave is that others blossom, and that's been happening.

We've also had some external recruitment. Nicholas Hennell, one of the really bright guys from Renault's aero department and Simon Lacey, former head of aero at Honda, have joined us. We've got a broader participation of individuals in the aero process, which in our judgement will make us stronger.

But the truth, really, is that the aerodynamic definition and layout of this year's car came from Adrian and the test will be next year. It's great to see people from your own organisation grow and develop, but if we sense they are not going to deliver, we are capable of head-hunting. That's considered aggressive but, when others do it, quite reasonable – big, bad McLaren!"

What do the Team McLaren Mercedes MP4-21
and the Mercedes-Benz SLR McLaren
have in common? Both rely on
Mobil 1 with SuperSyn technology
for advanced wear protection
and enhanced performance.
Mobil 1. Let it perform for you.

**THE MORE YOU KNOW ABOUT MOBIL 1,
THE BETTER IT IS FOR YOUR CAR.**

**TEAM McLAREN MERCEDES
TECHNOLOGY PARTNER**

Mobil 1

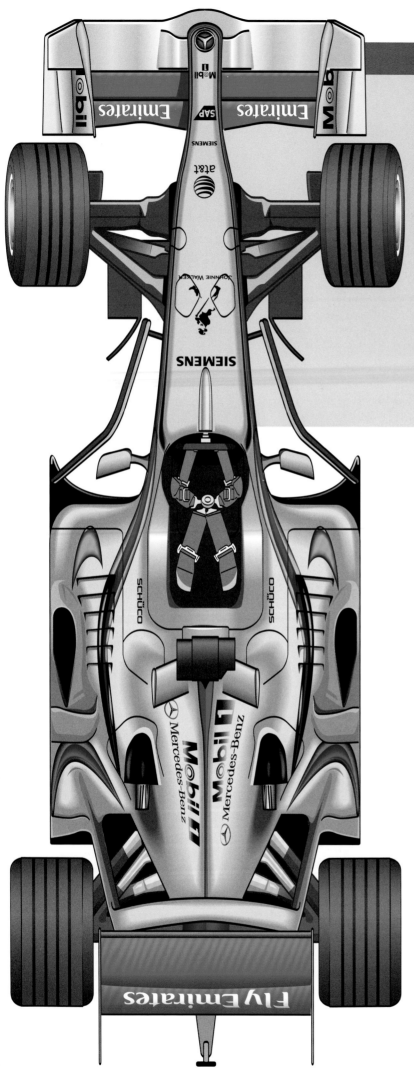

TECHNICAL SPECIFICATIONS

ENGINE
MAKE/MODEL Mercedes-Ilmor FO 108S
CONFIGURATION 2400cc V8 (90 degree)
SPARK PLUGS NGK
ECU McLaren Electronic Systems
FUEL Mobil 1
OIL Mobil 1
BATTERY GS Yuasa

TRANSMISSION
GEARBOX McLaren
FORWARD GEARS Seven
CLUTCH McLaren

CHASSIS
CHASSIS MODEL McLaren MP4-21
FRONT SUSPENSION LAYOUT
Inboard torsion bar/damper system operated by pushrod and bellcrank with a double wishbone arrangement
REAR SUSPENSION LAYOUT
Inboard torsion bar/damper system operated by pushrod and bellcrank with a double wishbone arrangement

DAMPERS McLaren
TYRES Michelin
WHEELS Enkei
BRAKE DISCS Hitco
BRAKE PADS AP Racing
BRAKE CALIPERS AP Racing
RADIATORS McLaren
FUEL TANK ATL
INSTRUMENTS McLaren Electronic Systems

DIMENSIONS
LENGTH 4600mm
WIDTH 1800mm
HEIGHT 950mm
WHEELBASE 3100mm
TRACK front 1450mm **rear** 1400mm
WEIGHT 600kg (including driver and camera)

Team McLaren Mercedes

1 Like many teams, McLaren struggled pre-season with heat rejection calculations, and the rear bodywork had to be revised to keep temperatures down
2 This front wing was introduced for the German Grand Prix as the team learned to cope with tyres that no longer had to last qualifying and the full race distance

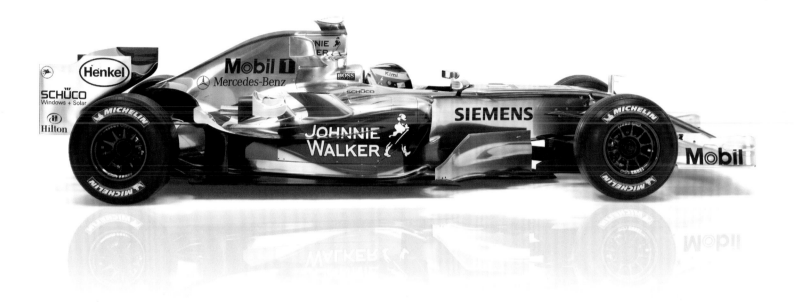

HONDA

By Jacky Eeckelaert
(Chief Engineer Advanced Research Programmes)
"Before the season, in winter testing, the car seemed to be quite fast, close to the pace of the Renault and Ferrari, but only on the first few laps. On longer runs, we lacked some pace. You could see it in the first races when we qualified much better than we raced.

Jenson qualified on pole in Australia, but the race pace was not there, and it got worse as the season went on, when our qualifying pace also started to desert us.

We were a little behind in different areas of development. One of the reasons was that the new wind tunnel was in its final stages of set-up as the season started, but a lot of effort went into setting it up and so the development on the aerodynamic side was lagging. The aero department was growing, we were hiring new people and that all eats up time, so the development was not quite following the path foreseen.

We had the first new aero kit at Imola. The profiled front wishbones and the mirror fairings were the obvious visual changes, and that was OK. Then we had a second new package in Magny-Cours. Part of that was a new front wing, with new flaps that were designed to take some loading off the mainplane and ease the loss of downforce when the front wheels were turned. The kit itself was good, but it harmed the engine cooling and we had to open the bodywork up so much that we ended up with less downforce than previously.

By then, we'd had some organisational changes as well, with Technical Director Geoff Willis leaving the team. With Honda taking over as owners, you would expect changes, but they didn't happen at the start of the season and I think it was a case of

waiting to see, as the car had been competitive in winter testing and at the first two races. When they saw the dip approaching mid-season that, for them, was the right moment to make changes.

Geoff, I suppose, didn't like one of the Japanese engineers (Nakamoto-san) taking overall control of the technical department. But Honda in Japan has a massive research and development centre – more than 10,000 people doing only R&D – and part of that helps develop the F1 engine and chassis.

My first job when I arrived from Sauber was to organise the co-ordination between the pair of headquarters in Japan and Brackley. It's important because they can do almost anything, not just designing and machining parts, but working on new alloys and whatever is needed. If you say that the Japan technical centre can become an important part of car development, then you need this co-ordination, and it's good that you have a man who is Japanese and also a racer, like Nakamoto-san, who also knows the European mentality after 20 years in motor racing. Before, Honda was more like an engine supplier who sometimes came up with ideas that may or may not have been adopted by Brackley. Now, they are a more integral part of the design and development process.

The car designed under Geoff's direction was good on the mechanical side – light, low centre of gravity, reliable, but we lacked aero development, and the rate of progress after the first race was too slow. We also had some reliability problems on the engine side that were not foreseen, and if the reliability is not there you don't test as well and so the performance suffers. It's a vicious circle, and when all these things combine you have a dip, which is what happened to us mid-season."

THE TEAM

PERSONNEL

CHIEF EXECUTIVE OFFICER Nick Fry
PRESIDENT OF HONDA RACING DEVELOPMENT Yasuhiro Wada
VICE PRESIDENT HONDA RACING DEVELOPMENT Otmar Szafnauer
SPORTING DIRECTOR Gil de Ferran
SENIOR TECHNICAL DIRECTOR Shuhei Nakamoto
DEPUTY TECHNICAL DIRECTOR Gary Savage
CHIEF DESIGNER Kevin Taylor
CHIEF ENGINEER ADVANCED RESEARCH PROGRAMMES Jacky Eeckelaert (above)
CHIEF AERODYNAMICIST Mariano Alperin-Bruvera
TEAM MANAGER Ron Meadows
DRIVERS Rubens Barrichello, Jenson Button
RACE ENGINEER (Barrichello) Jock Clear
RACE ENGINEER (Button) Andrew Shovlin
TEST TEAM MANAGER Andrew Alsworth
TEST/THIRD DRIVERS Anthony Davidson, James Rossiter
CHIEF MECHANIC Alastair Gibson
TOTAL NUMBER OF EMPLOYEES 550
NUMBER IN RACE TEAM 80
TEAM BASE Brackley, England
TELEPHONE +44 (0)1280 844000
WEBSITE www.hondaracingf1.com

TEAM STATS

IN F1 SINCE 1999 **FIRST GRAND PRIX** Australia 1999
STARTS 136 **WINS** 1 **POLE POSITIONS** 3
FASTEST LAPS 0 **PODIUMS** 18 **POINTS** 306
CONSTRUCTORS' TITLES 0 **DRIVERS' TITLES** 0

SPONSORS

Lucky Strike, Honda, Intercond, AVAYA, Ray Ban, Showa

11 RUBENS BARRICHELLO   **12 JENSON BUTTON**

THE FALL AND RISE

"The British GP was a shame, especially as it was Jenson's home race. We were struggling on the aero side for sure, the car was not well balanced and on a high-speed track it was a real problem.

After our Magny-Cours problems, we tested at Jerez and found a compromise. A few weeks after that, we got it all together and there was some engine evolution that gave us better performance and improved reliability. The wind tunnel was now working properly, and if Silverstone and Magny-Cours were our lows, from Hockenheim onwards we scored points all the time. Budapest, where Jenson took his fantastic win, gave everyone a boost and in the second half of the year we scored more than double the points we did in the first.

Rubens had a few problems at the start of the year and I can understand that because, for the last six years at Sauber, I was used to the Ferrari engine and software and I knew exactly where Rubens was coming from. The Ferrari philosophy of traction-control development was a step ahead of what I saw when I came to Honda. You could set it up so that coming out of low-speed corners you could floor the throttle and it would catch the car when it went into oversteer. That was not the case at Honda. It was optimised more for traction in a straight line, but in the corners it was not as far developed. Jenson had no problems with that because he is very smooth on the throttle and just uses the traction control a little. With Rubens, as soon as the nose was pointing in the right

direction he was used to flooring the throttle and letting the traction control do the rest, with him just controlling the car's attitude a little.

I went to Japan early in the year to explain this, the philosophy behind it, and they reacted and developed new software. Not only was the traction control different, but also the engine braking. They developed quite a powerful system of engine braking to avoid locking the rear wheels during downshifting. It was what Jacques Villeneuve found hard to cope with initially at Sauber.

This kind of thing is all very subtle, but some drivers are sensitive to it. On new tyres it's not such an issue, but as the tyres gets old and the car gets a bit more nervous, it's important to set up the systems to the driver's liking – nearly as important as the car set-up itself.

We are developing more sophisticated traction control/engine braking systems that can cope better with mixed track conditions. The grip level changes during a race weekend and if your system is not very sophisticated then you have massive set-up work every day, many hours to adapt it, and when it's wrong, it's wrong. So we try to develop systems that are more self-adapting and can cope with the evolution of the track or the tyre degradation. That work is never finished!

The important thing is that by the end of the season the rate of development was high and I am excited about prospects for 2007. The problem is that when you get to Ferrari/Renault territory, catching up gets more difficult!"

TECHNICAL SPECIFICATIONS

ENGINE
MAKE/MODEL Honda RA806E
CONFIGURATION 2400cc V8
(90 degree)
SPARK PLUGS NGK
ECU Honda
FUEL Elf
OIL Nisseki
BATTERY NGK

TRANSMISSION
GEARBOX Honda/XTrac
FORWARD GEARS Seven
CLUTCH AP Racing

CHASSIS
CHASSIS MODEL Honda RA106
FRONT SUSPENSION LAYOUT
Wishbones and pushrod-activated torsion springs and rockers with a mechanical anti-roll bar

REAR SUSPENSION LAYOUT
Wishbones and pushrod-activated torsion springs and rockers with a mechanical anti-roll bar
DAMPERS Showa
TYRES Michelin
WHEELS BBS
BRAKE DISCS Brembo
BRAKE PADS Brembo
BRAKE CALIPERS Alcon
RADIATORS IMI/Marston/Honda
FUEL TANK ATL
INSTRUMENTS Honda

DIMENSIONS
LENGTH 4675mm
WIDTH 1800mm
HEIGHT 950mm
WHEELBASE 3140mm
TRACK front 1460mm
rear 1420mm
WEIGHT 600kg (including driver and camera)

1 The first major modifications to Honda Racing's RA106 came with the introduction of an aerodynamically profiled front wishbone at the San Marino GP
2 The next main changes came at the French GP at Magny-Cours when the front wing was given reshaped flaps to take some pressure off the wing's mainplane

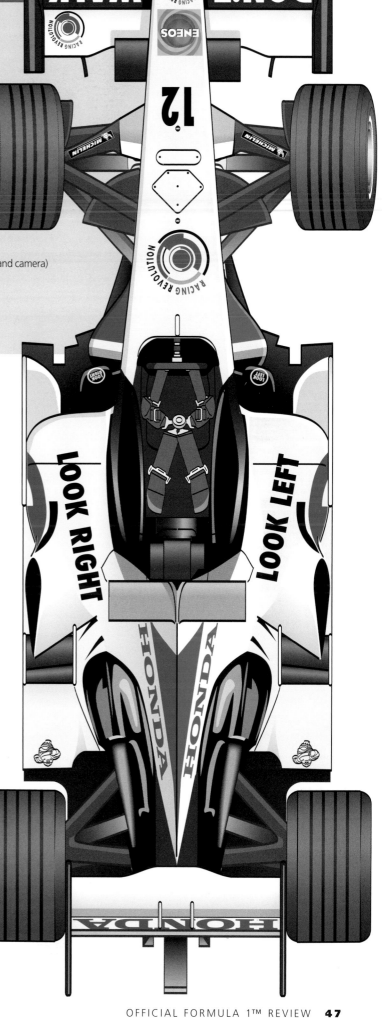

SAUBER BMW

THE TEAM

PERSONNEL

MOTORSPORTS DIRECTOR Mario Theissen
TECHNICAL DIRECTOR Willy Rampf (above)
CHIEF DESIGNER Jorg Zander
HEAD OF TRACK ENGINEERING Mike Krack
HEAD OF AERODYNAMICS Willem Toet
TEAM MANAGER Beat Zehnder
DRIVERS Nick Heidfeld, Robert Kubica, Jacques Villeneuve
RACE ENGINEER (Heidfeld) Andy Borne
RACE ENGINEER (Villeneuve, Kubica) Giampaolo Dall'Ara
TEST/THIRD DRIVERS Robert Kubica, Sebastian Vettel
CHIEF MECHANIC Urs Kuratle
TOTAL NUMBER OF EMPLOYEES 400
NUMBER IN RACE TEAM 80
TEAM BASE Hinwil, Switzerland
TELEPHONE +41 (0)1937 9000
WEBSITE www.bmw-sauber-f1.com

TEAM STATS

IN F1 SINCE 1993 **FIRST GRAND PRIX** South Africa 1993 **STARTS** 235 **WINS** 0 **POLE POSITIONS** 0 **FASTEST LAPS** 0 **PODIUMS** 8 **POINTS** 232 **CONSTRUCTORS' TITLES** 0 **DRIVERS' TITLES** 0

SPONSORS

Petronas, Credit Suisse, Intel, Malaysia, Syntium, Dell, O₂

16 NICK HEIDFELD   **17** JACQUES VILLENEUVE   **17** ROBERT KUBICA

By Willy Rampf (Technical Director)

"The biggest step in the car concept was adapting the chassis and aerodynamic package to the new V8 engines. There was 20% less capacity and 20% less horsepower and if you just took those figures you ended up with a car that was 20kph slower in top speed on a normal race track. That, for sure, was too low.

We had to estimate what would be the new top speed and end up with an overall figure by which to reduce the drag. When you gave this figure to the aerodynamicists they almost had to start with a new car. It is much easier to increase the downforce than to reduce the drag. Reducing drag meant taking off a lot of components, because the cross section is the same and the tyre size, which normally dictates drag, was also the same, so we had to shrink the bodywork wherever possible.

We had quite a lot of problems with vibrations on the dyno at the beginning of the year, but at the first test, although the drivers were complaining more, there was no real influence on the car.

The other thing that was different was the ability to change tyres in the race again. Most people found they could not go as soft with the tyres as they thought. In reality, with less torque on the wheels there is more capacity for lateral force and the cornering speeds increased quite a lot. More lateral load on the tyres meant that you could even end up with a harder tyre sometimes.

We had very few problems on the mechanical side. We started with a baseline car for the rollout and decided to introduce the next evolution mid-February. So, pre-season, we froze the design and told the aero guys to keep developing.

When you consider that we had a new team and a different engine as well, I think we made good progress.

One of the areas that we concentrated hard on was race starts. Renault showed us what was possible in 2005 and they provided our benchmark. By the later races we were at a really good level at our race starts and the drivers always managed to gain positions. We took advantage of the expertise at both BMW in Munich and at Hinwil.

The first big update came after the flyaway races, in time for Imola, and I think it was the biggest change. Then we concentrated on having new components for each race and continued that right through to the car we took to China.

For the Canadian and United States GPs, which are circuits that require a medium downforce set-up, it wasn't just a rear wing and a front wing, we considered all the bodywork and whether it still made sense and was efficient. The same applied at Monza, where Robert finished on the podium. We looked at all the features and asked if they were efficient enough and I think we proved there that it was the right direction to take: to start from scratch with a low downforce car and then concentrate on the drag target to make it efficient.

Our Canadian GP rear wing caused a bit of controversy, but we were always legal by the rule book. There were some grey areas of interpretation and we decided that if the FIA was not happy, we would modify it. It was on for Indianapolis a week later, but we had replaced it for the French GP.

At Magny-Cours, we ran our front pillars (see French GP race report) and had shown them to the FIA, who agreed they were OK. We thought that the drivers might have a problem with sight but, with Jacques, we took them off for a back-to-back test and he said, 'no, put them back again'. Officially it was more a safety concern for the FIA, but I think maybe they looked different and the FIA wanted to stop them before everyone else put them on. They were not about downforce, they were about tidying up the airflow.

At Monza, we were surprised at the qualifying result, because on fuel-adjusted figures we would have been on pole position. By that stage, we had more people on board and the aero guys did a very good job with the Monza low-downforce configuration.

On the mechanical side, we had a revision of the existing front suspension quite early in the season, aimed at improved feeling and better feedback for the driver. "

A GOOD FIRST YEAR

"I think that for the first year of the new BMW Sauber association the results were better than expected. We can be happy with our progress because we formed a new team and employed more than 100 people, mainly on the engineering side. We had to incorporate them into the team and consider their ideas. That's not easy because, at first, it slows you down. But this part of the development is now over and we'll see the benefits.

My role changed in 2006 because, before, we were alone in Hinwil and now we have very intensive co-operation with the guys in Munich. We have more test facilities available, more access to the engine characteristics and more integration. Munich comes up with a lot of ideas that have to be considered in testing, so the programme is not just tyre and aero work.

It was positive to bring Robert in as a racer from the Hungarian GP. He doesn't need a long introduction to a new track and gets on with it very quickly. Every driver has his preference on set-up. One can handle an understeering car, another an understeering car and you have to consider this in your basic set-up, but the characteristics of the car are the same for all the drivers.

Robert doesn't like an understeering car because he's got quite an aggressive turn-in. But I think the biggest difference was between Nick and Jacques. Jacques always tended towards an oversteering car and Nick likes an understeering car. But this, really, is just a balance issue and nothing drastic.

Our wind tunnel work is developing and we are currently in a phase where we are between two and three shifts. Not permanently six days a week, that will take a few months, but we are doing 24-hour shifts three or four days a week depending on the programme. To do six days a week you need a lot of people and we have more than doubled the head count in the aero department.

That's good. A large number of people have joined us because of the good working conditions and atmosphere that we offer – that, for 90% of the people, is more important than money.

Not a lot has yet changed with our facility because we are busy with a new building that will be finished next year, with an enlarged production area and more test rigs. That should help us to move even closer to the front runners."

Some think
heat, rubber,
and asphalt.

**We think the
right solution.**

Investment Banking • Private Banking • Asset Management

In Formula One™ it's often the equipment that decides the race. The BMW Sauber F1 Team makes their tire choice based on their race strategy, the circuit, and the prevailing weather conditions. That's why know-how and precision determine success. These are the qualities that we share with the racing team, and that inspire us to find the best solution for you. www.credit-suisse.com/f1

Thinking New Perspectives.

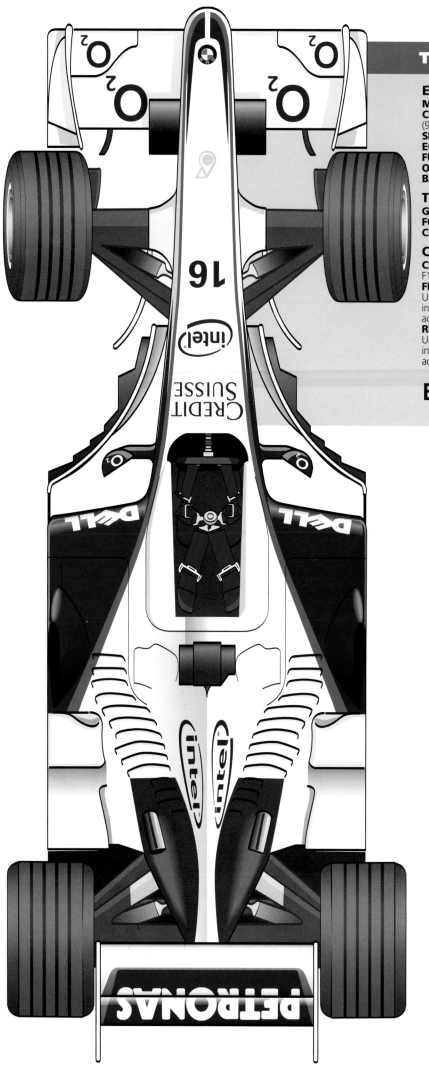

TECHNICAL SPECIFICATIONS

ENGINE
MAKE/MODEL BMW P86
CONFIGURATION 2398cc V8
(90 degree)
SPARK PLUGS Undisclosed
ECU Magneti Marelli
FUEL Petronas
OIL Petronas
BATTERY Undisclosed

TRANSMISSION
GEARBOX BMW Sauber
FORWARD GEARS Seven
CLUTCH AP Racing

CHASSIS
CHASSIS MODEL BMW Sauber
F1.06
FRONT SUSPENSION LAYOUT
Upper and lower wishbones,
inboard springs and dampers
activated by pushrods
REAR SUSPENSION LAYOUT
Upper and lower wishbones,
inboard springs and dampers
activated by pushrods

DAMPERS Sachs
TYRES Michelin
WHEELS OZ Racing

BRAKE DISCS Brembo or Carbone
Industrie
BRAKE PADS Brembo or Carbone
Industrie
BRAKE CALIPERS Brembo
RADIATORS Calsonic
FUEL TANK ATL
INSTRUMENTS Sauber Electronics

DIMENSIONS
LENGTH 4610mm
WIDTH 1800mm
HEIGHT 1000mm
WHEELBASE 3110mm
TRACK front 1470mm **rear**
1410mm
WEIGHT 600kg (including driver
and camera)

BMW Sauber F1 Team

1 These vertical pillars caused something of a stir when they were introduced at the French GP. The drivers said they didn't impede vision, but they were outlawed
2 This low-downforce rear wing was used at the Canadian GP and caused quite a bit of unrest before the team withdrew it for good after the United States GP

join the glitterati at the famous Monaco Grand Prix

You don't have to clear out the savings account to be at this fantastic event either!

Prices start from just £419 per person and included return charter flights, transfers and 3 nights accommodation with breakfast thrown in!

For that extra special weekend, we also have an excellent range of hospitality, private balconies, tables at the exclusive Monaco Grand Prix Ball and tickets to the most famous nightclub in town, the Amber Lounge!

for more details call our Crystal Sport reservation team on 0870 060 1375 (quote Racing)

TOYOTA

THE TEAM

PERSONNEL
CHAIRMAN AND TEAM PRINCIPAL
Tsutomo Tomita
PRESIDENT John Howett
ADVISOR Ove Andersson
EXECUTIVE VICE-PRESIDENT Yoshiaki Kinoshita
SENIOR GENERAL MANAGER, ENGINE
Luca Marmorini
SENIOR GENERAL MANAGER, CHASSIS
Pascal Vasselon (above)
DIRECTOR TECHNICAL CO-ORDINATION
Noritoshi Arai
HEAD OF AERODYNAMICS Mark Gillan
TEAM MANAGER Richard Cregan
DRIVERS Ralf Schumacher, Jarno Trulli
CHIEF RACE AND TEST ENGINEER Dieter Gass
RACE ENGINEER (Schumacher) Francesco Nenci
RACE ENGINEER (Trulli) Ossi Oikarinen &
Gianluca Tisanello
TEST DRIVERS Olivier Panis, Ricardo Zonta
CHIEF MECHANIC Gerard Lecoq
TOTAL NUMBER OF EMPLOYEES 600
NUMBER IN RACE TEAM 80
TEAM BASE Cologne, Germany
TELEPHONE +49 (0)223 4182 3444
WEBSITE www.toyota-f1.com

TEAM STATS
IN F1 SINCE 2002 **FIRST GRAND PRIX** Australia 2002
STARTS 88 **WINS** 0 **POLE POSITIONS** 2
FASTEST LAPS 1 **PODIUMS** 6 **POINTS** 150
CONSTRUCTORS' TITLES 0 **DRIVERS' TITLES** 0

SPONSORS
Panasonic, Denso, Intel, Karcher, EMC²

7 RALF SCHUMACHER

8 JARNO TRULLI

Pascal Vasselon (Senior General Manager, Chassis)
"The interim TF106 that we tested over the winter and started the season with was the logical consequence of what had gone before. The crossover point came when we introduced the new front suspension concept for the last two grands prix of 2005. That was really quite a big jump. We had to realign the rear and then realign the front. The TF106 was the realignment of the rear and we then had to prepare the front because the concept change was so big.

The second reason for the interim car was that we were changing tyre manufacturer and so there was a possibility that a car designed around Michelins could need a concept change. So, preparing the TF106B fulfilled all our targets. It bought us some analysis time.

The most urgent thing was to rework the rear end, because we were not happy about the mechanical layout. It was generally a lack of body control. The chassis movement was less controlled at the rear than the front. We initially had a spacer with the V8, which was not a brilliant engineering solution but, done properly, was no problem until we could introduce the TF106B at Monaco.

Technical Director Mike Gascoyne left the team early in the season, but most of the group stayed the same and, in modern F1, it's no longer about one person, so it wasn't too disruptive.

You have to manage two principal factors: tyres and aerodynamics. Most of the car concept can be aerodynamically orientated and then we manage the tyres with the set-up parameters; weight distribution, cambers, toes, suspension settings. With all that in your hands, you still have a lot to do in terms of tyre usage.

From our side, we had difficulty at the first race in Bahrain, but then strong tyres all year and, on many occasions, a competitive advantage.

It's normal to develop tyres for hot conditions and that's what Bridgestone did. As a consequence, in the winter we were struggling with these tyres, especially because they made quite a big concept change rather than detailed steps. We expected to go to Bahrain and find that the different weather ended the problems, but it wasn't hot enough to solve the temperature-window issues we had.

We had the same tyre selection as Ferrari and Williams but, as well as Bridgestone targeting hot conditions, we had been making sure we didn't put too much energy into the tyres. That combination meant that in Bahrain we were in trouble. People kept on talking about it a few races into the season but, really, it was a one-off. Next time out at Sepang, we had 52-degrees track temperature and were right in the working window with good pace. Ralf made two additional stops because of engine pneumatic consumption and ended up eighth, but his pace was less than 0.1s from Ferrari's best lap.

The Australian GP was interesting. We were expecting tyre warm-up issues because the track is demanding in terms of that and the weather was unsure, with cooler conditions possible. But then two things came up at the same time. We had time to test some set-up corrections, and Bridgestone came to Paul Ricard with a new compound that was targeted towards a lower temperature window and was really spot-on. The combination meant that we did not struggle. We had several safety-car periods and Ralf was among those who performed best at the restart.

While we got the Bahrain GP wrong, the next few races showed that the other teams didn't really have the tyre situation under control either. Maybe Ferrari got it right in Bahrain without really knowing why. In Melbourne, they did not really realise that tyre warm-up was so critical and ended up with both cars in the wall because they were running out of grip.

And at Williams, who were also on Bridgestone, we saw something really interesting with Nico Rosberg's driving style. He was brilliant in Bahrain and now we understand. Nico slides a lot and, in Bahrain, with the compound we had, the tyre was not graining and so you could slide without destroying them, and this was also giving the extra temperature the tyres needed. So Nico was brilliant.

After that, Bridgestone went to the compound that was more spot-on and gave the grip without sliding too much and Nico started to have huge graining problems. Every time Williams used compounds on the soft side, Nico destroyed his tyres because he was sliding. What was an advantage in Bahrain was now a problem, and Nico, compared to Mark Webber, struggled a lot with tyre consistency. It was very clear."

TURNING THE CORNER

"The introduction of the TF106B was our turning-point. When it came in Monaco it was a mechanical upgrade – a new monocoque and front suspension. It came together with a high-downforce package which we would have had anyway, but it opened up other aero developments for almost every race.

From there, our progress rate was really consistent until Turkey. The results were not always there, but we were much closer to the ultimate pace than we had been before. In terms of points-scoring, 2005 was much better for many reasons, better reliability included. But in terms of pace difference to the top we were often 1.5s behind McLaren and 1s behind Renault even though we were finishing in the points. This season we have scored fewer points, but our pace has rarely been more than 0.5s behind the leading car. We had a down at Monza, which is a one-off in terms of a low-downforce set-up, and in Shanghai we were compromised by the qualifying circumstances, which better suited Michelin.

Looking at the TF106B, we had a clear weakness in terms of the gearbox. Our shift time was too long and we lost quite a lot in terms of acceleration and with the launches. It's a combination of the mechanical systems and the control strategy. The suspension and body control was quite good, the aerodynamics can improve but were not bad at all, and the engine as well. There was no general weakness of the package apart from the gearbox.

You have to be careful analysing a season. Looking at the points is the obvious thing, but it's misleading and technicians have to extract the performance level from the circumstances. We have not scored a lot of points, but our performance was better than last year. That's what statistical analysis shows and that helps to maintain the motivation. Motorsport is never easy and all teams have ups and downs. The good teams come through the down times, stay together and come out the other side. If you cannot manage a down period, you are lost."

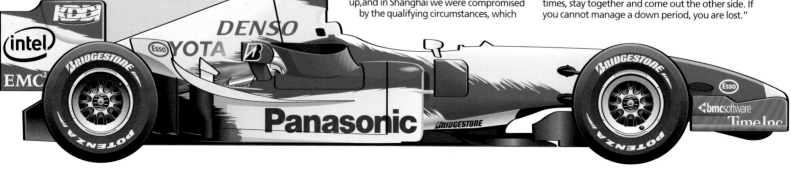

www.toyota-f1.com

One
Aim

Practice makes perfect

No matter how good you are you can always improve. That's why every
TOYOTA F1™ Team member is constantly seeking to perfect his or her skills, in
every aspect of the F1™ challenge. We call it 'Kaizen' – a Toyota philosophy built on
a unique spirit of optimism, hard work, innovative technologies and a shared
desire to be the very best we can.

TOYOTA

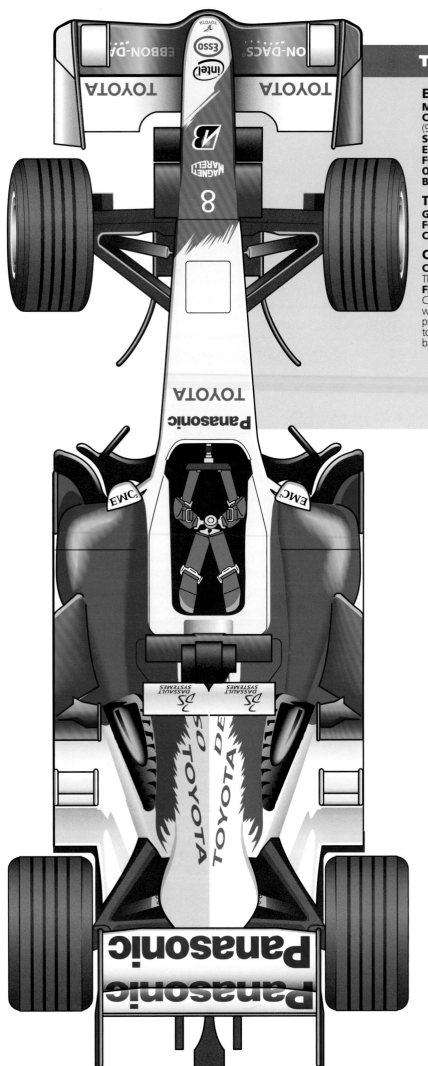

TECHNICAL SPECIFICATIONS

ENGINE
MAKE/MODEL Toyota RVX-06
CONFIGURATION 2398cc V8
(90 degree)
SPARK PLUGS Denso
ECU Toyota/Magneti Marelli
FUEL Esso
OIL Esso
BATTERY Panasonic

TRANSMISSION
GEARBOX Toyota
FORWARD GEARS Seven
CLUTCH Sachs/AP Racing

CHASSIS
CHASSIS MODEL Toyota
TF106/TF106B
FRONT SUSPENSION LAYOUT
Carbon-fibre double wishbones
with carbon-fibre trackrod and
pushrod. Pushrod-activated rocker,
torsion bar, damper and anti-roll
bar assembly

REAR SUSPENSION LAYOUT
Carbon-fibre double wishbones with
carbon-fibre toelink and pushrod.
Pushrod-activated rocker, torsion bar,
damper and anti-roll bar assembly
DAMPERS Sachs/Toyota
TYRES Bridgestone
WHEELS BBS
BRAKE DISCS Hitco
BRAKE PADS Hitco
BRAKE CALIPERS Brembo
RADIATORS Nippon-Denso
FUEL TANK ATL
INSTRUMENTS Toyota/
Magneti Marelli

DIMENSIONS
LENGTH 4530mm
WIDTH 1800mm
HEIGHT 950mm
WHEELBASE 3090mm
TRACK front 1425mm **rear**
1411mm
WEIGHT 600kg (including driver
and camera)

Panasonic TOYOTA *Racing*

1 The TF106B was introduced at Monaco, its engine cover topped with this triple
wing fitted for extra downforce on this unusual and exacting street circuit
2 The TF106B's sidepods were reprofiled for the British GP, as Toyota introduced
aero changes at almost every race following the car's Monaco debut

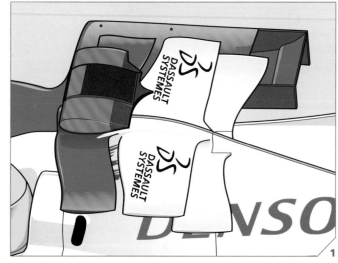

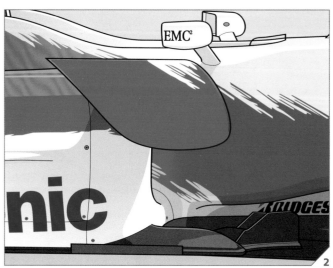

Get ready for 2007 with two great magazines...

12 issues for £36.50 (normally £47.40) SAVE 23%

This is the only magazine dedicated to the glamorous and adrenalin-fuelled sport of Formula 1. With stunning photography and unrivalled access, F1 Racing takes you into the heart of the F1 World Championship.

26 issues for £60 (normally £75.40) SAVE 20%

World-leading coverage of the best motorsport - from Formula 1 to club racing, including reports, analysis and experts' comments - packed into Autosport magazine every week.

RED BULL

THE TEAM

PERSONNEL

CHAIRMAN Dietrich Mateschitz
TEAM PRINCIPAL Christian Horner
TECHNICAL OPERATIONS DIRECTOR Adrian Newey
TECHNICAL DIRECTOR Mark Smith (above)
HEAD OF RACE AND TEST ENGINEERING
Paul Monaghan
CHIEF DESIGNER Rob Marshall
HEAD OF DEVELOPMENT Anton Stipovic
CHIEF AERODYNAMICIST Peter Prodromou
HEAD OF AERODYNAMICS Ben Agathangelou
HEAD OF R&D Andrew Green
TEAM MANAGER Jonathan Wheatley
DRIVERS David Coulthard, Robert Doornbos,
Christian Klien
RACE ENGINEER (Coulthard) Mark Hutcheson
RACE ENGINEER (Doornbos/Klien) Ciaron Pilbeam
TEST TEAM MANAGER Tony Burrows
TEST DRIVERS Michael Ammermuller, Robert Doornbos
CHIEF MECHANIC Kenny Handkammer
TOTAL NUMBER OF EMPLOYEES 485
NUMBER IN RACE TEAM 85
TEAM BASE Milton Keynes, England
TELEPHONE +44 (0)1908 279700
WEBSITE www.redbullracing.com

TEAM STATS

IN F1 SINCE 1997 as Stewart Grand Prix then Jaguar
Racing **FIRST GRAND PRIX** Australia 1997 **STARTS** 171
WINS 1 **POLE POSITIONS** 1 **FASTEST LAPS** 0
PODIUMS 6 **POINTS** 138 **CONSTRUCTORS' TITLES** 0
DRIVERS' TITLES 0

SPONSORS

Red Bull, Hangar-7

14 DAVID COULTHARD   **15** CHRISTIAN KLIEN   **15** ROBERT DOORNBOS

By Mark Smith, Technical Director
"For 2006, you had to think about weight distribution, as the V8 is 100mm shorter than the V10 we used in 2005. Secondly, there was the cooling, which we didn't get right. Thirdly, the impact on the transmission, as the reduced torque level allowed a little re-optimisation of the strength of the internal components.

Then we had fuel consumption and the way it influences the size of fuel cell, which in turn has knock-on effects on chassis length and weight distribution. It was one of the trickiest things and certainly wasn't a factor of capacity.

With the torque characteristics, you had to weigh up how that influenced all the control strategies – starts, traction, engine braking and gearshifts. Going from one engine supplier to another – Cosworth to Ferrari – obviously presented those issues anyway, but having a different configuration was another factor.

The transition to the Ferrari engine was not hard. The biggest difficulty was the change of ECU from Pi to Marelli, simply because it had knock-on effects with telemetry and data logging.

Our biggest issue was cooling. We got it wrong and were over-optimistic with the packaging. There were two things. First, we went a bit too far in terms of it being on the limit. Second, we had a different engine, and it's a fact of life that, thermally, no two engines behave the same.

It was no reflection on Ferrari. Had we made the step with the Cosworth, it would still have been a step too far. The fact we did it with an engine on which we didn't really understand the heat rejection meant we were faced with a big learning curve on something we'd taken too far. It was a very difficult thing to come back from. The only real way out is a monocoque redesign, but the logistics stopped us going down that route.

There was talk of the data not being correct from Ferrari, but it was more about the relationship between different groups in interpreting it. It was a small factor, and the main issue was that we went too far. There was never any question of two parties not co-operating and inevitably a couple of things were misquoted.

It took too long to sort out, no doubt about that. We swung the entry angle of the radiator out slightly and that had knock-on effects for the bodywork. It was all about trying to pull the radiator away from the chassis to give less of a pressure drop, get more of it working, at the same time increasing its surface area.

When we first ran the car, we had to cut holes in the bodywork to improve the flow exit, but that threw away 7% of rear downforce. We were dreading Malaysia, but we learned quite a bit about how the engine and the car ran in terms of average rpm and speed for a given cooling level. That definitely didn't map over from Cosworth. That first iteration was a mammoth effort from the aero and design groups over one weekend and that was the format we took to the first races.

We could run, but were on the limit of Ferrari's temperature specs and were throwing away efficiency. We made a reasonable step forward, but what happened then was that Adrian (Newey) was on board and wanted to push harder on RB3 and back off RB2. So, after Magny-Cours, there was no development of RB2."

TAKING THE HEAT

"One thing we can take pride in is that we developed a seamless-shift gearbox without the use of a transient dyno. The other key thing was a new front suspension geometry from Silverstone. The car suffered mid-corner understeer and we definitely moved that in the right direction.

We made good steps mechanically with things like installation stiffness and reduction of compliances, and it gave us a more responsive car. On a couple of occasions, Tonio Liuzzi drove it and always commented on how alive it felt.

Had we continued to develop the RB2, we would have finished the season better. It was disappointing, as in quite a few respects the car was well balanced, but always compromised by the aero inefficiency. Barcelona poor, Monaco podium, Silverstone bad tells its own story.

I was disappointed by David Coulthard's comments to the media in Suzuka, questioning whether we had the right people. I can forgive a driver making comments out of frustration, but the problem was that on Monday morning I was faced with a stream of demoralised people.

When I heard it, I thought, 'oh, he means me and one or two others'. I have enough confidence that it wasn't going to worry me, but I was amazed at how people took it personally right through the ranks.

It was not smart, in my opinion. Especially when you consider that there's a driver coming here next year (Mark Webber) that quite a lot of people in this team are very fond of. The other thing that frustrated me is that David knew we hadn't developed the car since France. So, get frustrated, have a knock at the people who made that decision, but don't diss everyone.

Christian Klien, although not universally popular within the Red Bull organisation, just got his head down and got on when we had our problems, which I appreciated. He had some bad luck and more than his fair share of reliability issues. The Monaco podium could just as easily have been his. I think he's been a bit unfortunate. And Robert Doornbos did a reasonable job on Fridays, and probably surpassed anyone's expectations when he replaced Christian.

There is a lot of restructuring going on. Peter Prodromou joins us from McLaren in November on the aero side, and then Neil Martin joins in the new year. Keith Saunt has already started on the operations and manufacturing side and I think we have the basis now, if we can keep it all together.

These kind of situations can all get a bit rocky. I saw that at Renault when the performance wasn't good. It's one of these things where whoever holds the purse strings has to remain unflustered. Clearly, that doesn't go on for ever, but certainly for a year or two you just have to be stable and give it a chance. I see that we've made a step back relative to where we were, albeit for a number of factors, but I firmly believe that the group of people we have with the tools we've got, and will have, will allow us to do the job."

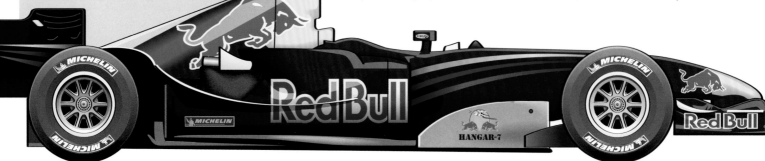

TECHNICAL SPECIFICATIONS

ENGINE
MAKE/MODEL Ferrari 056
CONFIGURATION 2398cc V8
(90 degree)
SPARK PLUGS NGK
ECU Magneti Marelli
FUEL Shell
OIL Shell
BATTERY Undisclosed

TRANSMISSION
GEARBOX Red Bull Racing
FORWARD GEARS Seven
CLUTCH AP Racing

CHASSIS
CHASSIS MODEL Red Bull RB2
FRONT SUSPENSION LAYOUT Aluminium-alloy
uprights with upper and lower wishbones and
pushrods. Torsion-bar springing and anti-roll bar

REAR SUSPENSION LAYOUT
Cast-titanium uprights with upper
and lower wishbones and pushrods.
Torsion-bar springing and
anti-roll bar
DAMPERS Multimatic
TYRES Michelin
WHEELS AVUS Racing
BRAKE DISCS Hitco
BRAKE PADS Hitco
BRAKE CALIPERS
Brembo
RADIATORS Red Bull
Racing
FUEL TANK ATL
INSTRUMENTS
Magneti Marelli

DIMENSIONS
LENGTH 4580mm
WIDTH 1800mm
HEIGHT 950mm
WHEELBASE 3135mm
TRACK front 1460mm **rear** 1415mm
WEIGHT 600kg (including driver and camera)

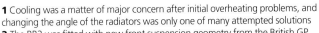

1 Cooling was a matter of major concern after initial overheating problems, and
changing the angle of the radiators was only one of many attempted solutions
2 The RB2 was fitted with new front suspension geometry from the British GP
onwards in a bid to get rid of mid-corner understeer, and it appeared to work

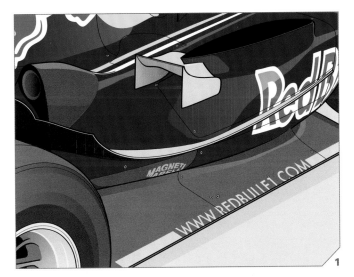

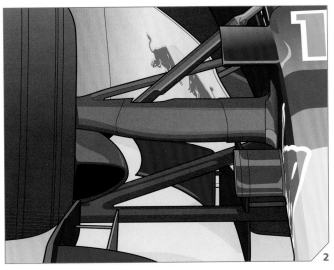

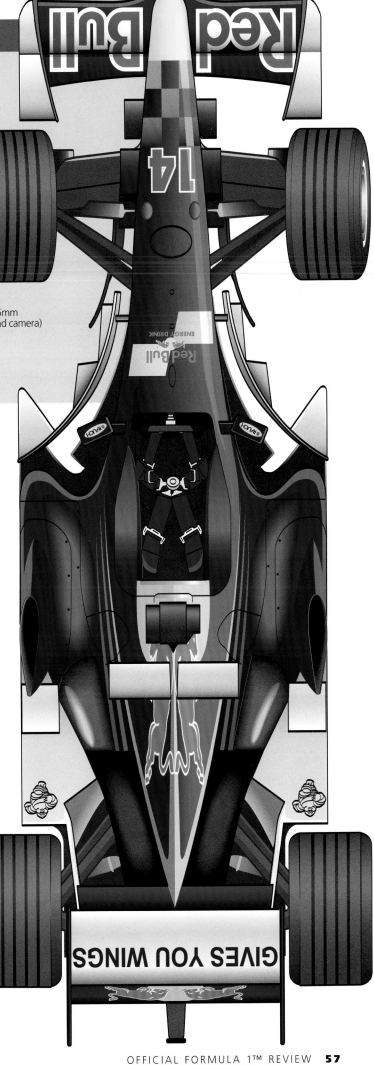

WILLIAMS

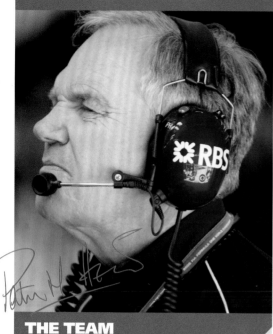

THE TEAM

PERSONNEL

TEAM PRINCIPAL Sir Frank Williams
DIRECTOR OF ENGINEERING Patrick Head (above)
CHIEF EXECUTIVE OFFICER Chris Chapple
TECHNICAL DIRECTOR Sam Michael
CHIEF DESIGNER Ed Wood
HEAD OF AERODYNAMICS Jon Tomlinson
CHIEF AERODYNAMICIST Loic Bigois
TEAM MANAGER Tim Newton
DRIVERS Nico Rosberg, Mark Webber
RACE ENGINEER (Rosberg) Tony Ross
RACE ENGINEER (Webber) Xevi Pujolar
TEST TEAM MANAGER Mike Condliffe
TEST DRIVERS Narain Karthikeyan, Alexander Wurz
CHIEF MECHANIC Carl Gaden
TOTAL NUMBER OF EMPLOYEES 520
NUMBER IN RACE TEAM 70 & 12 Cosworth
TEAM BASE Grove, England
TELEPHONE +44 (0)1235 777700
WEBSITE www.williamsf1.com

TEAM STATS

IN F1 SINCE 1973 **FIRST GRAND PRIX** Argentina
1973 **STARTS** 533 **WINS** 113 **POLE POSITIONS** 125
FASTEST LAPS 129 **PODIUMS** 293 **POINTS** 2512.5
CONSTRUCTORS' TITLES 9 **DRIVERS' TITLES** 7

SPONSORS

RBS, Petrobras, FedEx, Allianz, Budweiser, ORIS, Reuters,
Tata, Accenture, Hamleys, Mobilecast, MAN, Randstand

9 MARK WEBBER   **10** NICO ROSBERG

By Patrick Head (Director of Engineering)

"The main design element to focus on coming into 2006 was the change from the 3.0-litre V10s to the new 2.4-litre V8s. The new engines were shorter, but were similar in cross-section because the V10, in our case with BMW, was a 90-degree engine and the Cosworth V8 is 90 degrees too. We lost 120mm or so in length. We used some of it to carry a bit more fuel, and some of it in terms of gearbox length. We made our minds up on how to use that extra length from a weight distribution and a fuel capacity standpoint.

Although there was 20% less engine capacity, it did not follow that the fuel consumption reduced by 20%, because the amount of full-throttle running now is much more than we were doing last year. In quite a few places, we had as much power as we were able to use in 2005.

We made a decent start to the season in Bahrain and then, obviously, we had some problems. I'd put it down to two things. First of all, the performance was variable and some of that was down to us just adapting to the different tyre supplier. In previous years, we had been with Michelin and so we didn't have a data file of knowledge of Bridgestone's compounds. Taking into account the whole season, Bridgestone did a fantastic job but we, a bit like Toyota, had to learn quite a bit about their different compounds and the way they behave in different conditions.

Toyota had a tough start and noting Pascal Vasselon's comments about that first race (see Toyota review) and Nico's performance, he could well be right. Every driver has a slightly different way of working the car and these tyres are incredibly sensitive to the temperature window in which you are working them.

I would say that, generally, we didn't get the advantage from running as soft a tyre as Ferrari. They appeared to be able to take advantage from running a soft compound for good qualifying and then being able to look after it during the race. At some races, they've been so dominant that they have been able to deliberately go slower and look after the rubber.

Equally, the FW28 was stronger at some places than it was at others. It was quite strong at Monaco, where Mark was able to shadow Alonso and Räikkönen, yet there were also some places where we struggled. Coupled with that, we've been notably unreliable in a number of different areas, which was frustrating.

The unreliability was not consistent and mainly involved small problems but, annoyingly, problems that were significant enough to stop the car. We had cracked hydraulic pipes, burst water hoses, cracked exhaust collectors – basic engineering things needed to get the car to the finish.

It's in no way an excuse, and I haven't been counting up the points, but I think that given the performance of the car without the reliability issues, we could have been fifth or sixth in the championship. But, add the unreliability and it took us back to where we are – eighth. We have had tighter purse strings this year, of course, but I wouldn't say that it has impacted directly on the reliability side. Obviously, though, things are much tighter than they were with a manufacturer.

Looking at the Monaco performance and the places we've struggled, some may point the finger at aerodynamic efficiency. Clearly, we had some views internally but everyone has been working incredibly hard, the wind tunnels have been working around the clock, seven days a week, and it hasn't been for lack of effort.

Quite clearly, the results just haven't been good enough. We've made personnel changes and brought in some new blood. It's not that the people we have are bad – they're good people – but for whatever reason it just hasn't gelled."

IT WAS AN ANNUS HORRIBILIS

"Cosworth did a very good job on the engine side, but ultimately it just didn't happen for us both. We had a problem with one of the engines in Malaysia and then had to run them a little bit down for a while, but generally Cosworth did an exceptional job and it's really very sad for them that it doesn't look as if anyone will be taking up their engine next year.

From our side, if we hadn't taken up the V8 engine then I don't think it would have come into existence at all and, even if we'd gone out and won a number of races, I'm not sure it would have made any difference. We're extremely annoyed at ourselves over the overall results in 2006, but I don't think we feel we've caused the demise of Cosworth in Formula One.

Nico has shown great promise at times and maybe a bit of greenness at others. Hockenheim wasn't a very good home race for him, with an accident early on in first practice and then an accident early in the race. Overall, though, I think he's been very good and there have been races where he could have shown his capability but the unreliability hasn't enabled him to. He was in very good shape at Monza. He was ahead and pulling away from Trulli, who finished seventh, when a driveshaft joint failed.

Because of the shenanigans at the start in Turkey, he was lying in sixth place with a lot of fuel on board and holding that position well. I'm sure that he would have finished in fourth, fifth or sixth place but a water hose failed. I think he's done pretty well but, first race apart, hasn't had any stunning moments.

Equally, Mark has had some good qualifying and strong races and was going very well at Monaco when, again, the car let him down. That's been a great disappointment to us and him and I hope that when he moves on things will work out better for him. It hasn't been a great year for anybody at Williams.

We are hoping that this was an annus horribilis we can put behind us. We did contest the championship quite seriously in 2003, so it's not as if we haven't been competing but, equally, we've been saying for a few years, just watch us next season, and it hasn't happened. So I'm a bit reluctant to be too gung-ho, but quite clearly the performance we've had this year is not acceptable to Frank, it's not acceptable to me and it's not acceptable to most of the people within the team. As normal with these things, you've got to work out exactly why and put it right. It's a lot more than just gritting your teeth and trying harder."

WILLIAMSF1TEAM
OFFICIAL SPONSOR

New talent.

New power.

New dawn.

Make it happen.

As the 2006 season ends there's only one way to look. Forwards.
For the Williams F1 Team that means looking forward to working
with a new engine partner and a new driver.
In the new season, the entire team will be totally focused
and determined to make it happen.

Make it happen

The Royal Bank of Scotland Group

TECHNICAL SPECIFICATIONS

ENGINE
MAKE/MODEL Cosworth CA2006
CONFIGURATION 2398cc V8
(90 degree)
SPARK PLUGS Champion
ECU Pi/Cosworth
FUEL Petrobras
OIL Castrol
BATTERY Undisclosed

TRANSMISSION
GEARBOX WilliamsF1
FORWARD GEARS Seven
CLUTCH AP Racing

CHASSIS
CHASSIS MODEL Williams FW28
FRONT SUSPENSION LAYOUT
Carbon fibre double wishbones with
composite toelink and pushrod-
activated torsion springs
REAR SUSPENSION LAYOUT
Wishbones and pushrod-activated
torsion springs and rockers

DAMPERS WilliamsF1
TYRES Bridgestone
WHEELS OZ Racing
BRAKE DISCS Carbone Industrie
BRAKE PADS Carbone Industrie
BRAKE CALIPERS AP Racing
RADIATORS Marston
FUEL TANK ATL
INSTRUMENTS WilliamsF1

DIMENSIONS
LENGTH 4500mm
WIDTH 1800mm
HEIGHT 950mm
WHEELBASE 3100mm
TRACK front 1470mm
rear 1420mm
WEIGHT 605kg (including driver
and camera)

WILLIAMS F1

1 Major bodywork changes were introduced for the San Marino GP as the team fought to regain aerodynamic efficiency to make up for poor levels of grip
2 This triple airbox wing was introduced for Hungary, with the top set of wings acting as a flow conditioner, the lower two pairs more for producing downforce

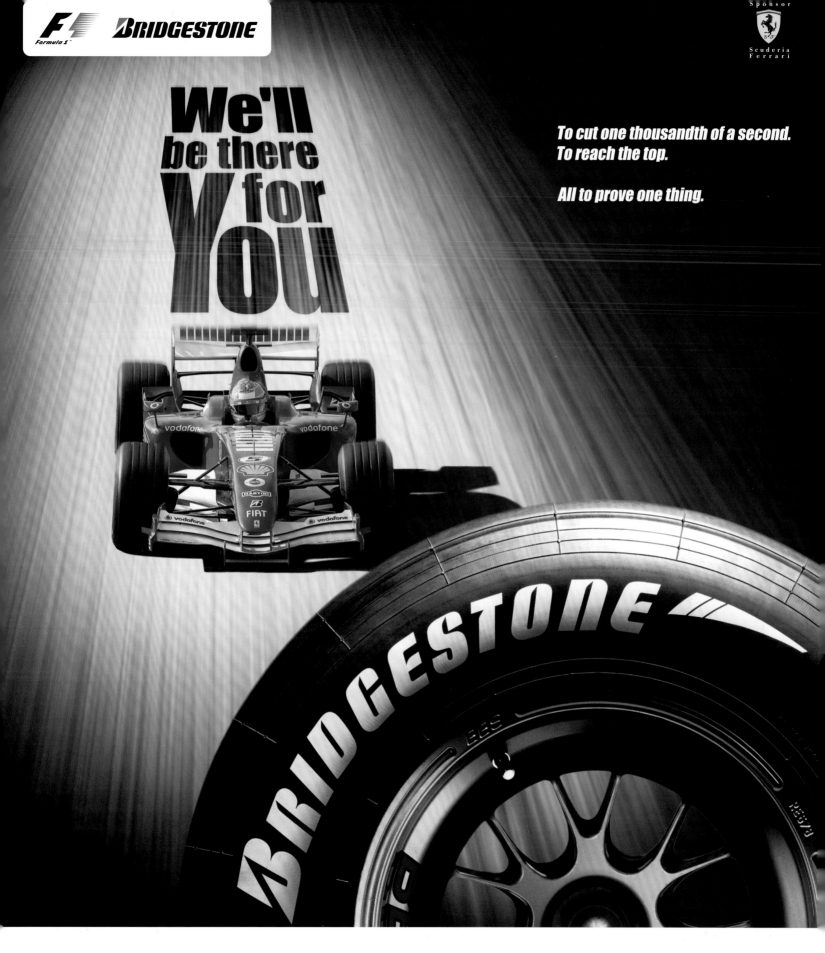

TORO ROSSO

THE TEAM

PERSONNEL

TEAM OWNERS Dietrich Mateschitz/Gerhard Berger
TEAM PRINCIPAL Franz Tost (above)
GENERAL DIRECTOR Gianfranco Fantuzzi
TECHNICAL DIRECTOR Gabriele Tredozi/Alex Hitzinger
CHIEF DESIGNER Ben Butler
CHIEF AERODYNAMICIST Matteo Frolino
TEAM MANAGER Massimo Rivola
DRIVERS Vitantonio Liuzzi, Scott Speed
CHIEF ENGINEER Laurent Mekies
RACE ENGINEER (Liuzzi) Riccardo Adami
RACE ENGINEER (Speed) Stefano Sordo
THIRD DRIVER Neel Jani
RACE ENGINEER (Jani) Graziano Michelacci
CHIEF MECHANIC Bruno Fagnocchi
TOTAL NUMBER OF EMPLOYEES 128
NUMBER IN RACE TEAM 60
TEAM BASE Faenza, Italy
TELEPHONE +39 (0)546 696111
WEBSITE www.tororosso.com

TEAM STATS

IN F1 SINCE 1985 **FIRST GRAND PRIX** Brazil 1985
STARTS 359 **WINS** 0 **POLE POSITIONS** 0
FASTEST LAPS 0 **PODIUMS** 0 **POINTS** 39
CONSTRUCTORS' TITLES 0 **DRIVERS' TITLES** 0

SPONSORS

Red Bull

20 VITANTONIO LIUZZI   **21** SCOTT SPEED

By Franz Tost (Managing Director)

"We started, of course, with the core of the Minardi team. When Red Bull took over, we had 108 employees. Currently, we have around 125 and anticipate bringing in another 12 employees for quality control, fabrication and engineering.

Alex Hitzinger will take over the position of Technical Director after Gabriele Tredozi's contract expires at the end of the season. We have around 12 people involved on the cars, including electronics, data analysis and the engineering of the cars and will, for next season, bring in another one or two. We have a design team, most of whom are with Adrian Newey in Milton Keynes working on the new car.

The STR01 was a development of the 2005 RB1, but next year's car will be a completely new construction. This year's car was changed a little on the aerodynamic and mechanical sides, but many components were carried over from the RB1.

Our key difference this year, of course, is that we were alone in using a rev-limited V10, a dispensation granted to Minardi before Red Bull bought the team. In F1, if you have to find a solution that includes a compromise, it's not always the best solution...

At the beginning of the season, everything was quite equal, but during the season the manufacturers did a fantastic job of developing the V8 engines in terms of horsepower and reliability.

The V8s generally started the season from around 19,000rpm and finished up closer to 20,000rpm. It was decided, therefore, because of the equivalency that, from the Hungarian GP onwards, we could increase the revs from 16,700 to 17,000. But that was only in qualifying, not the race. That was because most of our opposition were not revving so high in the race.

The V10 has many more disadvantages, as I personally thought. The experts said that in Monaco and Budapest we would finish in the top three, but we didn't have the advantage you get from a V10 versus a V8. You have a different torque curve and the V10 produces more torque than the V8, but the traction control reduces this. The drivers complained about how active the traction control was in comparison to the V8s. So, in Monaco and Budapest we didn't have good races. In fact, I think they were the worst races we had.

We changed a lot of traction-control software but, because of the regulation that we were not allowed to change anything in the engine, we couldn't change the crankshafts, nothing. We would like to have changed the hardware, but we were not allowed to.

The other thing we had to contend with was an aerodynamic compromise. In Formula One, the newest package is most often the best package. Our opposition could take advantage of the aerodynamic advantages offered by the shorter V8 engines, but we could not.

We ran in a 100 per-cent-scale wind tunnel in Stuttgart, which has been used by other teams in the past, and were there a couple of days. In a full-scale tunnel, however, you must be really very well prepared. I think we tested more than 120 parts in that test and pushed very hard.

Looking at developments throughout the season, the key steps were on the aerodynamic side with front endplates then sidepods. The sidepod intakes for the radiators were altered, and we tried to introduce aero changes gradually after wind-tunnel tests. We also made some small mechanical alterations and the braking system was changed.

We went from AP to Brembo and Hitco, and didn't necessarily stick with one solution, we mixed it up a little. With the brake material you must involve the driver because some drivers have a better feel with the Hitco material, while others feel more at home with Brembo, and it changes. We changed the brake discs during the winter tests and around Monaco time we changed the brake calipers. The master cylinders, as far as I remember, we changed at Nürburgring."

A YEAR OF COMPROMISE

"We knew that with Tonio Liuzzi and Scott Speed we had two young, inexperienced drivers. So far, they have developed well, and we will see in 2007 if they can profit from the learning process. I predict that we will have a good season with them next year. A driver needs two or three years in F1 to really understand what's going on.

It's quite hard to assess them realistically, because with the tyre degradation and our compromised package, we were a little bit disadvantaged. And we were not at the level demanded by top-level F1, therefore it was not so easy for them. Everything is in the process of being structured, and I hope that next season we can do a good job. We have a test team with some very good people and we did a lot of mileage with no technical failures. But we couldn't do any tyre testing for historical reasons. Minardi had Bridgestone and we had chosen to go with Michelin but, because of capacity, Michelin decided that only Red Bull would do the tyre tests, not us.

There were a couple of highs over the season. First of all, there was a really good race from Scott in Australia, then the first point for Tonio at Indianapolis. The most disappointing races were in Budapest and also the Chinese GP. I was a little bit disappointed afterwards, but the rest of the season was average.

I hope that we will make good progress next year because the philosophy of both Red Bull and Toro Rosso is that sooner or later we will be front runners. 'Red Bull gives you wings' is what it says on the car, and we want those wings too!

I have known Gerhard Berger a long time and it is good that he became involved. He has a lot of experience, both as a driver and with BMW. Everything is about organisation, and it's a question of humans being involved. If they want to co-operate, everything is possible. If they don't want to, everything is much more complicated. As people know, in F1 you never have technical problems, you only have human problems.

Obviously, we are linked to Red Bull and we have had a very good relationship with them. We worked especially closely regarding the tyres we had to choose, which helped our situation with not being able to do the tyre tests. And therefore the race engineers from Toro Rosso and Red Bull worked closely together.

In summary, I suppose I'd say that it has been a year of restrictions, not only on revs! We are looking forward to not having those restrictions in 2007. The handbrake, hopefully, will be off."

TECHNICAL SPECIFICATIONS

ENGINE
MAKE/MODEL Cosworth TJ2006
CONFIGURATION 2998cc V10 (90 degree)
SPARK PLUGS Champion
ECU Pi Systems
FUEL Shell
OIL Shell
BATTERY Undisclosed

TRANSMISSION
GEARBOX Undisclosed
FORWARD GEARS Seven
CLUTCH AP Racing

CHASSIS
CHASSIS MODEL Toro Rosso STR01
FRONT SUSPENSION LAYOUT
Cast-titanium uprights, upper and lower carbon wishbones and pushrods, torsion-bar springs and anti-roll bars
REAR SUSPENSION LAYOUT
Cast-titanium uprights, upper and lower carbon wishbones and pushrods, torsion-bar springs

and anti-roll bars
DAMPERS Koni
TYRES Michelin
WHEELS AVUS Racing
BRAKE DISCS Brembo and Hitco
BRAKE PADS Brembo and Hitco
BRAKE CALIPERS AP Racing
RADIATORS Undisclosed
FUEL TANK ATL
INSTRUMENTS Pi Systems

DIMENSIONS
LENGTH 4685mm
WIDTH 1800mm
HEIGHT 950mm
WHEELBASE Over 3000mm
TRACK front 1480mm
rear 1418mm
WEIGHT 600kg (including driver and camera)

SCUDERIA Toro Rosso

1 Brakes were something of an issue for Scuderia Toro Rosso, and two changes of supplier took place as the team strove to find a solution that offered 'feel'
2 Changes to the STR01's front wing endplates were seen as key, as the team fought to make up for the aerodynamic disadvantage of running the longer V10

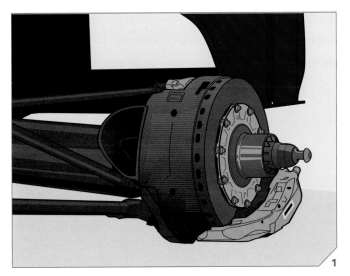

1

2

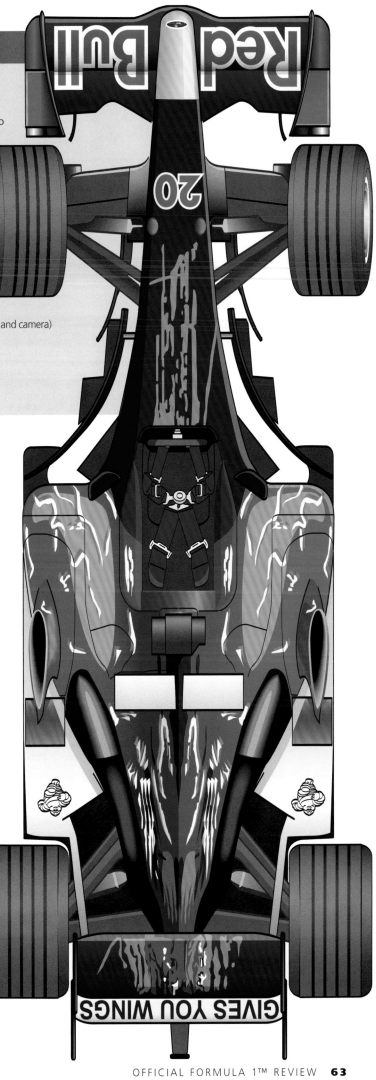

SPYKER

THE TEAM

PERSONNEL
TEAM OWNER Michiel Mol
TEAM PRINCIPAL Colin Kolles
CHIEF TECHNICAL OFFICER Mike Gascoyne
TECHNICAL DIRECTOR James Key (above)
HEAD OF DESIGN John McQuilliam
HEAD OF AERODYNAMICS Simon Phillips
TEAM MANAGER Andy Stevenson
DRIVERS Christijan Albers, Tiago Monteiro
CHIEF ENGINEER Dominic Harlow
RACE ENGINEER (Albers) Jody Eggington
RACE ENGINEER (Monteiro) Brad Joyce
TEST TEAM MANAGER Stewart Cox
TEST/THIRD DRIVERS Giorgio Mondini, Alex Premat, Adrian Sutil, Ernesto Viso, Markus Winkelhock
HEAD OF CAR BUILD Nick Burrows
CHIEF MECHANIC Andy Deeming
TOTAL NUMBER OF EMPLOYEES 209
NUMBER IN RACE TEAM 50
TEAM BASE Silverstone, England
TELEPHONE +44 (0)1327 850800
WEBSITE www.spykerf1.com

TEAM STATS
IN F1 SINCE 1991 **FIRST GRAND PRIX** USA 1991
STARTS 268 **WINS** 4 **POLE POSITIONS** 2
FASTEST LAPS 2 **PODIUMS** 20 **POINTS** 287
CONSTRUCTORS' TITLES 0 **DRIVERS' TITLES** 0

SPONSORS
Spyker, Rhino's, Superfund, ZIM, Zecco.com, Weigl, EuroPoker, JVC, MAN, TrekStor, Dremel, Garcia Jeanswear

19 CHRISTIJAN ALBERS   **18 TIAGO MONTEIRO**

By James Key (Technical Director)

"The switch to V8s was fairly seamless for us, because we were going from the Toyota V10 to the Toyota V8. The installation wasn't physically much different and it was actually quite a good programme. We went to an interim car based on our 2005 chassis and introduced the 2006 gearbox with a spacer.

We had to launch the new car in February because, from Toyota's side, they wanted everything complete by that date. When winter testing kicked off, people were talking about vibrations being an issue, but Toyota briefed us very well on that and gave us a good feel of what to look out for.

What happened on the speed traces with the V8s was quite funny. Some of it was obviously going back to pit stops and softer tyres but, because the rear axle was limiting the car performance less, as there was less torque going through it, we were actually quite a bit quicker out of corners, and into them as well. We could see it especially at places like Silverstone and Barcelona, where the quick corners got quicker with a V8 engine. That obviously seemed a bit perverse and was difficult to simulate too.

We were coming from a long way off the pace in 2005. With the takeover going on at the same time, it didn't make things easy. We had to plan as best we could to make a car that was a new platform to develop. The M16 was always intended as that, so we designed in a lot of capacity to change things, and pinpointed many development steps during the season that we didn't have time to cater for straight away.

The aerodynamic package we started with was OK, but we already had developments ready for the European season before we even ran the car. It was the same with the front suspension, because we had a feel for what to expect and, luckily, what we thought was correct. We did a lot of aero work towards the beginning of the season, particularly on the front end, and that yielded good results from the Nürburgring onwards, where suddenly we were quicker.

Some of it was difficult to see, but the work on the rear was around the diffuser and brake duct area where we opened up a lot of potential. It was things we hadn't realised during the winter because we just didn't have time to visit those areas. Then, with the front wing, the bi-flap looked good in the wind tunnel, improving stability and handling, and proved to be an even bigger step on the track. The lap-time gain we found from that aero package at Imola and the Nürburgring was more than expected.

We did some suspension updates before Monaco and that was a very competitive race for us, even if the result didn't show it. We were quicker than David Coulthard, who finished third with the Red Bull. That was a bit frustrating, but it was the first real sign that we weren't that far off.

After that, we tried to introduce new aero components and any chassis tweak we could at every event. The subsequent steps were small additions, and the next significant update which helped the handling was the Mk2 front suspension I mentioned previously. That came at Magny-Cours, where we went better than we expected. We tended to have an understeering car, and that characteristic began to disappear with the suspension modification. The next significant update was for Turkey, where we had a completely new front wing and bargeboard package."

GETTING THE BUZZ BACK

"I think we've done possibly 25% of the testing of pretty much all the guys ahead of us because, financially, we simply haven't been in a position to do more. We have survived fine and thank Midland for the season, but we haven't got the spending power to compete with the likes of BMW and Toyota and these huge companies. What we have ensured is that the testing work that we've done has been as efficient as possible. When we've done a shakedown, for example, we've tried to get as much out of the permitted 50km as we possibly could.

The engine at the start of the season was one of the most, if not the most, reliable engine out there and, in general, the performance level has been alright. But we then had a spate of failures, which was disappointing and affected Christijan quite badly in three consecutive races. That was a shame because he'd been really competitive but ended up at the back of the grid. I think it appeared to be a similar problem in each case and it's not an easy one to solve. I'm not going to say too much, but people speculating that it was pneumatic might not be in the wrong area.

Christijan and Tiago both did very well. It was great to have Tiago on board again this year because of the continuity it gave us, which we hadn't had in recent years. He is very reliable and very easy on the car as well, so you can tune the race strategy around the fact that you know he's going to be good on the tyres and the brakes and everything else. Christijan has done a really good job, he's a fun character to work with and he's shown some real pace.

We've had quite a few third drivers through the team, with Giorgio Mondini doing the most mileage. He's done a good job, and Markus Winkelhock and Adrian Sutil have both had very good inputs too. I think Adrian is a very clear talent. He's only done a few sessions with us, but he's always been very quick and his feedback has been excellent.

The future looks interesting, with Mike Gascoyne coming on board. I was at Jordan when Mike was there, not quite in the same capacity as now, so it will be a different working relationship and we will have to sit down and work out how we split the responsibilities.

Mike has a great deal of experience, which is going to be useful for us, but he's coming to a team which is much smaller and differently structured to what he's been used to recently. We'll have to see how it works out, but I'm sure it will be positive – back to the old style of racing team rather than the corporate entity.

I must say, the buzz around the team now is getting similar to how it was a few years back when we were successful as Jordan. We went through a sticky patch, but this year things have turned around and I'm quite certain that it's going to get better."

TECHNICAL SPECIFICATIONS

ENGINE
MAKE/MODEL Toyota RVX-06
CONFIGURATION 2398cc V8 (90 degree)
SPARK PLUGS Denso
ECU Magneti Marelli
FUEL/OIL Undisclosed
BATTERY GS Yuasa

TRANSMISSION
GEARBOX Spyker MF1
FORWARD GEARS Seven
CLUTCH AP Racing

CHASSIS
CHASSIS MODEL Spyker-Midland M16
FRONT SUSPENSION LAYOUT
Composite pushrods activating chassis-mounted in-line dampers and torsion bars, unequal length composite aerodynamic wishbones, front anti-roll bar
REAR SUSPENSION LAYOUT
Composite pushrods activating gearbox-mounted rotary dampers and torsion bars, unequal length composite aerodynamic wishbones
DAMPERS Titanium
TYRES Bridgestone
WHEELS BBS Racing
BRAKE DISCS Hitco
BRAKE PADS Hitco
BRAKE CALIPERS AP Racing
RADIATORS Secan
FUEL TANK ATL
INSTRUMENTS Undisclosed

DIMENSIONS
LENGTH 5000mm
WIDTH 1800mm
HEIGHT 950mm
WHEELBASE 3000mm
TRACK front 1480mm
rear 1418mm
WEIGHT 601kg (including driver and camera)

1 Both these graphics and the plan view show the M16 in early-season Midland livery. This one shows the revised front suspension and bi-flap front wing
2 Aerodynamic tweaks were introduced for almost every race, including this updated bargeboard package for tidying the airflow behind the front wheels

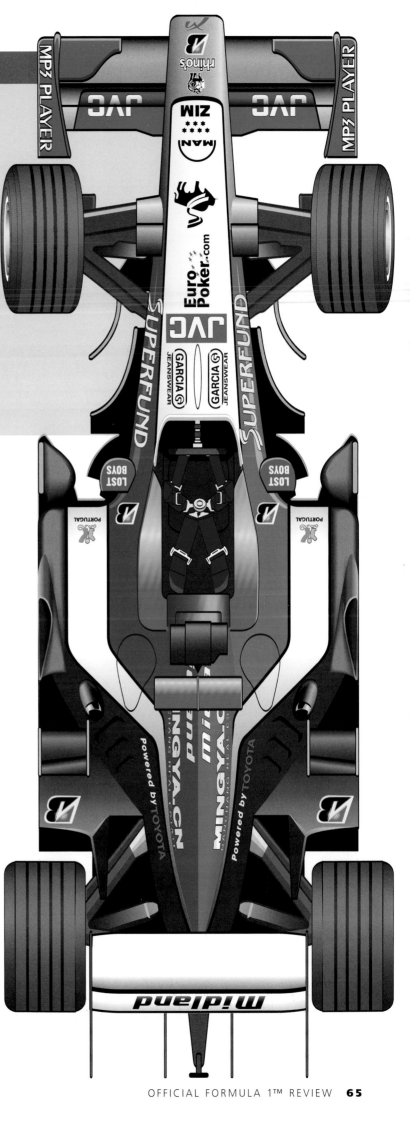

SUPER AGURI

THE TEAM

PERSONNEL

TEAM PRINCIPAL Aguri Suzuki
MANAGING DIRECTOR Daniele Audetto
TECHNICAL DIRECTOR Mark Preston (above)
SPORTING DIRECTOR Graham Taylor
CHIEF DESIGNER Peter McCool
CHIEF AERODYNAMICIST Ben Wood
TEAM MANAGER Mick Ainsley-Cowlishaw
DRIVERS Yuji Ide, Franck Montagny, Takuma Sato, Sakon Yamamoto
RACE ENGINEER (Sato) Gerry Hughes
RACE ENGINEER (Ide/Montagny/Yamamoto) Antonio Cuquerella
TEST/THIRD DRIVERS Franck Montagny, Sakon Yamamoto
CHIEF MECHANIC Phill Spencer
TOTAL NUMBER OF EMPLOYEES 152
NUMBER IN RACE TEAM 43
TEAM BASE Witney, England
TELEPHONE +44 (0)1993 871600
WEBSITE www.saf1.com

TEAM STATS

IN F1 SINCE 2006 **FIRST GRAND PRIX** Bahrain 2006
STARTS 18 **WINS** 0 **POLE POSITIONS** 0
FASTEST LAPS 0 **PODIUMS** 0 **POINTS** 0
CONSTRUCTORS' TITLES 0 **DRIVERS' TITLES** 0

SPONSORS

Honda, Bridgestone, Samantha Kingz, Life Card, Taisei

22 TAKUMA SATO **23** YUJI IDE **23** FRANCK MONTAGNY **23** SAKON YAMAMOTO

By Mark Preston (Technical Director)

"I think the Super Aguri story is one of those things that only happens in a 'do it' environment like Formula One. There I was working on some other plans, when last November there was a call from Daniele (Audetto) saying there was something going on with a new F1 team. It all just happened in such a huge rush.

A week later, it was a case of 'right, what's the plan?' Two weeks later it was 'OK, let's move into this building!' We called it, 'The 100 Days To The Grid'. We were working every hour God sent but, as far as I remember, we didn't actually work Christmas Day…

We had to adapt the old Arrows cars and it was an interesting time. Every day there was a problem and every day a solution. I was pulling together the technical side and Aguri (Suzuki) was organising engines, drivers, money and everything else. Myself, Daniele, Kevin (Lee), Wayne (Humphreys) and others were doing the organising in Leafield.

We had four monocoques; one that was doing the crash test, two that were destined to be race cars and one that was initially a systems car because Honda was supplying all the electronics and codes to help us integrate that with the old Arrows chassis and gearbox.

It was a really big rush and we first did three not so reliable days of testing in Barcelona at the end of February. That car was the old Arrows with the same old aero package and, in parallel, we had one car being modified to the 2006 rules and crash-tested. And we also had a model in the wind tunnel to decide on the first aerodynamic configuration.

Obviously, the old Arrows had run to less stringent aero regulations and when we drew the aero graph it was just phenomenal. It started at a fairly high aero level and immediately dropped more than 20% when it was adapted to the current rules. It didn't take long to get back up there and we were above that level well before the end of the year with the SA06.

In total, the team only had five weeks of wind-tunnel time before the start of the season. They focused on the body in the first week and signed it off. In the second week, it was top bodies, then wings and nose box.

Honda was massively supportive and, actually, their guys said it was the fastest engine installation they'd ever done, from the date of our first meeting to the systems car running.

The gearbox was probably the most difficult technical challenge. We were going to introduce the new one earlier but we had some timing issues and so used the old 'box to start with. Honda put a great deal of effort into the electronics and the control code. We were saying: 'Are you sure you can control this old gearbox with your new code?' And it was, 'Yeah, yeah, no problem', and they had it running in two days.

With two really excellent partners in Bridgestone and Honda, we just had to deal with the aerodynamic side. We pretty much left the monocoque alone, as a big bracket that held all the big aero bits together!"

PLAYING THE PERCENTAGES

"The best thing, for me, is that everyone said we were going to be 7s off the pace and we were actually 5–5.5s. I think we proved that the philosophy of concentrating on aero was the right one. We were using percentages to track our progress and we went from being 6.7% from the ultimate pace first time out, to 3.7% away from pole at Monza. We think that in anybody's book that's pretty impressive when Ferrari and Renault were pushing forward at such a rate that some of the others started to drop off the back.

Introducing the SA06, the development was focused on the rear end, which has a new quick-shift gearbox from Honda R&D. With the new gearbox came a lot of integration. It was a lot neater and, added to that, obviously the SA05 had suspension from 2002, and tyres have moved on a long way since then, so the rear suspension needed a lot of attention.

Running the SA05, we could at least see the areas that we needed to change, and we completed a lot of work with Bridgestone and developed new rear suspension. Integrating the gearbox and engine also saved weight, so we now had a reasonable amount of ballast on the car and a reduced centre of gravity, which gave the engineers a bit of room to play with weight distribution around the chassis, which is important for the tyres nowadays.

With the lower rear main plane of the SA06 wing we moved onto the twin-pylon arrangement, which allowed it to become much more aerodynamic, which in turn allowed changes to the floor and top bodywork. The SA06 had new sidepods, new-style radiator inlet ducts and a new top body, with the heat-shielding across the gearbox integrated properly with the engine, so that underbody and overbody flow was a lot better. The downforce gain, SA05 to SA06, was in the realm of 10%.

In terms of reliability, hydraulics were always an issue. You need a lot of miles and the ability to bash on through a testing programme. With something like a wing, you can put it on a test rig, bend it and stretch it, but with hydraulics you can't input the same amount of vibration, temperature, and so on, in the same way a car does.

We limited ourselves to running at the track and put more effort into doing our learning in front of the world! Post-Monza was only our second test. You could see it making leaps and bounds, but not enough to compete with the guys doing 50–70,000km of testing. It's just not the same ball park.

On the driving side, Takuma Sato has been really great and we've been impressed by his dedication and understanding of where we are. He kept a brave face on it and enjoyed himself where possible. Those first races, sometimes overtaking five cars on the first lap, were impressive. Sakon Yamamoto and Franck Montagny also did very well for us and it was hard on Yuji Ide because he didn't get any proper testing and we had lots of problems.

What we run chassis-wise next year might depend on the politics and, as an engineer, I just keep out of it and keep my head down…"

TECHNICAL SPECIFICATIONS

ENGINE
MAKE/MODEL Honda RA806E
CONFIGURATION 2400cc V8
(90 degree)
SPARK PLUGS NGK
ECU Honda
FUEL/OIL Undisclosed
BATTERY Undisclosed

TRANSMISSION
GEARBOX Honda/XTrac
FORWARD GEARS Seven
CLUTCH AP Racing

CHASSIS
CHASSIS MODEL Super Aguri SA06
FRONT SUSPENSION LAYOUT
Upper and lower carbon-wrapped steel
wishbones, pushrod-activated torsion springs
and rockers, with mechanical anti-roll bars
REAR SUSPENSION LAYOUT
Upper and lower carbon-wrapped steel
wishbones, pushrod-activated torsion springs
and rockers, with mechanical anti-roll bars

DAMPERS Ohlins
TYRES Bridgestone
WHEELS BBS
BRAKE DISCS Hitco
BRAKE PADS Hitco
BRAKE CALIPERS AP Racing
RADIATORS Undisclosed
FUEL TANK ATL
INSTRUMENTS
Super Aguri

DIMENSIONS
LENGTH 4666mm
WIDTH 1800mm
HEIGHT 950mm
WHEELBASE 3090mm
TRACK front 1472mm
rear 1422mm
WEIGHT 600kg
(including driver and
camera)

SUPER AGURI
F1 TEAM

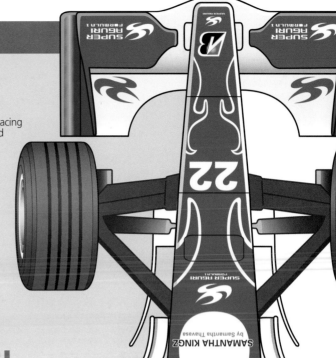

1 The SA06 was a major leap forward, with detailing such as this front wing
bringing it up to 2006 standards after the SA05 was effectively a 2002 Arrows
2 The rear end was the area of focus for the SA06, but there were also new
sidepods, a new style of inlet duct and a new top body to smooth overbody flow

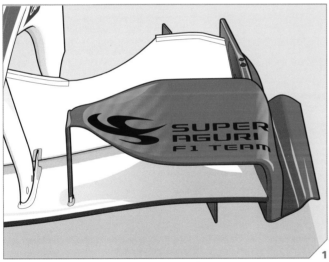

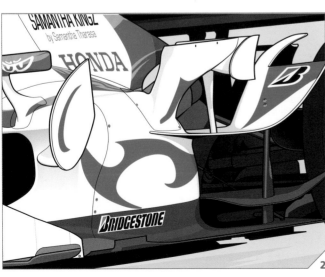

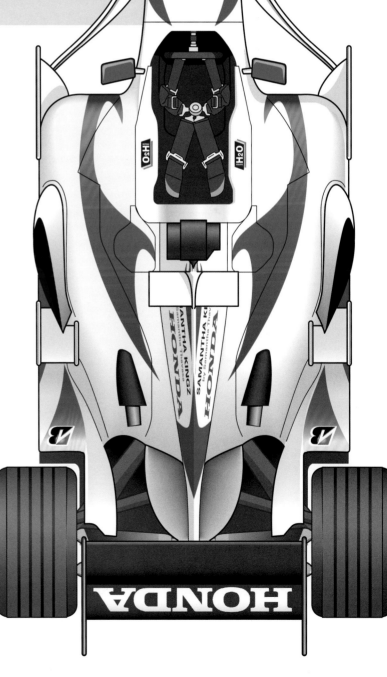

The car that even Formula 1™ drivers won't overtake.
The new CLK 63 AMG as the Official F1™ Safety Car

Mercedes-Benz

THE RACES

The 2006 season wasn't only about Ferrari versus Renault, as outlined in the reports for all 18 grands prix, with the inside story told by the drivers, team chiefs and tech men

2006 FORMULA 1™ GULF AIR
BAHRAIN GRAND PRIX
Sakhir

ONE-NIL TO RENAULT

Renault hoped their predominance would continue into 2006, and it did, but Ferrari showed that they had been busy over the winter and, with their new V8, could shine

Fernando Alonso started the season just as he finished in 2005, scoring a brilliant win after Renault's strategy helped to give him the jump on the opposition at the Bahrain Grand Prix. The big difference this year was that his rival at this opening race was not Kimi Räikkönen, but Michael Schumacher. The contrast between the German's charging performance and his lacklustre efforts in the 2005 finale in China could not have been greater. Indeed, Michael took pole position at the Sakhir circuit and led until the final round of pit stops, when Alonso charged out of the pits to block his rival with just metres to spare.

The real story of the weekend was the introduction of the new qualifying system. Six cars were eliminated after the first 15 minute session and six after the next session, leaving 10 to contest the final 20 minute period that would see them using up race fuel to record 'credit' laps for Sunday and leaving their final sprint on new tyres to the last possible moment.

Extensive winter testing in Bahrain had given Ferrari and Bridgestone an edge and went some way to explaining Michael's pole run. At the other extreme, the qualifying format's pitfalls were demonstrated by Räikkönen, as the Finn had a spectacular suspension

failure at the start of the first session, and was thus relegated to the back of the starting grid.

The new-style qualifying was an event in itself, and provided an interesting grid, but its legacy was far from over. For the previous three seasons, the fuel left in the car has had a direct effect on laps run in the race. This time, though, we had also to consider the number of 'credit' laps run in the final qualifying session, with an amount of fuel corresponding to that burned during the 'credit' laps being added to the cars for the race, plus how teams had used their tyres over the two days.

The laps completed by the key players certainly made for fascinating reading. By coming into the pits for only one tyre change, the Renaults had run 14 laps. In contrast, the Ferraris had run 12, while Honda had done two tyre changes and yet squeezed in 13 laps, one more than the Ferraris.

This was of course new ground for the teams, but also for the sport's governing body, the FIA, and its own procedures didn't run as smoothly as had been hoped. After issuing a signed document on Saturday night verifying the laps completed, Charlie Whiting had to amend it on race morning when the timekeepers realised that one of Michael's laps had been run outside 110% of his best time (he blamed traffic for this lap at 110.9% of his best), and was therefore discounted. McLaren's Juan Pablo Montoya was also penalised for the same 'offence', being docked two priceless laps.

Michael was now three laps down on Alonso, or 11 to 14 in terms of fuel put back into the car. Of course, no one outside the teams knew how much either man had left in the tank at the end of qualifying, but those three laps were a strong hint that the Ferrari man would be stopping first…

The tyre situation was also intriguing. Michael had used two sets of tyres on Friday, one on Saturday morning, one in the second qualifying session, and

two in final qualifying. He thus had just one new set left for the race, while Alonso had saved two sets. In contrast to the single-lap format, this year teams were now free to use whichever set of tyres they wished at the start of the race.

With two new sets to play with, it was a no-brainer for Alonso to fit new tyres for the start. Fourth on the grid, he needed every advantage he could get over that first lap as he tried to make up places. Michael didn't. Ferrari's thinking took various factors into account. Firstly, he had team-mate Felipe Massa riding shotgun behind him, and Alonso also had to get past Jenson Button's Honda. Therefore Michael could probably get away without the benefit of new rubber.

Secondly, the team knew that the timing of Michael's first stop meant that the first stint would be the shortest of the three stints by some margin, so it was worth using up older tyres. And thirdly, the likelihood was that after the first stop he would need to sprint in order to stay ahead of his pursuers, and that's when new rubber would be handy. If he had sufficient margin, he could also still save the new tyres for after the second stop, as a sprint then would be even more critical.

OPPOSITE TOP Williams fits a new nose to Nico Rosberg's FW28 after its first lap clash with Nick Heidfeld

OPPOSITE BOTTOM LEFT Scott Speed stands by his stranded Toro Rosso in practice, but the American went on to finish 13th on his debut

OPPOSITE BOTTOM RIGHT Jenson Button's Honda is refuelled during qualifying before going out to set third fastest time

BELOW Fernando Alonso heads Felipe Massa and Juan Pablo Montoya as they chase after Michael Schumacher in the opening stint of the race

INSIDE LINE
MICHAEL SCHUMACHER
FERRARI DRIVER

"It was great to get pole position for the opening round of the World Championship, not because it was my 65th, which equalled the record, but because I've had to wait a long time to get back on top. We have done a lot of hard work in the meantime and this was proof of it. All winter long we were

thinking that we had a good package, but you always have to wait for confirmation until everyone turns up at the first race and competes in the same conditions.

To have confirmation of what you have thought is always a relief because every engineer and every mechanic at Ferrari has been giving everything to put us back on top. There is quite a bit of emotion and good feeling because the 2005 season was a tough one.

The new qualifying format was certainly very exciting. Especially so in the first session, because we wanted to leave it towards the end to make our run, but then there was a red flag and everyone basically got one lap. The difference between hero and zero was really not very much at that point…

The second qualifying session was a little bit more straightforward and the

idea was just to play safe and stay in the top 10. Then we had a good strategy to go for the pole, which worked well. The team came here very focused, concentrated and organised and it was a great start.

In the race, OK, I only just lost out to Fernando [Alonso] at the second pit stop but, honestly, if you bear in mind where we were last year, if someone had told us beforehand that we would finish a close second in Bahrain, on merit, we would have been very happy about that. It's eight points and, while a win is always better of course, I'm honestly happy with pole position and second. The competitiveness was there and the ability to fight is the main thing.

Unfortunately, I didn't get the fuel allocation for one of my qualifying laps (outside 110% of his fastest time)

because I had to back off in traffic and if you look at it, maybe that was the one extra lap that I was missing at the second stop, in a way.

I think the TV pictures showed how close it was when Fernando came out of the pits. I was on the outside and I tried to get ahead, but there was no opportunity. Once behind him, it was a question of waiting for a mistake or a bad moment with a back-marker, but that didn't happen. However, I'm happy. I want to be able to challenge throughout the season and after this race there is no reason to think that I can't. "

INSIDE LINE
MARTIN WHITMARSH

McLAREN
CEO FORMULA ONE

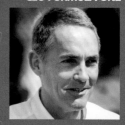

"It was a fantastic drive from Kimi to start back in 22nd and last place on the grid and yet work his way through the field to finish third, but it was still a bit frustrating for us because you end up wondering what might have been if he hadn't had the problem in the first place.

Kimi's problem was obviously the wishbone failure that put him out of qualifying in the first session. The root cause of the problem went back to Friday, though. In the front of the cockpit the electronics are tightly packaged and we suffered a few chafed cables as things started to get a bit warm! That, in turn, caused an electronic malfunction that triggered a downshift when there shouldn't have been one, which damaged the gearbox. We changed the 'box, but then a suspension joint failed and it looked to us like a manufacturing issue.

Kimi was obviously extremely frustrated at these events, but there had been so many predictions of doom and gloom in winter testing that I think he was actually very positive about the fact that, without problems, he could have been challenging for pole. The reality was that he was 22nd on the starting grid though and, of course, that frees you up to choose whatever race strategy you like. We opted for the one-stop race because it didn't look as though we were going to have any tyre-wear issues.

Kimi's first lap was pretty awesome and he came around in 13th place. He went around the outside of Turn 1 and then picked off a few more drivers as they were tripping over each other in Turn 4. He was going through the field very impressively indeed, but then got caught up for a while behind Jacques Villeneuve. Unfortunately, he was hitting the rev-limiter in seventh gear trying to pass Jacques, which made it a bit difficult, but he finally overtook him under braking.

I think you have to be happy finishing on the podium when you have started at the back and Kimi certainly seemed to have strong pace. Jenson was giving him a bit of pressure in the closing stages of the race, but I think he was on new rubber when Kimi's one-stop tyres were getting a bit worn and then he eased his pace.

Looking at the overall picture, it's hard to tell where everyone is at the opening race of the season. Sakhir is obviously sandy and that can make surface conditions relatively untypical. Also, Ferrari has tested in Bahrain ahead of the race, which obviously helped them, but they did seem pretty competitive. It was an excellent race, which is just what F1 wanted, and I think we could be in for a tremendously exciting year."

In the end, Michael did save his new set of tyres for the second stop, and he put in some fast times right at the start of his third and final stint. However, it still wasn't quite enough to beat Alonso. The Spaniard had run his rubber in the sequence new-new-old, but all that third, scrubbed set had to do was carry him to the end of the pit lane and allow him to scrabble out of Turn 1 in front of the Ferrari. After that, there was nothing Michael could do.

That was the key moment, and a reminder of just how critical a lap here and there can be in a race. Michael stopped on lap 15, Alonso on lap 19. The Spaniard didn't get ahead at that stage of the grand prix, but managed it at the second stops, which came on laps 36 and 39 respectively.

Although the pass came not at the first round of stops but at the second, it still related directly back to what had happened in qualifying. Ferrari put as little fuel in the tank as it dared at the first stop in order to keep Michael ahead, knowing that Renault could respond at Alonso's first stop and still ensure that he would definitely pit later second time around.

Michael rued losing the lap that the FIA had docked after qualifying, but in the end it was his mistake to lose too much time while jockeying for a clear piece of road in the 20 minute top-10 scramble. Ferrari also made the compromise of stopping twice for new tyres in qualifying: it helped to secure them the front row, but lost a lap of race fuel relative to Renault.

There was one factor that Michael could do nothing about: had Massa managed to keep Alonso behind him on the first lap, things might have turned out differently. As it was, Alonso's new tyres helped to give him that critical edge and helped him jump the second Ferrari. The only downside for Renault was an early V8 failure for Giancarlo Fisichella.

"It was a really exciting race, a really difficult race," said Renault Engineering Director Pat Symonds, clearly relishing the challenge. "But I think that's what the public likes to see, and it's what we enjoy as well. It was almost perfect, but we always feel disappointed when we have a second car that stops. Fernando's race was absolutely the way we like to go racing, though. He totally understood the race. He knew what he needed to do, and he did bloody well I think. It's what we expect of him.

"I said it in 2005, I think at times he was being very conservative in his driving, and I knew damn well

OPPOSITE **Vitantonio Liuzzi impressed by finishing on the same lap as winner Alonso in his Toro Rosso**

TOP **Felipe Massa's Ferrari debut was marked by this 190mph spin and then a wheel gun problem that cost him a points-scoring finish**

ABOVE **Suspension failure meant that Kimi Räikkönen started last, but his drive to third was most impressive**

that when he didn't need to be, he wouldn't be. You saw it in China. This is much more the Fernando that we enjoy seeing…"

Behind this duo, McLaren's Räikkönen put in a stunning performance, getting up from stone last to 13th place on the first lap and ultimately finishing the grand prix in third place.

"Kimi's race was fantastic," said McLaren Chief Executive Officer Martin Whitmarsh. "To come from 22nd place on the grid to third like that, it was a great race, and he did a fantastic job judging the risks that

you have to take in the first few laps to get yourself in a position to do that. Kimi did everything right. Later in the race, he was patient, he wasn't impetuous. It demonstrates that we are a little bit competitive, and clearly if we weren't starting 22nd then we would use that competitiveness to be competing for the top step of the podium, and not the bottom step."

Honda Racing had come to the Bahrain GP in confident mood after a close-season in which the renamed team had shown consistently strong form in testing, and Button did well to qualify third, but he bogged down at the start of the race, and had to work hard to recover to fourth place.

"I don't know what went wrong there, but it just didn't move," said Button. "It's really disappointing. I think I was back in about eighth place when I was braking for Turn 1 and I regained a couple of places there. I finally got past Rubens and Juan Pablo and I was looking good, but I lost so much ground at that start trying to fight past people that I wasn't able to get a podium finish.

"If everything had gone to plan, it would have been great. But one hiccup proved that everything has to go to plan to achieve success, and it didn't for us. It's something we really need to work on. It's very important to get the starts right, because everyone else got off the line well."

Montoya complained of a lack of engine performance all meeting and finished in fifth place ahead of the Williams pair of Mark Webber and Nico Rosberg, the latter getting involved in a first lap tangle but proving one of the stars of the race by setting fastest lap on a great recovery drive through the field which impressed more than a few onlookers since it was his Formula One debut. Klien took the last point for Red Bull, ahead of Massa, whose Ferrari debut included a spectacular spin at 190mph.

SNAPSHOT FROM
BAHRAIN

CLOCKWISE FROM RIGHT The architecture of the
grandstands has an appeal of its own at nightfall; 'losers
thataway', says the 2005 World Champion; the heat of
the desert can make life a little tiring; Takuma Sato, back
on the scene with Super Aguri F1, sits tight as a pair of
acrobats get busy; Ferrari versus Renault sounds about
right; fastest in the first sector, a collapsed suspension
rendered that effort meaningless for Kimi Räikkönen

WEEKEND HEADLINES

■ Rival teams expressed dissatisfaction with the degree
of flexibility apparent on Ferrari's rear wings, which
was reckoned to contribute to the cars' impressive
straightline speed. The consensus from the others was
that if the situation wasn't quickly clarified by the FIA,
then everyone else would have to follow suit and
produce similar designs.

■ The Bahrain GP was the first race in which the FIA
used a permanent steward. Britain's Tony Scott
Andrews landed the job of attending all the races to
provide a degree of consistency in the decision
making process. As previously, the other two stewards
were rotated through the season.

■ The Bahrain event organisers laid on a pro-celebrity
race using Chevrolet-badged Holdens prepared in
Australia by Tom Walkinshaw. The cars proved to be a
handful and had a few technical problems, but
Olympic rowing legend Steve Redgrave managed to
show that he is pretty handy behind the wheel.

■ Newcomers Super Aguri F1 beat the odds to get both
cars through practice and qualifying without major
problems. There was some chaotic action in the pits
come the race, and rookie Yuji Ide retired, but Takuma
Sato eventually made it home 18th and last, four laps
down on the winner.

■ After finishing 2005 in strong form, Toyota had a
terrible weekend as the team adjusted to life with
new partners Bridgestone. The drivers struggled with
unexpectedly low tyre temperatures all weekend, and
were well off the pace in the race as Ralf Schumacher
came home 14th and Jarno Trulli a lowly 16th.

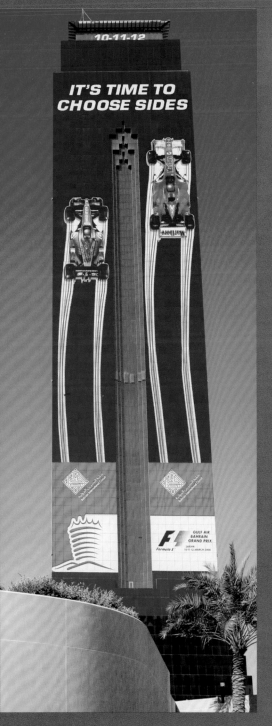

RACE RESULTS

BAHRAIN SAKHIR

RACE DATE March 12th
CIRCUIT LENGTH 3.363 miles
NO. OF LAPS 57
RACE DISTANCE 191.716 miles
WEATHER Warm & bright, 22°C
TRACK TEMP 44°C
RACE DAY ATTENDANCE N/A
LAP RECORD Michael Schumacher, 1m30.252s, 134.262mph, 2004

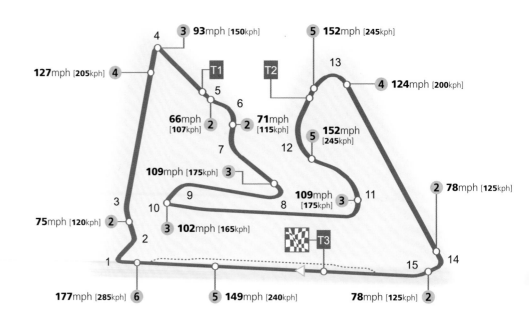

PRACTICE 1			
	Driver	Time	Laps
1	R Kubica	1m32.170s	20
2	A Wurz	1m32.184s	18
3	K Räikkönen	1m33.388s	6
4	M Schumacher	1m33.469s	5
5	C Klien	1m34.800s	6
6	N Jani	1m34.831s	15
7	JP Montoya	1m34.887s	6
8	F Massa	1m34.925s	6
9	D Coulthard	1m35.017s	4
10	V Liuzzi	1m35.083s	8
11	R Doornbos	1m35.203s	15
12	S Speed	1m35.371s	7
13	T Monteiro	1m36.542s	9
14	C Albers	1m36.930s	9
15	M Winkelhock	1m37.918s	16
16	T Sato	1m38.190s	15
17	Y Ide	1m40.782s	15
18	F Alonso	no time	2
19	A Davidson	no time	2
20	G Fisichella	no time	2
21	J Trulli	no time	2
22	N Heidfeld	no time	1
23	R Schumacher	no time	1
24	J Villeneuve	no time	1
25	R Barrichello	no time	0
26	J Button	no time	0
27	N Rosberg	no time	0
28	M Webber	no time	0

PRACTICE 2			
	Driver	Time	Laps
1	A Davidson	1m31.353s	28
2	M Schumacher	1m31.751s	15
3	A Wurz	1m31.764s	27
4	F Massa	1m32.175s	13
5	F Alonso	1m32.538s	13
6	V Liuzzi	1m32.703s	24
7	R Doornbos	1m32.926s	24
8	G Fisichella	1m33.215s	14
9	J Button	1m33.226s	12
10	R Kubica	1m33.244s	26
11	C Klien	1m33.557s	8
12	K Räikkönen	1m33.577s	11
13	JP Montoya	1m33.726s	15
14	N Heidfeld	1m33.848s	11
15	N Jani	1m33.900s	24
16	S Speed	1m34.284s	22
17	M Webber	1m34.333s	5
18	R Barrichello	1m34.384s	9
19	D Coulthard	1m34.432s	7
20	T Monteiro	1m34.459s	14
21	N Rosberg	1m34.953s	14
22	R Schumacher	1m35.170s	18
23	M Winkelhock	1m35.686s	24
24	J Trulli	1m35.898s	11
25	J Villeneuve	1m36.264s	8
26	C Albers	1m36.314s	16
27	T Sato	1m37.588s	19
28	Y Ide	1m39.021s	21

PRACTICE 3			
	Driver	Time	Laps
1	J Button	1m31.857s	16
2	M Schumacher	1m31.868s	8
3	F Alonso	1m31.975s	11
4	G Fisichella	1m32.050s	12
5	F Massa	1m32.826s	6
6	J Villeneuve	1m32.913s	14
7	J Trulli	1m33.038s	16
8	K Räikkönen	1m33.262s	12
9	R Schumacher	1m33.523s	14
10	M Webber	1m33.876s	11
11	C Klien	1m33.944s	14
12	R Barrichello	1m34.009s	15
13	N Heidfeld	1m34.094s	11
14	D Coulthard	1m34.142s	16
15	JP Montoya	1m34.406s	11
16	N Rosberg	1m34.434s	11
17	C Albers	1m34.541s	14
18	T Monteiro	1m35.026s	14
19	V Liuzzi	1m35.351s	13
20	S Speed	1m35.532s	13
21	T Sato	1m36.994s	15
22	Y Ide	1m41.889s	10

QUALIFYING 1		
	Driver	Time
1	F Alonso	1m32.433s
2	J Button	1m32.603s
3	G Fisichella	1m32.934s
4	N Rosberg	1m32.945s
5	JP Montoya	1m33.233s
6	M Schumacher	1m33.310s
7	N Heidfeld	1m33.374s
8	M Webber	1m33.454s
9	F Massa	1m33.579s
10	D Coulthard	1m33.678s
11	J Villeneuve	1m33.882s
12	R Barrichello	1m33.922s
13	J Trulli	1m33.987s
14	S Speed	1m33.995s
15	C Klien	1m34.308s
16	V Liuzzi	1m34.439s
17	R Schumacher	1m34.702s
18	C Albers	1m35.724s
19	T Monteiro	1m35.900s
20	T Sato	1m37.411s
21	Y Ide	1m40.270s
22	K Räikkönen	no time

QUALIFYING 2		
	Driver	Time
1	F Alonso	1m31.215s
2	JP Montoya	1m31.487s
3	G Fisichella	1m31.831s
4	N Heidfeld	1m31.958s
5	F Massa	1m32.014s
6	M Schumacher	1m32.025s
7	J Button	1m32.025s
8	C Klien	1m32.106s
9	M Webber	1m32.309s
10	R Barrichello	1m32.322s
11	J Villeneuve	1m32.456s
12	N Rosberg	1m32.620s
13	D Coulthard	1m32.850s
14	J Trulli	1m33.066s
15	V Liuzzi	1m33.416s
16	S Speed	1m34.406s

Best sectors – Practice		
Sec 1	A Wurz	29.427s
Sec 2	F Alonso	38.916s
Sec 3	A Wurz	22.623s

Speed trap – Practice		
1	R Kubica	193.8mph
2	K Räikkönen	192.8mph
3	J Villeneuve	192.7mph

Best sectors – Qualifying		
Sec 1	M Schumacher	29.517s
Sec 2	F Alonso	38.777s
Sec 3	JP Montoya	22.548s

Fernando Alonso
"This was a good win helped by fantastic stops. I almost went out when Massa spun past me. I looked after the tyres so I had something left at the crucial moment."

Michael Schumacher
"I'm not complaining about being second, but I have mixed feelings as we could've won. This year the fight for the title will be very close: there are several good teams."

Kimi Räikkönen
"We thought we had a chance of points, even from the back, but to get a podium is fantastic. I was up to 13th by lap 2 even though the cars in front were lighter."

Jenson Button
"This could have been great had I not had such a bad start. The strategy didn't work, as I lost places off the start and wasn't where we had aimed to be at the stops."

Jacques Villeneuve
"I managed to get through the first few corners, settled into a rhythm, overtook Coulthard and stayed in front of Räikkönen. Then, all of a sudden, I lost power."

Jarno Trulli
"We went with a two-stop strategy so we could make comparisons with Ralf's data. I pushed as hard as I could, but the harder I pushed the slower I seemed to go!"

Giancarlo Fisichella
"I had the same problem as in qualifying: a big loss of power. I was a long way from our potential. Then I had an hydraulic problem which forced me to retire."

Felipe Massa
"I was very close to Alonso and I touched the brakes, lost the rear end and spun off. I lost time changing the right rear and for the rest of the race I was flat-out."

Juan Pablo Montoya
"I've not been totally comfortable with my car's set-up. I'm a little disappointed finishing fifth as I know that the car could do more. However, it was a steady race."

Rubens Barrichello
"Early on we saw a great waste of our potential, although Jenson and I had a great race with each other. But, soon after, I had a gearbox problem and was unable to push."

Nick Heidfeld
"Rosberg spun in front of me at Turn 1. I fought back and had an exciting battle with Coulthard, but it's disappointing when you start 10th and don't score any points."

Ralf Schumacher
"After our problems in qualifying, we used the race as a test session to collect data. Of course, this was not the way we hoped to start off the 2006 season."

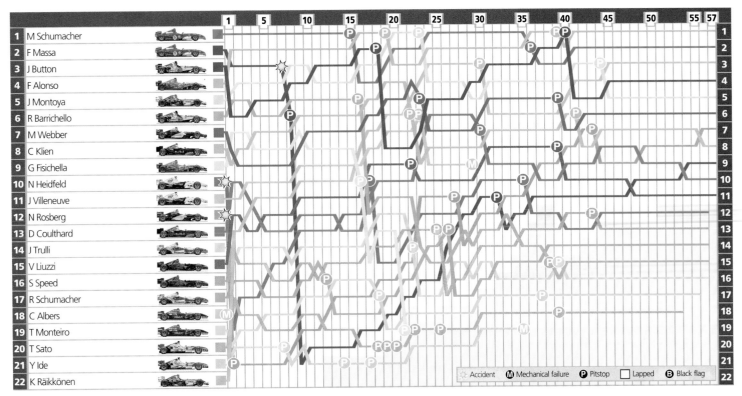

	Driver		1	5	10	15	20	25	30	35	40	45	50	55	57
1	M Schumacher														
2	F Massa														
3	J Button														
4	F Alonso														
5	J Montoya														
6	R Barrichello														
7	M Webber														
8	C Klien														
9	G Fisichella														
10	N Heidfeld														
11	J Villeneuve														
12	N Rosberg														
13	D Coulthard														
14	J Trulli														
15	V Liuzzi														
16	S Speed														
17	R Schumacher														
18	C Albers														
19	T Monteiro														
20	T Sato														
21	Y Ide														
22	K Räikkönen														

☼ Accident   Ⓜ Mechanical failure   ⓟ Pitstop   ☐ Lapped   Ⓑ Black flag

QUALIFYING 3

	Driver	Time
1	M Schumacher	1m31.431s
2	F Massa	1m31.478s
3	J Button	1m31.549s
4	F Alonso	1m31.702s
5	JP Montoya	1m32.164s
6	R Barrichello	1m32.579s
7	M Webber	1m33.006s
8	C Klien	1m33.112s
9	G Fisichella	1m33.496s
10	N Heidfeld	1m33.926s

GRID

	Driver	Time
1	M Schumacher	1m31.431s
2	F Massa	1m31.478s
3	J Button	1m31.549s
4	F Alonso	1m31.702s
5	JP Montoya	1m32.164s
6	R Barrichello	1m32.579s
7	M Webber	1m33.006s
8	C Klien	1m33.112s
9	G Fisichella	1m33.496s
10	N Heidfeld	1m33.926s
11	J Villeneuve	1m32.456s
12	N Rosberg	1m32.620s
13	D Coulthard	1m32.850s
14	J Trulli	1m33.066s
15	V Liuzzi	1m33.416s
16	S Speed	1m34.406s
17	R Schumacher	1m34.702s
18	C Albers	1m35.724s
19	T Monteiro	1m35.900s
20	T Sato	1m37.411s
21	Y Ide	1m40.270s
22	K Räikkönen	no time

RACE

	Driver	Car	Laps	Time	Avg. mph	Fastest	Stops
1	F Alonso	Renault R26	57	1h29m46.205s	128.761	1m32.534s	2
2	M Schumacher	Ferrari 248	57	1h29m47.451s	128.731	1m32.523s	2
3	K Räikkönen	McLaren-Mercedes MP4-21	57	1h30m05.565s	128.300	1m32.864s	1
4	J Button	Honda RA106	57	1h30m06.197s	128.285	1m32.729s	2
5	JP Montoya	McLaren-Mercedes MP4-21	57	1h30m23.253s	127.881	1m32.771s	2
6	M Webber	Williams-Cosworth FW28	57	1h30m28.137s	127.766	1m32.660s	2
7	N Rosberg	Williams-Cosworth FW28	57	1h30m49.248s	127.271	1m32.408s	3
8	C Klien	Red Bull-Ferrari RB2	57	1h30m52.976s	127.184	1m33.212s	2
9	F Massa	Ferrari 248	57	1h30m56.112s	127.111	1m32.739s	2
10	D Coulthard	Red Bull-Ferrari RB2	57	1h31m01.746s	126.980	1m33.376s	1
11	V Liuzzi	Toro Rosso-Cosworth STR01	57	1h31m12.202s	126.737	1m33.480s	2
12	N Heidfeld	BMW F1.06	56	1h29m56.330s	126.263	1m33.772s	2
13	S Speed	Toro Rosso-Cosworth STR01	56	1h30m01.841s	126.134	1m33.108s	2
14	R Schumacher	Toyota TF106	56	1h30m24.528s	125.606	1m34.112s	2
15	R Barrichello	Honda RA106	56	1h30m42.588s	125.190	1m33.840s	2
16	J Trulli	Toyota TF106	56	1h30m51.466s	124.986	1m34.852s	2
17	T Monteiro	Midland-Toyota M16	55	1h30m15.643s	123.564	1m35.940s	2
18	T Sato	Super Aguri-Honda SA05	53	1h31m13.629s	117.805	1m37.104s	6
R	Y Ide	Super Aguri-Honda SA05	35	Engine	-	1m38.302s	3
R	J Villeneuve	BMW F1.06	29	Engine	-	1m33.694s	1
R	G Fisichella	Renault R26	21	Hydraulics	-	1m34.320s	2
R	C Albers	Midland-Toyota M16	0	Driveshaft	-		0

CHAMPIONSHIP

	Driver	Pts
1	F Alonso	10
2	M Schumacher	8
3	K Räikkönen	6
4	J Button	5
5	JP Montoya	4
6	M Webber	3
7	N Rosberg	2
8	C Klien	1

Speed trap – Qualifying
1 F Alonso 189.5mph
2 M Schumacher 189.4mph
3 J Villeneuve 188.7mph

Fastest Lap
N Rosberg 1m32.408s
(131.773mph) on lap 42

Fastest speed trap
F Massa 193.6mph
Slowest speed trap
Y Ide 182.9mph

Fastest pit stop
1 JP Montoya 25.369s
2 J Button 25.424s
3 R Schumacher 25.497s

Constructor		Pts
1	Renault	10
2	McLaren-Mercedes	10
3	Ferrari	8
4	Honda	5
5	Williams-Cosworth	5
6	Red Bull-Ferrari	1

David Coulthard

"I flat-spotted when I was fighting with Heidfeld. It feels like you're sitting on top of a spin drier. The team wanted me to do an oil transfer, but I couldn't see the button."

Mark Webber

"Today's race was superb, a really good job by the team. Having both cars finishing was useful as we've collected a lot of data to help with our understanding of the tyres."

Vitantonio Liuzzi

"We were expecting a bit more. But it was good to see the chequered flag in a reasonable position. Sadly, we didn't have the pace we needed over the weekend."

Tiago Monteiro

"The T-Car wasn't set up for me, so it was a compromise. The car is definitely faster and better than it was last year, but it's not quick enough at the moment."

Takuma Sato

"The boys in the garage deserve to be happy as they worked so hard. We had radio and fuel rig problems, which is why there was some confusion during our pit stops."

Christian Klien

"I made up a few places, but the car's grip went away. I also had a clutch problem. It's a shame that Nico overtook me in the final laps as I fell from seventh to eighth."

Nico Rosberg

"I made a mistake at Turn 1, expecting Heidfeld might leave more room. I enjoyed battling with Coulthard and seventh with fastest lap is more than I expected."

Scott Speed

"I'm pleased to have got to the flag without making any mistakes in my first grand prix. My car's balance wasn't right, but we were able to fix that at the pit stop."

Christijan Albers

"It's a shame I didn't get to race. It's really unlucky, as we've never had that driveshaft problem before. It's just one of those things that's impossible to predict."

Yuji Ide

"I wanted to finish, but the engine stopped. Earlier, I couldn't get neutral so I over-ran my stop. The crew has been working hard so I feel bad for my lack of experience."

2006 FORMULA 1™ PETRONAS
MALAYSIAN GRAND PRIX
Kuala Lumpur

RENAULT RULES

Renault's superiority was such that
Giancarlo Fisichella led Fernando Alonso
home in a 1–2 finish despite the best
efforts of Jenson Button and Honda Racing

The race itself might not have been an edge-of-the-seat thriller like Bahrain, but the Malaysian GP weekend had plenty to recommend it, as it underlined that 2006 was going to be an intriguing season, with so many interwoven layers involving engine mileage, new tyres, fuel weights and qualifying strategy. Suddenly, the sport appeared to be more complex than at any time in the recent past.

And while Giancarlo Fisichella didn't put a foot wrong on his way to scoring a pretty straightforward victory for Renault, his team-mate Fernando Alonso's troubles proved that even the best organised teams could get it wrong.

Alonso was the last man on a hot lap in the crucial third qualifying session, and when a decent time didn't materialise and he ended up eighth, people were left scratching their heads. While Fisichella was whisked away to the press conference for the three top qualifiers, sombre looks in the Renault camp revealed that something had gone badly wrong.

In fact, in the rush to refuel the car before the third session, the team had given him double the intended fuel load, having thought that nothing had gone in at the first attempt. So he went into the fuel-burning session way overweight. His good fortune was that Michael Schumacher already had a penalty, Christian Klien opted out of the fight and Ralf Schumacher had suffered a blown engine. All of that meant he would start seventh. It could have been worse.

Renault had stumbled into an area of the new qualifying rules that no one had anticipated. The emphasis thus far had been on doing as many credit laps as possible in order to ensure that, having got them back, you could go as far as possible in the race with your commensurate fuel load. Now we had a team that didn't want to use its credit laps, making use of the fact that the rules say only that you may replace the fuel. Since Alonso had run 13 laps in Q3, he could start the race with the fuel he had left in the car, with that plus his 13 laps, or any permutation in between.

"We'd taken the downside of qualifying," said Engineering Director Pat Symonds. "The upside was that we had more options than we'd ever known, so we evaluated a helluva lot of them and came up with what might seem an oddball one."

Fisichella was joined on the front row by Jenson Button, while Nico Rosberg continued to impress by qualifying in third, ahead of Mark Webber and the

McLarens of Juan Pablo Montoya and Kimi Räikkönen.

Concerns over engine longevity due to a valve problem meant that Michael Schumacher's Ferrari had taken an engine change, so he went from his original fourth to 14th. Team-mate Felipe Massa was right at the back after also taking a penalty (he actually changed engines twice so that he could run a lot of practice laps), so it wasn't looking good for Ferrari.

It was clear that the McLarens had a heavy fuel load, and Ron Dennis remained bullish about prospects, but the risks inherent in qualifying on the third row became evident on the first lap, for while the two drivers were busy racing each other Räikkönen was nudged into a big accident by Klien's Red Bull.

"To finish first, first you've got to finish," said Dennis. "It was a pretty stupid mistake of Klien's. He hit Kimi straight up the back. I don't think Kimi was doing anything extraordinary. There was nothing wrong with the data: he didn't brake early. It was a straight incident from a guy who doesn't normally find himself in that position."

Apart from that, it was a relatively clean start as Fisichella headed Button. Alonso got a flier and took a few risks on the run to Turn 1 to end the first lap in an

BELOW Pole starter Giancarlo Fisichella leads Jenson Button, Fernando Alonso, Mark Webber, Juan Pablo Montoya (almost hidden) and Kimi Räikkönen, just before the Finn's McLaren was hit by Christian Klien's Red Bull

OPPOSITE Jenson Button composes himself with his crew on the grid before starting from the outside of the front row

amazing third place, helped by the fact that the Williams duo were falling over each other on the inside line. Suddenly things didn't seem so bad, as it was obvious that Alonso would be running a longer first stint than the two ahead.

Fisichella stopped on lap 19, and Button two laps later. By then, the gap from the Honda to the heavier Alonso had drifted to 14.9s, so the 2005 World Champion was not an immediate threat. But, after his late stop on lap 26, Alonso resumed less than 8s behind the Brit. Now it was a question of what would happen in and around the second stops.

Fisichella and Button came in on lap 38, with the Renault man 10s clear and under no threat from the Honda driver. Alonso had closed to within 4s of Button and, by running five very quick laps while the Honda was tanked up for the run to the flag, he was able to jump him for second place as he rejoined. After that, it was a controlled run to the flag for the Renault duo as they lodged the first 1–2 in fully 24 years for the team. There appeared to be something in reserve.

"We had a small problem with tyre graining after the pit stop," said Fisichella. "But, apart from that, there was a great balance to the car, great behaviour,

INSIDE LINE
GIANCARLO FISICHELLA

RENAULT DRIVER

"To win from pole position – I can't really ask for anything more! On Friday, the car did not feel perfect, probably due to the circuit conditions, with a bit too much slow-corner oversteer. However, after discussion, we made some adjustments to the car overnight and the balance felt great in both qualifying and the race.

You get high temperatures here at Sepang, of course, and even in the third qualifying session you are aware of it. It's the toughest race of the season physically. I'm confident that I'm strong both physically and mentally, but it's the same for everyone and I felt right.

We had some fuel-rig problems during qualifying which meant that Fernando's car actually took onboard a double load of fuel, which explains why he qualified only back in eighth place. The team could compensate in the race by not taking all of his allocated fuel credit laps (2.8kg per top-10 run-off lap in Sepang) but, in terms of grid slot and strategy for the race, I was in a good position.

Both Fernando and I had really strong races and scored Renault's first 1–2 finish as a constructor since the 1982 French Grand Prix. It was a great result and the weekend's target, but it was certainly hard to achieve because the others were close to us. I had a problem with tyre graining for a couple of laps after my first pit stop but, apart from that, I was very comfortable.

I was talking with my engineer (Alan 'Bat' Permane) about Fernando's pace because, obviously, after he made such a fantastic start and took third position, he could have been a threat. But we were always on target and so I was confident. I was pushing hard, but not going over the limit and I never made a mistake as I drove to my third Formula One victory.

I will take a win any way it comes, but sometimes there is nothing you can do. Last year in the Japanese Grand Prix at Suzuka I started third on the grid and was the race leader going onto the last lap, but I was 10mph slower than Räikkönen on the start/finish straight and I simply couldn't keep him behind me.

But this was my day and nobody was going to take it away. I wanted to really do everything I could here. It has been an emotional weekend. I dedicate both my pole position and the win to a friend of mine. We started karting together as eight-year-olds and unfortunately last Sunday he died in an accident. Ciao, Pietro."

remained the suggestion that he and the team should have somehow found a way to keep Alonso behind.

"We're a little bit too far off their pace to have pipped Alonso," said Honda technical director Geoff Willis. "If we were a little bit faster, we'd be in a slightly better position on the track and thus not caught by some of the traffic we have to get past. Some of the traffic happens when you appear to be genuinely racing them. Yes, you're ahead of them on your strategy, but you're running behind them on the track, and you're not lapping them, so you don't get the benefit of blue flags."

Montoya took fourth place, but it was a poor reward on a day when McLaren felt that Räikkönen could have got the job done. In fact, Montoya struggled throughout with understeer; the team would later surmise that hasty bodywork mods to aid cooling had compromised the balance.

Of more interest was what happened behind the Colombian. Fifth should have gone to Nick Heidfeld, the victim of a BMW engine failure on lap 49, after a great race by the German. It went instead to a Ferrari, but not the one we had expected... From the back of the grid, Massa ran a one-stop strategy, and as events unfolded it proved to be better than the two-stopper Michael used from 14th. The German was up to 10th on lap 1, helped by Räikkönen's demise, but he seemed a little surprised to find his new team-mate in front at the end of the race. Off-track events were of even more concern to Ferrari (see 'Snapshot').

The final points went to BMW Sauber's Jacques Villeneuve and Ralf Schumacher, the latter starting his Toyota from the back after an engine failure in second qualifying. He beat team-mate Jarno Trulli, who struggled with tyre problems again, and was further hampered by a first-lap nudge from Scuderia Toro Rosso's Tonio Liuzzi that damaged the diffuser.

Another to take an engine-change penalty, Rubens

ABOVE Rubens Barrichello had to start 20th after his engine was changed before qualifying and ended up out of the points in 10th

BELOW Jacques Villeneuve hustles his BMW Sauber to seventh place

OPPOSITE The Ferrari pit crew readies itself for Michael Schumacher, but his two-stop strategy left him one place behind his one-stopping team-mate

and I was really very comfortable."

"It means a lot to everyone," said Symonds. "1–2s are so rare that they give me such a thrill. Everyone loves winning, but 1–2s really are something. Even with all the success of last year, this is such a great result. Giancarlo takes a lot of unfair knocks, but he's got a lot of strength of character that people outside the team don't see. It was a big, big disappointment to retire last week [in Bahrain], but to come back in such style, it says so much about the character of the guy. Within the team, everyone loves Giancarlo, and we're so pleased to see him get this result."

Button took a comfortable third, but there

INSIDE LINE
BERNARD FERGUSON

**COSWORTH
COMMERCIAL DIRECTOR**

"It's been a long hard road for Cosworth ever since Ford put us up for sale. When we announced the deal with Williams there was a level of scepticism. And when we showed the V8 engine running to 20,000rpm on our website, there was a bit more. But I don't think there's any now. All these guys with their acoustic analysers probably know exactly what the rpm was when Nico Rosberg passed Christian Klien on his way to points in Bahrain. It was 20,000rpm – just like it said on the tin!

Seeing those flames around Nico's car in the race here are not exactly the kind of pictures you want to be looking at, but both we and and Williams came to the Malaysian Grand Prix with an aggressive strategy.

Nico's debut in Bahrain was fantastic really and Mark Webber is a real fighter, and then we had both cars on the second row here at Sepang. When talking to [Williams Technical Director] Sam Michael about Nico, it's clear that he's going to become a major force. In fact, he's come on a lot faster than Frank, Patrick or Sam thought he would. I think they were mentally giving him seven or eight grands prix to get with it, but he set fastest lap in his first grand prix, qualified third here and there's not much he's doing wrong at the moment. His target coming to Malaysia was to win, simple as that, and there was no point us coming here to be conservative and meander around hoping that other people fell off.

We came to Sepang to be aggressive and we lost an engine. And that's it. We don't get over-excited when we are doing well and we don't get too disappointed when we get kicked in the crutch. Life's like that. There was no warning, but we'll shovel the bits into a box, take them back to headquarters in Northampton and we should be able to diagnose the problem pretty soon.

I think that Cosworth has made a very promising start to the season and we've worked out a development programme with Williams that they are happy with. You can be successful as an independent, but it's extremely difficult for any business when you hear engine manufacturers talking about a collective billion dollar spend, or whatever, to put 22 cars on a track in 18 locations over the course of a year. When you talk to sponsors, it's certainly hard to convince them that it's not money being wasted… There's clear need for restraint with engines, but it has to be managed in a constructive fashion, and by negotiation rather than insistence."

ABOVE Takuma Sato displays banzai style under braking as he jousts with Vitantonio Liuzzi

BELOW LEFT Juan Pablo Montoya ran a faultless race to fourth place for McLaren

BELOW RIGHT Victory number three for Fisichella

Barrichello, still didn't seem to be coming to terms with the Honda. The Brazilian started from the back on a one-stopper and, with a drive-through penalty adding to his woes, was classified 10th.

It was a bad day for the two Red Bull teams. Liuzzi was the only man to make it home, taking 11th after a first-lap nose change ruined his day. What had started out as a good weekend for Williams ended in disappointment when Rosberg had an early engine failure, while Webber had a hydraulic problem when running a strong fourth on lap 16.

"I think, all in all, it was a good weekend for me again," said Rosberg. "I left a good impression in qualifying: P3 was great for me. Going off the grid wasn't quite so good, and then I tried to hold my position to Mark. When I raced in GP2, the guy would have backed off, but here, not really! I accepted that. I thought OK, P4 is fine, and then Alonso came flying down, so that was a big surprise to me."

This time, Renault didn't seem to have any serious challengers. Would anyone give them a hard time next time out in Melbourne?

SNAPSHOT FROM
MALAYSIA

CLOCKWISE FROM RIGHT The twin Petronas Towers are emblematic of the enormous growth of capital city Kuala Lumpur; the marshals are instructed on what to do with the kit laid out in front of them; Ferrari wings remained the focus of attention, due to concerns from other teams about their flexibility; one small truck, one large load of marshals; the welcoming face of Malaysia; soaring temperatures, towering humidity, one fan and a welcome breeze of cooling air, relief

WEEKEND HEADLINES

■ Teams' concerns about Ferrari's wings reached fever pitch in Malaysia when it emerged that the front wing flaps were apparently designed to move under load, adding fuel to the fire created by flexing rear wings. Rival teams wrote to the FIA and threatened a post-race protest until Ferrari capitulated before the start, and promised to bring new parts to the following round in Australia.

■ Speculation about Valentino Rossi's Ferrari prospects continued to mount, but Renault's points leader Fernando Alonso was underwhelmed when questioned on the subject, suggesting that the Italian's efforts were a waste of Ferrari's time and that Rossi would never be on the ultimate pace in Formula One.

■ A few days after the race, Williams revealed that chief designer Jorg Zander, who had only recently joined the Grove team, was leaving for 'personal reasons'. Nothing more was heard for a few weeks until BMW Sauber announced that the German was on his way to Hinwil…

■ On 24 March, Toyota was proud to confirm that the Japanese GP was destined for its Fuji Speedway in 2007, leaving Honda-owned Suzuka's in the cold – unless Bernie Ecclestone could justify a second race in the country, as he did in 1994–95 with the Pacific GP at Aida. The return to the revamped Fuji Speedway will coincide with the 30th anniversary of the last F1 race there.

■ Flavio Briatore stunned his fellow GPMA members when he and Renault technical bosses joined representatives of Ferrari and Cosworth in a 'secret' meeting with the FIA at Maranello on 24 March. Later, the FIA announced a package of 2008 engine rules discussed that day which soon became known as the 'Maranello Agreement'.

RACE RESULTS
MALAYSIA
SEPANG

Official Results © [2006]
Formula One Administration Limited,
6 Princes Gate, London SW7 1QJ.
No reproduction without permission.
All copyright and database rights reserved

RACE DATE March 19th
CIRCUIT LENGTH 3.444 miles
NO. OF LAPS 56
RACE DISTANCE 192.887 miles
WEATHER Humid & bright, 34°C
TRACK TEMP 38°C
RACE DAY ATTENDANCE 100,000
LAP RECORD Juan Pablo Montoya,
1m34.223s, 131.595mph, 2004

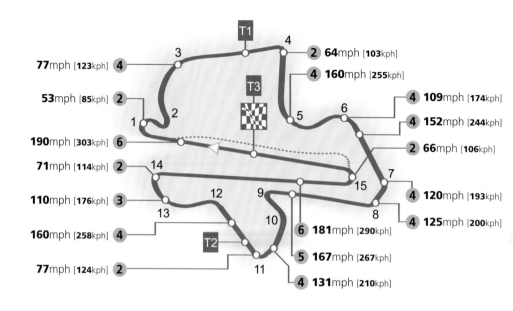

PRACTICE 1			
	Driver	Time	Laps
1	A Wurz	1m34.946s	19
2	R Kubica	1m35.733s	22
3	A Davidson	1m35.997s	25
4	JP Montoya	1m36.709s	4
5	D Coulthard	1m37.042s	7
6	M Schumacher	1m37.043s	4
7	F Massa	1m37.557s	18
8	R Doornbos	1m37.604s	18
9	R Schumacher	1m37.826s	9
10	C Klien	1m38.448s	5
11	N Jani	1m38.668s	21
12	J Trulli	1m38.837s	8
13	S Speed	1m39.599s	14
14	T Monteiro	1m39.899s	8
15	G Mondini	1m40.092s	22
16	V Liuzzi	1m40.123s	8
17	C Albers	1m40.608s	12
18	T Sato	1m41.072s	18
19	Y Ide	1m43.449s	19
20	F Alonso	no time	2
21	G Fisichella	no time	2
22	N Heidfeld	no time	1
23	K Räikkönen	no time	1
24	J Villeneuve	no time	1
25	R Barrichello	no time	0
26	J Button	no time	0
27	N Rosberg	no time	0
28	M Webber	no time	0

PRACTICE 2			
	Driver	Time	Laps
1	A Davidson	1m35.041s	14
2	A Wurz	1m35.388s	30
3	F Alonso	1m35.806s	14
4	F Massa	1m35.924s	22
5	K Räikkönen	1m36.132s	15
6	G Fisichella	1m36.182s	14
7	M Schumacher	1m36.617s	17
8	J Button	1m36.661s	12
9	J Villeneuve	1m37.045s	9
10	R Barrichello	1m37.270s	13
11	J Trulli	1m37.317s	23
12	N Heidfeld	1m37.418s	7
13	R Kubica	1m37.457s	28
14	JP Montoya	1m37.463s	12
15	V Liuzzi	1m37.590s	22
16	D Coulthard	1m37.603s	8
17	R Schumacher	1m37.695s	20
18	N Jani	1m37.831s	23
19	S Speed	1m37.926s	21
20	M Webber	1m38.081s	5
21	N Rosberg	1m38.205s	6
22	G Mondini	1m38.256s	20
23	C Klien	1m38.644s	10
24	C Albers	1m38.918s	20
25	R Doornbos	1m39.105s	28
26	T Monteiro	1m39.416s	20
27	T Sato	1m41.549s	22
28	Y Ide	1m43.164s	16

PRACTICE 3			
	Driver	Time	Laps
1	M Schumacher	1m34.126s	16
2	F Alonso	1m34.180s	13
3	G Fisichella	1m34.585s	13
4	J Button	1m34.616s	20
5	C Klien	1m34.815s	12
6	K Räikkönen	1m34.854s	10
7	R Schumacher	1m35.040s	7
8	N Rosberg	1m35.242s	14
9	D Coulthard	1m35.639s	14
10	J Trulli	1m35.690s	19
11	M Webber	1m35.700s	11
12	J Villeneuve	1m36.144s	9
13	N Heidfeld	1m36.505s	13
14	V Liuzzi	1m36.549s	15
15	R Barrichello	1m36.655s	13
16	JP Montoya	1m37.053s	8
17	F Massa	1m37.148s	21
18	C Albers	1m37.232s	18
19	S Speed	1m37.437s	19
20	T Monteiro	1m37.900s	17
21	T Sato	1m38.821s	15
22	Y Ide	1m40.542s	18

QUALIFYING 1		
	Driver	Time
1	JP Montoya	1m34.536s
2	K Räikkönen	1m34.667s
3	D Coulthard	1m34.839s
4	J Button	1m35.023s
5	F Massa	1m35.091s
6	N Rosberg	1m35.105s
7	C Klien	1m35.171s
8	R Schumacher	1m35.214s
9	M Webber	1m35.252s
10	J Villeneuve	1m35.391s
11	G Fisichella	1m35.488s
12	F Alonso	1m35.514s
13	J Trulli	1m35.517s
14	R Barrichello	1m35.526s
15	N Heidfeld	1m35.588s
16	M Schumacher	1m35.810s
17	S Speed	1m36.297s
18	V Liuzzi	1m36.581s
19	C Albers	1m37.426s
20	T Monteiro	1m37.819s
21	T Sato	1m39.011s
22	Y Ide	1m40.720s

QUALIFYING 2		
	Driver	Time
1	J Button	1m33.527s
2	G Fisichella	1m33.623s
3	F Alonso	1m33.997s
4	M Webber	1m34.279s
5	K Räikkönen	1m34.351s
6	C Klien	1m34.537s
7	N Rosberg	1m34.563s
8	JP Montoya	1m34.568s
9	M Schumacher	1m34.574s
10	R Schumacher	1m34.586s
11	D Coulthard	1m34.614s
12	R Barrichello	1m34.683s
13	J Trulli	1m34.702s
14	J Villeneuve	1m34.752s
15	N Heidfeld	1m34.783s
16	F Massa	no time

Best sectors – Practice		Speed trap – Practice		Best sectors – Qualifying	
Sec 1 A Wurz	24.783s	1 A Wurz	183.7mph	Sec 1 G Fisichella	24.659s
Sec 2 G Fisichella	30.845s	2 M Schumacher	183.0mph	Sec 2 J Button	30.677s
Sec 3 M Schumacher	38.421s	3 A Davidson	182.6mph	Sec 3 J Button	38.088s

Fernando Alonso
"Today was about advancing from P7. I got a great start and braked late into Turn 1 to get Webber. After that, it was a question of letting the strategy work itself out."

Michael Schumacher
"During my first stop I had to wait before going out, as another car was coming. I wasn't able to get past Felipe in the closing stages as I just wasn't fast enough."

Kimi Räikkönen
"I'm very disappointed as I had a great car set-up and very good strategy. It was fairly obvious that Klien made a basic mistake and ran into the back of me."

Jenson Button
"I'm pleased to be back on the podium, but it was the top step we had in mind. I was held up by traffic a few times, not least of all by Speed before the second pit stop."

Jacques Villeneuve
"I got held up by Trulli. I knew I should be in good shape as it was the first race for my engine. Our race pace was strong, so we need to work on qualifying."

Jarno Trulli
"We should have finished with both cars in the points but I had really bad luck, suffering a broken diffuser when someone hit me from behind at the start."

Giancarlo Fisichella
"It was a perfect race, but very tough physically and mentally. It was really, really hot and I felt it from mid-race, yet there was no choice but to push to the end."

Felipe Massa
"To start from the last row and end up fifth is a good result. I lost time behind some of the slower cars but when I had a free track I was able to keep a good pace."

Juan Pablo Montoya
"We lost time in the first stint as my fronts were graining, but my pace matched Button's later on. With the hot temperatures we had to look after the engine."

Rubens Barrichello
"It's been an eventful meeting and it was disappointing to end it with a stop-go penalty when I was in with a chance of points. I'm sure things will pick up for the next few races."

Nick Heidfeld
"I kept up with the McLaren and was faster than the Ferraris. After my second stop, it was close with Felipe, but I stayed ahead. The engine failure came without warning."

Ralf Schumacher
"We're very happy to have scored our first point and didn't expect that with a three-stop race from the back. We're happy that our times showed we're competitive."

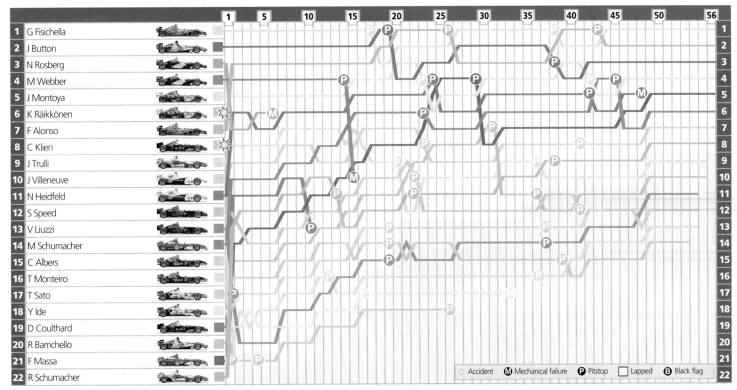

	Driver
1	G Fisichella
2	J Button
3	N Rosberg
4	M Webber
5	J Montoya
6	K Räikkönen
7	F Alonso
8	C Klien
9	J Trulli
10	J Villeneuve
11	N Heidfeld
12	S Speed
13	V Liuzzi
14	M Schumacher
15	C Albers
16	T Monteiro
17	T Sato
18	Y Ide
19	D Coulthard
20	R Barrichello
21	F Massa
22	R Schumacher

☼ Accident　Ⓜ Mechanical failure　Ⓟ Pitstop　☐ Lapped　Ⓑ Black flag

QUALIFYING 3

	Driver	Time
1	G Fisichella	1m33.840s
2	J Button	1m33.986s
3	N Rosberg	1m34.626s
4	M Schumacher	1m34.668s
5	M Webber	1m34.672s
6	JP Montoya	1m34.916s
7	K Räikkönen	1m34.983s
8	F Alonso	1m35.747s
9	C Klien	1m38.715s
10	R Schumacher	no time

GRID

	Driver	Time
1	G Fisichella	1m33.840s
2	J Button	1m33.986s
3	N Rosberg	1m34.626s
4	M Schumacher	1m34.668s
5	M Webber	1m34.672s
6	JP Montoya	1m34.916s
7	K Räikkönen	1m34.983s
8	F Alonso	1m35.747s
9	C Klien	1m38.715s
10	J Trulli	1m34.702s
11	J Villeneuve	1m34.752s
12	N Heidfeld	1m34.783s
13	S Speed	1m36.297s
14	V Liuzzi	1m36.581s
15	C Albers	1m37.426s
16	T Monteiro	1m37.819s
17	T Sato	1m39.011s
18	Y Ide	1m40.720s
19*	D Coulthard	1m34.614s
20*	R Barrichello	1m34.683s
21*	F Massa	no time
22*	R Schumacher	no time

* DENOTES 10-PLACE GRID PENALTY

RACE

	Driver	Car	Laps	Time	Avg. mph	Fastest	Stops
1	G Fisichella	Renault R26	56	1h30m40.529s	128.373	1m35.294s	2
2	F Alonso	Renault R26	56	1h30m45.114s	128.266	1m34.803s	2
3	J Button	Honda RA106	56	1h30m50.160s	128.146	1m35.604s	2
4	JP Montoya	McLaren-Mercedes MP4-21	56	1h31m19.880s	127.451	1m35.566s	2
5	F Massa	Ferrari 248	56	1h31m23.783s	127.360	1m35.954s	1
6	M Schumacher	Ferrari 248	56	1h31m24.383s	127.346	1m35.647s	2
7	J Villeneuve	BMW Sauber F1.06	56	1h32m00.990s	126.502	1m36.002s	2
8	R Schumacher	Toyota TF106	56	1h32m01.817s	126.483	1m35.686s	3
9	J Trulli	Toyota TF106	55	1h30m42.142s	126.043	1m36.380s	2
10	R Barrichello	Honda RA106	55	1h30m53.222s	125.787	1m36.188s	1
11	V Liuzzi	Toro Rosso-Cosworth STR01	54	1h31m05.666s	123.219	1m37.387s	3
12	C Albers	Midland-Toyota M16	54	1h31m12.211s	123.071	1m38.198s	2
13	T Monteiro	Midland-Toyota M16	54	1h32m18.242s	121.604	1m39.510s	2
14	T Sato	Super Aguri-Honda SA05	53	1h30m56.659s	121.137	1m40.199s	2
R	N Heidfeld	BMW Sauber F1.06	48	Engine	-	1m35.751s	2
R	S Speed	Toro Rosso-Cosworth STR01	41	Clutch	-	1m37.313s	1
R	Y Ide	Super Aguri-Honda SA05	33	Throttle	-	1m42.833s	1
R	C Klien	Red Bull-Ferrari RB2	26	Hydraulics	-	1m36.867s	2
R	M Webber	Williams-Cosworth FW28	15	Hydraulics	-	1m36.771s	1
R	D Coulthard	Red Bull-Ferrari RB2	10	Hydraulics	-	1m38.078s	0
R	N Rosberg	Williams-Cosworth FW28	6	Engine	-	1m37.366s	0
R	K Räikkönen	McLaren-Mercedes MP4-21	0	Accident	-	-	0

CHAMPIONSHIP

	Driver	Pts
1	F Alonso	18
2	J Button	11
	M Schumacher	11
4	G Fisichella	10
5	JP Montoya	9
6	K Räikkönen	6
7	F Massa	4
8	M Webber	3
9	N Rosberg	2
	J Villeneuve	2
11	C Klien	1
	R Schumacher	1

Speed trap – Qualifying

1	JP Montoya	184.0mph
2	N Heidfeld	183.5mph
3	K Räikkönen	182.6mph

Fastest Lap
F Alonso 1m34.803s
(130.794mph) on lap 45

Fastest speed trap
F Massa 186.4mph
Slowest speed trap
Y Ide 179.5mph

Fastest pit stop

1	F Alonso	25.455s
2	J Trulli	25.511s
3	N Heidfeld	25.701s

David Coulthard
"I lost hydraulic pressure, which meant I had no power assistance. As the gearbox is controlled by the hydraulics as well, I became stuck in sixth gear."

Mark Webber
"My start was OK, but Alonso's was phenomenal. This prevented us from running at our own pace. The hydraulic problem came on as I was on the start/finish line."

Vitantonio Liuzzi
"It was a pity that I tangled with another car on the first lap and had to pit for a new nose. Apart from that, the car was hard to drive, as I wasn't happy with my brakes."

Tiago Monteiro
"I got stuck behind two slower cars, so my engineers brought me in early. I had the pace to get by them, but it was hard as I was losing ground on the straights."

Takuma Sato
"We've improved on our pit stops since Bahrain so I was able to push a few cars. We still struggle on high-downforce corners and have some hard work to do."

Christian Klien
"I went into Turn 4 with the McLarens and was on the kerbs so couldn't go any further right and mine and Kimi's cars touched. I broke my front suspension."

Nico Rosberg
"I lost a few places at the start and also at Turn 1 where I could've been more aggressive. But, a few seconds before my engine gave up, I felt something was wrong."

Scott Speed
"After a poor qualifying, I didn't get off the line well at the start, but we showed decent pace and had a good track position before the car was hit by clutch failure."

Christijan Albers
"We had bad luck with the start, as Tiago and I ended up being held up. Afterwards, we got caught up in traffic. That was unfortunate, but it was nice to run a full race."

Yuji Ide
"The balance wasn't good and I had the same mechanical problem as I had in Bahrain. The problem got worse and the car's pace got slower, so I stopped."

Constructor

		Pts
1	Renault	28
2	Ferrari	15
	McLaren-Mercedes	15
4	Honda	11
5	Williams-Cosworth	2
6	BMW Sauber	2
7	Red Bull-Ferrari	1
	Toyota	1

2006 FORMULA 1™ FOSTER'S AUSTRALIAN GRAND PRIX
Melbourne

TWO OUT OF THREE

Reigning champion Fernando Alonso added a second win in three starts to his burgeoning tally, taking it easy as he was trailed home by McLaren's Kimi Räikkönen

The Australian Grand Prix might not have featured a close battle for the lead, but four safety car periods, a string of incidents from the formation lap to the chequered flag and some dramatic passes meant that Melbourne put on a great show. Much of the action resulted from a problem that afflicted most of the grid, as drivers struggled to get their tyres up to working temperature. The fact that some did it better than others contributed to the show immensely.

One of the few men not to encounter any troubles was race winner Fernando Alonso, and the scary thing for the opposition was that the team insisted that he had a great deal in hand. Indeed, after two wins and a second place in the first three grands prix he was already well on the way to building up the sort of points cushion that he enjoyed in 2005.

Team-mate Giancarlo Fisichella did a great job to beat the Spaniard in qualifying, although both Renault drivers were beaten by Jenson Button's Honda. Fisichella then blew his chance to outrace Alonso by stalling on the grid before the parade lap. He went to the back of the grid, while his misfortune helped Juan Pablo Montoya, who had managed to spin on the formation lap, but was able to re-take his place.

When the race finally got underway, Button took advantage of the vacant grid position immediately behind him to hang on to the lead, although Alonso gave him a hard time. However, there was an immediate safety car period triggered by a spectacular tangle involving Christian Klien, Nico Rosberg and Felipe Massa. The Brazilian had already had a big shunt earlier in the weekend, so things were not looking good for Ferrari. Worse was to come…

At the restart, we saw the first real signs of how the tyre temperature issue would play a crucial part in this race. Button led on to the pit straight, but he had lost a little momentum through the final two corners, allowing Alonso to drag past to take the lead.

On lap 5, Klien had a heavy crash under braking – possibly a legacy of the earlier bump – and the safety car came out again. For a second time, Button was embarrassed at the restart, this time Räikkönen dragging past to take second place in his McLaren. However, the Finn locked his right front wheel and paid the price with a serious vibration that would eventually damage his front wing.

Alonso pitted on lap 20, leaving Räikkönen in front until he stopped a lap later. That left local hero Mark Webber as an unexpected leader for two glorious laps. He still had the fuel to run a few more laps when a transmission failure stranded the Williams.

Alonso extended his lead over Räikkönen into the second stint, until on lap 33 the safety car was called for once again. The trigger for its deployment was none other than seven-time World Champion Michael Schumacher. A conservative decision to use an older specification Bridgestone proved rather costly as Ferrari struggled more than Toyota and Williams to get the tyres up to temperature, and Michael had to manhandle his car around. He went quickly when the tyres came into the optimum operating window, but finally lost it on the last turn. Two cars in the wall: that

hadn't happened to Ferrari for a long time…

The timing was right for pitting, and Alonso lost a 20s lead that had been built up, while that damaged wing meant that Räikkönen was unable to keep up. A nose change cost Räikkönen some track positions and ended any hope he had of pushing Alonso in the closing stages. It was also bad news for Montoya, who earlier had another spin behind the safety car. Much to his frustration, he lost some ground when he was stacked up behind Räikkönen in the pits.

No sooner was the Schumacher mess tidied up than the restart brought out the safety car for the fourth time. A defensive move by Jacques Villeneuve

OPPOSITE Juan Pablo Montoya was a driver who couldn't wait to leave Melbourne behind after a race packed with embarrassing gaffes

ABOVE Lap 1, Turn 2, and Red Bull Racing's Christian Klien clashes with Nico Rosberg's Williams and Felipe Massa's Ferrari, triggering the first of what would prove to be four safety-car periods

INSIDE LINE
JENSON BUTTON
HONDA RACING DRIVER

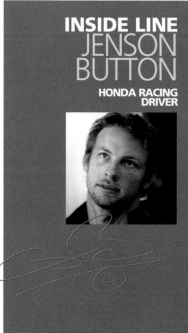

"It was great to get the pole and I didn't know beforehand that it was Honda's first as a constructor since the 1968 Italian Grand Prix. It was a manic qualifying session, with red flags in both the first and second period.

We were really struggling for grip when qualifying started and I had a brief 'off' in the first session. I've actually been going off quite a lot this weekend, which is unusual. I was off twice on Friday and the conditions have been so tricky out there: it was very, very windy and the combination of that and the low grip made it easy to make a mistake. A lot of cars were weaving on the straight to try to get tyre temperature and part of the problem is that the conditions are cooler than we expected when we made the tyre selection. So, to get pole position was fantastic.

Race day was cool again and I knew we were going to have the same problems. We kept the tyre blankets on until the last possible moment and I was aware how good the Renault starts are. Giancarlo had a problem on the grid and the first start was aborted, which removed half the threat, but I knew that Fernando would challenge and he did. I managed to keep him behind me in Turn 1 and when he tried at Turn 6, but the early safety car did me no favours at all.

I knew I had to try to get a decent exit from the last corner to keep Fernando at bay, but it was hopeless: it was like driving a car with no wings. There was no grip at all and I had understeer going in and oversteer out. He just blew past me as soon as we crossed the line. I had the same problem at each safety car period and,

of course, it didn't help our cause that it was deployed fully four times during the grand prix!

Fifth place was not what I was expecting, but then I even lost that when the engine failed on the last lap. I coasted to a halt just before the finish line, which meant that I scored no points but at least didn't pick up a 10-place grid penalty at Imola. I could feel the engine tightening but I didn't lift off and when it went, it was like having the sun behind my ears!

We've got only two weeks to solve the tyre issue and it's a big problem. It's similar to the problem we had in 2005 – not being able to get heat into the tyres during the race. The car is quick over one lap, so it's massively frustrating, but we don't seem to be able to make it work with the same tyres other people are running."

INSIDE LINE
PAT SYMONDS

**RENAULT
ENGINEERING DIRECTOR**

"Giancarlo was unfortunate at the start as he had a problem that was triggering the anti-stall mechanism. He caught it four times, but didn't manage to cancel the fifth one. The car has a safety system that cuts in after 10 seconds, which is specified in the regulations, and so the engine cut out and he lost a front row position and had to start from the pitlane.

In situations like that, people tend to blame the driver but as an engineer I don't like to apportion blame if a system has proved difficult to use. Fisi's drive to fifth place was actually a very good effort as the rest of his race was far from straightforward. He had a spin behind the first safety car when everyone was struggling for grip. In fact, we were so concerned about the safety car periods that we contacted the FIA to ask them to get it to go a little faster because we were losing so much heat from the tyres.

Giancarlo then found himself with quite a lot of understeer in the middle of the race. I'm not sure why, but he managed to get a better balance using the diff' and the traction control.

He was then very aggressive after the safety car periods and managed to catch Jenson. Although he dropped away for a while when he started to have a clutch problem, we put it right, but you have to let the systems know that there has been a clutch failure and that took a bit of time. When we got the control systems sorted out, Giancarlo was soon hassling Jenson again and we'd like to think that he pushed him hard enough to contribute to the engine failure!

Fernando's victory was relatively straightforward. He didn't quite manage to pass Jenson's Honda at the start. Our cars are good off the line, but expecting him to make up a two-slot deficit was asking a bit much. Actually, I think Fernando was caught out a little when Jenson braked a bit early – nothing underhand I'm sure, just a reflection of the lack of grip that he seemed to be struggling with.

Fernando took full advantage of the first safety car to take the lead. The rules say that you are not allowed to overtake before the start/finish line when the safety car goes in and Fernando handled it perfectly – he crossed the line with virtually a zero gap. For the later safety car period, we were quite fortunate to have the two Midlands as a buffer, and after that Fernando was able to take it easy. He really did have an awful lot in hand and we were able to turn the engine down and save it, with one eye on the next race at Imola."

saw Tonio Liuzzi pitched into a high-speed crash on the straight after the first complex, the BMW Sauber driver claiming that he hadn't seen the Italian.

The grand prix finally gained its momentum with the restart on lap 41. With traffic between himself and Räikkönen, Alonso was able to get a decisive jump, while Ralf Schumacher ran in a surprise third place ahead of Montoya. Pushing to recover ground, Montoya went over the kerb at the last corner on lap 46 and the jolt caused the engine to cut and the gearbox to fail. On the surface it was all smiles in the McLaren camp afterwards, but…

Meanwhile Alonso enjoyed a relatively easy run to the flag while trying to save his engine for the following grand prix at Imola. Räikkönen did his best to keep Alonso honest, and from nowhere produced the race's fastest lap right at the end, closing to within 1.8s of the Spaniard's Renault.

"The race was difficult in terms of keeping up the concentration and the motivation," said Alonso. "I pushed hard all the way through the first part of the race. I was 20s ahead in spite of one safety car period. I was ready to turn down everything at the end, and then the gap disappeared every time so I needed to push a little bit more again."

"It's a great start, but there are 15 races to go," said Renault's Engineering Director Pat Symonds. "I said at the beginning of the season that I thought it would be very much about how people developed their cars through the year. That's still the case. I'm very, very grateful for the fantastic car that our guys have produced, it has given us a great start, but we've got to keep pushing. One of the lessons I learned from last year was that early victories are mentally so good for you, they give everyone the confidence. I'm very glad to be learning that lesson again!"

Against all expectations, third place went to Ralf Schumacher and Toyota. The team had worked hard

on the tyre temperature issue that it encountered in Bahrain, and that paid dividends as the TF106 fared better than most. After starting sixth, Ralf was always in the hunt, despite a drive-through penalty, and the result was well deserved. Team-mate Jarno Trulli, feeling ill all weekend, tangled with David Coulthard on lap 1, but escaped censure from the stewards.

Nick Heidfeld earned a solid fourth place for BMW Sauber. He made a good start and ran a long first stint that enabled him to rise to second, but the car suffered more than most with cold tyres at restarts and he lost ground when it mattered. Without that problem, he could have finished third.

OPPOSITE Christian Klien's car didn't approve after his first lap contact, and he exited the event four laps later when his RB2 turned sharp left into a wall

ABOVE Fernando Alonso presses on to his 10th grand prix win

BELOW Ralf Schumacher puts Mark Webber under pressure before the local hero retired with transmission failure

ABOVE It's not often that Michael Schumacher drops it, but this is the accident still in progress after he'd lost control by hitting a bump as he closed in on Button

BELOW Another not to finish, just, was Jenson Button, who pulled off, his Honda's engine smoking, just metres from the finish line

After his startline mishap, Fisichella put in a storming drive, helped by the safety car periods. He even had to overcome a clutch problem on his way to what became fifth place at the very last corner, thanks to Button's spectacular demise. The four points for fifth place was going to be a poor reward for the Briton, but an engine failure going into the last turn on the final lap took even that away. The team told him to give up the three points he would have earned by coasting across the line to sixth, as parking the car guaranteed a new engine without a 10-place penalty for the following race at Imola.

Villeneuve started from the back with an engine penalty and made good progress to an eventual sixth place on a one-stopper. He was unlucky to be in the pits just as the safety car was deployed for the last time. Without that, he might have done better.

Rubens Barrichello had a terrible day for Honda, being stuck behind Takuma Sato's Super Aguri for 20 laps and suffering like team-mate Button with tyre problems. The only upside of Button's Melbourne retirement for Honda was that it moved Rubens from eighth place to seventh.

The real battle for the final championship point took place after the race... On the road, the position went to Scuderia Toro Rosso's Scott Speed, ahead of David Coulthard, but the Red Bull-backed cars had traded positions under yellow flags after Speed's team-mate Tonio Liuzzi had crashed. The stewards looked into the matter and reversed the order, and American rookie Speed also landed a fine for what the officials called "unacceptable behaviour", after swearing at his rival. Speed hadn't been quite on the pace of Liuzzi, who even passed Michael Schumacher (for the third time in his seven starts) before Villeneuve edged him onto the grass.

As noted, a fast-starting Sato led his Honda replacement Barrichello early on, who in turn had Coulthard stuck behind him. Such a scenario seemed impossible just a few weeks earlier when the ancient 2002 Arrows was being rebuilt and reliveried. Normal order was resumed after the pit stops and the others found clean air. Still, it had been fun for Aguri Suzuki's newcomers while it lasted.

The Australian GP proved to be an intriguing event, and while it was good to see Toyota and BMW Sauber joining the party, Alonso's form looked ominous. It seemed that McLaren and Honda couldn't quite get it right, while the threat from Ferrari, so apparent in Bahrain, had faded...

SNAPSHOT FROM
AUSTRALIA

CLOCKWISE FROM RIGHT As ever, the Melbourne race organisers put on a show, whether on the track or overhead; Honda Racing's Jock Clear explains matters to Rubens Barrichello; glamorous pre-race entertainment; one of a pair of human kangaroos – with giant springs concealed beneath their furry costumes; the Australian branch of the tifosi came more in hope than expectation; Sir Stirling Moss takes time out on the grid

WEEKEND HEADLINES

- Following the fuss in Malaysia about flexing wings, there were no scrutineering problems for Ferrari after the team apparently modified its wings to the satisfaction of the FIA. The biggest story of the season so far thus fizzled out, although the rumblings would resurface a few races down the line.

- Toyota technical director Mike Gascoyne parted company with the team just days after Ralf Schumacher finished third in Melbourne. Personality clashes with his immediate bosses were the reason, which was officially put down to a "difference of philosophy". Pascal Vasselon took over most of Gascoyne's duties.

- Much speculation surrounded the identities of the 22 teams that had expressed their interest in entering the 2008 World Championship before the deadline of 31 March. David Richards, Trevor Carlin, Eddie Jordan and Paul Stoddart were among the few of the 11 'unknowns' to declare their hands.

- After the Australian GP, Honda team boss Nick Fry made much of the fact that the team had the presence of mind to stop Jenson Button before the finish line. Had he finished sixth with his blown engine, he would have had to take a 10-place penalty at Imola. Curiously, by the San Marino GP, Fry insisted that Button was told to stop on safety grounds, this perhaps something to do with the FIA's ban on 'voluntary' retirements.

- The debate over the future of Silverstone continued to rage as a rebel group of British Racing Drivers' Club members stepped up a campaign to oust the board and defeat redevelopment proposals, with 1996 World Champion Damon Hill emerging as a surprise candidate for the presidency of the club.

RACE RESULTS
AUSTRALIA MELBOURNE

Official Results © [2006]
Formula One Administration Limited,
6 Princes Gate, London SW7 1QJ.
No reproduction without permission.
All copyright and database rights reserved

RACE DATE April 2nd
CIRCUIT LENGTH 3.295 miles
NO. OF LAPS 57
RACE DISTANCE 187.815 miles
WEATHER Sunny but cool, 19°C
TRACK TEMP 26°C
RACE DAY ATTENDANCE 103,000
LAP RECORD Michael Schumacher,
1m24.125s, 141.016mph, 2004

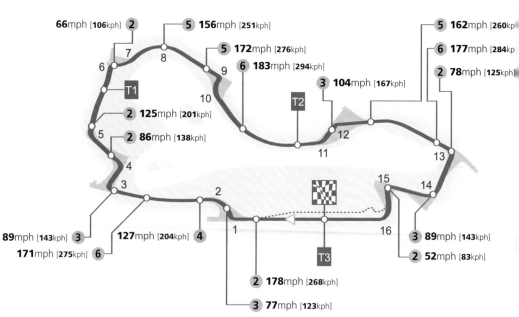

66mph [106kph] 2
5 156mph [251kph]
5 162mph [260kp]
7
8
6 177mph [284kph]
6
9
5 172mph [276kph]
2 78mph [125kph]
6 183mph [294kph]
T1
10
3 104mph [167kph]
T2
2 125mph [201kph]
5
12
2 86mph [138kph]
11
13
4
15
14
3
2
16
89mph [143kph] 3
127mph [204kph] 4
1
171mph [275kph] 6
T3
3 89mph [143kph]
2 52mph [83kph]
2 178mph [268kph]
3 77mph [123kph]

	PRACTICE 1		
	Driver	Time	Laps
1	A Davidson	1m28.259s	26
2	R Doornbos	1m28.559s	19
3	J Villeneuve	1m28.595s	16
4	K Räikkönen	1m28.713s	5
5	F Massa	1m29.025s	7
6	M Schumacher	1m29.041s	7
7	R Schumacher	1m29.411s	5
8	A Wurz	1m29.461s	19
9	R Kubica	1m29.576s	13
10	C Klien	1m29.601s	7
11	D Coulthard	1m29.676s	9
12	S Speed	1m31.017s	8
13	C Albers	1m31.039s	9
14	T Monteiro	1m31.812s	10
15	T Sato	1m34.036s	9
16	Y Ide	1m36.684s	19
17	M Winkelhock	1m36.859s	17
18	N Jani	1m40.818s	4
19	F Alonso	no time	2
20	G Fisichella	no time	2
21	V Liuzzi	no time	2
22	J Trulli	no time	2
23	R Barrichello	no time	1
24	N Heidfeld	no time	1
25	JP Montoya	no time	1
26	J Button	no time	0
27	N Rosberg	no time	0
28	M Webber	no time	0

	PRACTICE 2		
	Driver	Time	Laps
1	A Davidson	1m26.822s	28
2	A Wurz	1m26.832s	27
3	R Kubica	1m27.200s	25
4	J Button	1m27.213s	12
5	F Alonso	1m27.443s	14
6	M Schumacher	1m27.658s	16
7	K Räikkönen	1m27.773s	16
8	R Barrichello	1m28.075s	20
9	JP Montoya	1m28.200s	15
10	F Massa	1m28.227s	17
11	G Fisichella	1m28.280s	11
12	J Villeneuve	1m28.440s	22
13	D Coulthard	1m28.531s	18
14	M Webber	1m28.860s	10
15	N Heidfeld	1m29.053s	5
16	J Trulli	1m29.138s	20
17	S Speed	1m29.196s	18
18	R Schumacher	1m29.379s	16
19	T Monteiro	1m29.713s	21
20	R Doornbos	1m29.876s	32
21	C Klien	1m29.879s	9
22	N Rosberg	1m29.933s	11
23	N Jani	1m30.686s	26
24	V Liuzzi	1m30.734s	14
25	C Albers	1m30.830s	18
26	M Winkelhock	1m31.260s	25
27	T Sato	1m32.556s	27
28	Y Ide	1m34.224s	22

	PRACTICE 3		
	Driver	Time	Laps
1	N Heidfeld	1m35.335s	10
2	J Villeneuve	1m36.281s	16
3	V Liuzzi	1m36.373s	10
4	G Fisichella	1m36.414s	13
5	R Schumacher	1m36.445s	10
6	F Massa	1m36.506s	11
7	M Schumacher	1m37.332s	10
8	R Barrichello	1m37.481s	15
9	J Trulli	1m37.492s	10
10	S Speed	1m37.852s	11
11	C Klien	1m37.947s	12
12	M Webber	1m38.036s	7
13	J Button	1m38.505s	11
14	D Coulthard	1m38.683s	15
15	N Rosberg	1m39.401s	11
16	T Monteiro	1m39.515s	7
17	F Alonso	1m39.654s	11
18	Y Ide	1m40.261s	18
19	T Sato	1m41.448s	5
20	JP Montoya	1m44.350s	3
21	K Räikkönen	1m48.284s	3
22	C Albers	no time	3

	QUALIFYING 1	
	Driver	Time
1	JP Montoya	1m27.079s
2	K Räikkönen	1m27.193s
3	M Webber	1m27.669s
4	J Trulli	1m27.748s
5	G Fisichella	1m27.765s
6	N Heidfeld	1m27.796s
7	R Schumacher	1m28.007s
8	J Button	1m28.081s
9	M Schumacher	1m28.228s
10	N Rosberg	1m28.351s
11	D Coulthard	1m28.408s
12	J Villeneuve	1m28.460s
13	F Alonso	1m28.569s
14	C Klien	1m28.757s
15	F Massa	1m28.868s
16	V Liuzzi	1m28.999s
17	R Barrichello	1m29.943s
18	C Albers	1m30.226s
19	S Speed	1m30.426s
20	T Monteiro	1m30.709s
21	T Sato	1m32.279s
22	Y Ide	1m36.164s

	QUALIFYING 2	
	Driver	Time
1	F Alonso	1m25.729s
2	JP Montoya	1m25.902s
3	N Heidfeld	1m26.014s
4	M Webber	1m26.075s
5	K Räikkönen	1m26.161s
6	G Fisichella	1m26.196s
7	J Trulli	1m26.327s
8	J Button	1m26.337s
9	R Schumacher	1m26.596s
10	J Villeneuve	1m26.714s
11	M Schumacher	1m26.718s
12	D Coulthard	1m27.023s
13	V Liuzzi	1m27.219s
14	C Klien	1m27.591s
15	N Rosberg	1m29.422s
16	F Massa	no time

Best sectors – Practice		Speed trap – Practice			Best sectors – Qualifying	
Sec 1	R Kubica	28.756s	1	R Kubica	185.9mph	Sec 1	JP Montoya	28.614s
Sec 2	A Wurz	23.388s	2	M Schumacher	185.3mph	Sec 2	J Button	22.950s
Sec 3	A Davidson	34.268s	3	J Villeneuve	184.4mph	Sec 3	J Button	33.400s

Fernando Alonso

"I had a good lead after the first pit stops, then lost it during the second safety car. I was able to get a good gap on each restart. I'm pleased we were able to save the engine."

Michael Schumacher

"I was pushing to try to close on Jenson. He wasn't very quick and I tucked in behind him and unexpectedly got heavy understeer and finished on the grass."

Kimi Räikkönen

"I enjoyed a battle with Juan, but when I passed Jenson I flatspotted my right front. Then a front wing footplate broke. Luckily the safety car gave us time to change it."

Jenson Button

"I struggled for grip after each restart and lost so much time and so many places. I could feel that something was wrong with the engine in Turn 13."

Jacques Villeneuve

"Starting from 19th with a full tank and finishing sixth is better than I expected. The only problem I had was warming up the tyres after the safety car phases."

Jarno Trulli

"A couple of corners in, I was following Coulthard who was zigzagging. I went to the inside and was ahead at the corner but he closed the door, hitting me."

Giancarlo Fisichella

"I stalled and had to start from the pits. I then had no telemetry. The second stint was hard as the car understeered. After the final stop, the clutch failed."

Felipe Massa

"At Turn 1, I had Klien on my left and Speed on my right. Klien touched me, which spun me right, then I hit Rosberg and ended up in the barrier. I'm very unhappy."

Juan Pablo Montoya

"I spun as we were lining up, but the start was aborted. I spun in the race, too, but could've finished on the podium, but I hit a kerb and a default system killed the engine."

Rubens Barrichello

"I struggled with the brakes and it was impossible for me to overtake, although I was able to get past Speed and gain position. I have a couple of points at least."

Nick Heidfeld

"It's fantastic for a new team to get both cars in the points. Unluckily, I couldn't get heat into the tyres after the safety cars; it was really bad after the last one."

Ralf Schumacher

"The drivethrough was my fault as I hit the button twice. Some of the safety-car periods were a bit of a fight, but after the third period I gained a couple of places."

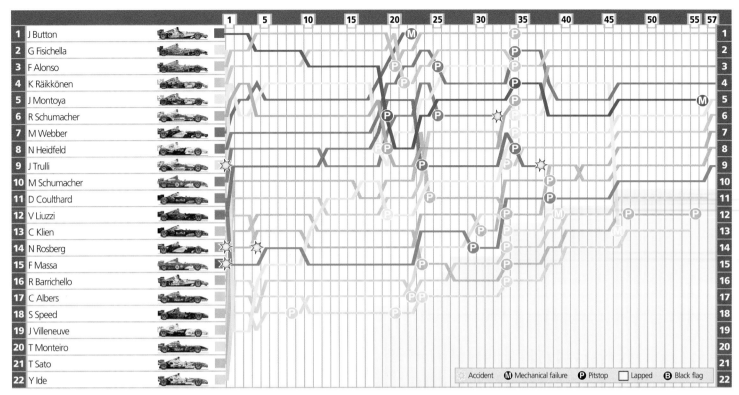

Key: ☼ Accident | Ⓜ Mechanical failure | Ⓟ Pitstop | ☐ Lapped | Ⓑ Black flag

QUALIFYING 3

	Driver	Time
1	J Button	1m25.229s
2	G Fisichella	1m25.635s
3	F Alonso	1m25.778s
4	K Räikkönen	1m25.822s
5	JP Montoya	1m25.976s
6	R Schumacher	1m26.612s
7	M Webber	1m26.937s
8	N Heidfeld	1m27.579s
9	J Villeneuve	1m29.239s
10	J Trulli	no time

GRID

	Driver	Time
1	J Button	1m25.229s
2	G Fisichella	1m25.635s
3	F Alonso	1m25.778s
4	K Räikkönen	1m25.822s
5	JP Montoya	1m25.976s
6	R Schumacher	1m26.612s
7	M Webber	1m26.937s
8	N Heidfeld	1m27.579s
9	J Trulli	1m26.327s
10	M Schumacher	1m26.718s
11	D Coulthard	1m27.023s
12	V Liuzzi	1m27.219s
13	C Klien	1m27.591s
14	N Rosberg	1m29.422s
15	F Massa	1m28.868s
16	R Barrichello	1m29.943s
17	C Albers	1m30.226s
18	S Speed	1m30.426s
19*	J Villeneuve	1m29.239s
20	T Monteiro	1m30.709s
21	T Sato	1m32.279s
22	Y Ide	1m36.164s

* DENOTES 10-PLACE GRID PENALTY

RACE

	Driver	Car	Laps	Time	Avg. mph	Fastest	Stops
1	F Alonso	Renault R26	57	1h34m27.870s	119.297	1m26.189s	2
2	K Räikkönen	McLaren-Mercedes MP4-21	57	1h34m29.699s	119.259	1m26.045s	2
3	R Schumacher	Toyota TF106	57	1h34m52.694s	118.777	1m27.810s	3
4	N Heidfeld	BMW Sauber F1.06	57	1h34m58.902s	118.647	1m27.700s	2
5	G Fisichella	Renault R26	57	1h35m06.291s	118.494	1m27.561s	2
6	J Villeneuve	BMW Sauber F1.06	57	1h35m17.424s	118.263	1m28.321s	1
7	R Barrichello	Honda RA106	57	1h35m19.774s	118.214	1m27.690s	2
8	D Coulthard	Red Bull-Ferrari RB2	57	1h35m21.853s	118.171	1m28.250s	2
9*	S Speed	Toro Rosso-Cosworth STR01	56	1h35m46.687s*	118.175	1m28.367s	2
10	J Button	Honda RA106	56	Engine	-	1m27.799s	2
11	C Albers	Midland-Toyota M16	56	1h35m40.604s	115.719	1m29.238s	2
12	T Sato	Super Aguri-Honda SA05	55	1h35m46.666s	113.533	1m30.574s	3
13	Y Ide	Super Aguri-Honda SA05	54	1h35m38.433s	111.628	1m33.737s	3
R	JP Montoya	McLaren-Mercedes MP4-21	46	Electrical	-	1m27.464s	2
R	T Monteiro	Midland-Toyota M16	39	Hydraulics	-	1m29.687s	2
R	V Liuzzi	Toro Rosso-Cosworth STR01	37	Accident	-	1m27.988s	2
R	M Schumacher	Ferrari 248	32	Accident	-	1m27.180s	1
R	M Webber	Williams-Cosworth FW28	22	Transmission	-	1m27.800s	0
R	C Klien	Red Bull-Ferrari RB2	4	Accident	-	1m41.351s	0
R	J Trulli	Toyota TF106	0	Accident	-	-	0
R	N Rosberg	Williams-Cosworth FW28	0	Crash damage	-	-	0
R	F Massa	Ferrari 248	0	Accident	-	-	0

* DENOTES 25s PENALTY FOR OVERTAKING UNDER YELLOW FLAGS

CHAMPIONSHIP

	Driver	Pts
1	F Alonso	28
2	G Fisichella	14
	K Räikkönen	14
4	J Button	11
	M Schumacher	11
6	JP Montoya	9
7	R Schumacher	7
8	N Heidfeld	5
	J Villeneuve	5
10	F Massa	4
11	M Webber	3
12	R Barrichello	2
	N Rosberg	2
14	D Coulthard	1
	C Klien	1

Speed trap – Qualifying

1	J Villeneuve	188.5mph
2	F Alonso	188.5mph
3	JP Montoya	188.4mph

Fastest Lap

K Räikkönen 1m26.045s
(137.866mph) on lap 57

Fastest speed trap

M Schumacher 188.9mph

Slowest speed trap

C Klien 176.6mph

Fastest pit stop

1	T Sato	19.486s
2	G Fisichella	19.612s
3	R Barrichello	19.667s

Constructor

	Constructor	Pts
1	Renault	42
2	McLaren-Mercedes	23
3	Ferrari	15
4	Honda	13
5	BMW Sauber	10
6	Toyota	7
7	Williams-Cosworth	5
8	Red Bull-Ferrari	2

 David Coulthard

"I passed Trulli at Turn 2. Going into Turn 3 I saw him coming and moved over, but he ran wide so I re-passed him. In Turn 6 he did the same, but I didn't see him coming."

Mark Webber

"We're not sure what happened, we think it's gearbox-related. I was running heavy and it might have been tough to beat Kimi and Fernando, but a podium was on."

Vitantonio Liuzzi

"What happened was a real shame as we had really good pace. I'm not happy as I think Jacques (Villeneuve) might have put me in the wall."

 Tiago Monteiro

"We had a great Friday, some problems on Saturday, but I was having a great race and there may have been the possibility of a top 10, but we had a technical issue."

Takuma Sato

"I was able to work my way up to the middle of the pack, but I had a problem with my left-front. At the end of the next lap I had a problem with my right-front."

 Christian Klien

"There was a safety car period early on and it was difficult to warm my tyres. On lap 7, I touched the brakes, the rear locked or something broke and I hit the wall."

Nico Rosberg

"Massa and Klien got in a tangle at Turn 1. Massa hit me from behind and my rear wing was off and my radiators were too damaged for me to continue."

Scott Speed

"To come from wherever we were on the grid, it's incredible to come away with a point. It was one of the greatest moments of my life." He was later penalised and demoted.

 Christijan Albers

"I got caught in the group behind Sato. After the first pit stop, I was still behind Sato but passed him on a straight, on the outside. That felt good."

Yuji Ide

"This is the first time both Taku and I have finished, so I'm happy. But I'm far from being competitive compared to the other drivers, so I want to improve my skills."

FORMULA 1™ GRAN PREMIO
FOSTER'S DI SAN MARINO
2006
Imola

SCHUEY HITS TOP

Michael Schumacher won but once for Ferrari in 2005, and that was a gift, so his title hopes bloomed when he delighted the tifosi with a home victory scored on merit

After the bleak 2005 season and a disappointing start to 2006, everything came right for Michael Schumacher and Ferrari at Imola's San Marino Grand Prix as the team scored a great win on home ground that really should not have been theirs.

The main talking point in the paddock after the race wasn't so much the way Ferrari won, but the way Renault lost. No one could quite understand why Fernando Alonso peeled into the pits several laps earlier than planned on lap 41, when it seemed all he had to do was to be a little patient and victory would come his way. Within a lap, leader Michael Schumacher, who had appeared to have no chance of staying in front, made his own second and final stop, emerging still safely in front, and what many felt was an unnecessary gamble by Renault failed to pay off.

Like Monaco and the Hungaroring, Imola is a track notorious for its lack of overtaking opportunities – Alonso's 2005 win proved that – so everything came down to the grid and the pit stops.

The previous week's Barcelona test suggested that Ferrari and Bridgestone had made serious progress. Renault erred on the heavy side with its fuel load in qualifying, assuming that Michael would do the

"We hoped to be strong at Imola and so it was. We started off with pole position on Saturday, my 66th and a new record. To be honest, though, these things are just numbers – they might be nice to look back on when you are older but they don't mean so much at the time.

Imola was really satisfying because we showed good pace in the first race in Bahrain but then made some mistakes in Malaysia and Melbourne. It was good to come here and perform so well. That was thanks to many things, including our partners Shell, who came up with a completely new fuel and some more horsepower, and Bridgestone, who had been working extremely hard on the tyre side.

I made a good start and was able to open up a lead in the first stint, while Fernando was behind Jenson and my team-mate Felipe. We suspected from the qualifying times that Fernando would do a longer first stint than us but that was OK and everything was fine until after my first pit stop, when we ran into some trouble. I had a degree of tyre graining, which wasn't a big issue honestly, but the car never really improved again or performed like it had in the first stint.

When my lap times fell away, I knew that Fernando would catch me and there was nothing I could do about it, so I concentrated on looking after the tyres so that we would have a chance when it came to the critical point around the 'in' laps. I also knew from last year, when it was me trying to pass Fernando at the end, that so long as I didn't make a mistake, it would be very difficult for him to pass me on the track.

When it came to the last pit stop, it was pretty straightforward. We saw that Renault had decided to pit early, so I had to push as hard as possible for one lap and then hope to get a good pit stop. It worked out better than I expected and I came out ahead. Then it was just a case of keeping Fernando behind until the end.

At the start of the third stint, I drove in a way that reduced the risk of having a similar problem with the last set of tyres, whereas I needed to attack in the second stint because I thought Fernando was running longer. At the end of the race, he was behind me and so all I had to do was keep him there.

For the World Championship it is looking much better now. We were very competitive here at Imola, apart from at one point in the race, and we've also had a good test at Barcelona, so I think we should be pretty good from now on."

opposite to guarantee pole. The hope was to follow Michael to the first stop and jump in front, but even from second place there was also a chance to get into the lead on the long drag to Turn 1 at the start.

Michael did indeed take pole position, but he was followed by Jenson Button, Rubens Barrichello and Felipe Massa. Alonso, who admitted that his lap was as good as it could have been, was only fifth. The Renault plan clearly didn't allow for as many as three cars sneaking into the gap between Alonso and Michael. Clearly the cars in between – and especially that of Massa – could slow the Spaniard's progress in the early stages of the race.

Alonso was on the favourable inside of the grid, but was blocked off the line by Massa's Ferrari and lost momentum. He did at least get past Barrichello, but still had Button and, crucially, Massa between himself and Michael. There was a brief safety car period after MF1's Christijan Albers was tipped into a spectacular first lap roll by Super Aguri's rookie Yuji Ide before the action resumed.

As Michael sped away, all Alonso could do was run at Massa's pace until the second Ferrari stopped, so he hung back to save tyres and keep temperatures down. The gap between Michael and Massa in third stretched out to around 12s before Felipe pitted on lap 19. Was that the best the Brazilian could do, or was he deliberately slowing Alonso?

There was nothing the Spaniard could do except wait for Massa to give him a clear track. It was obvious, too, that once the red cars were out of the way, Alonso didn't have enough laps with which to take the lead. The focus now was on how to sort things out at the second round of pit stops.

Alonso came in on lap 25, five laps after Michael. He took on enough fuel to run maybe three laps longer than the Ferrari to their second stops. But to make use of his advantage he had to be right with Michael when the Ferrari made its second stop. At the time, that looked as though it would be very difficult – even given the fact that Massa (and Button) were now out of the way, and he had a clear run.

But then a strange thing happened; Michael ran into tyre problems, and his lap times faded. At one point, he was 4.2s off his best lap time from the end of the first stint, although that was an extreme example.

"When we had problems in the second stint, I didn't understand what was going on," said Ferrari's Ross Brawn. "The car was quick at the beginning of the stint, but then we got a lot of understeer, and we lost the gap to Alonso. We would have been in trouble then, because we knew that they were going to go a little bit longer before their second stop, and we were going to be caught at the pit stop. We got a lot of graining on the front, and it wouldn't clean up."

"The middle stint was really difficult for them," said Renault's Pat Symonds. "I was surprised how quickly we caught them in the first laps. We could see that we could catch them easily, but we weren't convinced that we knew a way of getting past."

From 11.2s after his stop, the gap fell to nothing by lap 34. So within 10 laps of his first stop, and around 11–12 laps before his second stop was due, Alonso was right there, all over Michael. Yet there was nothing he could do to get past.

Michael's pace had slowed because he had the tyre problem, but it slowed further because he had to close all the doors, brake early, and generally mess with Alonso's head. All legitimate defensive stuff, of course, as employed by the Spaniard himself in 2005. Michael was also mindful of keeping the tyres alive, as best he could, until the very end of the stint.

In other words, the lap times he was doing – and therefore he was forcing Alonso to do as well – were

OPPOSITE TOP Giancarlo Fisichella had to play catch up on Italian soil as he qualified only 11th, but eighth was as high as he could climb

OPPOSITE BOTTOM Yuji Ide had a torrid weekend, with several offs, including a controversial incident in which he tipped Christijan Albers' MF1 out of the race on lap 1

ABOVE The timing of Fernando Alonso's second pit stop was crucial and many felt that Renault made an error in changing their tactic and bringing him in before Michael Schumacher pitted

slower than those he could have achieved, even allowing for the tyre issue. He had something in reserve, and Renault didn't know quite how much…

Nevertheless, everyone assumed that all Alonso had to do was wait, put in his three or so quick laps when Michael pitted, and cruise out of the pits in front. The prancing horse was a sitting duck. And that's when Renault surprised us by bringing Alonso in on lap 41, what appeared to be around four or five laps before the opposition expected him.

After the race, Renault Engineering Director Pat Symonds insisted that the true situation was much more marginal than everyone else thought, and that Renault's real concern was that they were possibly destined to pit on the same lap as Michael.

"What I didn't want to do was just follow him into the pits," said Symonds. "So we just said, well, follow him into the pits, we're going to follow him out of the pits, let's just have a go. We just thought that the best thing to do was to try and get out of his slipstream. We had nothing to lose, but maybe a small chance to gain, so we took it…"

Alonso's main problem was that his in-lap speed was determined by that of Michael up ahead, and only at the last second could he duck out of the Ferrari's slipstream and head down the pit lane.

Michael knew as he exited the final corner of the lap that the Renault had gone in. The only logical thing to do was come straight in after one more lap rather than waste any more time on that dodgy second set of tyres.

No need for defensive driving, no need to save the tyres for a few more laps, or indeed save fuel. He drove what must have been one of the most impressive laps of even his long career. He had found speed that Renault didn't expect him to find.

"It didn't work, but we didn't lose anything," insisted Symonds after the race. "The main reason it didn't work was that Michael's lap into the pits was 1.5s faster than anything he'd done in that stint, and that I just hadn't expected at all. If he hadn't managed that fantastic lap into the pits, and to be honest the lap before was pretty good too – about 0.6s faster than most of his laps – we would have had him, because we were only 0.7s behind him when he came out of the pits. So it was close, and we had to try something. I wasn't going to leave Alonso there to drive around behind him all bloody day."

The battle for the lead took everyone's attention away from what was going on behind. In fact, there was a

BELOW As ever, there was no need to guess which team the fans wanted to win, and their wishes were answered as Michael Schumacher put Ferrari back to the top of the pile

BOTTOM Williams continued to struggle for outright pace, but Mark Webber survived this gravelly off and showed his mettle in climbing from 10th to sixth place

OPPOSITE David Coulthard heads Nick Heidfeld early in the race

INSIDE LINE
PAT SYMONDS

RENAULT ENGINEERING DIRECTOR

"There were a lot of people thinking that we'd blown the race strategically, but a lot of that was based on pit stop times taken from TV screens, which are notoriously misleading.

It's true that Fernando's first pit stop was five laps after Michael's and that the stop times were not dissimilar,

but that doesn't mean that we had the potential to run five laps longer than Michael in the second stint.

We had short-fuelled Fernando at the first stop to make sure he stayed ahead of Felipe Massa in the second Ferrari. Felipe had stopped the lap before Michael and had been going quite quickly. We didn't want to risk coming out behind him. We also had a delay attaching the fuel rig, so not all of Fernando's stop was fuel-flow time.

When we looked at our fuel nozzle attachment time versus Ferrari's, we figured that Michael could run to lap 44 in the second stint, which was only a lap short of Fernando's planned second stop. We also knew that Michael had a new set of Bridgestones for the final stint and so he would have strong pace on his 'out' lap.

That meant that we would probably

have just the one extra lap to get ahead of Michael and, worst case scenario, he had slowed considerably in the second stint while Fernando was attacking, so could conceivably have got an extra lap out of the fuel, meaning that the potential was there for him to actually come in on the same lap as us. And we were unlikely to beat him if that was the case.

Given the speed that Michael was running, 2.5–3.5s slower than he had been, we thought that stopping early and giving Fernando an 'out' lap on new rubber and a clear track versus another lap for Michael on tyres he was obviously struggling with, was the better option. We took the gamble, but unfortunately it didn't pay off.

I have to admit that we were a little non-plussed when Michael suddenly produced a 1m25.7s lap on his 'in' lap.

He had fallen back into regular 1m27s laps and even dropped to a few in the high 1m28s. He was obviously struggling compared to his level of performance in the first stint and we didn't expect him to be able to increase his pace to that extent. These things are always fine with hindsight, but you don't have that luxury in a pressure situation during the race. The evidence suggested that our best chance of beating him was to make the early stop. Whether we could have beaten him by running longer is another question, and one we will never know the answer to."

ABOVE A Ferrari at speed remains a thing of beauty

BELOW LEFT Jenson Button's race was ruined by a fumbled second pit stop

BELOW RIGHT Michael Schumacher shows just what it means to win on one of Ferrari's home tracks

close contest for third, which ultimately saw Juan Pablo Montoya lead Massa and Kimi Räikkönen across the line, the Finn having faced an uphill struggle after a poor qualifying run saw him start only eighth.

Mark Webber was a solid sixth for Williams, while seventh place went to Button, who went for an unusual three-stop strategy. The race nearly turned to disaster for the British driver when he was waved out prematurely by chief mechanic Alistair Gibson, and ripped the nozzle out of the fuel hose. It could have been a disaster, but fortunately nobody was hurt,

although it was another grey day for Honda as Barrichello trailed home in 10th place.

Having failed to make the top-10 cut in qualifying, Giancarlo Fisichella claimed the final point, right on Button's tail. It was a bad day for Toyota, though, as Ralf Schumacher took ninth and Jarno Trulli posted an early retirement, while Nico Rosberg, Jacques Villeneuve and Nick Heidfeld all faced long afternoons with little reward.

So Ferrari and Michael were back. But was this, like Imola in 2005, a one-off?

SNAPSHOT FROM
SAN MARINO

CLOCKWISE FROM RIGHT Hands up if you want Ferrari to win...; Super Aguri's Yuji Ide left Imola more than a little chastened; memories of Ayrton Senna are still poignant 12 years on; no longer mere motorhomes, the teams' new hospitality facilities were given their first outing of 2006, with Red Bull's the biggest of all; this massive stonework displays theregion's martial past in all of its glory; a welcoming smile from a Foster's grid girl

WEEKEND HEADLINES

- Super Aguri's Yuji Ide escaped with a reprimand after he tipped MF1's Christijan Albers into a roll on lap 1. However, events moved on apace behind the scenes and the team was later told that Ide, who had also endured a few incidents in Australia, needed to go away and get more experience.

- Little was made of the fact that at Imola of all places Michael Schumacher eclipsed Ayrton Senna's pole record – the last great statistic that the German had to make his own. That was perhaps a reflection of the general feeling that pole had been devalued over the four years of the qualifying with race fuel era.

- As the first race in Europe, Imola saw the seasonal debuts of the new motorhomes. Red Bull stole the show with its massively extended Energy Centre, which now served its two teams, while perched above the trucks of both teams were so-called tree houses, offices on stilts to house the engineers. Meanwhile, BMW earned numerous plaudits with its classy new home.

- Shortly after the San Marino GP, the FIA confirmed that Prodrive had been granted the 12th and final entry for 2008, much to the frustration of Ron Dennis, who had backed the efforts of the Japanese Direxiv concern – fronted by Jean Alesi – to start what in effect would have been a McLaren B-team. The FIA also accepted the entries of all 11 current teams.

- Damon Hill was elected as President of the BRDC at the organisation's AGM at Silverstone. At the same time, the rebel group opposing redevelopment plans for the Northamptonshire track were defeated, bringing some stability in the run-up to the British GP.

RACE RESULTS
SAN MARINO IMOLA

RACE DATE April 23rd
CIRCUIT LENGTH 3.065 miles
NO. OF LAPS 62
RACE DISTANCE 190.030 miles
WEATHER Dry & bright, 28°C
TRACK TEMP 42°C
RACE DAY ATTENDANCE 65,000
LAP RECORD Michael Schumacher, 1m20.411s, 137.230mph, 2004

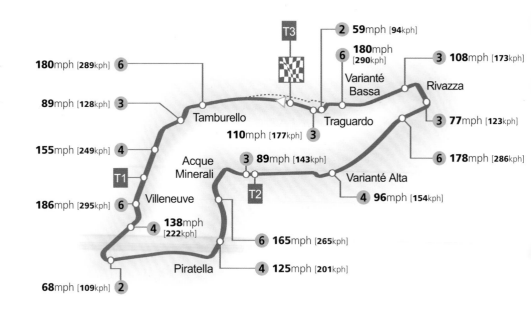

PRACTICE 1

	Driver	Time	Laps
1	M Schumacher	1m24.751s	4
2	A Wurz	1m25.132s	19
3	R Kubica	1m25.942s	24
4	A Davidson	1m26.012s	27
5	J Trulli	1m26.417s	7
6	R Doornbos	1m26.498s	18
7	F Massa	1m26.596s	4
8	D Coulthard	1m26.678s	7
9	K Räikkönen	1m26.938s	5
10	C Albers	1m28.048s	13
11	S Speed	1m28.498s	6
12	G Mondini	1m28.969s	20
13	C Klien	1m29.106s	6
14	N Jani	1m29.695s	13
15	T Monteiro	1m29.697s	13
16	V Liuzzi	1m30.348s	6
17	T Sato	1m31.217s	17
18	Y Ide	1m31.482s	17
19	F Alonso	no time	3
20	G Fisichella	no time	2
21	R Barrichello	no time	1
22	N Heidfeld	no time	1
23	JP Montoya	no time	1
24	R Schumacher	no time	1
25	J Villeneuve	no time	1
26	J Button	no time	0
27	N Rosberg	no time	0
28	M Webber	no time	0

PRACTICE 2

	Driver	Time	Laps
1	F Alonso	1m25.043s	15
2	M Schumacher	1m25.371s	13
3	R Kubica	1m25.421s	31
4	A Davidson	1m25.699s	31
5	F Massa	1m25.879s	16
6	G Fisichella	1m25.991s	15
7	J Trulli	1m26.029s	24
8	A Wurz	1m26.328s	31
9	JP Montoya	1m26.334s	15
10	N Heidfeld	1m26.387s	7
11	J Button	1m26.427s	12
12	K Räikkönen	1m26.500s	16
13	R Barrichello	1m26.653s	19
14	C Albers	1m26.783s	24
15	J Villeneuve	1m26.797s	13
16	R Doornbos	1m26.917s	27
17	N Rosberg	1m26.989s	10
18	V Liuzzi	1m27.128s	24
19	M Webber	1m27.157s	6
20	D Coulthard	1m27.503s	12
21	T Monteiro	1m27.544s	20
22	R Schumacher	1m27.639s	5
23	S Speed	1m27.719s	25
24	C Klien	1m27.990s	12
25	N Jani	1m28.361s	21
26	G Mondini	1m28.833s	27
27	T Sato	1m29.870s	23
28	Y Ide	1m31.042s	20

PRACTICE 3

	Driver	Time	Laps
1	M Schumacher	1m23.787s	14
2	F Alonso	1m24.068s	15
3	G Fisichella	1m24.377s	21
4	F Massa	1m24.383s	17
5	K Räikkönen	1m24.626s	12
6	R Schumacher	1m24.667s	21
7	J Button	1m24.850s	23
8	J Villeneuve	1m24.916s	13
9	C Klien	1m24.984s	13
10	V Liuzzi	1m24.994s	15
11	R Barrichello	1m25.041s	20
12	M Webber	1m25.205s	14
13	D Coulthard	1m25.575s	15
14	S Speed	1m25.662s	19
15	N Heidfeld	1m25.701s	9
16	C Albers	1m25.803s	22
17	J Trulli	1m25.806s	15
18	T Monteiro	1m26.476s	18
19	N Rosberg	1m27.019s	11
20	T Sato	1m28.267s	18
21	Y Ide	1m29.330s	20
22	JP Montoya	no time	1

QUALIFYING 1

	Driver	Time
1	F Alonso	1m23.536s
2	K Räikkönen	1m24.259s
3	R Schumacher	1m24.370s
4	G Fisichella	1m24.434s
5	J Trulli	1m24.446s
6	J Button	1m24.480s
7	N Rosberg	1m24.495s
8	M Schumacher	1m24.598s
9	R Barrichello	1m24.727s
10	D Coulthard	1m24.849s
11	V Liuzzi	1m24.879s
12	F Massa	1m24.884s
13	JP Montoya	1m24.960s
14	M Webber	1m24.992s
15	J Villeneuve	1m25.081s
16	N Heidfeld	1m25.410s
17	C Klien	1m25.410s
18	S Speed	1m25.437s
19	T Monteiro	1m26.820s
20	C Albers	1m27.088s
21	T Sato	1m27.609s
22	Y Ide	1m29.282s

QUALIFYING 2

	Driver	Time
1	M Schumacher	1m22.579s
2	K Räikkönen	1m23.190s
3	R Schumacher	1m23.565s
4	F Massa	1m23.595s
5	M Webber	1m23.718s
6	J Trulli	1m23.727s
7	F Alonso	1m23.743s
8	J Button	1m23.749s
9	R Barrichello	1m23.760s
10	JP Montoya	1m23.760s
11	G Fisichella	1m23.771s
12	J Villeneuve	1m23.887s
13	N Rosberg	1m23.966s
14	D Coulthard	1m24.101s
15	N Heidfeld	1m24.129s
16	V Liuzzi	1m24.520s

Best sectors – Practice

Sec 1	M Schumacher	23.607s
Sec 2	M Schumacher	27.268s
Sec 3	M Schumacher	32.807s

Speed trap – Practice

1	M Schumacher	182.5mph
2	F Massa	181.8mph
3	F Alonso	179.7mph

Best sectors – Qualifying

Sec 1	M Schumacher	23.260s
Sec 2	M Schumacher	26.788s
Sec 3	J Button	32.368s

Fernando Alonso
"We qualified with more fuel than the others, and the race showed we were right to pick that strategy. We could have won, but at Imola overtaking is almost impossible."

Michael Schumacher
"The result shows that work pays off. The key moment was staying ahead after the second stop. As we saw in 2005, overtaking at this track is almost impossible."

Kimi Räikkönen
"I lost a couple of positions at the start, then traffic hampered my progress. After the second stop, the car improved and I could push, but I got stuck behind Massa."

Jenson Button
"We missed out on a podium. I'd a problem at the first stop with the right rear wheel. In the second stop the lollipop was raised before the hose was disconnected."

Jacques Villeneuve
"It wasn't that exciting as I made a bad start and had a problem at the first stop. The balance was good and we should've been able to do some quick laps."

Jarno Trulli
"More bad luck. Something seemed to go wrong with the steering column and that meant I had to retire. It's a pity because we have been good all weekend."

Giancarlo Fisichella
"The start was fantastic, but I got crowded out. We took off some front wing and I made up ground. At the second stop, I came out just behind Button and Webber."

Felipe Massa
"I would've liked to have been on the podium, but I'm still pleased with this as it was important to score some points after I had some problems in my second stint."

Juan Pablo Montoya
"I'm pleased we managed to get a podium. I made a good start but got squeezed into the first chicane. I then hit traffic. Once I was in clear air, the leaders were 13s ahead."

Rubens Barrichello
"I'd a bad start, then lost time at my first stop when the nozzle failed. My lack of pace mid-race was due to the rear tyres locking; even though the brakes have got better."

Nick Heidfeld
"One of my main problems was lack of grip, but at the second pit stop we changed the front wing settings and the tyre pressures so the last stint was better."

Ralf Schumacher
"We were unlucky with traffic, but struggled for grip, though I don't think it's tyre-related. The pace improved later on when I was catching Fisichella and Button."

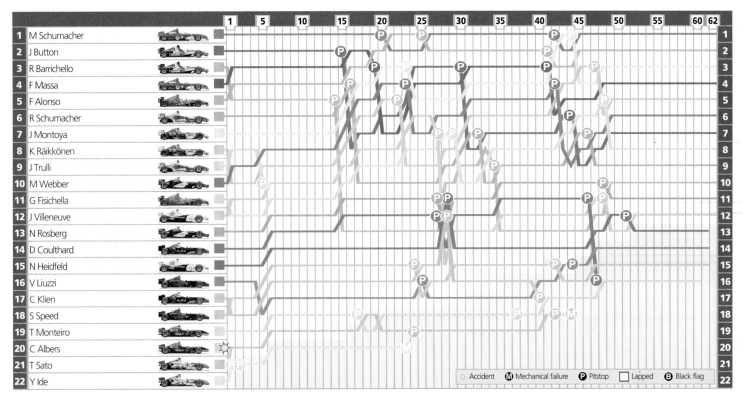

				1	5	10	15	20	25	30	35	40	45	50	55	60 62	
1	M Schumacher																1
2	J Button																2
3	R Barrichello																3
4	F Massa																4
5	F Alonso																5
6	R Schumacher																6
7	J Montoya																7
8	K Räikkönen																8
9	J Trulli																9
10	M Webber																10
11	G Fisichella																11
12	J Villeneuve																12
13	N Rosberg																13
14	D Coulthard																14
15	N Heidfeld																15
16	V Liuzzi																16
17	C Klien																17
18	S Speed																18
19	T Monteiro																19
20	C Albers																20
21	T Sato																21
22	Y Ide																22

☼ Accident   Ⓜ Mechanical failure   Ⓟ Pitstop   ☐ Lapped   Ⓑ Black flag

QUALIFYING 3

	Driver	Time
1	M Schumacher	1m22.795s
2	J Button	1m22.988s
3	R Barrichello	1m23.242s
4	F Massa	1m23.702s
5	F Alonso	1m23.709s
6	R Schumacher	1m23.772s
7	JP Montoya	1m24.021s
8	K Räikkönen	1m24.158s
9	J Trulli	1m24.172s
10	M Webber	1m24.795s

GRID

	Driver	Time
1	M Schumacher	1m22.795s
2	J Button	1m22.988s
3	R Barrichello	1m23.242s
4	F Massa	1m23.702s
5	F Alonso	1m23.709s
6	R Schumacher	1m23.772s
7	JP Montoya	1m24.021s
8	K Räikkönen	1m24.158s
9	J Trulli	1m24.172s
10	M Webber	1m24.795s
11	G Fisichella	1m23.771s
12	J Villeneuve	1m23.887s
13	N Rosberg	1m23.966s
14	D Coulthard	1m24.101s
15	N Heidfeld	1m24.129s
16	V Liuzzi	1m24.520s
17	C Klien	1m25.410s
18	S Speed	1m25.437s
19	T Monteiro	1m26.820s
20	C Albers	1m27.088s
21	T Sato	1m27.609s
22	Y Ide	1m29.282s

RACE

	Driver	Car	Laps	Time	Avg. mph	Fastest	Stops
1	M Schumacher	Ferrari 248	62	1h31m06.486s	125.724	1m24.624s	2
2	F Alonso	Renault R26	62	1h31m08.582s	125.675	1m24.569s	2
3	JP Montoya	McLaren-Mercedes MP4-21	62	1h31m22.354s	125.359	1m25.096s	2
4	F Massa	Ferrari 248	62	1h31m23.582s	125.331	1m25.528s	2
5	K Räikkönen	McLaren-Mercedes MP4-21	62	1h31m24.010s	125.321	1m25.027s	2
6	M Webber	Williams-Cosworth FW28	62	1h31m44.225s	124.862	1m25.488s	2
7	J Button	Honda RA106	62	1h31m46.121s	124.819	1m25.347s	3
8	G Fisichella	Renault R26	62	1h31m46.686s	124.806	1m25.353s	2
9	R Schumacher	Toyota TF106	62	1h31m51.977s	124.685	1m25.316s	3
10	R Barrichello	Honda RA106	62	1h32m24.337s	123.958	1m26.129s	2
11	N Rosberg	Williams-Cosworth FW28	62	1h32m26.161s	123.917	1m26.418s	2
12	J Villeneuve	BMW Sauber F1.06	62	1h32m28.856s	123.857	1m25.438s	2
13	N Heidfeld	BMW Sauber F1.06	61	1h31m14.621s	123.510	1m25.996s	2
14	V Liuzzi	Toro Rosso-Cosworth STR01	61	1h31m16.127s	123.477	1m23.679s	2
15	S Speed	Toro Rosso-Cosworth STR01	61	1h31m17.717s	123.440	1m26.248s	2
16	T Monteiro	Midland-Toyota M16	60	1h32m04.462s	120.388	1m27.160s	2
R	D Coulthard	Red Bull-Ferrari RB2	47	Driveshaft	-	1m26.855s	2
R	T Sato	Super Aguri-Honda SA05	44	Accident	-	1m29.100s	2
R	C Klien	Red Bull-Ferrari RB2	40	Hydraulics	-	1m26.759s	1
R	Y Ide	Super Aguri-Honda SA05	23	Suspension	-	1m31.032s	2
R	J Trulli	Toyota TF106	5	Steering	-	1m28.039s	0
R	C Albers	Midland-Toyota M16	0	Accident	-	-	0

CHAMPIONSHIP

	Driver	Pts
1	F Alonso	36
2	M Schumacher	21
3	K Räikkönen	18
4	G Fisichella	15
5	JP Montoya	15
6	J Button	13
7	F Massa	9
8	R Schumacher	7
9	M Webber	6
10	N Heidfeld	5
11	J Villeneuve	5
12	R Barrichello	2
	N Rosberg	2
14	D Coulthard	1
	C Klien	1

Speed trap – Qualifying
1 M Schumacher 183.4mph
2 F Massa 182.7mph
3 JP Montoya 181.3mph

Fastest Lap
F Alonso 1m24.569s
(131.177mph) on lap 23

Fastest speed trap
M Schumacher 184.9mph
Slowest speed trap
T Monteiro 175.6mph

Fastest pit stop
1 G Fisichella 22.856s
2 K Räikkönen 22.918s
3 R Schumacher 23.150s

	Constructor	Pts
1	Renault	51
2	McLaren-Mercedes	33
3	Ferrari	30
4	Honda	15
5	BMW Sauber	10
6	Williams-Cosworth	8
7	Toyota	7
8	Red Bull-Ferrari	2

 **David Coulthard**

"I had a broken driveshaft, maybe as a result of something that happened after the pit stop, as when I pulled away I had a problem with the engine taking revs."

Mark Webber

"We had a great race with the boys doing a good job on the strategy. The only tricky part was the first few laps on high fuel which made the car hard work."

Vitantonio Liuzzi

"We had a decent race pace, but couldn't pass anyone as it's so hard at this track. I had a brake problem from lap 3 on so I could not push as I was locking up."

 **Tiago Monteiro**

"We had two strategy options, depending on how the start went. I managed to stay in front of Sato and from that point I was pushing hard to follow the Torro Rossos."

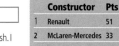 **Takuma Sato**

"It's disappointing not to finish. I had a reasonable start and was able to make up a position, but the car was lacking in pace so I could not improve any further."

Christian Klien

"In qualifying, I had a problem with the speed limiter. In the race, I had a hydraulic problem. I started behind Speed and with it being so hard to pass here, I lost time."

Nico Rosberg

"I didn't feel 100% comfortable on used tyres. My main problem was racing in traffic and when I should have pushed to gain ground, there was someone ahead."

Scott Speed

"I might have passed Heidfeld if I hadn't got held up around the pit stops. I was unlucky in that I let Michael by a couple of corners before he pitted so I lost about 5s."

 Christijan Albers

"The Super Aguri drivers are being too aggressive at the start. I had a lot of fuel on board, so I wasn't trying to hold anyone up, but Ide just pushed me off."

Yuji Ide

"I didn't think I was pushing too hard, but when I was exiting the second chicane Albers was on the racing line and I couldn't avoid hitting his car."

2006 FORMULA 1™
GRAND PRIX OF EUROPE
Nürburgring

MICHAEL DOUBLES

This was as much a battle between the teams' strategists as it was between the drivers, but Michael Schumacher wasn't complaining as he usurped Alonso again

The European GP produced another great contest between Michael Schumacher and Fernando Alonso, but whether it was an actual race is a moot point. It was a game of chess, a battle of nerves between top strategists Ross Brawn and Pat Symonds, that, as ever, came down to the timing of the pit stops.

Once he knew that he was stuck in second place, Alonso turned his engine revs down and cruised to the flag, doing just enough to keep Felipe Massa behind. The difficulties of overtaking, the points system, the need to save an engine for a second race…so many things contributed to this state of affairs. Nevertheless, the first two stints had been gripping stuff.

The race followed a truly thrilling qualifying session, made all the more dramatic by the 'phantom' red flag that appeared fleetingly on the timing screens and caused some drivers to abort their laps. Then there was Giancarlo Fisichella's remonstration with a bemused Jacques Villeneuve after the Renault man was blocked by the BMW Sauber and failed to make it into the Top 10 for the second race running.

Adding to the interest, for the first time Renault gave Alonso the luxury of two runs on new tyres in Q3, a ploy used previously by Ferrari and Honda. That and the

INSIDE LINE
FELIPE MASSA
FERRARI DRIVER

"After the performance at Imola, which many people had been expecting, it was good for us to come here and underline it. Michael qualified on the front row with me on the second row. It was a little bit windy during qualifying which meant that it wasn't easy to get an optimum lap, but the package was good following on from Imola: we were quick in free practice and the team is doing a really good job.

It was quite tricky to find the right time to go out in qualifying to ensure that you could avoid the traffic. There were six or seven cars together with only a very small gap between them, so the timing of my run was important, but things worked out for me.

I was really happy with my race performance and my first ever podium. I made a really good start and was alongside Michael coming into Turn 1. But at the Nürburgring the first corner is pretty tight and we have seen quite a few tangles there in the past, so I had to be careful. Michael was on the inside and had the line, and I really don't think I would have been very popular if I had tried any heroics and they hadn't come off!

The whole car was very strong, especially at the beginning when Michael and I were pushing Fernando [Alonso], then suddenly he found some more pace. My car was quite consistent all race and I think Bridgestone did an excellent job with the tyres for the Nürburgring and we made a good choice. Only in the last stint, when I had scrubbed tyres, was the car not quite so good. It was a great result for the team – two wins in seven days for Michael – and it made up for the first three races when we weren't quite on the pace. We had really good strategy and the race was well managed, but the last five laps were not so easy for me because I was getting closer and closer to Fernando, and Kimi was getting closer and closer to me. Because I was so close to the Renault, I was losing downforce and that was giving me a bit of a hard time, especially when the wind changed at the same time.

In the end, everything was fine and it was great for me to produce such a strong race with no mistakes. It's important for the team to have us both scoring well so that we can mount a challenge for the constructors' championship. Everything worked perfectly for us this weekend and we were really strong. It has changed the shape of the championship and I hope that we will be in a position to challenge Renault and Fernando very strongly over the rest of the season."

fact that he had no other worries (such as a double load of fuel as befell his car at Imola) helped to put him on pole by just over 0.2s over Schumacher. Michael's gloomy reaction afterwards indicated that all had not gone well, and that he had expected to be on top.

As ever at the 'Ring, there was some first corner aggro, which eliminated David Coulthard and Tonio Liuzzi, while culprit Ralf Schumacher escaped unharmed. After a brief safety-car interlude, Alonso set about building a lead. It was great stuff as Michael stayed right with Alonso throughout the first stint, and third fastest qualifier Massa did a more than respectable job to hang on.

Who would crack first and pit? In the event it was Alonso, but only just, coming in on lap 17. Michael pre-empted Renault by going quickly at just the right moment, cutting the gap from 1.2s on lap 15, to 0.6s on lap 16. Ferrari had a pretty good idea when Renault was going to stop and Michael was ready to pounce.

He came in on lap 18, but that one clear lap wasn't quite enough for Michael to make the difference, even though his in-lap was 0.225s quicker than his rival's. He resumed right on Alonso's tail, and stop times suggested that there wasn't much in it in terms of how much fuel went on board.

In fact, Michael had nearly an extra lap in hand when he made that first stop. But the reason he didn't stay out until lap 19 was just that – it was nearly a lap of fuel, and nearly is not good enough.

"It was a little unfortunate, as we didn't quite gain a lap under the safety car," Ross Brawn explained. "It's where your lap falls, because even with the equipment we have, you never get a lap to be 18.0, it's always 18.2, or 18.3. That lap was 18.97, and we could have taken a risk on going to 19, which I think would have really made the difference, but is it worth taking a risk in that situation? We knew that, all being well, we would have another opportunity later in the race to attack again. We pretty much did what we did, we just didn't quite gain a lap under the safety car period."

The bottom line was that Michael had pitted a lap later, and had that 'spare' lap. So when he made that first stop in effect he only had to put a lap's worth more fuel in the car than Alonso had taken (or 1.03 to be precise!) in order to give himself a critical three-lap advantage at the second stop.

And three laps' fuel was enough to do the job, with more than a little help from Bridgestone tyres that were in extremely good shape at the end of the

OPPOSITE TOP Trouble at the first corner seems an annual event. This time it was triggered by Ralf Schumacher who clipped Tonio Liuzzi and sent his car crashing into David Coulthard's

OPPOSITE BOTTOM Scott Speed produced another strong run, bringing his Toro Rosso home 11th, right on the tail of Nick Heidfeld's BMW Sauber

ABOVE Fernando Alonso leads the two Ferraris easily back up the hill from the Dunlop Kehre in the opening stint

second stint, and allowed Michael to push as hard as he wanted. Alonso pitted on lap 38, and Michael won the race with his speed on laps 39–41.

For those three crucial laps, Michael was around 1.5s quicker than Alonso, who had come out of the pits with a massive 22-lap fuel load for the run to the flag. Alonso also didn't have the advantage of a new set of tyres for those laps – a legacy of the strategy of using the extra set in the third qualifying session.

So when Michael finally came in, filled to the flag, and dashed out again, he resumed still comfortably in front. And that's when Alonso, mindful that he had to take this engine to his home race in Spain, backed off.

In fact, that allowed Michael to ease off as well, although those chasing the leaders didn't play the game. When historians look back at this race, they will be astonished to see that four cars from three teams were covered by just 4.879s at flagfall as Massa closed up in third, for the first podium of his career, with Kimi Räikkönen and McLaren right there in fourth. Yet few probably came away with the impression that the silver car was anything like as competitive as that.

McLaren's problem was finding the pure speed needed for qualifying, and that was exacerbated here

at the Nürburgring. The tyres the team chose were simply not soft enough, and on Friday the drivers had a terrible time finding any grip. The situation improved, but the team went into qualifying knowing that it was going to be a struggle.

Räikkönen started fifth with what turned out to be fuel to run six laps longer than Alonso, and five more than Michael. If he had been right on the tail of the others when they pitted, he would have jumped them, but the extra weight and the fact that Michael's Bridgestones stayed so consistent, meant they stayed tantalisingly out of reach. Pretty much the same happened at the second stops, and Räikkönen then had the frustration of catching the leading group. At Imola, too, we saw the McLarens catching up in the final stint, but at tracks where passing opportunities are rare, it was a case of too little, too late.

"Given where we were on Friday and Saturday morning, it was a reasonable outcome," said Martin Whitmarsh. "We selected a tyre, as did a number of the other Michelin runners, that was too hard, and we then had difficulty getting it into the operating window. Kimi made a reasonable start, was within 5–10 seconds of the lead throughout, and he led twice. We weren't quite there, close, we thought we might be able to sneak it by going long in the second stint. We gave him the opportunity of a few more revs at the end to have a go, but he couldn't get by."

Meanwhile Juan Pablo Montoya was on the second race with his engine, and in the latter stages was out of the points, having made a bad start and generally getting caught in the wrong place at the wrong time. Given more revs for a late shot at the points, it blew.

It was another race of frustration for Honda in the wake of much talk about underperforming in the opening races. Jenson Button didn't qualify as well as usual, but the message was that he would be alright in the race. He ran fifth early on, but would not have

BELOW With both Mark Webber and Nico Rosberg needing new Cosworth V8s in their Williams after third practice, they had little reason to smile, although Rosberg bagged two points in the race

BOTTOM McLaren's Juan Pablo Montoya had another race to forget as he ran ninth and then dropped out with engine failure

ABOVE **BMW Sauber driver Nick Heidfeld gained four places on lap 1 to climb to ninth place and lead Giancarlo Fisichella and Juan Pablo Montoya, but ended up 10th to team-mate Jacques Villeneuve's eighth**

INSIDE LINE
ROSS BRAWN

FERRARI
TECHNICAL DIRECTOR

"Our 1–3 finish was a tremendous result for us after so much hard work and a difficult start to the season. We always had confidence in the car's pace, but knowing it and proving it are two different things.

Winning at Imola a week ago was one thing, but Renault's pace was such that many people thought they would go on to the Nürburgring and win. Pat Symonds admitted that the strength of their performance at Imola surprised him and I think that our pace here did the same.

As well as the drivers, we have to acknowledge the progress made by Bridgestone and the excellent tyre performance we had here. There wasn't another tyre in the range that would have been as good as the one we used. It was extremely good – fast and consistent – and it was that consistency that won us the race.

Choosing the tyre compounds so far in advance without being allowed on the relevant circuit in the previous week has never been easy and it's more difficult than ever this year as the V8 cars place an entirely different set of demands on a tyre to the V10s. The longitudinal demands are lower as there is less acceleration through the rear tyres, lower terminal speeds and higher entry speeds meaning less braking requirement. The lateral forces, however, are higher. The implications of that narrow the window of effective choices. Less energy being fed into the tyres from the engines means that they don't heat up as quickly, while higher lateral forces mean they are more prone to graining – especially when you go softer on compound to help get heat into them.

Michael was a bit disappointed not to get pole position, as he'd been very quick from first thing on Friday morning and he set the fastest time in Q2. But Fernando also did a very good lap. Michael was able to stay with the Renault in the race and we thought he might be able to take the lead at the first pit stop. But he only ran one lap longer than Fernando and also had a bit of a moment at Turn 6, pushing hard on his in-lap. I think he would have had to do two extra laps to make it and, actually, the safety car on the opening lap brought us very close to being able to stop on lap 19 instead of lap 18. Our computer said 18.97 laps. We were tempted to go for it, but running out of fuel is always a bit embarrassing...

Also, we knew we'd get another opportunity later in the race as Michael was saying that he had performance in hand following Fernando. That's the way it turned out and he drove a great race. Not bad for an old man!"

ABOVE Rubens Barrichello's
Honda struggled for grip in the
race, but the Brazilian showed
improved form to finish fifth

LEFT Ferrari fun on the podium as
Felipe Massa shares his delight at
finishing third with the jubilant,
grand prix-winning Schumacher

finished any higher even if his engine hadn't failed. His position was inherited by Barrichello, who had outqualified Jenson. But while 4.879s covered the top four, Rubens was another 1m07.707s further back!

After his qualifying problems, Fisichella couldn't better sixth for Renault. Nico Rosberg did a great job for Williams to advance from last – the result of a penalty for an engine change – to seventh. He ran a mammoth 33-lap opening stint, and while it looked as though he might make it a one-stopper, he managed to squeeze a second stop in. It was a drive of good judgement and maturity from a difficult situation. Team-mate Mark Webber would have finished a place or two ahead after he also took a penalty, and made up for it with a strong first lap. A hydraulic problem claimed him and so the final point went to Jacques Villeneuve, who had outrun team-mate Nick Heidfeld for most of the weekend.

Jarno Trulli was a useful sixth for Toyota early on, but faded with handling problems after the sort of performance for which he has so often been criticised in the past. Ralf Schumacher was nowhere in the early laps, but put in a surprisingly feisty drive that looked likely to gain some points, only for the engine to let go.

So Imola wasn't a fluke, and Ferrari now appeared to be Renault's real title rivals.

SNAPSHOT FROM
EUROPE

CLOCKWISE FROM RIGHT Where's Michael? Schumacher Sr remains the biggest draw in Germany; Meanwhile, the sofa might have looked comfortable, but younger brother Ralf didn't in this interview for Germany's Premier Sport; the paddock remains the place to be for those who want to be seen; a phone call from Super Aguri's Daniele Audetto put Franck Montagny into the grand prix ring for the first time; Keke Rosberg combines the role of father and mentor for Nico

WEEKEND HEADLINES

■ Yuji Ide's troubles with the authorities gave Franck Montagny the unexpected chance to make his grand prix debut, having originally agreed to be non-participating third driver at the 'Ring. With no testing, the former Renault man was in at the deep end, but he had a respectable race until suffering an engine failure.

■ A pair of GP2 victories for the ever-impressive Lewis Hamilton really caught the attention of the Nürburgring paddock hierarchy. Ron Dennis noted that the long-time McLaren protégé could be in F1 as early as 2007, and admitted that it wasn't impossible that he could go straight into a McLaren race seat.

■ Jacques Villeneuve lost his three fastest qualifying times from Q3 for not getting out of Giancarlo Fisichella's way in the middle session, and thus contributing to the Italian failing to make the cut. Afterwards, Giancarlo went along to the BMW garage to remonstrate with Jacques who insisted that he couldn't compromise his own out lap. Despite the penalty, Jacques still started ninth.

■ Driver safety in testing became a talking-point at the Nürburgring following discussions within the GPDA. Mark Webber was keen to point out that medical and marshalling facilities were not up to the standard expected on race weekends.

■ Moves towards modifying the qualifying system gathered momentum during the Nürburgring weekend, with Bernie Ecclestone among those who felt that the third session might perhaps be better with the cars running one at a time rather than whenever the teams pleased. Several drivers agreed with him, but the idea quickly ran out of momentum and change was not pursued.

RACE RESULTS
EUROPE
NÜRBURGRING

Official Results © [2006]
Formula One Administration Limited,
6 Princes Gate, London SW7 1QJ.
No reproduction without permission.
All copyright and database rights reserved

RACE DATE May 7th
CIRCUIT LENGTH 3.199 miles
NO. OF LAPS 60
RACE DISTANCE 191.940 miles
WEATHER Dry & bright, 20°C
TRACK TEMP 40°C
RACE DAY ATTENDANCE 121,000
LAP RECORD Michael Schumacher,
1m29.468s, 128.718mph, 2004

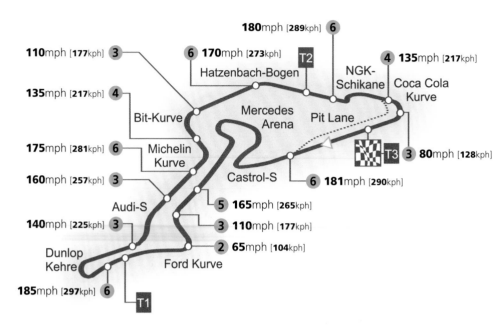

	PRACTICE 1		
	Driver	Time	Laps
1	A Wurz	1m32.079s	20
2	A Davidson	1m32.399s	29
3	R Kubica	1m32.852s	22
4	M Schumacher	1m32.858s	4
5	R Doornbos	1m32.944s	19
6	J Button	1m33.635s	7
7	R Barrichello	1m34.213s	6
8	K Räikkönen	1m34.402s	5
9	R Schumacher	1m34.995s	6
10	A Sutil	1m35.332s	21
11	N Jani	1m35.365s	19
12	S Speed	1m35.612s	8
13	C Albers	1m35.985s	8
14	T Monteiro	1m36.062s	10
15	T Sato	1m37.817s	20
16	F Montagny	1m37.933s	16
17	F Alonso	no time	2
18	G Fisichella	no time	2
19	V Liuzzi	no time	2
20	D Coulthard	no time	1
21	C Klien	no time	1
22	JP Montoya	no time	1
23	J Trulli	no time	1
24	N Heidfeld	no time	0
25	F Massa	no time	0
26	N Rosberg	no time	0
27	J Villeneuve	no time	0
28	M Webber	no time	0

	PRACTICE 2		
	Driver	Time	Laps
1	A Wurz	1m32.675s	27
2	F Alonso	1m33.579s	14
3	M Schumacher	1m33.619s	14
4	R Doornbos	1m33.799s	25
5	A Davidson	1m33.870s	29
6	R Schumacher	1m33.883s	19
7	J Button	1m33.920s	12
8	R Kubica	1m33.991s	30
9	G Fisichella	1m34.030s	19
10	A Sutil	1m34.179s	23
11	N Rosberg	1m34.215s	19
12	C Albers	1m34.472s	23
13	K Räikkönen	1m34.536s	13
14	F Massa	1m34.546s	18
15	R Barrichello	1m34.631s	11
16	M Webber	1m34.825s	14
17	JP Montoya	1m34.968s	14
18	C Klien	1m35.066s	19
19	D Coulthard	1m35.241s	14
20	N Heidfeld	1m35.308s	12
21	V Liuzzi	1m35.406s	19
22	N Jani	1m35.479s	26
23	S Speed	1m35.669s	21
24	J Villeneuve	1m35.688s	12
25	T Monteiro	1m35.902s	18
26	T Sato	1m36.255s	25
27	F Montagny	1m36.665s	16
28	J Trulli	no time	5

	PRACTICE 3		
	Driver	Time	Laps
1	M Schumacher	1m30.788s	12
2	F Massa	1m31.093s	10
3	R Schumacher	1m31.395s	21
4	J Villeneuve	1m31.531s	13
5	G Fisichella	1m31.584s	12
6	F Alonso	1m31.807s	14
7	J Button	1m32.104s	16
8	C Klien	1m32.197s	13
9	V Liuzzi	1m32.290s	17
10	K Räikkönen	1m32.320s	11
11	N Rosberg	1m32.459s	15
12	S Speed	1m32.505s	18
13	R Barrichello	1m32.534s	18
14	M Webber	1m32.711s	16
15	N Heidfeld	1m32.773s	16
16	D Coulthard	1m32.779s	15
17	JP Montoya	1m32.989s	12
18	J Trulli	1m33.120s	24
19	T Monteiro	1m33.744s	19
20	C Albers	1m34.469s	21
21	F Montagny	1m35.706s	20
22	T Sato	1m36.082s	15

	QUALIFYING 1	
	Driver	Time
1	F Alonso	1m31.138s
2	M Schumacher	1m31.235s
3	K Räikkönen	1m31.263s
4	J Button	1m31.420s
5	N Heidfeld	1m31.457s
6	R Schumacher	1m31.470s
7	J Villeneuve	1m31.545s
8	G Fisichella	1m31.574s
9	R Barrichello	1m31.671s
10	M Webber	1m31.712s
11	D Coulthard	1m31.742s
12	JP Montoya	1m31.774s
13	J Trulli	1m31.809s
14	F Massa	1m31.921s
15	N Rosberg	1m32.053s
16	V Liuzzi	1m32.621s
17	C Klien	1m32.901s
18	C Albers	1m32.936s
19	S Speed	1m32.992s
20	T Monteiro	1m33.658s
21	T Sato	1m35.239s
22	F Montagny	1m46.505s

	QUALIFYING 2	
	Driver	Time
1	M Schumacher	1m30.013s
2	K Räikkönen	1m30.203s
3	F Alonso	1m30.336s
4	R Barrichello	1m30.469s
5	JP Montoya	1m30.671s
6	F Massa	1m30.732s
7	J Trulli	1m30.733s
8	J Button	1m30.755s
9	J Villeneuve	1m30.865s
10	M Webber	1m30.892s
11	R Schumacher	1m30.944s
12	N Rosberg	1m31.194s
13	G Fisichella	1m31.197s
14	D Coulthard	1m31.227s
15	N Heidfeld	1m31.422s
16	V Liuzzi	1m31.728s

Best sectors – Practice		
Sec 1	J Villeneuve	30.024s
Sec 2	F Massa	37.564s
Sec 3	M Schumacher	23.110s

Speed trap – Practice		
1	M Schumacher	181.6mph
2	F Massa	181.3mph
3	F Alonso	180.1mph

Best sectors – Qualifying		
Sec 1	M Schumacher	29.428s
Sec 2	F Alonso	37.236s
Sec 3	F Alonso	23.080s

Fernando Alonso
"I had a good start from pole. We came in two laps earlier than the Ferraris on the second stop, and they moved ahead. After that, I just turned down the engine."

Michael Schumacher
"I was in Alonso's slipstream. I couldn't see anything in my mirrors, but then I realised that Felipe was coming alongside, but I was able to stay ahead."

Kimi Räikkönen
"I got past Barrichello, but Button was able to squeeze through at the first corner, then on lap 4 I passed him before the chicane. But it wasn't enough for a podium."

Jenson Button
"I fought Räikkönen in Turns 1–3 before I got ahead to take fourth. The car was inconsistent and I'd have been happy to finish fifth. Instead, the engine tightened."

Jacques Villeneuve
"I had a good battle with Fisichella. With the car he had, I thought he'd overtake me, but he stayed behind until the second stop, so that was good."

Jarno Trulli
"I pushed all race, but struggled with the balance. The team tried different set-up adjustments, but I just didn't seem to increase my pace until the last 10 laps."

Giancarlo Fisichella
"I had only one or two clear laps all race, but we had a good strategy. I was aggressive on the pit-entry at the second stop as it was my one chance to pass Villeneuve."

Felipe Massa
"I'm happy as I stood on the podium for the first time. I made a great start and was alongside Michael but, as he had the inside line, he was able to stay ahead."

Juan Pablo Montoya
"I lost a few places at the first corner. After that, I was always stuck in traffic at points when I needed clean air to benefit from the heavier fuel load I was carrying."

Rubens Barrichello
"Fifth place is not what we were hoping for, but I was struggling with the balance of the car and it was just a case of surviving and doing the best we could."

Nick Heidfeld
"I made a super start and was able to make up four places. I then tried very hard but I couldn't keep up with the drivers in front of me. I was struggling with balance."

Ralf Schumacher
"I lost time at the first corner, but made up for this with a long first stint which put me into sixth. We were doing competitive times, but then we had an engine failure."

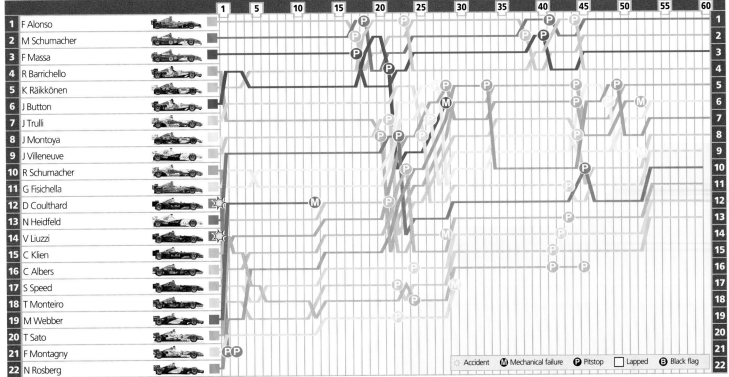

	Driver			
1	F Alonso			
2	M Schumacher			
3	F Massa			
4	R Barrichello			
5	K Räikkönen			
6	J Button			
7	J Trulli			
8	J Montoya			
9	J Villeneuve			
10	R Schumacher			
11	G Fisichella			
12	D Coulthard			
13	N Heidfeld			
14	V Liuzzi			
15	C Klien			
16	C Albers			
17	S Speed			
18	T Monteiro			
19	M Webber			
20	T Sato			
21	F Montagny			
22	N Rosberg			

☆ Accident   Ⓜ Mechanical failure   Ⓟ Pitstop   ☐ Lapped   Ⓑ Black flag

QUALIFYING 3

	Driver	Time
1	F Alonso	1m29.819s
2	M Schumacher	1m30.028s
3	F Massa	1m30.407s
4	R Barrichello	1m30.754s
5	K Räikkönen	1m30.933s
6	J Button	1m30.940s
7	J Trulli	1m31.419s
8	JP Montoya	1m31.880s
9	M Webber	1m33.405s
10	J Villeneuve	1m36.998s

GRID

	Driver	Time
1	F Alonso	1m29.819s
2	M Schumacher	1m30.028s
3	F Massa	1m30.407s
4	R Barrichello	1m30.754s
5	K Räikkönen	1m30.933s
6	J Button	1m30.940s
7	J Trulli	1m31.419s
8	JP Montoya	1m31.880s
9	J Villeneuve	1m36.998s
10	R Schumacher	1m30.944s
11	G Fisichella	1m31.197s
12	D Coulthard	1m31.227s
13	N Heidfeld	1m31.422s
14	V Liuzzi	1m31.728s
15	C Klien	1m32.901s
16	C Albers	1m32.936s
17	S Speed	1m32.992s
18	T Monteiro	1m33.658s
19*	M Webber	1m33.405s
20	T Sato	1m35.239s
21	F Montagny	1m46.505s
22*	N Rosberg	1m31.194s

* DENOTES 10-PLACE GRID PENALTY

RACE

	Driver	Car	Laps	Time	Avg. mph	Fastest	Stops
1	M Schumacher	Ferrari 248	60	1h35m58.765s	119.981	1m32.099s	2
2	F Alonso	Renault R26	60	1h36m02.516s	119.902	1m32.532s	2
3	F Massa	Ferrari 248	60	1h36m03.212s	119.888	1m33.099s	2
4	K Räikkönen	McLaren-Mercedes MP4-21	60	1h36m03.644s	119.879	1m32.472s	2
5	R Barrichello	Honda RA106	60	1h37m11.351s	118.487	1m33.952s	2
6	G Fisichella	Renault R26	60	1h37m12.881s	118.456	1m32.964s	2
7	N Rosberg	Williams-Cosworth FW28	60	1h37m13.330s	118.447	1m33.579s	2
8	J Villeneuve	BMW Sauber F1.06	60	1h37m28.129s	118.147	1m34.037s	2
9	J Trulli	Toyota TF106	59	1h36m00.978s	117.936	1m33.953s	2
10	N Heidfeld	BMW Sauber F1.06	59	1h36m08.187s	117.788	1m34.035s	2
11	S Speed	Toro Rosso-Cosworth STR01	59	1h36m09.384s	117.763	1m34.091s	2
12	T Monteiro	Midland-Toyota M16	59	1h37m26.121s	116.218	1m35.504s	2
13	C Albers	Midland-Toyota M16	59	1h37m28.526s	116.170	1m35.428s	2
R	R Schumacher	Toyota TF106	52	Engine	-	1m33.607s	2
R	JP Montoya	McLaren-Mercedes MP4-21	52	Engine	-	1m33.571s	2
R	T Sato	Super Aguri-Honda SA05	45	Hydraulics	-	1m36.706s	2
R	F Montagny	Super Aguri-Honda SA05	29	Engine	-	1m37.214s	1
R	J Button	Honda RA106	28	Engine	-	1m34.042s	1
R	C Klien	Red Bull-Ferrari RB2	28	Transmission	-	1m34.553s	1
R	M Webber	Williams-Cosworth FW28	12	Hydraulics	-	1m35.415s	0
R	D Coulthard	Red Bull-Ferrari RB2	2	Accident damage	-	2m24.500s	2
R	V Liuzzi	Toro Rosso-Cosworth STR01	0	Accident damage	-	-	0

CHAMPIONSHIP

	Driver	Pts
1	F Alonso	44
2	M Schumacher	31
3	K Räikkönen	23
4	G Fisichella	18
5	F Massa	15
6	JP Montoya	15
7	J Button	13
8	R Schumacher	7
9	R Barrichello	6
10	M Webber	6
11	J Villeneuve	6
12	N Heidfeld	5
13	N Rosberg	4
14	D Coulthard	1
15	C Klien	1

Speed trap – Qualifying
1 M Schumacher 183.7mph
2 G Fisichella 183.6mph
3 F Massa 182.9mph

Fastest Lap
M Schumacher 1m32.099s
(125.042mph) on lap 39

Fastest speed trap
M Schumacher 183.5mph
Slowest speed trap
K Räikkönen 175.0mph

Fastest pit stop
1 R Schumacher 22.711s
2 G Fisichella 23.098s
3 R Barrichello 23.129s

Constructor

	Constructor	Pts
1	Renault	62
2	Ferrari	46
3	McLaren-Mercedes	38
4	Honda	19
5	BMW Sauber	11
6	Williams-Cosworth	10
7	Toyota	7
8	Red Bull-Ferrari	2

David Coulthard

"At the first corner, Ralf touched Tonio, who got knocked onto me. It was one of those racing incidents. We were able to replace the nose, but then we had another issue."

Mark Webber

"It was going fantastically until what we think was a hydraulics problem meant that I lost all the controls. I'd made up seven places and was still carrying lots of fuel."

Vitantonio Liuzzi

"I passed some cars off the grid, then got hit from behind by Ralf. He hit me in the right rear tyre and then David couldn't avoid hitting me. A shame as the car felt good."

Tiago Monteiro

"This was the first time Christijan and I got to mix it up. I got a good start and was able to pass a few cars. After that, it was a matter of staying focused out of the pit stops."

Takuma Sato

"It was a great race until the last moment when I had a hydraulic problem. The start was exciting, but the car's straight-line speed got increasingly slower."

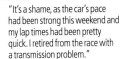

Christian Klien

"It's a shame, as the car's pace had been strong this weekend and my lap times had been pretty quick. I retired from the race with a transmission problem."

Nico Rosberg

"Two points from dead last. In the first stint I didn't feel comfortable in the car, but after the first stop I could attack and I even thought about passing Fisichella."

Scott Speed

"I think I was quicker than Heidfeld and the Toyotas. We need to sharpen up our pit stops – me and the team – as that's where we lost time. But the race pace is great."

Christijan Albers

"After I passed Montagny, I was behind Tiago, who was behind Sato who let Tiago get by. I got past after a few laps, but by that time Tiago had run away."

Franck Montagny

"It's disappointing not to finish my first race for the team, but that's racing! I was having a reasonable run until I had a hydraulic problem. I'd like to thank Aguri Suzuki."

FORMULA 1™ GRAN PREMIO
TELEFÓNICA DE ESPAÑA 2006
Catalunya

ALONSO'S BIG DAY

Fernando Alonso really wanted to win his home grand prix and Renault team-mate Giancarlo Fisichella helped him break clear from the start to beat Michael Schumacher

The Spanish Grand Prix proved to be round four of the Fernando Alonso v Michael Schumacher battle. Following consecutive victories for the Ferrari ace at Imola and the Nürburging, Alonso made it two wins and two second place finishes apiece, ensuring that honours were even after the duo's fights in Bahrain, Imola, the Nürburgring and Barcelona. The problem for the seven-time World Champion was that the Spanish race was the sixth round of the championship, and in the two races in which Ferrari had messed up, Alonso had taken 18 points out of a possible 20 for a win in Australia and a second place in Malaysia.

The Spanish GP didn't have the knife-edge tension of the previous three encounters, in part because an interloper got in the way of these arch-rivals in the form of Giancarlo Fisichella, who rode shotgun for his Renault team-mate. Nevertheless, until the second stops were done, there was still an interesting race underway, although ultimately it was to be a straightforward win for Renault.

As ever, the race swung on qualifying. Was Ferrari tricked, either deliberately or by circumstances, into believing that the Renaults weren't as fast as they proved to be? Alonso in particular underperformed in

ABOVE **Ralf Schumacher runs wide in the wake of Toyota team-mate Jarno Trulli. Although they qualified well, neither would score**

OPPOSITE **Nico Rosberg leads Tonio Liuzzi, Christian Klien and David Coulthard in a midfield battle that yielded no points**

the crucial middle session, the one that normally gives rivals an indication of true speed.

Ferrari duly put a heavy fuel load in Michael's car for Q3 in the hope that Michael would still have a shot at the front row, but the team had no way of knowing that Alonso would suddenly find nearly half a second.

"We weren't sand bagging," said Renault's Engineering Director Pat Symonds. "I think that we were looking for grip, and every time it got warmer we were finding a bit. Obviously you don't lay it on the line in Q2. They weren't great laps to be honest, for either driver, but it certainly wasn't intentional…"

Whatever, Michael went to the start a disappointed

third, albeit knowing that he had the capability of going several laps further than Alonso. It should have been enough to jump him at the first stops, but this time Fisichella was in the way in second place, unable to match the Spaniard's pace. By the time Alonso pitted on lap 17, the Italian was over 10s behind, and of course Michael was trapped behind the second Renault, totally helpless. He turned out to have enough fuel to run six laps longer than Alonso, but it was never going to be enough to make up that deficit.

"This wasn't a race about strategy, really," said Symonds. "This was a race about pace. I was surprised in the first stint. I didn't think we'd pull out that much,

INSIDE LINE
FERNANDO ALONSO

RENAULT DRIVER

"It's a fantastic feeling racing in Spain, so to take my first pole position and race win at home was great. It was an amazing atmosphere, and the party started when I took pole. The times were pretty close and I was only just ahead of my team-mate Giancarlo. For me, it was pretty similar to what

happened at the Nürburgring – Q2 was just so-so and then I put in a very good lap in Q3 to take pole position.

Actually, we changed the car quite a lot because it was handling differently in Saturday morning free practice. There was a lot of oversteer and so we made some changes for Q1 and everything worked well. You're always a bit concerned whether the problem was actually the conditions in free practice, but we made the right call and it was great to see the reaction from the grandstands when I took pole. It's good to see people really enjoying themselves and I was thinking that 66 laps in the race won't be enough for me! But I was wrong. When you're leading and you're not under a lot of pressure you have time to worry about things going wrong and you just want to see the chequered flag.

On race morning, I drove the King around the circuit in a Renault Megane and meeting him again on the podium is the best thing that has happened to me in Formula One, apart from Brazil last year where I won the championship. Maybe this one was an even better feeling because I crossed the line winning the race. In Brazil, it was more dramatic as I had to defend third position to be sure of the title and that's a different feeling. Here, with nothing like that in my mind, I was free to drive to win.

I think Giancarlo got a better start than me, but I was able to defend the inside line. It's always better to fight with your team-mate than another driver. Then the strategy worked out well. It was a bit different from the previous race at the Nürburgring because to get pole position we had

been lighter than Ferrari and we knew we had to make a gap in the first stint. I found the gap quite quickly and it could have been a defensive race from then on, but that wasn't actually the case. This time, Ferrari wasn't coming on really strong and so I was just maintaining the gap, especially in the last stint. I was controlling the revs and conserving the car.

I think we achieved our maximum race performance here in Barcelona and I am a little surprised that the last two races have been straight fights with Ferrari. Some others, I think, can come back, especially McLaren."

but neither did Fernando. I was saying let's try for a 5s gap coming into the first stops, and he said 'I don't think we can do it'. I said 'I know!' So I was surprised there. As I say, the pace into the stop was great…"

The inevitable question was had Fisichella been asked to run to a pace to block Michael? That had certainly occurred to Ferrari Technical Director Ross Brawn: "I think you have to look at Fisichella's times when he was free. He was a little bit slower than Alonso but, at times, he was 1s a lap slower. Maybe he had problems. Who knows?"

However, Symonds denied that the Italian was asked to do anything untoward, although admitting that it had been a possibility.

"We obviously discussed it – you have to – but if we'd done that I think the overall effect on the year would have been negative. It's a terrible thing to ask a driver to do. It's one thing to do it in the last race when you're fighting for the championship, but to do it in round six, with a guy who's already won a race and got the potential to finish high in the championship, it's just not the way to go racing is it? I won't say it wasn't discussed, but the discussion was very short."

Was Michael really being held up at all, though? Brawn made a big point of it, but Michael himself was less vocal on the subject, hinting that the pace just wasn't there. After all, he was carrying six laps' worth of fuel more than Alonso – that amounted to 15kg, using the FIA standard for Barcelona.

Brawn said that Michael had deliberately hung back a little from Fisichella to save engine, tyres and so on – sticking to the Italian's gearbox would have achieved nothing since passing is all but impossible – but it certainly appeared that he couldn't have gone very much quicker than he actually did.

"We had a discussion on the pit wall," said Symonds. "We know Ferrari are going long, but are they saving tyres or anything? Just watching the car, I

got the impression that he was driving absolutely as fast as it could go.

"Sometimes after five or six laps you can't see what's happening, it's still a bit of a mess, but it was actually establishing itself quite well quite early. The gap we had coming into that first pit stop was more than I expected. If that had been followed by a poor stint, we still wouldn't have made it. It really was a real race all the way up to the second stop." Having jumped Fisichella for second at the first stops, Michael made a pretty good effort in the middle stint, but Alonso was equal to him. The Ferrari was still too far behind to take advantage of six extra laps on near empty tanks after Alonso's last fill-up. The pace wasn't quite there, and the ever-fickle Barcelona track had on this day tipped the balance in favour of the Renault/Michelin package.

Even Symonds admitted that he was surprised by the apparent ease of Alonso's victory: "Yeah, I was a little bit, because I honestly didn't think we were going to win it, when I looked at yesterday. The tyres worked really well, the car was quick, and it was won on speed, not on strategy."

Fisichella was outdriven by team-mate Alonso, and he even had a brief off when chasing Michael (he said he was disturbed by a radio message), but nevertheless the team was happy: "He was really good," said Symonds. "One little mistake, but he pushed all the way, had a bit more pressure on him. Faultless, other than one little run through the gravel. Luckily, it didn't cost him."

Felipe Massa was a little left behind this time, but he still finished an easy fourth place in the second Ferrari, and from somewhere produced fastest lap.

The Spanish GP brought some hard lessons for the opposition, and especially for McLaren. In the previous two grands prix, Kimi Räikkönen had picked up pace through the race, and at the Nürburgring he had

BELOW It was another retirement for Juan Pablo Montoya, this time after spinning out of the race

OPPOSITE TOP Nick Heidfeld blasts out of the pits en route to picking up the final point for eighth

OPPOSITE BOTTOM Ferrari's Ross Brawn ponders how he might get Michael Schumacher anywhere close to leader Fernando Alonso

INSIDE LINE
ALAIN DASSAS
RENAULT PRESIDENT

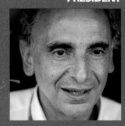

"The manufacturers have finally reached a commercial settlement over the future of Formula One.

The Grand Prix Manufacturers Association statement is as follows: 'A memorandum of understanding (MOU) on the commercial structure of F1, as developed between CVC, FOA (Formula One Administration) and the GPMA was unanimously agreed and signed by representatives from the five GPMA teams: BMW Sauber, Honda GP, McLaren Mercedes, Renault F1 and Toyota Racing. The GPMA are committed to Formula One until 2012.'

So, we have an agreement with Bernie [Ecclestone] and have reached a level where everybody should feel happy.

Importantly, this shows that Renault has the willingness to pursue its presence in F1. It's a 2008–2012 agreement and so the team is committed to being there. We show the market, we show the other teams and we show the sponsors that we are there to continue.

It's a good agreement because the breakdown of F1 income is more balanced than before. Now we can concentrate on other tasks, such as finding good drivers and good sponsors. Before we committed to being there for a period of time, people were hesitating, which is why it was important for us to reach this agreement.

Talking of drivers, it's true that we like to grow our talent from within. We have our Renault Driver Development Programme, which is very successful, but it's also true that we are there to have top performances. We need a top driver to do that, just as we need young talent. Fernando Alonso has done a great job for Renault and performed superbly in winning the championship last year. Fernando will not be easy to replace.

Having said that, we are the reigning World Champions and I'm sure that Flavio Briatore has had serious talks with many drivers. As I say, it's an important step to reach this commercial agreement. We've been talking about this agreement for a long time and, in the end, you have to decide what you're going to do.

All the improvements that we have obtained in these negotiations have been obtained jointly with the other manufacturers and we are now in a position to get on and go forward. As for Flavio, he has been with us in his current role since 2000 and it is true that his contract expires at the end of this year. It is up to us to convince him that Renault remains capable of operating as a front-running team. What interests Flavio is that he wants to be at the top of the races, so if we give him the means to be at the top, I think he will be happy to sign again."

finished right behind the Ferrari/Renault battle. He was behind it this time as well in fifth, but miles behind – nearly a minute at the flag. To some degree, he had backed off to protect an engine at the end of its two-race cycle, but the package just wasn't quick enough. Having qualified ninth, he saved his day with a brilliant charge to fifth place at the start.

For the second race running, Juan Pablo Montoya was mired in midfield in his McLaren, this time after a fuelling mistake by the team in qualifying. He started heavy, and an early spin put him out of the race.

Honda continued to be the fourth team in the equation, and in Spain the car was pretty much a match for the McLaren. Had Jenson Button not been passed at the start by Räikkönen, and then got stuck behind his team-mate Rubens Barrichello early on, he might have beaten the Finn. Sixth and seventh places brought useful points, but it was not where the team thought it would be.

The last point went to Nick Heidfeld. Against, the odds, the German driver had been overshadowed by BMW Sauber team-mate Jacques Villeneuve of late, and the Canadian was again very quick during the weekend. But he had to take a 10-place grid penalty after the team damaged his Nürburgring engine in transit, and thus had to change it.

It was an average weekend for Williams, at a track that punishes aerodynamic inefficiency. Mark Webber finished in ninth place and Nico Rosberg 11th, but that was little to write home about. It was even worse for Toyota. Yet again, both cars qualified in the top 10, but Jarno Trulli faded badly to 10th, while Ralf Schumacher retired after an early delay when he broke his wing – against Trulli's rear wheel!

Things were about as bad as they could be for the Red Bull quartet. The Ferrari-engined RBR cars just weren't in the picture in Spain, and matters weren't helped when a water leak put David Coulthard in the barrier in qualifying. As usual, the MF1s and Super Aguris were fighting at the back, and the war escalated when Super Aguri rookie Franck Montagny made clumsy contact with Tiago Monteiro, spinning him out. MF1 tried to take the matter further, but the stewards weren't interested.

It now seemed clear that Renault and Ferrari were well clear of the rest, and incredibly evenly matched, with a few degrees of track temperature tipping the balance in favour of one or the other. Monaco was next – and anything could happen there…

LEFT **There can be no mistaking what it means to Fernando Alonso to win on home ground. That he extended his points advantage to 15 was only a bonus**

SNAPSHOT FROM
SPAIN

CLOCKWISE FROM RIGHT
Barcelona remains one of the great
cities visited by Formula One,
thanks to Gaudi's architecture;
David Coulthard chalked up his
200th start; Michael Schumacher
couldn't resist a game of football;
M is for Movistar; Ron Dennis
advocates a little more fun in F1

WEEKEND HEADLINES

■ The first meeting of the new Sporting Working Group, a forum within which the team managers could vote
on rule changes for 2008, was held a few days before the Spanish GP. The engine freeze rules were the
major point of discussion and the teams wrong-footed the sport's governing body, the FIA, when they voted
against the entire principle of the freeze. That wasn't meant to happen…

■ Some 131,000 people were claimed to have turned out to see local hero Fernando Alonso in action on
Sunday, including regular grand prix guest King Juan Carlos. A week later, even more turned up in Seville for
a free show on the streets of the city, during which Alonso demonstrated last year's V10-powered car.

■ Peace broke out on the morning of the Spanish GP when McLaren chief Ron Dennis revealed to the media
that the GPMA teams had finally done a deal with Bernie Ecclestone for 2008. Instigators Renault quickly
responded with a press release confirming its own arrangement – with no mention of the others – and then
the GPMA issued a 'collective' statement.

■ Paul Ricard and Valencia circuits were mentioned as possible hosts of a Mediterranean GP that would move
between venues. There were even suggestions from the Paul Ricard camp that, due to lack of spectating
facilities, their event would be run with only VIPs and the media present. Bernie Ecclestone would later
claim that he would not consider such an event.

■ Shortly after the Spanish GP, the FIA announced the opening of the tendering process to find an official tyre
supplier for 2008–10. Due to have a monopoly anyway in 2007, Bridgestone remained the logical option,
but at least there was the formal possibility for others to pitch for the job.

RACE RESULTS
SPAIN
CATALUNYA

RACE DATE May 14th
CIRCUIT LENGTH 2.875 miles
NO. OF LAPS 66
RACE DISTANCE 189.777 miles
WEATHER Dry & bright, 28°C
TRACK TEMP 39°C
RACE DAY ATTENDANCE 132,000
LAP RECORD Giancarlo Fisichella,
1m15.641s, 136.840mph, 2005

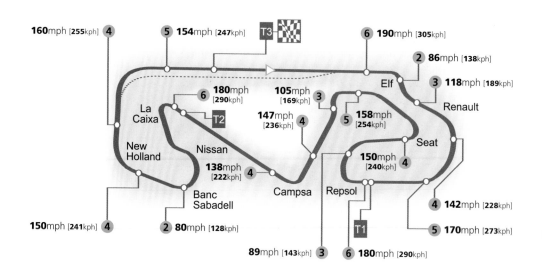

PRACTICE 1

	Driver	Time	Laps
1	F Massa	1m15.796s	4
2	M Schumacher	1m16.099s	4
3	A Wurz	1m16.125s	21
4	R Kubica	1m16.628s	21
5	A Davidson	1m16.961s	24
6	R Doornbos	1m17.424s	20
7	N Jani	1m19.720s	20
8	G Mondini	1m20.708s	21
9	T Sato	1m20.744s	9
10	F Montagny	no time	3
11	S Speed	no time	3
12	F Alonso	no time	2
13	G Fisichella	no time	2
14	J Villeneuve	no time	2
15	C Albers	no time	1
16	R Barrichello	no time	1
17	J Button	no time	1
18	D Coulthard	no time	1
19	N Heidfeld	no time	1
20	C Klien	no time	1
21	V Liuzzi	no time	1
22	T Monteiro	no time	1
23	JP Montoya	no time	1
24	N Rosberg	no time	1
25	R Schumacher	no time	1
26	J Trulli	no time	1
27	M Webber	no time	1
28	K Räikkönen	no time	0

PRACTICE 2

	Driver	Time	Laps
1	A Davidson	1m16.533s	38
2	R Doornbos	1m16.824s	29
3	F Alonso	1m16.860s	16
4	A Wurz	1m17.075s	30
5	C Klien	1m17.086s	10
6	M Schumacher	1m17.100s	21
7	G Fisichella	1m17.291s	17
8	J Button	1m17.414s	12
9	R Barrichello	1m17.417s	16
10	R Schumacher	1m17.506s	25
11	J Trulli	1m17.610s	30
12	N Heidfeld	1m17.622s	18
13	R Kubica	1m17.844s	34
14	M Webber	1m17.908s	14
15	K Räikkönen	1m17.933s	4
16	J Villeneuve	1m18.007s	13
17	F Massa	1m18.223s	19
18	JP Montoya	1m18.261s	5
19	N Rosberg	1m18.283s	18
20	D Coulthard	1m18.410s	6
21	N Jani	1m18.774s	32
22	G Mondini	1m18.910s	22
23	S Speed	1m19.257s	22
24	V Liuzzi	1m19.334s	18
25	C Albers	1m19.358s	15
26	T Sato	1m19.616s	30
27	T Monteiro	1m20.311s	19
28	F Montagny	1m22.222s	21

PRACTICE 3

	Driver	Time	Laps
1	M Schumacher	1m15.658s	14
2	G Fisichella	1m15.707s	14
3	N Heidfeld	1m16.057s	13
4	C Klien	1m16.277s	12
5	D Coulthard	1m16.352s	16
6	R Barrichello	1m16.399s	16
7	F Massa	1m16.410s	15
8	F Alonso	1m16.595s	10
9	JP Montoya	1m16.660s	9
10	K Räikkönen	1m16.705s	9
11	J Button	1m16.999s	18
12	S Speed	1m17.004s	13
13	R Schumacher	1m17.199s	19
14	V Liuzzi	1m17.240s	19
15	N Rosberg	1m17.645s	14
16	M Webber	1m17.743s	14
17	J Villeneuve	1m17.924s	16
18	J Trulli	1m18.411s	18
19	T Monteiro	1m18.747s	22
20	T Sato	1m18.857s	20
21	C Albers	1m19.587s	19
22	F Montagny	1m20.031s	24

QUALIFYING 1

	Driver	Time
1	F Alonso	1m15.816s
2	G Fisichella	1m16.046s
3	M Schumacher	1m16.049s
4	J Button	1m16.054s
5	J Villeneuve	1m16.066s
6	J Trulli	1m16.174s
7	JP Montoya	1m16.195s
8	R Schumacher	1m16.234s
9	R Barrichello	1m16.266s
10	N Heidfeld	1m16.322s
11	F Massa	1m16.359s
12	K Räikkönen	1m16.613s
13	C Klien	1m16.627s
14	M Webber	1m16.685s
15	V Liuzzi	1m17.105s
16	N Rosberg	1m17.213s
17	S Speed	1m17.361s
18	T Monteiro	1m17.702s
19	C Albers	1m18.024s
20	T Sato	1m18.920s
21	F Montagny	1m20.763s
22	D Coulthard	no time

QUALIFYING 2

	Driver	Time
1	M Schumacher	1m14.637s
2	G Fisichella	1m14.766s
3	J Trulli	1m15.068s
4	F Alonso	1m15.124s
5	J Button	1m15.150s
6	R Schumacher	1m15.164s
7	F Massa	1m15.245s
8	R Barrichello	1m15.258s
9	K Räikkönen	1m15.422s
10	N Heidfeld	1m15.468s
11	M Webber	1m15.502s
12	JP Montoya	1m15.801s
13	N Rosberg	1m15.804s
14	J Villeneuve	1m15.847s
15	C Klien	1m15.928s
16	V Liuzzi	1m16.661s

Best sectors – Practice
Sec 1	G Fisichella	22.519s
Sec 2	G Fisichella	30.234s
Sec 3	M Schumacher	22.689s

Speed trap – Practice
1	J Villeneuve	194.4mph
2	M Schumacher	193.6mph
3	F Massa	193.0mph

Best sectors – Qualifying
Sec 1	M Schumacher	22.134s
Sec 2	F Massa	29.727s
Sec 3	G Fisichella	22.480s

Fernando Alonso
"I didn't get a good start and Fisico reacted better than me, but after that, everything was perfect. It was a day of many emotions, especially the in-lap in front of my people."

Michael Schumacher
"The race was decided in the first stint, as I didn't have the pace to stay with Alonso. After the lap times we'd done earlier in the weekend, this was surprising."

Kimi Räikkönen
"I made a good start, from ninth to fifth and that was all the progress I was able to make. It simply wasn't possible to keep up with the Renaults and Ferraris."

Jenson Button
"Though I was behind Rubens and Räikkönen was able to pull away, as soon as I had clear air, I reeled Räikkönen in, making it a shame that I had problems in qualifying."

Jacques Villeneuve
"The Super Aguris had amazing starts and then there were cars in front and nowhere to go. I was next to Coulthard, but he pushed me wide, which was fair."

Jarno Trulli
"Ralf and I had similar strategies, but I was on old tyres. When he made his move, I took my usual line. I didn't deliberately close the door and didn't feel the collision."

Giancarlo Fisichella
"Things were close into Turn 1, but Fernando had the advantage. When I came out behind Michael, I was pushing, and made a mistake which put me in the Turn 3 gravel."

Felipe Massa
"I had some traffic in a few crucial phases of the race and that's one of the reasons I couldn't close on Giancarlo to try and get past him for third in the run of pit stops."

Juan Pablo Montoya
"I made a dreadful start but was able to gain some ground again in Turn 1. Then I don't know what happened but I lost the car, got stuck on the kerb and that was it."

Rubens Barrichello
"I lost a place off the start and then lost time due to a fuel pressure problem on my in-lap. After that, things ran according to plan, apart from a vibration in the last stint."

Nick Heidfeld
"It was important to overtake Barrichello, as his car was heavy. If he had held me off, I wouldn't have made it into the points, but I passed him on the outside in Turn 1."

Ralf Schumacher
"I was following Jarno and tried to get by on the entry to Turn 1. It wasn't a heavy impact but I lost my wing so had to pit, then was hit by an electronic problem."

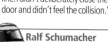

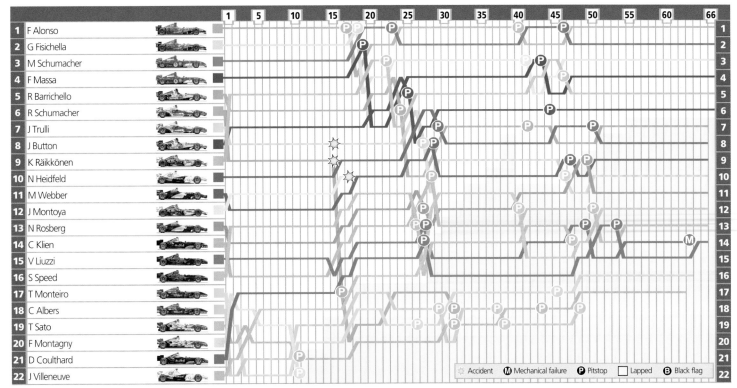

	1	5	10	15	20	25	30	35	40	45	50	55	60	66	
1	F Alonso														1
2	G Fisichella														2
3	M Schumacher														3
4	F Massa														4
5	R Barrichello														5
6	R Schumacher														6
7	J Trulli														7
8	J Button														8
9	K Räikkönen														9
10	N Heidfeld														10
11	M Webber														11
12	J Montoya														12
13	N Rosberg														13
14	C Klien														14
15	V Liuzzi														15
16	S Speed														16
17	T Monteiro														17
18	C Albers														18
19	T Sato														19
20	F Montagny														20
21	D Coulthard														21
22	J Villeneuve														22

☼ Accident   Ⓜ Mechanical failure   Ⓟ Pitstop   ☐ Lapped   Ⓑ Black flag

QUALIFYING 3

	Driver	Time
1	F Alonso	1m14.648s
2	G Fisichella	1m14.709s
3	M Schumacher	1m14.970s
4	F Massa	1m15.442s
5	R Barrichello	1m15.885s
6	R Schumacher	1m15.885s
7	J Trulli	1m15.976s
8	J Button	1m16.008s
9	K Räikkönen	1m16.015s
10	N Heidfeld	1m17.144s

GRID

	Driver	Time
1	F Alonso	1m14.648s
2	G Fisichella	1m14.709s
3	M Schumacher	1m14.970s
4	F Massa	1m15.442s
5	R Barrichello	1m15.885s
6	R Schumacher	1m15.885s
7	J Trulli	1m15.976s
8	J Button	1m16.008s
9	K Räikkönen	1m16.015s
10	N Heidfeld	1m17.144s
11	M Webber	1m15.502s
12	JP Montoya	1m15.801s
13	N Rosberg	1m15.804s
14	C Klien	1m15.928s
15	V Liuzzi	1m16.661s
16	S Speed	1m17.361s
17	T Monteiro	1m17.702s
18	C Albers	1m18.024s
19	T Sato	1m18.920s
20	F Montagny	1m20.763s
21	D Coulthard	no time
22*	J Villeneuve	1m15.847s

*10-PLACE GRID PENALTY

RACE

	Driver	Car	Laps	Time	Avg. mph	Fastest	Stops
1	F Alonso	Renault R26	66	1h26m21.759s	131.783	1m16.723s	2
2	M Schumacher	Ferrari 248	66	1h26m40.261s	131.258	1m16.922s	2
3	G Fisichella	Renault R26	66	1h26m45.710s	131.177	1m17.083s	2
4	F Massa	Ferrari 248	66	1h26m51.618s	131.028	1m16.648s	2
5	K Räikkönen	McLaren-Mercedes MP4-21	66	1h27m18.634s	130.353	1m17.357s	2
6	J Button	Honda RA106	66	1h27m20.106s	130.316	1m17.367s	2
7	R Barrichello	Honda RA106	65	1h26m34.248s	129.477	1m17.399s	2
8	N Heidfeld	Sauber-BMW F1.06	65	1h26m41.014s	129.305	1m17.869s	2
9	M Webber	Williams-Cosworth FW28	65	1h26m42.377s	129.272	1m17.900s	2
10	J Trulli	Toyota TF106	65	1h27m05.221s	128.706	1m18.465s	2
11	N Rosberg	Williams-Cosworth FW28	65	1h27m05.739s	128.694	1m17.861s	2
12	J Villeneuve	Sauber-BMW F1.06	65	1h27m06.907s	128.665	1m18.050s	1
13	C Klien	Red Bull-Ferrari RB2	65	1h27m22.416s	128.284	1m18.516s	2
14	D Coulthard	Red Bull-Ferrari RB2	65	1h27m27.008s	128.172	1m17.862s	2
15	V Liuzzi	Toro Rosso-Cosworth STR01	63	1h24m48.720s	128.090	1m18.488s	2
16	T Monteiro	Midland-Toyota M16	63	1h26m36.951s	125.423	1m19.265s	2
17	T Sato	Super Aguri-Honda SA05	62	1h26m29.247s	123.614	1m20.411s	3
R	C Albers	Midland-Toyota M16	48	Spun off	-	1m19.532s	3
R	S Speed	Toro Rosso-Cosworth STR01	47	Engine	-	1m18.541s	1
R	R Schumacher	Toyota TF106	31	Electronics	-	1m18.621s	1
R	JP Montoya	McLaren-Mercedes MP4-21	17	Spun off	-	1m19.482s	0
R	F Montagny	Super Aguri-Honda SA05	10	Driveshaft	-	1m22.389s	0

CHAMPIONSHIP

	Driver	Pts
1	F Alonso	54
2	M Schumacher	39
3	K Räikkönen	27
4	G Fisichella	24
5	F Massa	20
6	J Button	16
7	JP Montoya	15
8	R Barrichello	8
9	R Schumacher	7
10	N Heidfeld	6
11	M Webber	6
12	J Villeneuve	6
13	N Rosberg	4
14	D Coulthard	1
15	C Klien	1

Speed trap – Qualifying

1	F Massa	198.7mph
2	M Schumacher	195.2mph
3	G Fisichella	193.4mph

Fastest Lap

F Massa 1m16.648s
(135.036mph) on lap 42

Fastest speed trap

F Massa 197.0mph

Slowest speed trap

C Albers 182.7mph

Fastest pit stop

1	D Coulthard	21.187s
2	N Heidfeld	21.449s
3	C Klien	22.288s

Constructor

	Constructor	Pts
1	Renault	78
2	Ferrari	59
3	McLaren-Mercedes	42
4	Honda	24
5	BMW Sauber-BMW	12
6	Williams-Cosworth	10
7	Toyota	7
8	Red Bull-Ferrari	2

David Coulthard

"That was a lonely race. I had a problem with the brakes when going to the grid and locked up a few times. That wasn't confidence inspiring and so I couldn't attack."

Mark Webber

"Our strategy was similar to others, but we weren't fast enough. Barcelona has been a tough venue for us all winter. Finishing a lap down isn't good."

Vitantonio Liuzzi

"It was a mistake to start on used tyres. The second stint was better. The car was going well, but I had to stop with a hydraulic problem with the steering on the last lap."

Tiago Monteiro

"Perhaps it wasn't very apparent, but we had a very good car. It's just too bad that Montagny spun me off early in the race, because it destroyed my race strategy."

Takuma Sato

"I was next to Monteiro when he put me onto the dirt. I regained my place under braking and passed a few cars, but as the tyres were covered in dust I lost it into Turn 4."

Christian Klien

"I lost places to the Toro Rossos at the start. I passed Liuzzi and got closer to Rosberg. After my first stop it was harder to keep pace and I lost ground to Rosberg."

Nico Rosberg

"There was a mistake in my second stop, so I fell behind Trulli, which cost time. I also had my first experience of being lapped and it's not pleasant!"

Scott Speed

"My engine started to let go in the second stint, which is a shame as I made an aggressive move on Rosberg and it paid off. I was 11th, so I thought a point was on."

Christijan Albers

"We didn't have the top speed to be competitive. I was gaining in the corners but losing out on the straights. To make matters worse, my front wing broke."

Franck Montagny

"It's bad that we stopped after 10 laps, but I passed Taku at the start and the two Midlands. We had a little bit of fighting and then after that I had a little bit of space."

FORMULA 1™ GRAND PRIX
DE MONACO 2006
Monte Carlo

LUCKY ALONSO

It's said that luck comes to the good, and this was the case as Alonso's challengers fell by the wayside to let him win, but it will be Michael's actions that will be remembered

Fernando Alonso may have filled another gap on his CV, but the Monaco GP was all about Michael Schumacher and his extraordinary lapse of judgement in qualifying. After the seven-time World Champion had spent years convincing the world to forget about transgressions earlier in his career, he blew it all when he attempted to sabotage the final qualifying runs of his main rivals, and keep pole for himself.

Michael was already on top of the time sheets when the timing monitors revealed that his final effort was not going to be quicker. Behind him, Alonso was on a lap that was going to knock him off the top spot, and there was no time to reply to it. So, when he got to Rascasse, Michael slid straight on and indulged in a bizarre series of steering movements that saw him come to a halt just short of the barrier on the exit. He made no attempt to manoeuvre out of the way, and after apparently killing the engine, climbed out. Meanwhile the yellow flag he created had spoiled the laps of Alonso and several other frustrated top-10 runners. With no time for a restart, pole position was his, for the time being.

The fall-out began almost immediately as rivals expressed their feelings about his tactics. Michael was

FORMULA 1™ GRAND PRIX DE MONACO 2006

stunned by the aggressive questioning he faced in the press conference for the top-three qualifiers, and gradually it dawned on Ferrari's hierarchy that this was a story they could not bury. The stewards announced that they would look into the incident.

Around 10.30pm, came their conclusion: it was decreed that Michael had deliberately tried to hamper other cars and his qualifying times were cancelled. He wouldn't start from pole, but instead from the back of the grid. Unluckily for Ferrari, Felipe Massa was already there, after crashing right at the start of qualifying.

It was an extraordinary turn of events, and even more extraordinary was the way that Ferrari refused to acknowledge that their man could have committed any wrong. Team technical director and tactician Ross Brawn simply got on with planning a way out of the hole: the only solution was to fill up Michael's fuel tank and start him from the pit lane.

In the end, it all turned out well for Alonso, since Ferrari and Bridgestone were clearly going to be strong in the race. Alongside him on the front row, he had Williams racer Mark Webber, who seemed unlikely to be a serious threat over a race distance. His main concern was McLaren's Kimi Räikkönen in third.

Alonso led away at the start, but his life was made harder when Räikkönen sneaked past Webber at the start of the second lap. The Finn stayed close to the Spaniard throughout the first stint, but the first question about their respective fule loads was answered when he pitted on lap 22. Alonso went one lap further, and resumed in front. However, Räikkönen had the fuel to go a lot further in the second stint, so all he had to do was stay in touch and prepare for a sprint after Renault's race leader pitted.

"He was pushing quite hard but it's almost impossible to overtake at Monaco," said Alonso. "I knew that there were important parts of the race, laps close to the pit stops and the laps after the pit stops,

INSIDE LINE
FRANCK MONTAGNY
SUPER AGURI DRIVER

"Alright, I might have been three laps down at the finish and the last car running, but I've finished a grand prix and that was an ambition that at the start of the year looked as though it might not happen.

I had a lot of links with Renault – through Formule Campus, Formule Renault, F3, F3000, Formula Nissan, the Le Mans 24 Hours. I did an F1 test at the same time as Sebastien Bourdais and we set similar times, a tenth or two apart, but in the end they picked me. Why, I really don't really know. Maybe I was better with feedback.

I signed a deal with Renault and then, a year later, when I got the third driver role for 2004, with Flavio Briatore. Part of the deal was that he would find me a race drive, but it didn't happen. I don't know why and I don't really want to know. It's past and I don't think it's important to stir things up, but I'm a free agent now.

Renault gave me the chance to be in F1, so I have to say 'thank you' first and with Super Aguri everything happened very quickly when I wasn't expecting it. I had no drive and was struggling to get something to do this year and they put me into F1, so I'm very happy. They have about 80 people and at Renault it's more like 800, so it's a big difference. Everything at Renault is so professional and perfect, but here everyone is pushing to do their best and things are improving, although it's not easy.

Nor is it easy to get money out of France for F1. It may have been in the Elf days [in the 1970s], but not now. I work quite hard at that side with my manager Gilles Bellec. I've worked with him for 10 years. I set up a kart team with my own mechanics when I was younger. We had five or six kids and one of them was Gilles' son. Gilles is not someone with a book full of contacts, but he knows racing and is very helpful with the communications side, which allows me to get on with driving.

I've got a big, big month coming up – all the F1 plus Le Mans. Every weekend – bang, bang, bang. It's going to be tough and we'll see what happens after that. I don't have long-term plans. At first it was one race with Super Aguri, then two others and now they have contracted me until after the US GP. If I can go to the end of the year and sign a deal for the next five years I'll be more than happy!"

and I wanted to have the tyres in good condition for those laps. For me, it wasn't important to push on lap 30. I pushed two or three laps, he was behind me with no problems, so when I saw that it was impossible to open up a gap, I said 'OK, I will manage the tyres and when it's time to push my tyres will be ready'."

There was an unexpected surprise in the middle of the race as Webber closed in on the leading duo. The Australian's Bridgestones were working well, and we had a three-way battle for the lead in prospect. Alas, Webber had more trouble getting through traffic, and then on lap 49 his race came to a smoky end at Ste Devote after an exhaust failure caused a fire. Later a

OPPOSITE TOP Michael Schumacher was very uncomfortable in the post-qualifying press conference

OPPOSITE BOTTOM Man of the moment Fernando Alonso watches the timing screens

ABOVE Franck Montagny brought his Super Aguri home, three laps down

BELOW Webber and Williams were set for a top finish, until...

similar problem would afflict Nico Rosberg, causing him to hit the barrier at the final corner.

"We knew how much fuel we had on board compared to Fernando and Kimi, because they stopped before us," said Williams technical director Sam Michael. "We put enough fuel to cover both of them. We calculated that Fernando put in enough to get to lap 52/53, and Kimi around 60, so we put in 61 for Mark, but we never saw that unravel. He got caught behind Fisichella, otherwise he had no problem at all sticking with them. He would have been strong."

Those pit stop estimates meant nothing, as Webber had pulled off in an awkward spot, so the safety car had to be deployed. Alonso and Räikkönen pitted immediately, then left together. Much to the frustration of McLaren, Räikkönen wasn't able to use his fuel advantage by running to the planned stops, and it seemed that he'd have to settle for second.

However, even that wasn't to be. Running slowly behind the safety car, Räikkönen had a bodywork fire, the legacy of a revised engine cover, and had to pull off before the tunnel. He'd had a similar incident on the Thursday when running slowly after a practice start at the end of the session and the team had failed to fully address the problem.

"In the pitstop, we had a long period with the engine on high revs," said McLaren chief Ron Dennis. "It heated the exhaust system up to high temperature, and then you go out behind the safety car, and you don't get enough airflow to cool the exhaust. Of course, we normally sort out these things in testing, but this is a new engine cover and new system in that area. So we had a fire in the engine compartment that damaged the wiring loom. It wasn't bad luck, more a reflection of our intensity of development."

A furious Räikkönen walked straight from his car to a yacht on which friends were staying, and never returned to the paddock…

At the restart, Alonso had a lot of traffic between himself and his nearest pursuer, Juan Pablo Montoya, and he enjoyed a cruise to the finish. It certainly made up for 2005, when Renault dropped the ball on its Monaco tyre choice.

Montoya was happy to claim second and his best result of the year, but once again he had been no match for his team-mate. "We were competitive all weekend," said the Colombian. "I lost of a bit of ground in the first stint. I passed a backmarker into the

BELOW Monaco's millionaire paradise spans out in front of Alonso as he races to victory

BOTTOM Rubens Barrichello came home fourth for Honda, wearing friend Tony Kanaan's helmet

OPPOSITE Perhaps one of the most privileged viewing spots of all, at the Grand Hotel hairpin

INSIDE LINE
CHRISTIAN HORNER

**RED BULL
SPORTING DIRECTOR**

"I knew I could be in trouble as soon as I said I'd jump naked into the Red Bull energy station pool if we got a podium. DC was fast all weekend and had it not been for being held up in Q3, he could have started on the first three rows. Fisichella blocked him and, as a result, we started behind Barrichello and

Trulli, both of whom were running one-stop fuel loads. That's why we took the decision to switch DC from a two-stop to a one-stop race, which was the right move but meant him doing 49 laps on his second set of tyres.

Before Monaco, we had just a couple of points to show for the first third of the season. After the strong season we had in 2005, then the excitement of signing Adrian (Newey), some people were a bit deflated. And there have been one or two jibes about how we ought to be winning races, but you can't do things overnight.

Everyone assumes it was the lure of an open cheque book that enticed Adrian, but I first spoke to him informally at Barcelona last year, then invited him to the *Star Wars* bash here in Monte Carlo a year ago. We spoke again at Guy Laliberté's post-Canadian

GP party and it was then that I sensed that he wasn't entirely happy at McLaren and that we may have a chance of signing him. Dietrich (Mateschitz) told me to do what was necessary and, in the end, I think the negotiations took about 10 minutes.

People assume it's money that persuades people to join Red Bull but we try to listen to people and appreciate their personal situations. I'm not talking about Adrian, but some of those who joined us have left positions with other teams where perhaps it was difficult for them to progress. It was 'Dead Man's Shoes' syndrome in certain cases. We try to give them responsibility and they thrive.

Adrian's main role is to concentrate on next year's car and already there is a lot of talk about 2007. Driver-wise, we don't have to make any decisions yet

and I'd say we are 12–18 months away from being able to do justice to the top three drivers. So long as DC is still doing the business on a Sunday afternoon, why change him? He's a great professional, still fully committed, he trains hard, his testing and feedback qualities are excellent and he's a superb ambassador. He's very good at the marketing and PR side. I haven't discussed this player/manager role that people talk about. DC doesn't like to be pigeon-holed and if you suggest he's getting on a bit, he gets a bit tetchy… And you can't argue with a man in a Superman cape!"

fast all weekend, but his qualifying run had been compromised by an unhelpful Fisichella. In turn, that meant that in the race he got stuck behind cars on much heavier fuel loads, so he deserved a little luck.

Rubens Barrichello had an eventful run to fourth, despite a late drive-through penalty for speeding in the pitlane. He still just managed to hold off Michael Schumacher. From his pitlane start, Michael had made great progress in the early laps. Inevitably, he got held up at times behind a driver who had no wish to make his life easy, but an early pit stop on lap 36 got him out of traffic, and later he was able to show his true pace.

Michael lost out when the safety car came out and, ironically, his originally planned stop would have been well-timed. But he continued to charge, and took great chunks out of Barrichello's advantage in the closing laps. Like Räikkönen, he clearly had the pace to beat Alonso in a straight fight.

After moving to the back of the top-10 following a qualifying penalty, Fisichella took a low-key sixth, while the final points went to Nick Heidfeld and Ralf Schumacher. In stark contrast to his team-mate, Massa could recover only to ninth.

"It's been a disappointing and frustrating weekend," said Ferrari chief Jean Todt. "When you know you have a winning potential, and you finish fifth and ninth… If there is a grand prix when you have to be in a good position at the start, it's Monte Carlo. I know that it was a big storm outside of the team among the F1 world about Michael stating that he did it on purpose. We have tried to demonstrate that it was a racing incident. It wasn't considered, so we didn't have any option but to accept it and try to make the best out of the situation."

The smiles as he left parc fermé suggested that Michael had enjoyed his afternoon, but there was no doubt that his behaviour had handed points to his rival. And they were going to be very hard to get back…

ABOVE Kimi Räikkönen and Mark Webber lap Felipe Massa's Ferrari

BELOW LEFT Juan Pablo Montoya stays off the marbles en route to second

BELOW RIGHT If the cape fits... David Coulthard brought a certain style to the podium ceremony after finishing third

chicane, got sideways and lost a bit of time. From there, it was just a matter of trying to keep up, and when Renault and Fernando upped the pace, my car was pretty good so I managed to close the gap."

The biggest surprise was the identity of the driver in third place. For a while, it looked likely to go to Jarno Trulli and Toyota's revised TF106B, but a late retirement put paid to that. A one-stop run from Christian Klien should have seen the Austrian claim his first podium finish, but he too dropped out. So it went instead to his team-mate David Coulthard. The Scot had been

SNAPSHOT FROM
MONACO

CLOCKWISE FROM RIGHT Monaco doesn't
normally take so much out of the tyres; Kimi
Räikkönen proves that he really is 'The Ice Man';
Monaco always manages to make even large
yachts look small; Red Bull's headquarters was
home to *Superman Returns*; Renault F1's MD Flavio
Briatore can never keep away from the pretty
ladies; three generations of the Montoya clan

WEEKEND HEADLINES

- Following their 2005 deal with the final *Star Wars*
  movie, Red Bull linked up with Hollywood once again to
  promote *Superman Returns*. Kevin Spacey was among
  the stars to attend a party, while David Coulthard wore
  a cape when he took to the podium after finishing third.

- The saga of Valentino Rossi's romance with Ferrari came
  to an end when the Italian ace announced that he was
  to stay with Yamaha in Moto GP, having had his hands
  full with a difficult start to the season. Ross Brawn
  admitted he was disappointed that he would not get the
  chance to work with the two-wheeled superstar, who
  had made quite an impression in testing.

- The Monaco paddock was stunned to hear of the death
  of Eduoard Michelin in a boating accident off the
  French coast. The 42-year-old tyre company boss had a
  very hands-on approach to the F1 programme, and in
  2005 had come to Spa-Francorchamps to make an
  impassioned speech that criticised the FIA's plans to
  get rid of tyre competition.

- Rubens Barrichello sported a new look in Monaco
  having agreed to swap helmet designs with IRL racer
  and close friend Tony Kanaan, who in turn ran in
  Barrichello's colours in the Indy 500. Rubens finished
  fourth while Kanaan managed fourth in the US classic,
  which saw Sam Hornish beat teenage rookie Marco
  Andretti in a dash to the line.

- Johnny Servoz-Gavin, the star of the 1968 Monaco GP,
  died at the age of 64 in late May. The Frenchman had led
  the street race for Matra before retiring after clipping a
  barrier. His career stuttered to a halt in 1970 after an eye
  injury meant that he struggled to get the best out of Ken
  Tyrrell's second March 701.

RACE RESULTS
MONACO
MONTE CARLO

RACE DATE May 28th
CIRCUIT LENGTH 2.075 miles
NO. OF LAPS 78
RACE DISTANCE 161.887 miles
WEATHER Dry & bright, 24°C
TRACK TEMP 27°C
RACE DAY ATTENDANCE 120,000
LAP RECORD Michael Schumacher,
1m14.439s, 100.373mph, 2004

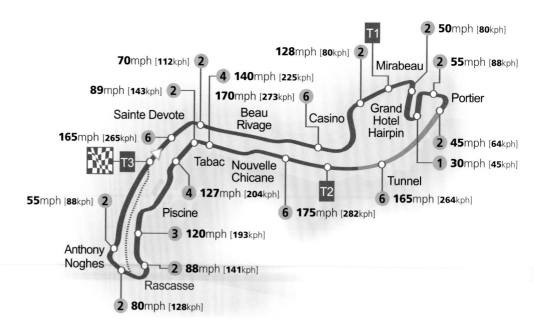

T1
2 **50**mph [**80**kph]
128mph [**80**kph] 2
Mirabeau
2 **55**mph [**88**kph]
70mph [**112**kph] 2
4 **140**mph [**225**kph]
Portier
89mph [**143**kph] 2
170mph [**273**kph] 6
Beau Rivage
Casino
Grand Hotel Hairpin
Sainte Devote
2 **45**mph [**64**kph]
165mph [**265**kph] 6
1 **30**mph [**45**kph]
Tabac Nouvelle Chicane
T2
Tunnel
55mph [**88**kph] 2
4 **127**mph [**204**kph]
6 **165**mph [**264**kph]
Piscine
6 **175**mph [**282**kph]
3 **120**mph [**193**kph]
T3
Anthony Noghes
2 **88**mph [**141**kph]
Rascasse
2 **80**mph [**128**kph]

PRACTICE 1

	Driver	Time	Laps
1	F Alonso	1m16.712s	13
2	A Davidson	1m16.872s	31
3	G Fisichella	1m16.888s	12
4	M Schumacher	1m16.973s	8
5	JP Montoya	1m17.458s	7
6	R Kubica	1m17.869s	19
7	A Wurz	1m17.949s	28
8	J Button	1m18.329s	12
9	R Doornbos	1m18.394s	23
10	R Barrichello	1m18.406s	12
11	D Coulthard	1m18.447s	10
12	N Rosberg	1m18.480s	15
13	M Webber	1m18.571s	17
14	F Massa	1m18.695s	15
15	J Trulli	1m18.703s	11
16	R Schumacher	1m19.021s	14
17	J Villeneuve	1m19.246s	16
18	C Klien	1m19.543s	10
19	N Jani	1m19.651s	25
20	G Mondini	1m19.669s	29
21	T Monteiro	1m19.730s	17
22	V Liuzzi	1m19.857s	16
23	S Speed	1m20.137s	13
24	C Albers	1m20.552s	17
25	T Sato	1m21.144s	23
26	F Montagny	1m21.594s	21
27	K Räikkönen	2m06.592s	3
28	N Heidfeld	no time	1

PRACTICE 2

	Driver	Time	Laps
1	A Wurz	1m15.907s	27
2	A Davidson	1m16.075s	15
3	JP Montoya	1m16.138s	24
4	F Alonso	1m16.221s	18
5	R Doornbos	1m16.292s	36
6	K Räikkönen	1m16.707s	18
7	G Fisichella	1m16.721s	23
8	D Coulthard	1m16.870s	19
9	J Button	1m16.903s	20
10	F Massa	1m17.251s	25
11	J Trulli	1m17.325s	25
12	T Monteiro	1m17.439s	30
13	R Barrichello	1m17.456s	24
14	G Mondini	1m17.497s	30
15	M Schumacher	1m17.603s	25
16	V Liuzzi	1m17.638s	31
17	M Webber	1m17.744s	19
18	R Schumacher	1m17.793s	26
19	N Rosberg	1m17.845s	15
20	J Villeneuve	1m17.874s	13
21	C Klien	1m18.123s	22
22	N Heidfeld	1m18.257s	10
23	S Speed	1m18.420s	29
24	C Albers	1m18.430s	24
25	F Montagny	1m18.731s	19
26	R Kubica	1m19.273s	22
27	N Jani	1m19.445s	27
28	T Sato	1m19.803s	31

PRACTICE 3

	Driver	Time	Laps
1	F Alonso	1m13.823s	19
2	M Schumacher	1m14.031s	20
3	G Fisichella	1m14.056s	20
4	D Coulthard	1m14.550s	19
5	N Rosberg	1m14.623s	17
6	JP Montoya	1m14.785s	21
7	M Webber	1m14.804s	16
8	F Massa	1m14.842s	24
9	J Button	1m15.020s	21
10	K Räikkönen	1m15.124s	17
11	R Barrichello	1m15.283s	20
12	C Klien	1m15.476s	19
13	N Heidfeld	1m15.591s	20
14	T Monteiro	1m15.809s	26
15	C Albers	1m16.066s	26
16	V Liuzzi	1m16.147s	27
17	S Speed	1m16.201s	21
18	J Villeneuve	1m16.285s	27
19	J Trulli	1m16.456s	24
20	T Sato	1m17.148s	24
21	R Schumacher	1m17.860s	21
22	F Montagny	1m17.934s	21

QUALIFYING 1

	Driver	Time
1	K Räikkönen	1m13.887s
2	F Alonso	1m14.232s
3	M Webber	1m14.305s
4	R Schumacher	1m14.412s
5	JP Montoya	1m14.483s
6	C Klien	1m14.489s
7	G Fisichella	1m14.614s
8	R Barrichello	1m14.766s
9	J Trulli	1m14.883s
10	N Rosberg	1m14.888s
11	J Button	1m15.085s
12	D Coulthard	1m15.090s
13	M Schumacher	1m15.118s
14	V Liuzzi	1m15.314s
15	J Villeneuve	1m15.316s
16	N Heidfeld	1m15.324s
17	C Albers	1m15.598s
18	T Monteiro	1m15.993s
19	S Speed	1m16.236s
20	T Sato	1m17.276s
21	F Montagny	1m17.502s
22	F Massa	no time

QUALIFYING 2

	Driver	Time
1	K Räikkönen	1m13.532s
2	F Alonso	1m13.622s
3	G Fisichella	1m13.647s
4	D Coulthard	1m13.687s
5	M Schumacher	1m13.709s
6	M Webber	1m13.728s
7	N Rosberg	1m13.909s
8	J Trulli	1m14.211s
9	JP Montoya	1m14.295s
10	R Barrichello	1m14.312s
11	R Schumacher	1m14.398s
12	C Klien	1m14.747s
13	V Liuzzi	1m14.969s
14	J Button	1m14.982s
15	J Villeneuve	1m15.052s
16	N Heidfeld	1m15.137s

Best sectors – Practice
Sec 1	F Alonso	19.505s
Sec 2	M Schumacher	36.477s
Sec 3	G Fisichella	17.784s

Speed trap – Practice
1	F Massa	176.3mph
2	G Fisichella	176.0mph
3	F Alonso	175.5mph

Best sectors – Qualifying
Sec 1	M Schumacher	19.359s
Sec 2	K Räikkönen	36.293s
Sec 3	D Coulthard	17.522s

Fernando Alonso
"This is a special place for a driver to win. I was surprised by Kimi's speed, but knew I had to look after the tyres. We seemed to have more rear wear problems than our rivals."

Michael Schumacher
"I'm happy to have got up to fifth. I was amazed at how tough the stewards' decision was. I can understand that, from the outside, things might seem a bit strange."

Kimi Räikkönen
"I'd have taken the lead after the second stops, but we lost out when the safety car came out. Then there was a fire caused by a heat shield which damaged a wiring loom."

Jenson Button
"I lost rear grip and had to stop a lot earlier than I wanted. We put on scrubbed tyres and took front wing off. After that the car was doing OK. This was a race to forget."

Jacques Villeneuve
"I caught Button at Ste Devote. Mid-race I had to let the leaders by and Coulthard also got past. I got dirt on my tyres and they were gone. Then I got a drive-through."

Jarno Trulli
"Once again it's a tale of woe! Our pace was good and the tyres consistent. I was bringing the car home and everything was fine until the sudden hydraulic problem."

Giancarlo Fisichella
"I lost my chance of a good finish after the penalty in qualifying. I was behind a lot of traffic for most of the race, but managed to pass Rosberg, Villeneuve and Coulthard."

Felipe Massa
"At the start, I managed to get ahead of the Super Aguris but was slowed by the collision between the Midlands. In the first stint, I lost so much time behind slower cars."

Juan Pablo Montoya
"I struggled with traffic and lost too much time to Alonso to mount a challenge. The car was good, and I think we could have won if things had gone our way."

Rubens Barrichello
"I'm disappointed as I was set for third. I was carrying a lot of fuel but did a good job to keep pace as I was struggling for balance. It was a blow to be called in for the drive-through."

Nick Heidfeld
"I gained four places at the start, but slowed as I thought I'd damaged the car. It turned out I just used the tyres too hard and so I pitted earlier than planned."

Ralf Schumacher
"We lost too many places at the start and I spent the first half of the race behind Heidfeld. We were faster but our strategy didn't allow us to break out of the traffic."

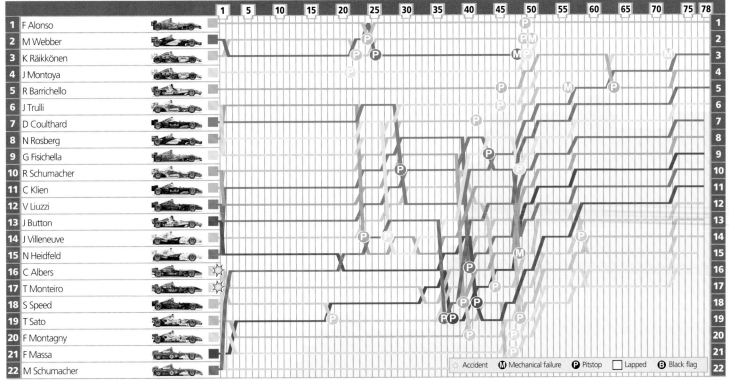

Accident   **M** Mechanical failure   **P** Pitstop   ☐ Lapped   **B** Black flag

QUALIFYING 3

	Driver	Time
1	M Schumacher	1m13.898s
2	F Alonso	1m13.962s
3	M Webber	1m14.082s
4	K Räikkönen	1m14.140s
5	G Fisichella	1m14.396s
6	JP Montoya	1m14.664s
7	R Barrichello	1m15.804s
8	J Trulli	1m15.857s
9	D Coulthard	1m16.426s
10	N Rosberg	1m16.636s

GRID

	Driver	Time
1	F Alonso	1m13.962s
2	M Webber	1m14.082s
3	K Räikkönen	1m14.140s
4	JP Montoya	1m14.664s
5	R Barrichello	1m15.804s
6	J Trulli	1m15.857s
7	D Coulthard	1m16.426s
8	N Rosberg	1m16.636s
9*	G Fisichella	1m14.396s
10	R Schumacher	1m14.398s
11	C Klien	1m14.747s
12	V Liuzzi	1m14.969s
13	J Button	1m14.982s
14	J Villeneuve	1m15.052s
15	N Heidfeld	1m15.137s
16	C Albers	1m15.598s
17	T Monteiro	1m15.993s
18	S Speed	1m16.236s
19	T Sato	1m17.276s
20	F Montagny	1m17.502s
21	F Massa	no time
22^	M Schumacher	1m13.896s

* AFTER REMOVAL OF HIS THREE FASTEST LAPS
^ ALL TIMES CANCELLED FOR CAUSING AN ACCIDENT

RACE

	Driver	Car	Laps	Time	Avg. mph	Fastest	Stops
1	F Alonso	Renault R26	78	1h43m43.116s	93.650	1m15.707s	2
2	JP Montoya	McLaren-Mercedes MP4-21	78	1h43m57.683s	93.431	1m16.008s	2
3	D Coulthard	Red Bull-Ferrari RB2	78	1h44m35.414s	92.869	1m17.849s	1
4	R Barrichello	Honda RA106	78	1h44m36.453s	92.854	1m17.320s	2
5	M Schumacher	Ferrari 248	78	1h44m36.946s	92.841	1m15.143s	1
6	G Fisichella	Renault R26	78	1h44m45.188s	92.725	1m15.919s	2
7	N Heidfeld	BMW-Sauber F1.06	77	1h44m24.512s	91.839	1m17.319s	1
8	R Schumacher	Toyota TF106B	77	1h44m25.993s	91.817	1m17.540s	1
9	F Massa	Ferrari 248	77	1h44m26.526s	91.809	1m16.612s	1
10	V Liuzzi	Toro Rosso-Cosworth STR01	77	1h44m29.101s	91.771	1m17.660s	1
11	J Button	Honda RA106	77	1h44m38.234s	91.637	1m17.300s	1
12	C Albers	Midland-Toyota M16	77	1h44m50.776s	91.455	1m17.603s	2
13	S Speed	Toro Rosso-Cosworth STR01	77	1h44m52.206s	91.434	1m17.481s	1
14	J Villeneuve	BMW-Sauber F1.06	77	1h44m58.768s	91.339	1m17.767s	2
15	T Monteiro	Midland-Toyota M16	76	1h44m18.837s	90.728	1m17.329s	2
16	F Montagny	Super Aguri-Honda SA05	75	1h43m53.299s	89.901	1m19.104s	1
17	J Trulli	Toyota TF106B	72	Hydraulics	-	1m17.180s	1
R	C Klien	Red Bull-Ferrari RB2	56	Transmission	-	1m17.930s	1
R	N Rosberg	Williams-Cosworth FW28	51	Throttle	-	1m17.227s	2
R	K Räikkönen	McLaren-Mercedes MP4-21	50	Fire	-	1m15.325s	2
R	M Webber	Williams-Cosworth FW28	48	Fire	-	1m15.680s	1
R	T Sato	Super Aguri-Honda SA05	46	Electrical	-	1m18.793s	1

CHAMPIONSHIP

	Driver	Pts
1	F Alonso	64
2	M Schumacher	43
3	G Fisichella	27
4	K Räikkönen	27
5	JP Montoya	23
6	F Massa	20
7	J Button	16
8	R Barrichello	13
9	R Schumacher	8
10	N Heidfeld	8
11	D Coulthard	7
12	M Webber	6
13	J Villeneuve	6
14	N Rosberg	4
15	C Klien	1

Speed trap – Qualifying

1	M Schumacher	179.0mph
2	G Fisichella	177.2mph
3	F Alonso	177.0mph

Fastest Lap

M Schumacher 1m15.143s
(99.430mph) on lap 74

Fastest speed trap

	M Schumacher	179.8mph
Slowest speed trap		
	T Monteiro	170.8mph

Fastest pit stop

1	F Alonso	23.553s
2	K Räikkönen	23.555s
3	G Fisichella	24.510s

David Coulthard
"It's been two years since I was on the podium, so it's great to finish on it here in Monaco. It's the first for Red Bull Racing too, a great reward for the team's hard work."

Mark Webber
"I was going longer than Alonso in the second stint and Montoya wasn't a threat, so a podium finish was on. It was an hour of running at qualifying pace."

Vitantonio Liuzzi
"We picked the wrong moment to refuel. At least we finished, but the safety car spoilt our strategy. Tenth place is quite good, but we really should have got points."

Tiago Monteiro
"We had that unnecessary incident at the start, and I lost time on the ensuing pit stop. I had to make up 30s and get past the Super Aguris, so my race was effectively shot."

Takuma Sato
"Our strategy enabled me to push, but I had an electrical issue and the speed dropped, so I pitted and we made a change, but after one lap we suffered total failure."

Christian Klien
"I lost drive. It's such a shame as I was up for a good points finish. It's frustrating that the car wasn't reliable and we need to work harder to get more finishes."

Nico Rosberg
"I was on a two-stop strategy when those around me were one-stopping. Then I had a problem with the throttle sticking open and it pushed me into the barriers."

Scott Speed
"The first lap was ace. After that, I didn't have the pace. I had problems with the rear and I'm finding it difficult to walk as my knee rubbed against the monocoque."

Christijan Albers
"At one point, we were almost the fastest on track. It was a shame to get a drive-through. I have no clue why, as my front wing was ahead. But everyone has their opinion."

Franck Montagny
"I'm happy to have finished for the first time. I had a good fight with Monteiro for 40 laps, but I'm sure that he won't say the same. I enjoyed it."

Constructor

	Constructor	Pts
1	Renault	91
2	Ferrari	63
3	McLaren-Mercedes	50
4	Honda	29
5	BMW Sauber	14
6	Williams-Cosworth	10
7	Toyota	8
8	Red Bull-Ferrari	8

2006 FORMULA 1™ FOSTER'S
BRITISH GRAND PRIX
Silverstone

ALONSO AGAIN

Picking a harder compound tyre than their rivals helped Renault and Fernando Alonso take the glory at Silverstone as Michael Schumacher usurped Räikkönen for second

We had waited a long time to see Fernando Alonso, Kimi Räikkönen and Michael Schumacher line up at the front of the grid together, so the buzz in the run-up to the British GP was quite something. Which of the three drivers – and teams – would get it right?

In the event, the race was a bit of an anti-climax, and even before the strategists showed their hands at the first round of pit stops, Alonso appeared to have things well under control. Furthermore, rather than adding spice to the battle between Renault and Ferrari, Räikkönen's presence actually served to spoil it.

Nevertheless, there was a great scrap for second place between Alonso's two main rivals, and while the Spaniard was pacing himself for much of the race, he wasn't that far ahead. There also remained the nagging question of how much closer Michael would have been had Räikkönen not been in the way for two-thirds of the race.

The big surprise of qualifying was Räikkönen. Fourth on the grid in Australia and Monaco (he was promoted to third by Michael's penalty at the latter), he had been nothing like as competitive over one lap as he had been in 2005 when it seemed that he could be first or second regardless of the fuel load he was

carrying. This season, the package had not had the pace, and more often than not McLaren had erred towards a higher fuel load and in effect opted out of the fight for pole position

This time Räikkönen was very much in it, and he produced an astonishing lap right at the end of the session to go second, splitting Alonso and Michael. What made Räikkönen joining the party fascinating was that the three top teams all had two rivals to try and outguess, rather than the usual one.

From the early laps, Alonso crept away, slowly but surely, and put enough daylight between himself and Räikkönen to make sure that, whatever happened in the stops, he would stay ahead. When Michael peeled into the pits from third place on lap 18, Alonso was already 3.7s clear of Räikkönen – not much, but plenty considering that Renault knew he was going further than his rivals. Räikkönen came in next time around, and then Fernando had three laps on near zero fuel and carefully nursed tyres to hammer home his advantage. And he did it in style.

As soon as Michael signalled the start of the opening pit stop sequence, Alonso banged in three laps that were substantially quicker than the pace at

INSIDE LINE
JENSON BUTTON

HONDA DRIVER

"I get such fantastic support from my home crowd that I was hoping to be able to give them something to cheer about. Being realistic, I knew that we weren't coming in with a real chance of taking on Michael and Fernando. What I didn't expect was to be starting the race 19th after not making it out of Q1! One of the statisticians came up with the fact that it was my worst starting position since 2003, when I was 20th. Guess where? Silverstone again.

On my first run, I felt a lack of grip and didn't want to risk going off. We obviously weren't in the best shape, but Rubens ultimately qualified sixth, so it wasn't disastrous.

I reckoned on improving on my second run but, due to to a combination of circumstances, I didn't get one. I was called in for a random weight-check with about five minutes of the session remaining and it took longer than normal. I think there was also some discussion going on among the team guys and by the time I was ready to go out again I had just missed my slot. There wasn't enough time to complete the out-lap and a flying lap and all I could do was get out of the car and watch everyone else knock me down the order.

Silverstone is high-speed, but it's quite a tough place to overtake.

We saw a cracking race with lots of passing a couple of years ago, but that was down to a combination of changing track conditions and varying tyre performance. I knew I was in for a tough race. I actually made a good start and made up five or six places on the first lap. I was starting to think that if I pushed hard and the strategy worked well, we might even get some points, when suddenly I was in the gravel at Brooklands. An oil leak coated the rear tyres with oil and I was a passenger.

Rubens ended up finishing 10th and what he said about his race kind of mirrors what we are experiencing at the moment. The car seems to work well with new tyres and then the grip and performance seems to go away during the race and we are left fighting it.

It's a bit frustrating, but you have to keep your motivation strong and look for solutions. We have some aerodynamic developments coming through in the next few races and hopefully we'll make progress. The crowd was disappointed, but I still got a fantastic reception as I walked back to the pits, which was pretty moving."

which he had been running, and which were obviously much faster than those of his rivals on heavy fuel loads. The fourth, his in-lap, was a second quicker even than that of Michael.

Able to adjust his fuel load in response to what the others had taken on board, Alonso emerged with his lead having stretched from 3.7s to an astonishing 10.7s between laps 18 and 23. It was a great performance, both on the pit wall and in the cockpit. After that, it was a question of managing the gap, which stayed at around 11–12s throughout the middle stint, although it wasn't all straightforward.

"That's the way we always race, to manage the gap," said Symonds. "We get what we can in the first stint, we check our targets on the second stop, and then we manage it from there.

"We had a lot of graining on the second set of tyres with Fernando. I was becoming concerned then, not worried, just concerned. We could see the understeer was building up, and the lap time wasn't on the targets that we anticipated. But it wasn't enough to put us in danger. It was the only bit that wasn't quite to plan, really."

The second round of pit stops followed a similar pattern to the first, with Michael coming in on lap 41, Räikkönen on lap 42, and Alonso two rather than three laps later, on lap 44. Before it all kicked off he had an 11.3s lead on Räikkönen, and after it he had 12.4s over Michael.

Beating the Renault was always going to be a difficult job, but McLaren were none too pleased to ultimately lose second place in the race to Michael at the final round of pit stops, thanks to a typical Michael/Ross Brawn double act.

As the second stops approached, Brawn tried exactly the same ploy that Renault used in an attempt to get past Schumacher at Imola. It didn't work for Alonso, but it did work this time for Michael…

Like Symonds in Italy, Brawn suspected that Michael would follow Räikkönen into the pits and, that being the case, the chances were that he would follow him straight out again. So what he did was gamble and bring Michael in early. In fact, Ferrari had tried the same thing at the first stops, and it very nearly worked. Brawn wouldn't say when Michael was due to stop first time around, but it did mean that Michael had not been four laps, or 12kg, lighter than Fernando in qualifying, as would otherwise be the case.

OPPOSITE Kimi Räikkönen harnessed all of his powers of concentration for a front row slot

BELOW The Silverstone crowd willed Honda's Jenson Button to succeed, but it wasn't to be

INSIDE LINE
OTMAR SZAFNAUER
VICE PRESIDENT, HONDA RACING DEVELOPMENT

"At Silverstone, there was constant talk about [FIA President] Max Mosley's plan to introduce homologated engines in 2008 and attempts to move that date forward to 2007. Politics, yes, but important politics.

Honda is completely against homologation. There will be no opportunity to develop engines and you'll know every race where everyone is going to start and finish. Do we want that? You'll be taking out one big variable at a time when you are already taking out another by having a single tyre supplier. We've already got a situation where the chassis are very similar due to the tight constraints of the rules. What we'll end up with is a situation where the drivers are the only variable. Some people will say that's good, but there are already lots of formulae that are all about drivers. And they don't get an audience.

Max came here and said that the rules will be as already published for 2008, but we've got to remember that one of the premises of making the 2008 sign-up process so very short — the time window went from a year-and-a-half to two weeks — was that we needed to know who the participants were so that they could have an active role in making the regulations! Besides, there's proper process for making changes and it's written in the sporting regulations, Appendix 5. That includes engine homologation.

Max can't deny that, as those are the FIA's rules. This only happened a couple of months ago and our memories aren't that short!

Then there's this facility to make 'reliability changes' at the discretion of the FIA. That happened in the Indy Racing League in the USA when, behind the backs of some of the manufacturers, there were a lot of changes. It's a dangerous situation.

Max says that when a manufacturer doesn't win, they will leave.

But, at the same time, when a manufacturer isn't winning and doesn't have the ability to develop into a winner, it damages the brand. If you're not winning and you're stuck with that for three years, then people will leave.

In IRL, the cars were similar and so a bit of difference in horsepower had a huge effect. Honda said, 'Look, we can't continue to lose every race, you're going to have to allow us to change,' and so the IRL said 'OK'. The change we made was massive, so then Toyota came back and said that they weren't going to lose either. But the IRL didn't tell Honda that they were allowing Toyota to change. We discovered it by comparing two engines and noticing that they were different.

When people think that the regulator is not being fair, they leave. For example, Toyota left the IRL. Now we're looking at the same situation in F1 for three years."

BELOW Jarno Trulli gave it his all, but starting from dead last made the expectation of points unrealistic

OPPOSITE TOP Jacques Villeneuve demonstrated that getting married hadn't blunted his speed

OPPOSITE BOTTOM Time to deliver: Becketts. Fernando Alonso used his speed through here to claim another pole for Renault

To make the early second stop work, the team couldn't tip off McLaren, because if the Woking team was on the ball it could also bring Räikkönen in early and negate the Ferrari tactic. Thus the Ferrari crew did not head into the pit lane until the very last second, so that McLaren had no time to change plans. Interestingly, Brawn admitted that to make that work the crew wasn't told until the very last moment. Had they been given an early warning, the body language would have been a bit of a give-away, even if they didn't head straight out into the pit lane.

It worked. Michael was right behind Räikkönen, but drove an exceptionally quick in-lap followed by a typically brilliant out-lap. The Finn lost 0.2s to Michael on his own in-lap and a little more in the pit lane. He then seemed to make a sluggish departure – the result of a brief fire – and as he headed out of the pit exit, Michael swept past with more than enough advantage to steal the position.

"There was a little problem in that we had a small airbox fire that cost us a little bit of a time," said McLaren Chief Executive Officer Martin Whitmarsh. "In an F1 engine, it's not a very rare thing but it's not something that you want. There's quite a lot of fuel around with the airbox system, and it can catch alight, and the consequence of course is that it consumes the oxygen that the engine is about to see, so it gives a cough and a splutter and it can stall the engine. So that made us a little bit slow away."

The change in the identity of his pursuer didn't make much difference to Alonso, and while Michael did briefly look like a threat, much to his frustration, Fernando responded with ease.

For once the gap didn't shrink in the closing laps as the leader backed off – Alonso was at the end of the two-race cycle with this engine – and in fact it was the opposition who went slower and allowed the gap to grow, but only from a low of 10.8s with four laps to go, to 13.9s at the flag.

The bottom line was that Alonso won the race with his qualifying performance, which saw him carrying some 9kg more than Räikkönen. Ferrari team supremo Jean Todt had to concede that Alonso was faster: "It was two or three tenths, which is not a lot," said the Ferrari chief. "But if you multiply that by 60 it makes 12–18s. And definitely they were quicker yesterday in qualifying. Michael at the beginning probably could have been quicker if we had not been behind Räikkönen, but he was behind."

We saw at races like Imola and Barcelona that McLaren was nearly but not quite there on race pace,

and it was more of the same at Silverstone. Räikkönen was frustratingly close to Alonso when he made his first stop – he was carrying 9kg less after all – and in the end his choice to go with the harder Michelin might have made the difference.

The rest of the field really were in a different race. Felipe Massa ran fourth in the first stint, much to the frustration of Giancarlo Fisichella, who was stuck behind the second Ferrari. They traded places when the Italian ran two laps longer to the first round of pitstops. Juan Pablo Montoya, winner at Silverstone in 2005, finished a distant sixth, way off the pace of his team-mate. He wasn't helped by a first corner nudge from BMW Sauber's Jacques Villeneuve which damaged the sidepod and left him trapped behind the Canadian's team-mate Nick Heidfeld.

The incident did Villeneuve no favours, but the double Silverstone winner had a good run to eighth place, finishing behind team-mate Heidfeld. Indeed, BMW Sauber had looked very strong all meeting, although their qualifying form had been compromised by carrying heavy fuel loads.

Nico Rosberg was outside the points-scoring positions in ninth, one place ahead of Rubens Barrichello in another dire weekend for Honda. Jenson Button had failed to make it through the first round of qualifying after the team underestimated the pace needed to get through the 15-minute session and the home crowd favourite failed to go out for a second run, which was a massive disappointment for all concerned. As a result, he started 19th but, after passing a few stragglers, spun to a smoky halt after oil leaked onto his rear tyres. At least he got further than Mark Webber, whose Williams was harpooned by Ralf Schumacher on the first lap after the German was nudged off line out of Becketts by Scott Speed and came back across the track to take him out.

After the race, the big question around the paddock was what could Michael have done had he not been stuck behind Räikkönen for the first stint of the race. The seven-time World Champion certainly ran at a near identical pace to the Renault driver for the latter two-thirds of the race, but Brawn admitted that Alonso had the edge on the day. Even Ferrari's Todt praised the Spaniard's efforts.

"He's scored 74 points out of 80," said the Frenchman. "It's remarkable. He's quick, competitive, and reliable, so it's made things more difficult for the others. Michael has 51 points, so it all depends on how we perform in the next 10 races."

ABOVE LEFT Schumacher scorches around his out-lap to advance to second place as Räikkönen (on the screen) makes his second stop

LEFT Alonso completes another excellent day at the office, winning as he pleased

SNAPSHOT FROM
BRITAIN

CLOCKWISE FROM RIGHT Silverstone's grandstands were packed, but not every fan was shouting for victory by Button or Coulthard; heading out for a quick lap...; "Pull up here Herr Schumacher"; a novel rear wing was sported by newly-married Jacques Villeneuve on his BMW Sauber; I'll raise you a bag of sweets that my Fernando beats your Michael; some come for the racing, others for the reflected glory

WEEKEND HEADLINES

■ A dreadful weekend for Honda brought the team's current problems sharply into focus, and a few days after the race it was announced that Technical Director Geoff Willis had gone on 'gardening leave', although team boss Nick Fry continued to insist that Willis could still have some role with the team.

■ Following his indiscretion at the end of qualifying in Monaco when he brought the session to a premature close, Michael Schumacher was the subject of much criticism from other drivers, and some made it clear that they felt he was not the right man to be championing safety issues for the Grand Prix Drivers' Association. However a meeting at Silverstone proved to be a damp squib after the majority of members chose to stay silent.

■ On a positive note, the GPDA had made progress with plans to improve safety in testing after drivers had become uncomfortable with the lack of medical and marshalling cover compared to race weekends. The GPDA vowed to find out what was required, while the teams agreed to fund improvements.

■ Having forsaken his Formula Nippon campaign back home in Japan, Sakon Yamamoto drove a third car for Super Aguri on Friday in preparation for taking over the second race seat later in the year. His lack of experience and the need to get him mileage meant that Franck Montagny would continue to race until further notice.

■ FIA President Max Mosley reiterated in a press conference his support for a 'greener' future for F1, and in particular the use of regenerative power devices. Meanwhile, the battle over the introduction of an engine freeze for 2008 gathered momentum as the manufacturers continued to push for a degree of flexibility.

RACE RESULTS
BRITAIN
SILVERSTONE

RACE DATE June 11th
CIRCUIT LENGTH 3.193 miles
NO. OF LAPS 60
RACE DISTANCE 191.064 miles
WEATHER Sunny & dry, 26°C
TRACK TEMP 42°C
RACE DAY ATTENDANCE 78,000
LAP RECORD Michael Schumacher,
1m18.739s, 146.059mph, 2004

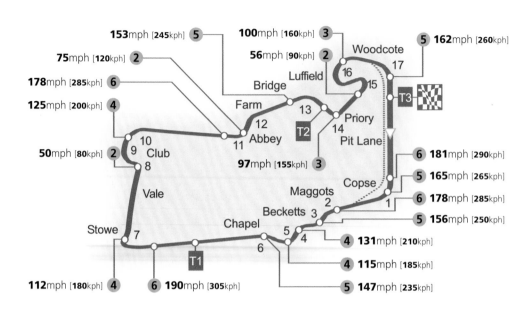

PRACTICE 1

	Driver	Time	Laps
1	A Wurz	1m21.946s	26
2	A Davidson	1m22.003s	31
3	R Kubica	1m22.365s	30
4	J Trulli	1m22.877s	7
5	M Schumacher	1m22.925s	3
6	R Barrichello	1m23.128s	5
7	J Button	1m23.415s	6
8	F Massa	1m23.816s	4
9	C Albers	1m24.019s	6
10	T Monteiro	1m24.070s	6
11	G Mondini	1m24.087s	19
12	N Jani	1m24.145s	22
13	T Sato	1m27.724s	10
14	S Yamamoto	1m29.678s	22
15	R Doornbos	no time	9
16	F Montagny	no time	3
17	R Schumacher	no time	2
18	F Alonso	no time	1
19	D Coulthard	no time	1
20	G Fisichella	no time	1
21	N Heidfeld	no time	1
22	C Klien	no time	1
23	V Liuzzi	no time	1
24	JP Montoya	no time	1
25	K Räikkönen	no time	1
26	S Speed	no time	1
27	J Villeneuve	no time	1
28	N Rosberg	no time	0
29	M Webber	no time	0

PRACTICE 2

	Driver	Time	Laps
1	R Kubica	1m21.082s	29
2	G Fisichella	1m22.294s	3
3	A Wurz	1m22.300s	30
4	A Davidson	1m22.310s	34
5	J Trulli	1m22.437s	17
6	F Massa	1m22.476s	19
7	F Alonso	1m22.603s	13
8	M Schumacher	1m22.825s	14
9	M Webber	1m23.099s	15
10	R Barrichello	1m23.104s	17
11	R Schumacher	1m23.114s	22
12	R Doornbos	1m23.140s	25
13	T Monteiro	1m23.194s	23
14	JP Montoya	1m23.199s	10
15	C Albers	1m23.499s	14
16	G Mondini	1m23.529s	25
17	J Button	1m23.707s	18
18	J Villeneuve	1m23.750s	13
19	N Rosberg	1m23.816s	16
20	N Heidfeld	1m23.895s	14
21	K Räikkönen	1m23.915s	4
22	V Liuzzi	1m24.012s	19
23	C Klien	1m24.158s	12
24	S Speed	1m24.167s	19
25	D Coulthard	1m24.392s	13
26	N Jani	1m24.666s	22
27	T Sato	1m25.870s	26
28	F Montagny	1m26.248s	22
29	S Yamamoto	1m27.908s	27

PRACTICE 3

	Driver	Time	Laps
1	M Schumacher	1m20.919s	13
2	N Heidfeld	1m21.361s	13
3	F Massa	1m21.633s	15
4	K Räikkönen	1m21.771s	12
5	G Fisichella	1m21.859s	12
6	F Alonso	1m21.870s	13
7	R Barrichello	1m22.023s	12
8	J Villeneuve	1m22.229s	14
9	V Liuzzi	1m22.456s	18
10	S Speed	1m22.532s	14
11	J Button	1m22.596s	15
12	D Coulthard	1m22.681s	15
13	T Monteiro	1m22.812s	19
14	C Klien	1m22.921s	14
15	JP Montoya	1m23.412s	7
16	J Trulli	1m23.459s	13
17	M Webber	1m23.964s	12
18	N Rosberg	1m24.010s	11
19	R Schumacher	1m24.386s	12
20	F Montagny	1m27.229s	10
21	T Sato	1m27.525s	12
22	C Albers	no time	3

QUALIFYING 1

	Driver	Time
1	F Alonso	1m21.018s
2	J Villeneuve	1m21.637s
3	F Massa	1m21.647s
4	K Räikkönen	1m21.648s
5	N Heidfeld	1m21.670s
6	M Schumacher	1m22.096s
7	JP Montoya	1m22.169s
8	G Fisichella	1m22.411s
9	D Coulthard	1m22.424s
10	S Speed	1m22.541s
11	V Liuzzi	1m22.685s
12	C Klien	1m22.773s
13	T Monteiro	1m22.860s
14	R Schumacher	1m22.886s
15	R Barrichello	1m22.965s
16	N Rosberg	1m23.083s
17	M Webber	1m23.129s
18	C Albers	1m23.210s
19	J Button	1m23.247s
20	T Sato	1m26.158s
21	F Montagny	1m26.316s
22	J Trulli	no time

QUALIFYING 2

	Driver	Time
1	F Alonso	1m20.271s
2	K Räikkönen	1m20.497s
3	G Fisichella	1m20.594s
4	N Heidfeld	1m20.629s
5	M Schumacher	1m20.659s
6	J Villeneuve	1m20.672s
7	JP Montoya	1m20.816s
8	F Massa	1m20.929s
9	R Barrichello	1m20.929s
10	R Schumacher	1m21.043s
11	D Coulthard	1m21.442s
12	N Rosberg	1m21.567s
13	V Liuzzi	1m21.699s
14	C Klien	1m21.990s
15	S Speed	1m22.076s
16	T Monteiro	1m22.207s

Best sectors – Practice

Sec 1	F Massa	25.376s
Sec 2	R Kubica	35.118s
Sec 3	M Schumacher	20.236s

Speed trap – Practice

1	F Massa	179.8mph
2	M Schumacher	178.5mph
3	F Alonso	178.5mph

Best sectors – Qualifying

Sec 1	F Alonso	25.166s
Sec 2	K Räikkönen	34.522s
Sec 3	K Räikkönen	20.204s

Fernando Alonso
"This is one of the classic races you want to win. Britain is the home of motorsport, I live half an hour from the track and, of course, we have a big part of our team nearby."

Michael Schumacher
"Second was the best we could do. We weren't quick enough. For much of the race I was behind Kimi though I had more potential, which is why second isn't so bad."

Kimi Räikkönen
"I wasn't fast enough on the straights to pass Alonso. I could close the gap, but that was it. I had oversteer towards the end, letting Fisichella close up."

Jenson Button
"We weren't as fast as the leaders, but the car was working well and had a good balance. But then I saw flames out of the back of the car and went off due to oil on the tyres."

Jacques Villeneuve
"Rosberg got me into Turn 1 as Montoya and I crashed. I was stuck behind Nico for 75% of the race, but when he pitted three laps before me, I took risks on old tyres."

Jarno Trulli
"It was always hard from the back of the grid, but I enjoyed it. I made it past a lot of cars in the first few laps. Thanks to good strategy, we were able to gain more places."

Giancarlo Fisichella
"There was graining in the second stint. I was then faster than Kimi in the first sector, but he was quicker in the second and third parts as they had more downforce."

Felipe Massa
"Renault showed itself to be very strong. I lost a place to Fisichella in the way the stops played out. I don't think I could have done better than this fifth place."

Juan Pablo Montoya
"A shame that Villeneuve hit my car going into the first corner, as our strategy would have seen us have a much stronger race. After that, I struggled with the balance."

Rubens Barrichello
"I'm really disappointed to finish 10th. The car works well with new tyres and then the performance just goes away during the race and I just seem to be fighting the car."

Nick Heidfeld
"I passed two cars off the grid and a third at the first corner. I was able to keep ahead of Montoya as I stayed out longer. Unluckily, first gear didn't work in my first stop."

Ralf Schumacher
"I lost too many places at the start. I had cars all around me and was hit from behind. That sent me into a spin, which meant that I couldn't help veering into Mark's path."

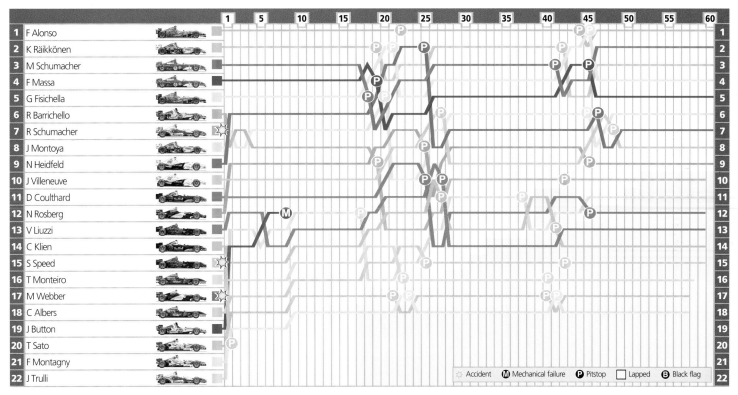

	Driver		1	5	10	15	20	25	30	35	40	45	50	55	60	
1	F Alonso															1
2	K Räikkönen															2
3	M Schumacher															3
4	F Massa															4
5	G Fisichella															5
6	R Barrichello															6
7	R Schumacher															7
8	J Montoya															8
9	N Heidfeld															9
10	J Villeneuve															10
11	D Coulthard															11
12	N Rosberg															12
13	V Liuzzi															13
14	C Klien															14
15	S Speed															15
16	T Monteiro															16
17	M Webber															17
18	C Albers															18
19	J Button															19
20	T Sato															20
21	F Montagny															21
22	J Trulli															22

Accident   (M) Mechanical failure   (P) Pitstop   ☐ Lapped   (B) Black flag

QUALIFYING 3

	Driver	Time
1	F Alonso	1m20.253s
2	K Räikkönen	1m20.397s
3	M Schumacher	1m20.574s
4	F Massa	1m20.764s
5	G Fisichella	1m20.919s
6	R Barrichello	1m20.943s
7	R Schumacher	1m21.073s
8	JP Montoya	1m21.107s
9	N Heidfeld	1m21.329s
10	J Villeneuve	1m21.599s

GRID

	Driver	Time
1	F Alonso	1m20.253s
2	K Räikkönen	1m20.397s
3	M Schumacher	1m20.574s
4	F Massa	1m20.764s
5	G Fisichella	1m20.919s
6	R Barrichello	1m20.943s
7	R Schumacher	1m21.073s
8	JP Montoya	1m21.107s
9	N Heidfeld	1m21.329s
10	J Villeneuve	1m21.599s
11	D Coulthard	1m21.442s
12	N Rosberg	1m21.567s
13	V Liuzzi	1m21.699s
14	C Klien	1m21.990s
15	S Speed	1m22.076s
16	T Monteiro	1m22.207s
17	M Webber	1m23.129s
18	C Albers	1m23.210s
19	J Button	1m23.247s
20	F Montagny	1m26.316s
21*	T Sato	1m26.158s
22	J Trulli	no time

*10-PLACE GRID PENALTY

RACE

	Driver	Car	Laps	Time	Avg. mph	Fastest	Stops
1	F Alonso	Renault R26	60	1h25m51.927s	133.892	1m21.599s	2
2	M Schumacher	Ferrari 248	60	1h26m05.878s	133.531	1m21.934s	2
3	K Räikkönen	McLaren-Mercedes MP4-21	60	1h26m10.599s	133.408	1m22.461s	2
4	G Fisichella	Renault R26	60	1h26m11.903s	133.375	1m22.238s	2
5	F Massa	Ferrari 248	60	1h26m23.486s	133.077	1m22.371s	2
6	JP Montoya	McLaren-Mercedes MP4-21	60	1h26m56.696s	132.230	1m22.780s	2
7	N Heidfeld	BMW Sauber F1.06	60	1h27m03.521s	132.057	1m22.706s	2
8	J Villeneuve	BMW Sauber F1.06	60	1h27m10.226s	131.888	1m22.921s	2
9	N Rosberg	Williams-Cosworth FW28	60	1h27m10.935s	131.870	1m22.916s	2
10	R Barrichello	Honda RA106	59	1h26m07.481s	131.263	1m23.224s	2
11	J Trulli	Toyota TF106B	59	1h26m15.457s	131.061	1m22.744s	2
12	D Coulthard	Red Bull-Ferrari RB2	59	1h26m35.684s	130.551	1m23.995s	2
13	V Liuzzi	Toro Rosso-Cosworth STR01	59	1h26m46.427s	130.281	1m24.221s	1
14	C Klien	Red Bull-Ferrari RB2	59	1h26m51.727s	130.149	1m23.712s	2
15	C Albers	Midland-Toyota M16	59	1h27m05.479s	129.807	1m23.977s	2
16	T Monteiro	Midland-Toyota M16	58	1h26m08.346s	129.016	1m24.636s	2
17	T Sato	Super Aguri-Honda SA05	57	1h26m37.391s	126.083	1m26.520s	2
18	F Montagny	Super Aguri-Honda SA05	57	1h27m03.191s	125.460	1m27.167s	2
R	J Button	Honda RA106	8	Oil leak	-	1m25.207s	0
R	S Speed	Toro Rosso-Cosworth STR01	1	Crash damage	-	2m08.623s	0
R	R Schumacher	Toyota TF106B	0	Accident	-	-	0
R	M Webber	Williams-Cosworth FW28	0	Accident	-	-	0

CHAMPIONSHIP

	Driver	Pts
1	F Alonso	74
2	M Schumacher	51
3	K Räikkönen	33
4	G Fisichella	32
5	JP Montoya	26
6	F Massa	24
7	J Button	16
8	R Barrichello	13
9	N Heidfeld	10
10	R Schumacher	8
11	D Coulthard	7
	J Villeneuve	7
13	M Webber	6
14	N Rosberg	4
15	C Klien	1

	Constructor	Pts
1	Renault	106
2	Ferrari	75
3	McLaren-Mercedes	59
4	Honda	29
5	BMW Sauber	17
6	Williams-Cosworth	10
7	Toyota	8
8	Red Bull-Ferrari	8

Speed trap – Qualifying

1	M Schumacher	182.4mph
2	F Massa	181.4mph
3	F Alonso	179.8mph

Fastest Lap

F Alonso 1m21.599s
(140.940mph) on lap 21

Fastest speed trap

M Schumacher 182.9mph

Slowest speed trap

T Sato 174.9mph

Fastest pit stop

1	J Villeneuve	21.047s
2	F Massa	21.301s
3	JP Montoya	21.529s

David Coulthard

"The car had a lot of understeer. I thought I might have damaged its underside when I was pushed over the kerb at Stowe by Jacques on the opening lap."

Mark Webber

"It looked like Speed clipped Ralf into Becketts which caused Ralf to spin. Ralf was trying to save his car, but he came back across the track, so I had nowhere to go."

Vitantonio Liuzzi

"Early on, I couldn't keep up with the group ahead of me, so we changed our strategy. Silverstone was likely to be tough for us, as the V10 was never going to be ideal."

Tiago Monteiro

"The advantage we gained by making it to Q2 hindered us as we had to use all the tyres we had and didn't have new tyres for the race. We gambled, and it didn't pay off."

Takuma Sato

"We were quite off the pace today and it proved to be a tough race for us, but the next two rounds have different track characteristics to Silverstone."

Christian Klien

"I had a lot of understeer and struggled in high-speed corners. The second stint was better, but unfortunately not enough to jump ahead of Tonio."

Nico Rosberg

"It's disappointing pushing all race and coming away with zero. I gained three places at the start, but was surprised not to get ahead of Villeneuve after his second stop."

Scott Speed

"I had an awesome start and got past Tonio and Christian. I tried to pass Ralf in the left-hander at Becketts. I came alongside him in the right-hand part, and we tangled."

Christijan Albers

"Everybody passed me when I let out the clutch. Tiago held me up a little bit. But, when he made his stop, I was able to push ahead and stay out front."

Franck Montagny

"I don't know if it was the tyres or not, but the car was unstable. After a few laps, the track improved and the car got a little better, but I still had no traction at all."

FORMULA 1™ GRAND PRIX DU CANADA 2006
Montréal

FORMULA FERNANDO

Safety car interruptions made Fernando Alonso work all the harder, but he was untouchable as he raced to his fourth straight victory, his sixth of the season

The Canadian GP represented the halfway mark of the championship, and to keep the title fight alive we really needed to see Michael Schumacher finishing ahead of Fernando Alonso. However, the Spaniard's relentless march towards his second consecutive Formula One crown continued unabated. His German opponent lost only two points to his rival, but the numbers were starting to become harder.

Strangely, it was Alonso who came to the Canadian Grand Prix hoping not to lose out too much to his main rival. "I think it will be difficult to increase [the lead] coming to two races where probably Ferrari are the favourites for the straightline speed they have," he said on Thursday. "I think we have to defend here a little bit, and hopefully finish in front of them, but it will be extremely difficult…"

Alonso was keen to put the memories of 2005's Canadian GP behind him. On that occasion, he spent a chunk of the race stuck behind team-mate Giancarlo Fisichella and, once in free air, he was told to push by his team in order to ensure that he dealt with the threat from Juan Pablo Montoya. He did so, but subsequently hit the wall.

This time, nothing went wrong. Alonso claimed

INSIDE LINE
JACQUES VILLENEUVE

BMW SAUBER DRIVER

"Coming into my home race in Montréal, everything was going well, both in and out of the car. (Jacques had both married and released a record within the past month). We scored good points at Silverstone on merit when we got both cars to the finish and nobody broke down. That was a good indication of our progress and I was hoping to carry it through with a good performance in Montréal.

Expectations were high from the whole team. The tyre geometry seemed to be working very well and I think that's the area where we have made the main gain. You are always a bit careful not to be too overconfident ahead of a race because you can always have a bad surprise but, in general, Montréal is a track where we thought we would be competitive.

I qualified 11th and was seventh at the end of the first lap. We were pretty heavy with fuel and ran 33 laps before our first pit stop. We were looking good for another double helping of points with me seventh and Nick eighth, but then I lost a bit of time at my second stop and he got by me.

It was still going to be a point but, with about 10 laps to go, I came up to lap Ralf Schumacher, who was struggling. He eventually moved out of the way, but unfortunately he did it in a corner and was still on the line. There was a huge build-up of marbles off the line, bigger this year because of the softer tyres, and it was just like being on ice. I went straight off, pretty hard. It was very annoying.

In general, 2006 has been a good and busy year. Life outside the car is going great, so there's nothing to complain about, but 100 per cent of my focus is still on racing and, right now, the contract talks beyond the end of the year are a calm area. The earlier it is sorted the better and I definitely want to be with BMW in 2007.

I don't consider myself old and I don't really understand the notions people have that you should bring in young, inexperienced drivers who aren't necessarily going to do as good a job, just because they are different. You notice different attitudes about that in America. In the US, there's an Establishment and drivers can have 30-year careers. Sure, they might slow down in their 40s and 50s, but their reputations don't suffer and the fans still want to see them. In Europe, it's the opposite. F1 wants to replace its established drivers with young unknowns who are largely over-hyped, and that's damaging F1's reputation as the pinnacle of motorsport because it suggests anyone can handle an F1 car."

another pole position, and with Fisichella putting in a great effort to qualify second and in theory ride shotgun, he looked well set, certainly as far as Michael's prospects were concerned. Kimi Räikkönen and Jarno Trulli had both sneaked into the picture, demoting the Ferrari star to fifth.

"We didn't expect Trulli to be there. That was the key," said Ferrari Technical Director Ross Brawn. "If he hadn't been in there everything would have been perfect. But he was, and maybe we should have run a little bit lighter [in qualifying] to avoid that. That was really the story of the race…"

Ferrari gambled on rushing in a new start procedure that had been tested by Luca Badoer. If it worked well, from fifth place Michael might be able to hustle past one of the lighter cars even before Turn 1.

Much rested on the new procedure. And while he had done lots of practice starts at the pit exit, when it really mattered he got away badly (as did Massa further back). Not only did he fail to beat Trulli away, but Nico Rosberg got past before Turn 1. Perhaps a little flustered, Michael was then hustled out of the way by an aggressive Juan Pablo Montoya. Luck played a part when Rosberg and Montoya collided, but the real problem was Trulli.

"We're trying to develop the start," said Brawn. "We're obviously looking to win, not finish second, so we took a bit more of a risk, and it didn't work very well. We will have to go back and understand it. As it turned out, I don't think it cost us anything, because Montoya helped us out [by colliding with Rosberg]. But it wasn't a great start…"

At Silverstone, Alonso was fastest and still pitted later than his rivals, but things worked out differently here. Indeed, for the first third of the race life was anything but easy for Alonso. His biggest problem was that Fisichella screwed up the start by creeping forward and duly earning a jumped start penalty. To

add insult to injury, he hesitated and was still beaten away by Räikkönen from third on the grid. This was the second time that Fisichella had blown a front row slot, after stalling in the Australian GP.

So, the first third of the race was pretty good as Alonso and Räikkönen pulled well clear of the rest. When Fisichella took his drive-through penalty, he emerged behind Trulli and Michael, and the Toyota man ensured that the gap to the leaders grew by the lap. Michael finally got past just before Trulli pitted.

"Jarno was probably costing us the best part of a second a lap early on," said Brawn. "For a while, he wasn't bad, but then he started to suffer and was costing us a lot of time. Just before he came in, his tyres were finished, and Michael was able to overtake quite easily."

Räikkönen kept Alonso honest and at one point had a serious go at him on the run to the final turn. That turned out to be his one big effort as the gap between the pair varied with their tyre performance.

The crucial moment came when Alonso was the first to dive into the pits on lap 23, and Räikkönen kept going not just for one lap, but for two. That should have been enough to give him a real chance of getting out of the pitlane and scrabbling around Turn 1 just in front of his rival, but the crew struggled to get the rear wheel nuts on, as the wheels were trying to turn due to a dragging clutch.

Of course, Alonso did his bit by driving a couple of simply brilliant laps after his stop but, as far as the win was concerned, it was over and the Finn was never close to him again.

Resurfacing on all the corners had made them more slippery than usual, but the real problem was that tyre debris created ice rink conditions at some turns, and every driver struggled to stay on the road.

Even Alonso had a few moments, but he dealt with them without fuss and put in another near

OPPOSITE Jacques Villeneuve was determined to shine on home ground, but his run to eighth ended in the wall

BELOW LEFT Ralf Schumacher had a torrid time on the harder Bridgestones, eventually withdrawing from the race

BELOW RIGHT Christijan Albers climbs out of his car after being assaulted by his team-mate Tiago Monteiro on lap 1

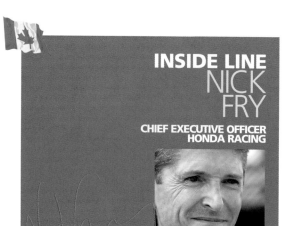

"Obviously, Honda is the talk of the paddock here in Montréal with the decision to appoint Shuhei Nakamoto Senior Technical Director while (Technical Director) Geoff Willis's future with the team is officially under review.

After our disappointing start to the season, the decision was taken that something had to be done. Wada san and I put in our ideas because nobody was debating the requirement for change. It would be silly just to continue doing the same thing and so we participated, but it was a group level – a board level – decision. Whether I was for or against is not relevant, because one person's opinion is neither here nor there. You have to go with the group.

The main issue we are trying to address is performance development of the car. The key to improving is to leverage all the resources of Honda, such as the people in Japan who work on the engine and chassis. In some areas it's good and in other areas it's not so good. It's something we have now got Jacky Eeckelaert involved in, but the key reason for Shuhei Nakamoto's appointment is that he spent six years working in the UK and has 17 years of Honda experience.

However, if anyone regards Nakamoto san as doing the same job as Geoff, I think they will be very mistaken. Geoff has vast F1 experience and Nakamoto san isn't an expert on F1 necessarily, but someone who can bring to bear resources in Japan and in Europe. What we would expect is our chief engineers to rise to the challenge to fill the experience void left by Geoff, while Nakamoto san brings in resources from elsewhere. They'll be doing different jobs.

F1 cars up until relatively recently were designed by one or two people, but I think times have changed. We are working towards a flatter management structure, with a larger number of people at senior level who work on specialist subjects. More departmental heads rather than a technical director who is all-seeing, all-hearing.

As regards Jenson, he signed up with Honda, not Nick Fry, Geoff Willis or any other individual. His confidence was in Honda as a company that had been successful in F1 and nothing's changed. If I was Jenson, I would take this as a sign of determination. If Honda had sat back and said 'Let's not change anything', I think Jenson would be very worried.

People have asked why it was Geoff who's gone and not me. The answer is that it is an engineering restructuring and I run the overall company, which is a totally different thing. Changing Nick Fry for another Nick Fry isn't going to help a design issue with the engineering of the car. Apart from making somebody happy that they had done something, it wouldn't have changed the situation."

faultless performance. By now, Michael had settled for third, but there was still a twist in the tale of this race. When Jacques Villeneuve's crash brought out the safety car Michael was some 39.2s down on Alonso and about 18s behind Räikkönen. Luck went his way once again and the gaps disappeared as the track went yellow, and Michael had his fire lit by the possibility of hunting down Räikkönen for second.

Three lapped drivers were between them in the queue – Honda's Jenson Button and Red Bull duo Christian Klien and David Coulthard – and at the restart, with six laps to go, it didn't take Michael long to deal with them. Räikkönen eventually lost his second place to the flying German with two laps to go when he ran wide at the hairpin.

For Michael, second place was a real bonus from where the team started on Friday, when both its Bridgestone compound choices proved problematic. Damage limitation was the perfect description. The interesting thing was that Michael ran nine laps longer to the first pit stop than Alonso, and seven laps longer than Räikkönen, so his qualifying performance could have been a lot better.

"It's two points in the wrong direction, but it's not finished," said Brawn. "It was alright in the race, but we weren't quite quick enough, so we've got to find some performance from somewhere. I don't think there was another tyre we could have used. There was a whole spread of tyres out there, and I don't think anyone did as good a job as we did."

Once again, Räikkönen was left to rue an expensive technical glitch which resulted in him stalling at his second pit stop. The fact that he seemed not too bothered about losing second with his own late error said a lot about how his relationship with McLaren was unravelling.

"We had a car in the first stint that was as quick as anyone else's out there," said McLaren CEO Martin Whitmarsh. "That's one of the raw ingredients of winning races, and I think we had that. So I think we had an opportunity to win. We obviously had two problematic stops because of a clutch problem, and that let the initiative slip. And then obviously at the end a mistake by Kimi gifted Michael second place."

The three big names filled the podium positions, but it was a day of mixed fortunes for their team-mates. After his penalty, Fisichella just didn't have

ABOVE Jenson Button's Honda gained ground on lap 1, but a lack of traction led to him falling down the order to an eventual ninth-place finish

BELOW Fernando Alonso offers praise to his Renault R26 that helped him race to yet another race win

the speed of Alonso and was never a threat to Michael, when really he should have been. He did at least get past Trulli to secure fourth, but his best lap was fully 0.7s off Alonso's. From the back of the top 10, Felipe Massa went for an unusual one-stop strategy that paid dividends and earned him fifth place, but he was nowhere near Michael. Montoya had a wild race, the second lap brush with Rosberg followed by an impact with the last corner wall and retirement on an ominous lap 13.

Sixth place for Trulli was a reasonable reward. For

once he got one over team-mate Ralf Schumacher. After chosing a different tyre, Ralf had a terrible time, eventually retiring after a series of excursions.

Once again, Nick Heidfeld finished seventh for BMW after a tidy performance. He should have been beaten by an inspired Villeneuve, but a pit stop glitch swapped their positions, and later the local hero had a huge accident when he got on the marbles after he was wrongfooted by the lapped Ralf.

Coulthard started at the back of the grid after an engine change, but made all the right moves at the right times, and the final safety car period (for JV) gave him a chance to launch an assault on Button that earned him the final point. He should have been beaten by Vitantonio Liuzzi, but an early brush with Mark Webber's Williams forced the Italian to stop for a new nose, and he never recovered.

For the second race in a row, Webber didn't get into the second round of qualifying, blaming his team-mate for holding him up. In the race, the soft Bridgestones the team had chosen made life impossible and he crept home 12th. Rosberg was mighty in qualifying, but his race ended when he was pitched into the wall by Montoya.

It was another awful weekend for Honda, distracted by its technical management shake-up. Button managed only ninth, while Rubens Barrichello retired when he felt his engine tighten.

MF1 drivers Tiago Monteiro and Christijan Albers contrived to collide on the first lap, with Albers eliminated on the spot and Monteiro able to continue after a pit stop for repairs. Straight after the race, Holland played Portugal in the Football World Cup – Tiago's boys eliminated the Dutch from the competition in a bloodbath of a match that saw two players from each side ejected from the field. It was a fair reflection on how the MF1 team-mates got on…

SNAPSHOT FROM
CANADA

CLOCKWISE FROM RIGHT Michelin was delighted that it beat Bridgestone to reach its 100th F1 win; water taxis ferry personnel down the rowing lake to the back of the paddock; 'Give us a J. Give us a V. And what have you got? JV!'; yes, this Jacques Villeneuve, the polymath with his latest CD; the trackside marmots starred as usual

WEEKEND HEADLINES

- In the run-up to the Canadian GP, the sport's governing body, the FIA, asked all teams to fit a 'slot gap separator' to their rear wings in order to reduce the prospects of wings flexing. In effect, the governing body acknowledged that the static load tests conducted in the scrutineering bay were ineffective.

- With the US GP imminent, Bernie Ecclestone made some mischievous comments about the race, noting that the race provided nothing but "aggravation", and that F1 had more TV viewers in Malta! The 2006 race was the last of the original contract, so negotiations with Indianapolis's Tony George were in motion…

- Kimi Räikkönen insisted in Canada that he wasn't waiting on news of Michael Schumacher's plans before deciding for which team he wanted to race in 2007: "My decision is my own," said the Finn. "I'll make the decision that I think is right for me."

- Frustrated by the ongoing debate over the future engine rules, Renault team chief Flavio Briatore branded his fellow engine manufacturers "hooligans" for failing to understand that the sport was about racing and not about developing technology. "I don't want to waste my time on it any more," said the Italian. The story was far from over, however…

- Midland F1 boss Alex Shnaider admitted in Montréal that he was in negotiation to sell his team to a group of Dutch investors, but insisted that he had yet to make up his mind about whether he was ready to cash in on his investment or not. He was reported to have been offered substantially more than he had paid in January 2005.

RACE RESULTS
CANADA
MONTREAL

Official Results © [2006]
Formula One Administration Limited,
6 Princes Gate, London SW7 1QJ.
No reproduction without permission.
All copyright and database rights reserved

RACE DATE June 25th
CIRCUIT LENGTH 2.710 miles
NO. OF LAPS 70
RACE DISTANCE 189.695 miles
WEATHER Sunny & dry, 28°C
TRACK TEMP 44°C
RACE DAY ATTENDANCE 119,000
LAP RECORD Rubens Barrichello, 1m13.622s, 132.511mph, 2004

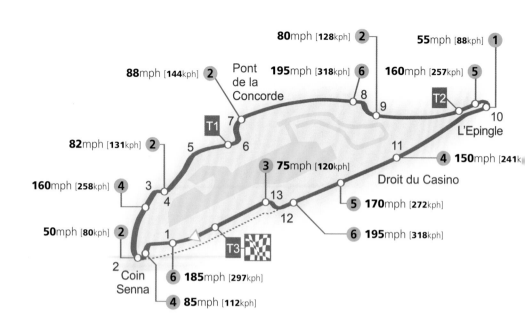

	PRACTICE 1		
	Driver	**Time**	**Laps**
1	R Kubica	1m16.390s	30
2	A Davidson	1m18.306s	26
3	A Wurz	1m18.941s	23
4	M Schumacher	1m18.994s	5
5	R Barrichello	1m19.070s	6
6	J Button	1m19.165s	6
7	N Jani	1m19.258s	24
8	R Doornbos	1m19.681s	20
9	V Liuzzi	1m20.154s	7
10	C Albers	1m20.646s	9
11	T Monteiro	1m20.799s	8
12	R Schumacher	1m20.861s	6
13	F Montagny	1m21.783s	17
14	T Sato	1m21.891s	20
15	S Yamamoto	1m23.159s	29
16	F Massa	1m23.179s	5
17	J Trulli	1m24.029s	7
18	F Alonso	no time	2
19	G Mondini	no time	2
20	D Coulthard	no time	1
21	G Fisichella	no time	1
22	N Heidfeld	no time	1
23	C Klien	no time	1
24	S Speed	no time	1
25	J Villeneuve	no time	1
26	JP Montoya	no time	0
27	K Räikkönen	no time	0
28	N Rosberg	no time	0
29	M Webber	no time	0

	PRACTICE 2		
	Driver	**Time**	**Laps**
1	R Kubica	1m16.965s	33
2	F Alonso	1m17.095s	15
3	A Wurz	1m17.337s	21
4	K Räikkönen	1m17.490s	10
5	A Davidson	1m17.627s	32
6	G Fisichella	1m17.805s	21
7	M Webber	1m17.848s	13
8	V Liuzzi	1m18.009s	18
9	N Heidfeld	1m18.015s	13
10	J Villeneuve	1m18.035s	14
11	R Doornbos	1m18.201s	32
12	R Barrichello	1m18.279s	16
13	J Button	1m18.429s	18
14	C Albers	1m18.503s	20
15	M Schumacher	1m18.549s	17
16	R Schumacher	1m18.614s	23
17	JP Montoya	1m18.761s	14
18	C Klien	1m18.865s	15
19	J Trulli	1m18.868s	17
20	S Speed	1m18.907s	21
21	N Rosberg	1m19.048s	10
22	F Massa	1m19.099s	15
23	G Mondini	1m19.138s	24
24	D Coulthard	1m19.313s	15
25	N Jani	1m19.541s	28
26	T Sato	1m19.624s	22
27	S Yamamoto	1m20.197s	26
28	T Monteiro	1m20.262s	18
29	F Montagny	1m21.434s	22

	PRACTICE 3		
	Driver	**Time**	**Laps**
1	F Alonso	1m15.455s	20
2	G Fisichella	1m15.521s	19
3	J Villeneuve	1m15.554s	13
4	N Heidfeld	1m15.616s	12
5	K Räikkönen	1m15.902s	12
6	M Schumacher	1m15.959s	13
7	JP Montoya	1m15.975s	12
8	R Barrichello	1m16.334s	17
9	F Massa	1m16.348s	18
10	S Speed	1m16.493s	18
11	C Klien	1m16.660s	17
12	J Button	1m16.673s	15
13	M Webber	1m16.710s	13
14	D Coulthard	1m16.765s	11
15	N Rosberg	1m16.829s	19
16	V Liuzzi	1m16.928s	19
17	J Trulli	1m17.503s	24
18	T Monteiro	1m17.747s	18
19	R Schumacher	1m18.212s	18
20	T Sato	1m18.926s	18
21	F Montagny	1m19.160s	19
22	C Albers	1m19.531s	16

	QUALIFYING 1	
	Driver	**Time**
1	F Alonso	1m15.350s
2	K Räikkönen	1m15.376s
3	M Schumacher	1m15.716s
4	N Heidfeld	1m15.906s
5	G Fisichella	1m15.917s
6	JP Montoya	1m16.251s
7	F Massa	1m16.259s
8	N Rosberg	1m16.404s
9	J Trulli	1m16.455s
10	J Villeneuve	1m16.493s
11	D Coulthard	1m16.514s
12	V Liuzzi	1m16.581s
13	C Klien	1m16.585s
14	J Button	1m16.594s
15	R Schumacher	1m16.702s
16	R Barrichello	1m16.735s
17	M Webber	1m16.985s
18	S Speed	1m17.016s
19	T Monteiro	1m17.121s
20	C Albers	1m17.140s
21	T Sato	1m19.088s
22	F Montagny	1m19.152s

	QUALIFYING 2	
	Driver	**Time**
1	F Alonso	1m14.726s
2	M Schumacher	1m15.139s
3	JP Montoya	1m15.253s
4	N Rosberg	1m15.269s
5	K Räikkönen	1m15.273s
6	G Fisichella	1m15.295s
7	J Trulli	1m15.506s
8	F Massa	1m15.555s
9	R Barrichello	1m15.601s
10	J Button	1m15.814s
11	J Villeneuve	1m15.832s
12	C Klien	1m15.833s
13	N Heidfeld	1m15.885s
14	R Schumacher	1m15.888s
15	V Liuzzi	1m16.116s
16	D Coulthard	1m16.301s

Best sectors – Practice	
Sec 1 F Alonso	20.984s
Sec 2 G Fisichella	24.039s
Sec 3 G Fisichella	30.276s

Speed trap – Practice		
1	F Massa	199.3mph
2	M Schumacher	199.2mph
3	J Villeneuve	198.8mph

Best sectors – Qualifying	
Sec 1 F Alonso	20.836s
Sec 2 K Räikkönen	23.754s
Sec 3 F Alonso	30.075s

Fernando Alonso
"Kimi pressured me in the opening stint. After the first stop, the team told me that he was going longer on the middle stint and I had a few scares as I pushed to the limit."

Michael Schumacher
"The race was complicated by my grid position and was made even harder by a start that left me behind Trulli. Kimi's mistake helped me to make up a place."

Kimi Räikkönen
"I was pushing Alonso in the first stint and had a go at the hairpin. When the safety car came back out, I went wide at the hairpin which allowed Michael past."

Jenson Button
"I had no grip with the front or rear tyres, plus understeer and a lack of traction. There's so much rubber going down here which leaves marbles on each corner."

Jacques Villeneuve
"Ralf was very slow and when he decided to let me by it was in a corner. He lifted and to avoid him I had to go wide where there was old rubber. It was like being on ice."

Jarno Trulli
"We've made a big step forward, especially since we introduced the TF106B. But, even today I had a misfire and we ran the engine in recovery mode."

Giancarlo Fisichella
"I jumped the start and though I tried to slow down and Kimi got past me, I got a drive-through. That was when I lost the chance of a podium finish."

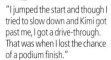

Felipe Massa
"We'd a different strategy based on one stop. Even with a heavy fuel load, I was able to run a good pace. Only after the safety car did I feel a slight lack of grip."

Juan Pablo Montoya
"I was next to Rosberg, but we touched. I thought I'd damaged the nose and pitted. I was trying to make up places, but touched the wall and damaged the rear."

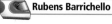

Rubens Barrichello
"The engine felt quite tight from the start, then after my 11th lap, I was losing a lot of places as everyone was able to pass me on the straights as I began to lose power."

Nick Heidfeld
"I got stuck behind Massa and Jacques, but I gained a place at my second stop. I was faster than Trulli, but after the safety-car period I had trouble getting heat into my tyres."

Ralf Schumacher
"I couldn't find any grip. It was my mistake, as I went for the wrong tyres. Every time I went on the marbles with my hard tyres I'd lose control. In the end, I had to retire."

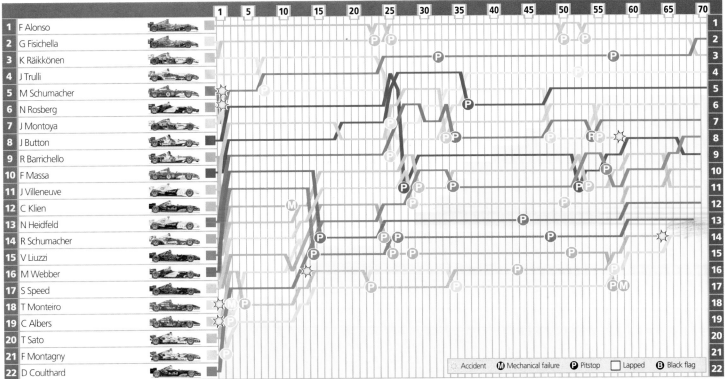

	Driver																
1	F Alonso
2	G Fisichella
3	K Räikkönen
4	J Trulli
5	M Schumacher
6	N Rosberg
7	J Montoya
8	J Button
9	R Barrichello
10	F Massa
11	J Villeneuve
12	C Klien
13	N Heidfeld
14	R Schumacher
15	V Liuzzi
16	M Webber
17	S Speed
18	T Monteiro
19	C Albers
20	T Sato
21	F Montagny
22	D Coulthard

☼ Accident Ⓜ Mechanical failure Ⓟ Pitstop ☐ Lapped Ⓑ Black flag

QUALIFYING 3

	Driver	Time
1	F Alonso	1m14.942s
2	G Fisichella	1m15.178s
3	K Räikkönen	1m15.386s
4	J Trulli	1m15.968s
5	M Schumacher	1m15.986s
6	N Rosberg	1m16.012s
7	JP Montoya	1m16.228s
8	J Button	1m16.608s
9	R Barrichello	1m16.912s
10	F Massa	1m17.209s

GRID

	Driver	Time
1	F Alonso	1m14.942s
2	G Fisichella	1m15.178s
3	K Räikkönen	1m15.386s
4	J Trulli	1m15.968s
5	M Schumacher	1m15.986s
6	N Rosberg	1m16.012s
7	JP Montoya	1m16.228s
8	J Button	1m16.608s
9	R Barrichello	1m16.912s
10	F Massa	1m17.209s
11	J Villeneuve	1m15.832s
12	C Klien	1m15.833s
13	N Heidfeld	1m15.885s
14	R Schumacher	1m15.888s
15	V Liuzzi	1m16.116s
16	M Webber	1m16.985s
17	S Speed	1m17.016s
18	T Monteiro	1m17.121s
19	C Albers	1m17.140s
20	T Sato	1m19.088s
21	F Montagny	1m19.152s
22*	D Coulthard	1m16.301s

* 10-PLACE GRID PENALTY

RACE

	Driver	Car	Laps	Time	Avg. mph	Fastest	Stops
1	F Alonso	Renault R26	70	1h34m37.308s	120.286	1m15.911s	2
2	M Schumacher	Ferrari 248	70	1h34m39.419s	120.242	1m15.993s	2
3	K Räikkönen	McLaren-Mercedes MP4-21	70	1h34m46.121s	120.100	1m15.841s	2
4	G Fisichella	Renault R26	70	1h34m52.987s	119.955	1m16.669s	3
5	F Massa	Ferrari 248	70	1h35m02.480s	119.755	1m17.308s	1
6	J Trulli	Toyota TF106B	69	1h34m48.881s	118.326	1m17.503s	2
7	N Heidfeld	BMW Sauber F1.06	69	1h34m50.306s	118.297	1m17.454s	2
8	D Coulthard	Red Bull-Ferrari RB2	69	1h34m56.187s	118.175	1m17.619s	2
9	J Button	Honda RA106	69	1h34m58.332s	118.130	1m18.001s	2
10	S Speed	Toro Rosso-Cosworth STR01	69	1h34m58.735s	118.122	1m17.720s	2
11	C Klien	Red Bull-Ferrari RB2	69	1h35m02.984s	118.034	1m17.576s	2
12	M Webber	Williams-Cosworth FW28	69	1h35m08.859s	117.913	1m17.705s	2
13	V Liuzzi	Toro Rosso-Cosworth STR01	68	1h35m16.298s	116.052	1m18.078s	3
14	T Monteiro	Midland-Toyota M16	66	1h35m22.575s	112.516	1m19.291s	3
15	T Sato	Super Aguri-Honda SA05	64	Accident	-	1m20.490s	3
R	J Villeneuve	BMW Sauber F1.06	58	Accident	-	1m 17.394s	2
R	R Schumacher	Toyota TF106B	58	Withdrew	-	1m18.793s	5
R	JP Montoya	McLaren-Mercedes MP4-21	13	Suspension	-	1m18.493s	1
R	R Barrichello	Honda RA106	11	Engine	-	1m19.286s	0
R	F Montagny	Super Aguri-Honda SA05	2	Engine	-	2m07.709s	0
R	N Rosberg	Williams-Cosworth FW28	1	Crash damage	-	1m26.579s	0
R	C Albers	Midland-Toyota M16	0	Accident	-	-	0

CHAMPIONSHIP

	Driver	Pts
1	F Alonso	84
2	M Schumacher	59
3	K Räikkönen	39
4	G Fisichella	37
5	F Massa	28
6	JP Montoya	26
7	J Button	16
8	R Barrichello	13
9	N Heidfeld	12
10	R Schumacher	8
11	D Coulthard	8
12	J Villeneuve	7
13	M Webber	6
14	N Rosberg	4
15	J Trulli	3
16	C Klien	1

Speed trap – Qualifying

1	F Massa	199.2mph
2	M Schumacher	199.2mph
3	S Speed	196.7mph

Fastest Lap

K Räikkönen 1m15.841s
(128.633mph) on lap 22

Fastest speed trap

M Schumacher 202.8mph

Slowest speed trap

F Montagny 188.3mph

Fastest pit stop

1	M Schumacher	23.639s
2	G Fisichella	24.283s
3	N Heidfeld	24.293s

Constructor

		Pts
1	Renault	121
2	Ferrari	87
3	McLaren-Mercedes	65
4	Honda	29
5	BMW Sauber	19
6	Toyota	11
7	Williams-Cosworth	10
8	Red Bull-Ferrari	8

David Coulthard

"The amount of rubber that comes off the tyres is incredible, so if you go an inch off line, the debris can suck you in. Jenson got sucked in, so I was able to overtake."

Mark Webber

"We picked the wrong tyres. I got a bit of grip back towards the end of the stints but, when all four tyres were completely grained, it was impossible to drive."

Vitantonio Liuzzi

"I was in about 10th after a few laps. Then I came up behind Webber who was very slow and, as I tried to pass him, his rear tyres touched my wing and I had to pit."

Tiago Monteiro

"I must apologise for my mistake. I was on the dirty part of the track, locked my rears and hit Christijan. After that, we changed what we could and brought the car home."

Takuma Sato

"I passed the Midlands at the start. But, after the first safety car came out, David squeezed past me, damaging my front wing. I then pushed hard, but crashed."

Christian Klien

"I broke first gear in the hairpin, which is why I went off line. There was one narrow driving line and the car understeered. I went into the gravel and lost three places."

Nico Rosberg

"I left room for Montoya to come inside me, as I knew if he passed me I'd get ahead coming out. But he came in tight, so we were never going to get through together."

Scott Speed

"Towards the end, the hairpin was almost undriveable. At my first stop, I had a problem with my left rear. We didn't have a fast car, but we muscled our way up the order."

Christijan Albers

"It was a shame to be out early, as our pace could have been strong. I passed Montagny and Monteiro. I was fighting with Sato, then Tiago hit me from behind at Turn 10."

Franck Montagny

"We didn't have a great start to the weekend, but we worked hard and I was confident for the race. It's a shame that we had an engine problem, but that's racing."

2006 FORMULA 1™
UNITED STATES GRAND PRIX
Indianapolis

ACTION STATIONS

A spectacular accident at the first corner got the US GP off to a flying start, but not even this could prevent Ferrari claiming a 1–2 headed by Michael Schumacher

Before the Canadian Grand Prix, Fernando Alonso had expressed his fear that Renault would lose out badly to Ferrari in the pair of back-to-back North American races, and that his participation would be focusing on damage limitation. In fact, it turned out to be the other way around at Montréal's Circuit Gilles Villeneuve as Michael Schumacher overcame dire troubles on Friday to eventually salvage second place behind Alonso. However, what happened at the United States GP proved that the Spaniard had indeed been correct to be cautious.

On Friday, Ferrari already had a good idea of how successful the weekend at the Indianapolis Motor Speedway would be, as Felipe Massa and Michael Schumacher were fourth and sixth fastest overall at the end of the second session, up among the other teams' third drivers who regularly end up atop the timesheets. While that didn't suggest dominance, the Italian team knew how much fuel it was running and could extrapolate forward from there.

Speaking after having studied the lap times and done his sums, Ferrari Technical Director Ross Brawn was especially optimistic, in marked contrast to the glum reaction everyone in the team had had on the opening day of the Canadian Grand Prix.

"We'll wait and see how things go, but it's far too early to say," he said. "Our tyres are probably looking a bit soft, which is a good sign, because when they look a little bit soft on a Friday, normally by Saturday or Sunday they come good, giving us confidence that the tyres will get better as the weekend progresses. In Montréal, we had problems with the tyres on the Friday, and it wasn't so clear whether they would really evolve in a good way over the course of the weekend. In fact, I'm much more confident here that the tyres are going to improve."

The real story was told on Saturday morning, when the teams' third drivers are out of the way and most teams make some effort to run their cars in low-fuel qualifying trim. Michael and Felipe were first and second, and their nearest challenger – Renault's Giancarlo Fisichella – was almost 1.2s behind. The rest knew in what trim they had been running and came to the conclusion that there was no point in even attempting to fight for pole position. Instead, they'd have to aim for the third grid slot. Furthermore, Ferrari's long runs in practice suggested that the dominance would carry over to the race.

It didn't hurt that a large chunk of the pursuing pack was eliminated in a pair of first-lap accidents. In fact, it certainly got a bit crowded between the first and second turns on the opening lap, and Juan Pablo Montoya managed to knock his McLaren team-mate Kimi Räikkönen into a spin after they had started from back in ninth and 11th places. Team principal Ron Dennis wasn't impressed, and the incident was to have huge ramifications for the Colombian…

Meanwhile, Jenson Button's Honda hit the Finn and Nick Heidfeld's BMW was launched over his front wheel into a spectacular somersault, from which he fortunately emerged with just a shaking. Local hero Scott Speed also piled in.

Further back in the pack, there was a separate incident that took care of Christian Klien, Mark Webber and Christian Albers. Ironically, once the dust settled, the field wasn't much larger than the one that contested the 2005 race when seven of the teams withdrew after the formation lap…

Once it was all cleared up and the safety car pulled in, at least there was something of a contest at the front, if only over the opening stint of the race, after Massa jumped ahead of Michael at the start.

BELOW Michael Schumacher had to run second behind team-mate Massa in the opening stint, but emerged ahead and stayed there for his record fifth win at Indy

"Nothing was planned," said Brawn, "we obviously just told them not to get in the way of each other. And that was all we asked. In fact, Michael dropping in behind Felipe gave Fernando a chance to go around the outside. But, because the tyres are so good here, we had grip at the start as well, and that makes a difference."

The fun ended at the first round of pit stops, at which, despite stopping earlier, Michael managed to sneak ahead of his Brazilian team-mate.

"He did a great run – no mistakes, nothing, very clean, very good, very tough to keep on," said Michael. "Obviously, you can't really stay that close in the slipstream and it was very hard, but I pushed extremely hard on the out lap and luckily our new tyres gave us the edge and made me go forward."

After that, it really was a demonstration run for the two red cars and it was a cruise to the line, as Michael became the first man to win five races at Indianapolis, and the team scored its first 'proper' 1–2 since the 2004 Italian GP. Even better, Alonso finished only fifth.

"We definitely performed extremely well all weekend long," Michael noted. "We prepared ourselves very thoroughly for these two flyaway races. We knew we had a very good car in our hands. In Canada, for whatever reason, it just didn't work out.

ABOVE Here's a sight that no team chief wants to see: both of his cars taken out in an accident. Button joins McLaren pair Räikkönen and assailant Montoya

INSIDE LINE
RALF SCHUMACHER
TOYOTA DRIVER

"This was my third attempt to make it around Turn 13 without hitting the wall and it was great that I achieved it!

Seriously, though, Turn 13 is full throttle and so long as the car sticks together and the tyres do, then it's very easy. And what's the alternative? Downshifting? You either do this job, or you don't. And I've never doubted that it's a job I want to do.

The previous two years here obviously weren't good. My Williams shunt in 2004 was by far the worse of the two accidents and I was out of the cockpit for three months after that. Then, last year, in the Toyota, I hit the wall at a better angle.

Actually, it was funny: Charlie Whiting (the FIA Safety Delegate) came and joked to me that they'd changed the wall after I'd hit it in 2004, so that I'd have a softer impact. Then I went straight out and did it again. And, you know what, it really was softer. But I had the same nurse in hospital. She just said, 'Not you again!' But I don't have nightmares about it…

This year was better all round and I was heading for my best result since my podium at the Australian GP before a wheel bearing failure stopped me with 11 laps to go when I was fifth.

Things didn't start too well and I had a vibration on Friday that was hard to trace. I got through into the final session of qualifying and qualified eighth, but spent most of the opening stint behind Rubens [Barrichello]. After that, the car had really good pace and Jarno [Trulli] proved it when he finished fourth on a one-stop strategy after starting from the pit lane.

The start of the season was difficult for us and it was particularly tough coming on the back of a strong 2005. We had the tyre shift from Michelin to Bridgestone and tyres are such a fundamental part of the performance package that it takes time to get the car and tyres working in harmony.

Then we had the end of the relationship with [Technical Director] Mike Gascoyne. I think, actually, that the team is functioning well on the technical side, as we have good depth and the motivation is there to work hard and achieve our targets. However, we don't have as much experience as some of the teams we are trying to compete against who have been in the sport for decades, some since the championship began.

Our fastest laps at Indianapolis were beaten only by the podium finishers and I think that's a good indication of the progress we've made, especially since the introduction of the TF106B. Our target was to win a race this year and that will be hard, but I don't think it's impossible."

With Ferrari controlling proceedings, the major point of interest was Alonso's uncharacteristic struggle to get on the pace. For, while his team-mate Fischella led the pursuit for Renault in third place, Alonso had to settle for a distant fifth, behind Jarno Trulli's Toyota.

Renault's Executive Director of Engineering Pat Symonds had admitted on Saturday afternoon that Indianapolis simply wasn't Fernando's circuit, for reasons no one in the team could really explain. He struggled here against then team-mate Trulli a couple of years ago, and against Fisichella in 2005, then again this time he just couldn't get a handle on the place. Throw in a bit of a tyre disadvantage and he was all at sea, at least by his own stellar standards.

That said, Alonso still salvaged four points. Just as at Monaco in 2005, he showed he could make the best out of a bad situation, and that of course is the sign of a true champion. As ever, luck went his way: Toyota's Ralf Schumacher gifted him a point later in the race, and who knows how many of the first lap crashers Button, Räikkönen, Montoya and Heidfeld – most if not all running the one-stop strategy that worked so well for Trulli – might have finished ahead.

It's interesting to note while Alonso was used to easing off the revs and saving his engine in the closing laps, on this occasion he set his best time on the penultimate lap. He was obviously aware that his V10 was coming to the end of its life (Fisichella had a new one and correspondingly had to protect it), but he was also trying to make a point.

While Alonso didn't quite hit the sweet spot, Fisichella certainly did. Twice this year when he has started on the front row something has gone horribly wrong. This time it all fell into place for him and, buoyed by the security that came with his recent contract extension, the Italian was flying.

"I did my best, and I think that was the best result I could do today with our pace, which was good, but

ABOVE Out of Turn 13, the start/finish straight is long and notably wide, excellent for lining up an overtaking manoeuvre

OPPOSITE TOP Toyota's Jarno Trulli was one of the stars of the show, working his way up to fourth after starting from the pitlane

OPPOSITE BOTTOM Giancarlo Fisichella chases down his Renault team-mate Fernando Alonso

Here, everything was just spot on and to have Felipe alongside is just a dream result."

A smiling Brawn admitted that everything had gone to plan, certainly as far as the tyres getting even better as the weekend went on: "It just developed as we hoped it would. You get a feel for the tyres on the first day, and we had the grip, that was the important thing. Although there was some graining happening, as happened in the race, the graining disappeared and it wasn't a problem. We had an extremely comfortable race. You get the tyres right, and even on a circuit like this that's a huge advantage, and the tyres were perfect. It was much sweeter than last year."

INSIDE LINE
JOIE CHITWOOD
PRESIDENT INDIANAPOLIS MOTOR SPEEDWAY

"We've made a huge investment in Formula One. It's been seven years so far and we'd like to see it continue. I think F1 needs a good spot in America and I think Indianapolis is as good a spot as there is.

There was an initial frustration period after last year, lots of letters and calls, but I'm optimistic at the way the spectator numbers looked this year.

Bernie might have been saying some slightly inflammatory things about America, but our company tends not to negotiate in the press, so we'll take our time after this event and sit down with Mr Ecclestone and talk about the future…

F1 is a quality event and the local economy embraces it. A lot of the restaurants here change their hours to reflect a more European schedule, which is to stay open later. They do say that they move a lot more bottles of wine than bottles of beer when F1 comes to town…

We had some legal issues to face after the 2005 fiasco but, happily, the court has ruled in our favour, although I guess they will appeal. They were suing for a number of things, not just ticket compensation but also travel, accommodation, all sorts of things. The American legal system is interesting and these things can be lengthy. Lawsuits definitely dampen the enthusiasm of all involved.

As far as Michelin is concerned, I think they stepped up above and beyond the call of duty. Voluntarily, they offered a refund for all the race-day tickets for last year, they purchased 20,000 tickets for race day this year and they were also involved in the local organising committee to help welcome all the customers and visitors to town. As a company, I applaud what they did.

As for increasing the awareness of F1, Scott Speed has done so well in Europe to be attractive at this level, but he's created his name outside America, which is challenging. Would a driver making his name in America before going over to F1 help? Absolutely.

Scott is running great so far and if we could see some great finishes from him that would give the media more reason to cover it. People ask about Marco Andretti and obviously the Andretti name is very popular in motorsport, globally. If he was to go down the F1 path, I think there would be a significant following.

Marco, at 19, had a phenomenal run in the Indy 500. He lost it by a car length and got passed by Sam Hornish with about 200 yards to go. It was a great race and showed what kind of talent his is. I think people will expect great things of him in the future and he definitely has the pedigree."

ABOVE Vitantonio Liuzzi gained nine places on lap 1 by staying out of trouble and raced on to score Toro Rosso's first point

BELOW Michael Schumacher rewards Ross Brawn with a slug of bubbly after he'd masterminded a Ferrari 1–2

not good enough to beat Ferrari," Fisichella smiled. "It was important to overtake Fernando as I was quicker than him, and it was important to push and go to the end. I made no mistakes at all."

Even Fisichella couldn't pinpoint why he had been so far ahead of Alonso: "I have no idea. You know, sometimes I'm just comfortable in the car, and I'm able to be quicker than him. It's a good time to do it, and it's really important for the next race, which is our home grand prix. I'm also very happy with the new contract that I've signed for next year."

Trulli started the race from the pitlane with an ultra-heavy load in his Toyota. There are worse races to attempt a one-stopper, and good fortune smiled on him at the first corner – he was straight up to 13th place having gained nine places without even getting up to full speed. Trulli seemed to stay out forever and when he finally stopped on lap 39 he dropped back briefly to seventh. However, the team knew that he would pick up some of those ahead when they peeled off for their second round of pit stops.

In the end, Trulli came within a whisker of getting down to Turn 1 in front of Fisichella when the Renault man pitted on lap 53, but that still left him in a more than respectable fourth place: "It was very quick all through the race. There was a bit of a question mark at the beginning, because I didn't know about the set-up as we had never run the car so heavy. But I knew we had a quick car, I knew we had a big chance today, with a bit of luck, and in the end it worked out."

Barrichello qualified fourth but, despite the first lap chaos, he couldn't finish higher than sixth on race day as the Toyotas proved faster. Seventh place went to David Coulthard, the Scot scoring for the third time in four races, with Tonio Liuzzi scoring Scuderia Toro Rosso's first point in eighth. Meanwhile, a frustrated Nico Rosberg struggled to get on the pace throughout and came home ninth for Williams.

So, Bridgestone got its sums right to a spectacular degree at Indianapolis and it left one wondering whether Michelin erred on the conservative side as a result of its dramas here in 2005. It was an obvious conclusion to draw, and it was more apparent than ever that tyres would decide the title battle.

"We're reasonably optimistic," said Brawn of the next race in France. "Again, it's down to the tyre war. I think the cars are probably quite similar, and it's a question of how the tyres work."

SNAPSHOT FROM
USA

CLOCKWISE FROM RIGHT
"Do they really give these kids licences?"; Jenson Button and team chief Nick Fry discuss where Honda Racing is heading; a local beauty; Captain America was in attendance, watching from the packed grandstands, but sadly American hero Scott Speed got only as far as Turn 2; Juan Pablo Montoya has no idea at this point that he'll leave Indianapolis under a cloud for taking his team-mate out on lap 1

WEEKEND HEADLINES

- Double Champcar champion Sebastien Bourdais took advantage of a weekend free from racing to talk to any F1 team boss who would listen. The Frenchman famously missed out on a Renault test deal at the end of 2002 when he declined to do a management deal with Flavio Briatore, but the pair have since made peace, and were spotted in conversation.

- The British media got a little overexcited when it was revealed that GP2 frontrunner Lewis Hamilton was due to drive a McLaren at Jerez. The team did its best to downplay the event by pointing out that the purpose was for filming an advertisement, and that occasional test driver Darren Turner was also involved in the shoot.

- A few days after the United States Grand Prix, the FIA revealed that the tender to supply a common ECU for 2008 and beyond had been won by a joint proposal from Microsoft and McLaren Electronic Systems (MES). The rival bid of longtime Ferrari partners Magneto Marelli and Pi Research was thus defeated.

- Exactly a year after the post-Indy war of words between Michelin and the FIA had stolen the headlines came the not unexpected news that Bridgestone had won the FIA contract to be the sole tyre supplier from 2008. Michelin, sticking to its withdrawal plans, did not make a bid.

- The BMW Sauber flexi-wing story continued to rumble on through the United States Grand Prix meeting, but in the days after the race the team was asked to make changes in time for the following Grand Prix in France. For the time being, that would put an end to a subject that had been garnering considerable attention thus far through the season.

RACE RESULTS
UNITED STATES
INDIANAPOLIS

Official Results © [2006]
Formula One Administration Limited,
6 Princes Gate, London SW7 1QJ.
No reproduction without permission.
All copyright and database rights reserved

RACE DATE July 2nd
CIRCUIT LENGTH 2.605 miles
NO. OF LAPS 73
RACE DISTANCE 190.139 miles
WEATHER Sunny & dry, 35°C
TRACK TEMP 49°C
RACE DAY ATTENDANCE N/A
LAP RECORD Rubens Barrichello,
1m10.399s, 133.229mph, 2004

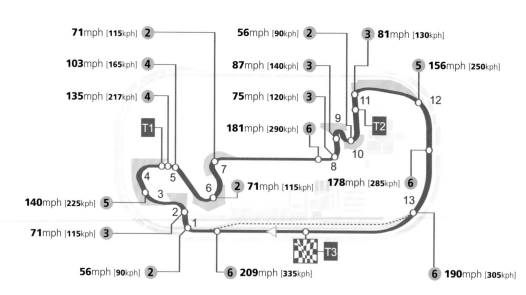

PRACTICE 1				PRACTICE 2				PRACTICE 3		
	Driver	Time	Laps		Driver	Time	Laps		Driver	Time	Laps
1	A Davidson	1m12.083s	27	1	A Davidson	1m12.013s	38	1	M Schumacher	1m10.760s	15
2	M Schumacher	1m12.458s	3	2	R Kubica	1m12.809s	39	2	F Massa	1m11.039s	8
3	R Kubica	1m13.008s	31	3	G Fisichella	1m12.933s	14	3	G Fisichella	1m11.940s	15
4	R Barrichello	1m13.090s	5	4	F Massa	1m13.264s	26	4	N Heidfeld	1m12.049s	18
5	J Button	1m13.189s	6	5	G Mondini	1m13.327s	33	5	R Barrichello	1m12.149s	13
6	N Jani	1m13.710s	24	6	M Schumacher	1m13.346s	18	6	F Alonso	1m12.202s	15
7	G Mondini	1m14.654s	33	7	T Monteiro	1m13.387s	21	7	J Button	1m12.269s	18
8	A Wurz	1m14.745s	38	8	J Button	1m13.397s	16	8	J Villeneuve	1m12.327s	13
9	S Speed	1m14.791s	8	9	F Alonso	1m13.474s	14	9	K Räikkönen	1m12.569s	13
10	R Doornbos	1m15.018s	22	10	K Räikkönen	1m13.554s	9	10	JP Montoya	1m12.592s	10
11	T Monteiro	1m15.091s	8	11	S Speed	1m13.688s	26	11	V Liuzzi	1m12.675s	18
12	V Liuzzi	1m15.532s	8	12	M Webber	1m13.691s	15	12	M Webber	1m12.904s	15
13	C Albers	1m15.647s	10	13	N Heidfeld	1m13.725s	14	13	T Monteiro	1m12.913s	18
14	T Sato	1m15.971s	17	14	V Liuzzi	1m13.735s	24	14	J Trulli	1m13.091s	21
15	S Yamamoto	1m16.116s	31	15	JP Montoya	1m13.825s	10	15	R Schumacher	1m13.101s	19
16	F Montagny	1m16.489s	17	16	J Villeneuve	1m13.857s	17	16	S Speed	1m13.103s	17
17	G Fisichella	no time	3	17	N Jani	1m13.946s	31	17	C Klien	1m13.113s	15
18	R Schumacher	no time	2	18	R Barrichello	1m14.011s	20	18	C Albers	1m13.172s	19
19	J Trulli	no time	2	19	A Wurz	1m14.050s	39	19	N Rosberg	1m13.230s	12
20	J Villeneuve	no time	2	20	C Klien	1m14.084s	15	20	D Coulthard	1m13.364s	17
21	F Alonso	no time	1	21	C Albers	1m14.169s	19	21	T Sato	1m13.806s	16
22	D Coulthard	no time	1	22	T Sato	1m14.391s	24	22	F Montagny	1m14.454s	10
23	N Heidfeld	no time	1	23	J Trulli	1m14.449s	16				
24	C Klien	no time	1	24	N Rosberg	1m14.562s	17				
25	JP Montoya	no time	1	25	D Coulthard	1m14.676s	18				
26	K Räikkönen	no time	1	26	R Doornbos	1m14.839s	13				
27	F Massa	no time	0	27	R Schumacher	1m15.063s	10				
28	N Rosberg	no time	0	28	S Yamamoto	1m15.120s	33				
29	M Webber	no time	0	29	F Montagny	no time	2				

QUALIFYING 1			QUALIFYING 2	
	Driver	Time		Driver	Time
1	F Massa	1m11.088s	1	M Schumacher	1m10.636s
2	M Schumacher	1m11.588s	2	F Massa	1m11.146s
3	R Schumacher	1m11.879s	3	G Fisichella	1m11.200s
4	N Heidfeld	1m11.891s	4	R Barrichello	1m11.263s
5	J Villeneuve	1m12.114s	5	R Schumacher	1m11.673s
6	R Barrichello	1m12.156s	6	N Heidfeld	1m11.718s
7	J Button	1m12.238s	7	J Villeneuve	1m11.724s
8	G Fisichella	1m12.287s	8	J Button	1m11.865s
9	F Alonso	1m12.416s	9	F Alonso	1m11.877s
10	JP Montoya	1m12.477s	10	K Räikkönen	1m12.135s
11	T Monteiro	1m12.627s	11	JP Montoya	1m12.150s
12	C Albers	1m12.711s	12	M Webber	1m12.292s
13	C Klien	1m12.773s	13	S Speed	1m12.792s
14	K Räikkönen	1m12.777s	14	C Albers	1m12.854s
15	M Webber	1m12.935s	15	T Monteiro	1m12.864s
16	S Speed	1m13.167s	16	C Klien	1m12.925s
17	D Coulthard	1m13.180s			
18	T Sato	1m13.496s			
19	N Rosberg	1m13.506s			
20	J Trulli	1m13.787s			
21	V Liuzzi	1m14.041s			
22	F Montagny	1m16.036s			

Best sectors – Practice		Speed trap – Practice		Best sectors – Qualifying	
Sec 1 M Schumacher	21.967s	1 M Schumacher	209.2mph	Sec 1 M Schumacher	21.850s
Sec 2 F Massa	28.445s	2 G Fisichella	207.3mph	Sec 2 M Schumacher	28.397s
Sec 3 M Schumacher	20.134s	3 F Massa	206.2mph	Sec 3 M Schumacher	20.200s

Fernando Alonso
"I wasn't competitive and the car lacked grip as well as completing race two of a hard engine cycle. So I did the maximum possible, and made sure I scored points."

Michael Schumacher
"It was a great weekend with pole yesterday and this victory today! We had prepared well for these last two races, but in Canada were unable to demonstrate that fact."

Kimi Räikkönen
"I made a good start. However, things got messy at Turn 2 and Juan Pablo hit me from behind. There's no point blaming anyone as these things happen in racing."

Jenson Button
"We were three-abreast into Turn 2 when Montoya decided to pass. He had room up the inside so I don't know why he hit my wheel, but that pushed me into Heidfeld."

Jacques Villeneuve
"I was quite a bit faster than the three ahead, so I was waiting for the stops to see what happened. The engine just gave up, sad, as it was the first race on this engine."

Jarno Trulli
"Even though I was starting from the pits, we had a chance. I profited from the Turn 1 pile-up. But I'm happy as I matched the others despite carrying more fuel."

Giancarlo Fisichella
"I was cautious under braking into Turn 1, which let Fernando past. But when the safety car went in, I had a speed advantage and he didn't make life difficult for me."

Felipe Massa
"The start went very well and I managed to pass Michael. I had a strong first stint, but he passed me during the first pit stop, when I had a clutch problem."

Juan Pablo Montoya
"When you start so far back you have to race to make up places. Unluckily, as everybody braked for Turn 2, I was squeezed by one of the Hondas and sadly I hit Kimi."

Rubens Barrichello
"It was a shame that only nine cars finished as I wanted the fans to have a great race. There was a lot of action for them, but the lap 1 incident was unfortunate."

Nick Heidfeld
"I escaped unhurt, but don't know what happened. I had a good start, and had made up three places so was almost next to Jacques. Then, all of a sudden, I was airborne."

Ralf Schumacher
"We were looking good for points but I had a very long brake pedal so I had to come in when I was in fifth. Then the team found we had a wheel bearing failure."

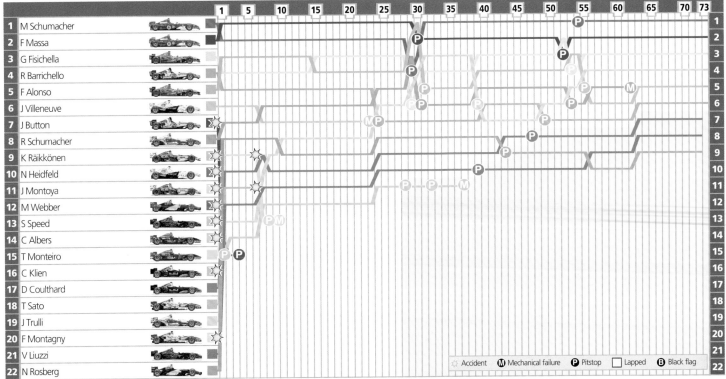

		1	5	10	15	20	25	30	35	40	45	50	55	60	65	70	73	
1	M Schumacher																	1
2	F Massa																	2
3	G Fisichella																	3
4	R Barrichello																	4
5	F Alonso																	5
6	J Villeneuve																	6
7	J Button																	7
8	R Schumacher																	8
9	K Räikkönen																	9
10	N Heidfeld																	10
11	J Montoya																	11
12	M Webber																	12
13	S Speed																	13
14	C Albers																	14
15	T Monteiro																	15
16	C Klien																	16
17	D Coulthard																	17
18	T Sato																	18
19	J Trulli																	19
20	F Montagny																	20
21	V Liuzzi																	21
22	N Rosberg																	22

☼ Accident　Ⓜ Mechanical failure　Ⓟ Pitstop　▢ Lapped　Ⓑ Black flag

QUALIFYING 3

	Driver	Time
1	M Schumacher	1m10.832s
2	F Massa	1m11.435s
3	G Fisichella	1m11.920s
4	R Barrichello	1m12.109s
5	F Alonso	1m12.449s
6	J Villeneuve	1m12.479s
7	J Button	1m12.523s
8	R Schumacher	1m12.795s
9	K Räikkönen	1m13.174s
10	N Heidfeld	1m15.280s

GRID

	Driver	Time
1	M Schumacher	1m10.832s
2	F Massa	1m11.435s
3	G Fisichella	1m11.920s
4	R Barrichello	1m12.109s
5	F Alonso	1m12.449s
6	J Villeneuve	1m12.479s
7	J Button	1m12.523s
8	R Schumacher	1m12.795s
9	K Räikkönen	1m13.174s
10	N Heidfeld	1m15.280s
11	JP Montoya	1m12.150s
12	M Webber	1m12.292s
13	S Speed	1m12.792s
14	C Albers	1m12.854s
15	T Monteiro	1m12.864s
16	C Klien	1m12.925s
17	D Coulthard	1m13.180s
18	T Sato	1m13.496s
19	F Montagny	1m16.036s
20*	V Liuzzi	1m14.041s
21^	N Rosberg	no time
22	J Trulli	1m13.787s

* 10-PLACE GRID PENALTY
^ SENT TO BACK FOR MISSING A WEIGHT CHECK

RACE

	Driver	Car	Laps	Time	Avg. mph	Fastest	Stops
1	M Schumacher	Ferrari 248	73	1h34m35.199s	120.625	1m12.719s	2
2	F Massa	Ferrari 248	73	1h34m43.183s	120.455	1m12.954s	2
3	G Fisichella	Renault R26	73	1h34m51.794s	120.273	1m13.131s	2
4	J Trulli	Toyota TF106B	73	1h34m58.803s	120.125	1m13.269s	1
5	F Alonso	Renault R26	73	1h35m03.609s	120.024	1m13.316s	2
6	R Barrichello	Honda RA106	73	1h35m11.715s	119.854	1m13.611s	2
7	D Coulthard	Red Bull-Ferrari RB2	72	1h34m59.009s	118.476	1m14.730s	1
8	V Liuzzi	Toro Rosso-Cosworth STR01	72	1h35m05.359s	118.344	1m14.286s	1
9	N Rosberg	Williams-Cosworth FW28	72	1h35m09.147s	118.265	1m14.707s	2
R	R Schumacher	Toyota TF106B	62	Wheel bearing	-	1m13.225s	2
R	C Albers	Midland-Toyota M16	37	Gearbox	-	1m14.731s	3
R	J Villeneuve	BMW Sauber F1.06	23	Engine	-	1m13.934s	0
R	T Monteiro	Midland-Toyota M16	9	Accident	-	1m22.036s	1
R	T Sato	Super Aguri-Honda SA05	6	Accident	-	1m43.802s	0
R	J Button	Honda RA106	3	Accident	-	2m04.692s	0
R	K Räikkönen	McLaren-Mercedes MP4-21	0	Accident	-	-	0
R	N Heidfeld	BMW Sauber F1.06	0	Accident	-	-	0
R	JP Montoya	McLaren-Mercedes MP4-21	0	Accident	-	-	0
R	M Webber	Williams-Cosworth FW28	0	Accident	-	-	0
R	S Speed	Toro Rosso-Cosworth STR01	0	Accident	-	-	0
R	C Klien	Red Bull-Ferrari RB2	0	Accident	-	-	0
R	F Montagny	Super Aguri-Honda SA05	0	Accident	-	-	0

CHAMPIONSHIP

	Driver	Pts
1	F Alonso	88
2	M Schumacher	69
3	G Fisichella	43
4	K Räikkönen	39
5	F Massa	36
6	JP Montoya	26
7	J Button	16
8	R Barrichello	16
9	N Heidfeld	12
10	D Coulthard	10
11	R Schumacher	8
12	J Trulli	8
13	J Villeneuve	7
14	M Webber	6
15	N Rosberg	4
16	V Liuzzi	1
	C Klien	1

Speed trap – Qualifying

1	F Massa	207.7mph
2	M Schumacher	207.3mph
3	G Fisichella	206.1mph

Fastest Lap

M Schumacher 1m12.719s
(128.957mph) on lap 56

Fastest speed trap

G Fisichella	208.7mph

Slowest speed trap

T Monteiro	199.5mph

Fastest pit stop

1	G Fisichella	21.784s
2	R Schumacher	22.160s
3	F Massa	22.732s

Constructor — Pts

	Constructor	Pts
1	Renault	131
2	Ferrari	105
3	McLaren-Mercedes	65
4	Honda	32
5	BMW Sauber	19
6	Toyota	16
7	Red Bull-Ferrari	11
8	Williams-Cosworth	10
9	Toro Rosso-Cosworth	1

David Coulthard

"I was next to Christian into Turn 1 and could see Tonio on the outside, so I backed off. Montoya created a shunt. From there, it was just a battle with Liuzzi and Rosberg."

Mark Webber

"There was someone slow in the middle of the track and I was minding my own business and got harpooned by somebody on the right rear. I got launched."

Vitantonio Liuzzi

"We've come close, but now we've got the team's first point. I was racing with Coulthard, but he was a bit quicker than me in the second stint. We're on fire now!"

Tiago Monteiro

"I saw a gap and found myself in ninth. Unluckily, at the restart, Sato made an unrealistic move on me heading into the corner, locking his wheels and ramming into me."

Takuma Sato

"At the restart, I caught DC and Monteiro and I was half a length up beside Monteiro into Turn 1. He kept pushing across, so I couldn't go anywhere and I ran out of space."

Christian Klien

"I passed both Midlands and, heading into Turn 1, was on the inside. But then it got very tight. I was next to a Williams and then a lot of cars crashed together."

Nico Rosberg

"It's a disappointing result as I was up to eighth after lap 1, but the car was a handful. Apart from affecting our pace, it made the race really physically demanding."

Scott Speed

"I got by Webber and Ralf at Turn 1 and then it all fell apart at Turn 2. It wouldn't have mattered if I'd tried to go inside or outside as the track was blocked with cars flipping."

Christijan Albers

"I collided at the start and lost my front wing, which is why I pitted early. I also sustained damage to my bargeboard and sidepod wing, and then my transmission failed."

Franck Montagny

"I'm normally careful at the start. I think Coulthard pushed against Klien and he spun in front of me and you can't stop from 200kph when the car in front is 5m away."

FORMULA 1™ GRAND PRIX
DE FRANCE 2006
Magny-Cours

MICHAEL AGAIN

Michael Schumacher did all he could to cut Fernando Alonso's points lead, but second place for the reigning champion on the team's homeground restricted the impact

Michael Schumacher kept the World Championship battle alive with a superb victory for Ferrari in the French Grand Prix, but once again Renault's points leader Fernando Alonso limited the damage to his lead by securing second place. Alas, the race itself was an anti-climax, and the nail-biting contest that the grid line-up had suggested never really materialised.

There was plenty to talk about off the track, however. The biggest story of the week was Juan Pablo Montoya's announcement on the Sunday before the French GP that he was going to NASCAR with Chip Ganassi in 2007. That didn't sit too well with McLaren team principal Ron Dennis and, on Tuesday, it was announced that Montoya would be put on the bench, in Ron's own words, and test driver Pedro de la Rosa would have the drive for the foreseeable future. The sudden departure of one of the sport's most colourful stars, albeit one having a mediocre season, came as a huge surprise.

Just as dramatic was the ongoing future engine rules saga. With a nominal deadline for agreement set by the FIA for 16:00 on Sunday, there were endless discussions and meetings through the Magny-Cours weekend. The issue was clouded further after FIA President Max Mosley came up with the suggestion that the

manufacturers should subsidise a customer engine supply. An offer finally came just before the start of the race and Mosley rejected it as being inadequate.

After Schumacher's win in the United States GP, even Ferrari insiders admitted that it would be hard to sustain the momentum at Magny-Cours, but Bridgestone again brought a good tyre. Michael used it to secure pole position despite a pit fire that left him with virtually no running on Saturday morning. With team-mate Felipe Massa alongside to protect him from Alonso, who'd qualified third, the prospects for an exciting race looked good.

Michael duly got away well at the start and never looked under any serious threat, as Massa did his bit by just containing Alonso's attack, and then helping Michael to open a gap. From the outside, it looked as though Massa was delaying Alonso, but the Renault driver was in fact pretty much at full stretch in that first stint, and he could barely hang on to Massa.

"It was close, and I was nearly on the grass at one point," said Alonso of the first-lap scramble, "so I had to back off after I tried to overtake him, but obviously it's very difficult on this track so we would have to wait for the pit stops. We hoped at that stage to have perfect consistency in the tyres, so we knew that we should be in front of Felipe."

"It was quite hard, especially at the start," Massa admitted. "He got alongside at the first corner and it was tight, but I managed to stay in position and he was pushing a little bit, especially in the first five laps. Then I managed to improve my pace and to find a gap between us, and it was comfortable to the first stop."

Alonso certainly couldn't match the pace of leader Schumacher, whose tyres held up rather better than the Renault team had anticipated.

"We did get a surprise in qualifying as we didn't think that they had that pace for a single lap," said Renault's Executive Director of Engineering Pat

Symonds. "In a way, that sort of led us to believe that maybe their degradation was going to be a bit higher in the race. We were sure that they were going to go for three stops, and that backed up our feeling. But the surprise in the race was that it wasn't high. In fact, it was actually better than ours, so that made it difficult."

The three frontrunners pitted on consecutive laps, with Alonso the second to come in. That was crucial. Having seen how long Massa was stationary, and thus confirmed that he was going – like Michael – for three stops, Renault put in a little extra fuel in order to put Alonso onto a two-stopper.

"After starting behind the two Ferraris, we guessed

OPPOSITE It was a less than shining meeting for Honda. Rubens Barrichello was their better qualifier, in 13th position. Neither car finished

ABOVE Felipe Massa keeps Fernando Alonso at bay on lap 1 as Ferrari team-mate Michael Schumacher escapes in the lead

INSIDE LINE
JARNO TRULLI

TOYOTA DRIVER

"There was no great result to speak of, and I'm talking about a retirement when it could have been a podium, but the car was competitive and I qualified fourth, which equalled my best starting position of the season in Canada.

When I arrived at Magny-Cours, all everyone wanted to talk about was

the World Cup final. Being Italian, I enjoyed it of course, but it doesn't change my life. It was an interesting game and I think both teams deserved to win. There, how's that! Do I get a job as a diplomat?

Actually, I really like France and I've always had a good time, both professionally and personally. This year was really good. I celebrated my 32nd birthday on Thursday and then I went to the *Pink Floyd* concert on Friday evening. With the race and the concert it was a very special atmosphere, almost like a carnival.

The car felt competitive right from the start of the weekend and my fourth on the grid was in spite of a heavy fuel load. I was doing a two-stop race, so we were looking very good and although the Ferrari and Renault pace was strong, as usual, we definitely had

the potential to finish on the podium. I was in a podium position in Monte Carlo late in the race and I was hoping to make up for it here. But suddenly the brake pedal went long and I had no choice but to stop, which was frustrating.

As far as next year is concerned, I have agreed a new deal with the team and it's now in the detail stages. I am more than happy to stay at Toyota because my ambition is the same as the team's, which is to challenge for the World Championship. You don't get to that stage overnight, which is why I'm more than happy to look towards a longer-term future. I think I've proved my worth over the past two seasons and, when the team reaches a position to challenge, which I am sure it will, I want to be a part of that.

Last year, we made such a strong

start to the season, which was perhaps unexpected by a lot of people, and I was running at the front in the early races. This year, we changed tyre supplier and it takes time to tune the car and the suspension to the tyres. We had some other issues too, so things were much more difficult, but the impressive thing is that heads did not go down in the team and everybody kept working hard. It's easy to do that when things are going well, not so easy when results are less good. The character and spirit of the team has impressed me."

at that point that they were on three stops," reported Alonso. "It's difficult to overtake on this track, or nearly impossible actually, so if we were going to stay on the same strategy we would finish behind the Ferrari drivers. But if we did a different strategy, we had the possibility of finishing in front of them.

"We always have two options. Especially so here, as it's wide open between two and three stops and the first stop was similar in both cases around lap 17, 18 and 19 and from there we decided. I think it was quite clear and our tyres seemed to be a little more constant in the long runs, so we chose to go for two stops."

It was soon evident that Massa would be unable to resist Alonso, and the Spaniard was easily able to jump him for second in the latter stages, securing eight vital points. That put a damper on Michael's celebrations, but a two-point gain was better than nothing.

"We had a good start and we drove our race from there," said the German. "We weren't sure how the race would go as we didn't do any long runs because of some problems we had on Saturday morning. But I have to say that the car, the tyres, the whole package worked superbly, and it's a great result. I'm sorry for Felipe that he couldn't keep his second place."

"It was clear Fernando was in trouble, certainly in the first stint," explained Ferrari Technical Director Ross Brawn. "So he was dropping back behind Felipe, but there were different phases. Michael's tyres were good the whole time, while Felipe was good at the beginning and then lost a bit of performance towards the end. It went in phases. We tried to tune the car as it went along and with Michael there were no problems. They went away for Felipe in the middle of the race, and it was disappointing that he couldn't beat Fernando. It's not the gain in the points that we'd hoped for, but it's a good gain in the constructors' and that's important. We're going in the right direction…"

Toyota continued to show good form, and both

cars were in the top five in qualifying, emphasising that Bridgestone had got its sums right. Ralf Schumacher had a good drive to fourth place, despite a delay in his first pit stop. However, he should have been beaten by team-mate Jarno Trulli, but after a strong early run the Italian retired as the victim of engine and brake problems.

It was a difficult weekend for McLaren as Kimi Räikkönen couldn't better fifth place, finishing just ahead of Giancarlo Fisichella, who had a frustrating afternoon.

"It looked quite good until the second stint," said Symonds of Fisichella's afternoon, "and then he got a lot of graining, which was funny as Fernando didn't. Fisi also had a dreadful qualifying lap – mistakes I'm afraid."

Meanwhile, Pedro de la Rosa's return proved to be spectacular. Despite spending much of the race stuck behind Mark Webber's Williams, he impressed on his way to seventh. He even set the third fastest lap of the race behind the two Ferrari drivers and a little under 0.1s faster than the best by Räikkönen.

"I was pretty careful with Kimi and Fisichella," de la Rosa said of the start. "When we got to Turn 8 I was looking for a way past Giancarlo, and Webber overtook me on the inside. I didn't want to close the door because I wanted to finish the race. After that, I thought he was a little bit unsporting. To cover one side is OK, but then he was moving from side to side and I didn't know where he was going to throw the car next. It was a little bit too much, to be honest."

Good work at the first round of pitstops allowed de la Rosa to jump the Williams, but then he got caught behind BMW's Jacques Villeneuve, who had yet to pit and stayed out for another nine laps. Only when the Canadian stopped could de la Rosa run at his true pace.

"It was frustrating when after the first pit stop I saw Jacques. I thought 'man, it's not my race'! But, once I was in clean air, I was pushing very nicely, the car was well balanced and we could recover what we lost."

The final point went to BMW's Nick Heidfeld after

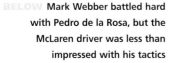

BELOW Mark Webber battled hard with Pedro de la Rosa, but the McLaren driver was less than impressed with his tactics

OPPOSITE The BMW Sauber sprouted new nose wings and Nick Heidfeld used his F1.06 to race to the final point for eighth place

INSIDE LINE
WILLY RAMPF

SAUBER BMW TECHNICAL DIRECTOR

"The nose wings that we ran in France came purely from computational fluid dynamics (CFD) followed by wind tunnel optimisation. The aim was to improve the airflow around the engine cover and onto the rear wing. They had a similar effect to the roll-hoop wings fitted to other cars. They were not actively creating downforce, but they improved the airflow around the car. Also, if you were following another car they smoothed out the wake a little.

We started wind-tunnel work a couple of weeks before the Magny Cours race and we track-tested the wings at Jerez. The results translated just the way we expected and the drivers said the car was more stable. There was a small lap-time benefit too, something in the region of a tenth of a second at Magny Cours.

Surprisingly, there were no negative comments in terms of visibility. I was a bit surprised because when I first saw the parts in the wind tunnel I thought there may be a distracting or disturbing element as far as the drivers were concerned. But we showed it to them early enough, and we also mocked it up to see if there were any downsides, and to be honest, none of the drivers had a problem with them or even really noticed them while driving. At one of the tests we ran a back-to-back and when we took them off the drivers asked for them to be put back because of the additional stability.

And then the FIA stepped in. We showed them to the FIA before we used them, but afterwards I think there was a general feeling that they might obstruct the view and so Charlie Whiting came up with a clarification, which we respected. I don't think they were very pretty, and maybe it was a bit like the X-wings that people used to run on the sidepods.

I think the official line to ban the X-wings was 'dangerous construction', but our nose wings were never rated as a dangerous construction. Let's just say that the car looked different!

It's always a bit frustrating when you have a good idea and then it gets banned, more for reasons of safety than technical matters, but it's all part of the game.

The other thing about Magny Cours was that Jacques Villeneuve was the only one who ran the soft Michelin tyres, with everyone else thinking they wouldn't last. He actually put them on to get a good starting position, although he ended up in traffic and qualified 16th, but they also turned out to be very good race tyres. Jacques was never very hard on the tyres and I think more drivers could have used the soft compound, Nick (Heidfeld) included."

another solid race, while David Coulthard just missed out points by finishing in ninth place after a strong performance for Red Bull Racing.

Magny-Cours was a bad venue for Honda as its cars were well off the pace, and neither Jenson Button nor Rubens Barrichello made it to the chequered flag after hitting engine problems. Williams had an equally difficult time, with Webber damaging his car after a rear tyre failure and Nico Rosberg managing only 14th after picking up a 10-place grid penalty for having an engine change and struggling throughout.

To sum up, the French GP wasn't the most exciting race of the season, but at least that battle for World Championship honours became marginally closer and Michael was confident that he could keep on gaining.

"To me, Indianapolis wasn't really the reference in a way. We were too dominant," Michael mused. "Looking at this race, yes, it's a reference point. We have clearly made up ground on Renault and we have to keep on working at that pace and for sure everybody will just keep pushing for the last seven races. It's far from being over…"

SNAPSHOT FROM
FRANCE

CLOCKWISE FROM RIGHT Former Renault racer Rene Arnoux celebrates another Renault landmark with Alonso and Fisichella; this is what happens if you run wide...; national colours; dark and light; David Richards was on the prowl; Honda's Nick Fry; Michael celebrates Italy's winning of the World Cup

WEEKEND HEADLINES

■ Highlight of the French GP for many was the Roger Waters concert on Friday evening. Despite heavy rain, the Pink Floyd founder member put on a great show that included a full run through of *Dark Side of the Moon*, with Nick Mason joining him behind the drums. Tickets for paddock insiders were hard to come by, but Michael Schumacher, Jean Todt and Ross Brawn managed to get backstage at the interval.

■ Just before the French GP, the World Motor Sport Council confirmed that the third session of qualifying would be reduced from 20 to 15 minutes with immediate effect. It was felt generally that the final session dragged on for too long. Also rubber-stamped were plans to outlaw third cars running on Fridays from 2007 onwards.

■ Super Aguri confirmed that, having let Franck Montagny contest his home race, the team would give its second car to Sakon Yamamoto from the German GP onwards. The team also tested its revised SA06 at Silverstone a few days after the French GP, in preparation for its planned debut in Germany.

■ Straight after the French GP weekend, Renault Managing Director Flavio Briatore went into hospital in Rome for what was announced as an operation on a kidney stone. It was later revealed that he had in fact shown early signs of cancer that had fortunately been spotted in time. The Italian admitted that the scare had made him have a serious think about his lifestyle.

■ Two days after the French GP, 1996 World Champion Damon Hill got back behind the wheel of a Renault F1 car when he conducted a brief demonstration in London's Whitehall in front of Prime Minister Tony Blair. The event, part of a promotion for the return of the Motor Show to London, was designed to promote Britain's motorsport industry.

RACE RESULTS
FRANCE
MAGNY-COURS

RACE DATE July 15th
CIRCUIT LENGTH 2.739 miles
NO. OF LAPS 70
RACE DISTANCE 189.630 miles
WEATHER Sunny & dry, 35°C
TRACK TEMP 54°C
RACE DAY ATTENDANCE 84,000
LAP RECORD Michael Schumacher,
1m15.377s, 130.910mph, 2004

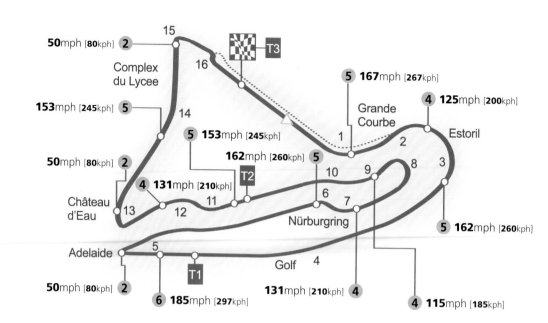

PRACTICE 1

	Driver	Time	Laps
1	R Kubica	1m16.794s	31
2	A Davidson	1m17.133s	29
3	J Button	1m18.160s	4
4	R Schumacher	1m18.752s	6
5	A Sutil	1m18.777s	32
6	N Jani	1m18.962s	21
7	A Wurz	1m19.055s	17
8	J Villeneuve	1m19.063s	6
9	R Doornbos	1m19.311s	20
10	N Rosberg	1m19.401s	6
11	C Albers	1m19.465s	7
12	J Trulli	1m19.806s	7
13	T Monteiro	1m20.335s	7
14	F Montagny	1m20.790s	11
15	T Sato	1m21.160s	10
16	S Yamamoto	1m23.891s	11
17	V Liuzzi	no time	2
18	F Alonso	no time	1
19	D Coulthard	no time	1
20	P de la Rosa	no time	1
21	G Fisichella	no time	1
22	C Klien	no time	1
23	K Räikkönen	no time	1
24	S Speed	no time	1
25	R Barrichello	no time	0
26	N Heidfeld	no time	0
27	F Massa	no time	0
28	M Schumacher	no time	0
29	M Webber	no time	0

PRACTICE 2

	Driver	Time	Laps
1	R Kubica	1m16.902s	33
2	F Alonso	1m17.498s	14
3	A Davidson	1m17.750s	37
4	A Wurz	1m17.859s	29
5	G Fisichella	1m17.916s	13
6	M Schumacher	1m17.938s	16
7	A Sutil	1m18.049s	31
8	R Doornbos	1m18.175s	28
9	R Schumacher	1m18.274s	21
10	N Jani	1m18.639s	32
11	J Trulli	1m18.721s	23
12	J Button	1m19.005s	18
13	F Massa	1m19.013s	20
14	N Heidfeld	1m19.108s	15
15	K Räikkönen	1m19.140s	9
16	C Albers	1m19.183s	21
17	R Barrichello	1m19.259s	5
18	M Webber	1m19.413s	10
19	V Liuzzi	1m19.589s	14
20	N Rosberg	1m19.692s	19
21	T Monteiro	1m19.701s	19
22	P de la Rosa	1m19.809s	14
23	T Sato	1m19.996s	22
24	S Speed	1m20.003s	12
25	D Coulthard	1m20.135s	12
26	J Villeneuve	1m20.154s	11
27	C Klien	1m20.409s	14
28	F Montagny	1m21.132s	14
29	S Yamamoto	1m21.969s	32

PRACTICE 3

	Driver	Time	Laps
1	J Villeneuve	1m17.005s	13
2	N Heidfeld	1m17.049s	16
3	J Trulli	1m17.056s	18
4	N Rosberg	1m17.188s	16
5	M Webber	1m17.358s	12
6	J Button	1m17.476s	19
7	K Räikkönen	1m17.556s	12
8	P de la Rosa	1m17.653s	16
9	R Schumacher	1m17.666s	18
10	D Coulthard	1m17.859s	19
11	G Fisichella	1m17.995s	17
12	C Albers	1m18.059s	24
13	V Liuzzi	1m18.199s	20
14	M Schumacher	1m18.214s	5
15	F Massa	1m18.396s	8
16	F Alonso	1m18.447s	16
17	T Monteiro	1m18.487s	23
18	S Speed	1m18.545s	20
19	C Klien	1m18.631s	17
20	R Barrichello	1m18.961s	20
21	F Montagny	1m19.497s	18
22	T Sato	1m21.497s	10

QUALIFYING 1

	Driver	Time
1	J Trulli	1m15.550s
2	M Schumacher	1m15.865s
3	R Schumacher	1m15.949s
4	K Räikkönen	1m16.154s
5	F Massa	1m16.277s
6	F Alonso	1m16.328s
7	D Coulthard	1m16.350s
8	M Webber	1m16.531s
9	N Rosberg	1m16.534s
10	P de la Rosa	1m16.679s
11	N Heidfeld	1m16.686s
12	G Fisichella	1m16.825s
13	C Klien	1m16.921s
14	C Albers	1m16.962s
15	R Barrichello	1m17.022s
16	S Speed	1m17.117s
17	V Liuzzi	1m17.164s
18	J Villeneuve	1m17.304s
19	J Button	1m17.495s
20	T Monteiro	1m17.589s
21	F Montagny	1m18.637s
22	T Sato	1m18.845s

QUALIFYING 2

	Driver	Time
1	M Schumacher	1m15.111s
2	R Schumacher	1m15.625s
3	F Massa	1m15.679s
4	F Alonso	1m15.706s
5	K Räikkönen	1m15.742s
6	J Trulli	1m15.776s
7	G Fisichella	1m15.901s
8	P de la Rosa	1m15.902s
9	N Rosberg	1m15.926s
10	D Coulthard	1m15.974s
11	M Webber	1m16.129s
12	N Heidfeld	1m16.294s
13	C Klien	1m16.433s
14	R Barrichello	1m17.027s
15	S Speed	1m17.063s
16	C Albers	1m17.105s

Best sectors – Practice		Speed trap – Practice		Best sectors – Qualifying	
Sec 1 F Alonso	25.112s	1 F Alonso	187.4mph	Sec 1 M Schumacher	24.619s
Sec 2 R Kubica	26.875s	2 G Fisichella	187.2mph	Sec 2 M Schumacher	26.443s
Sec 3 A Davidson	24.635s	3 N Rosberg	186.4mph	Sec 3 M Schumacher	24.049s

Fernando Alonso
"We went into the race with two strategies and, once we saw that Ferrari would be three-stopping, we knew it would be hard to pass them so we chose to stop twice."

Michael Schumacher
"That was a fantastic result, even if in all honesty it was unexpected. I got a good start and from then on I could run my own race. Now I must keep this momentum going."

Kimi Räikkönen
"A disappointing race, as the car was handling well. We were lacking the speed to win, but I lost a few tenths in the second stop which cost me fourth place."

Jenson Button
"We were going much better today and I was up to 11th place and catching Speed when I felt a loss of power as I came onto the back straight."

Jacques Villeneuve
"I had to pass Barrichello at the start, but after that it was quite a boring race. The car was very good and the only problem was my qualifying result."

Jarno Trulli
"That was a pity, as everything was going well. After the first stop, I felt a drop-off from the engine. Soon after that the brake pedal started getting longer and longer."

Giancarlo Fisichella
"The car was getting more and more difficult to drive, with tyre graining in the second stint that meant I couldn't build a gap over Ralf and Kimi to stay ahead."

Felipe Massa
"I was on a three-stop strategy and Alonso switched to a two-stopper and that meant I wasn't able to fight with him on the track. I also hit a lot of traffic."

Pedro de la Rosa
"The car had the speed and I feel I could have scored more points if I hadn't lost position to Webber at the start. This meant that I lost time in the opening stint."

Rubens Barrichello
"It looks as though the engine failed because there was a lot of smoke and I lost all the power. However, I believe in this team and we will react to this."

Nick Heidfeld
"My car was OK, I scored a point and more wasn't possible. Unusually for me, my start was average, but I passed Coulthard in the hairpin on the opening lap."

Ralf Schumacher
"It's a pity that we had a problem with the wheel nut at the first stop, as we could have made the podium. The car was quick and the tyres were very good too."

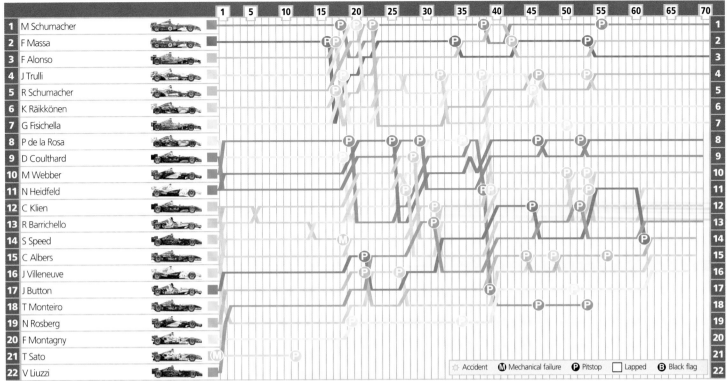

	Driver	
1	M Schumacher	
2	F Massa	
3	F Alonso	
4	J Trulli	
5	R Schumacher	
6	K Räikkönen	
7	G Fisichella	
8	P de la Rosa	
9	D Coulthard	
10	M Webber	
11	N Heidfeld	
12	C Klien	
13	R Barrichello	
14	S Speed	
15	C Albers	
16	J Villeneuve	
17	J Button	
18	T Monteiro	
19	N Rosberg	
20	F Montagny	
21	T Sato	
22	V Liuzzi	

Legend: ☼ Accident Ⓜ Mechanical failure Ⓟ Pitstop ☐ Lapped Ⓑ Black flag

QUALIFYING 3

	Driver	Time
1	M Schumacher	1m15.493s
2	F Massa	1m15.510s
3	F Alonso	1m15.785s
4	J Trulli	1m16.036s
5	R Schumacher	1m16.091s
6	K Räikkönen	1m16.281s
7	G Fisichella	1m16.345s
8	P de la Rosa	1m16.632s
9	N Rosberg	1m18.272s
10	D Coulthard	1m18.663s

GRID

	Driver	Time
1	M Schumacher	1m15.493s
2	F Massa	1m15.510s
3	F Alonso	1m15.785s
4	J Trulli	1m16.036s
5	R Schumacher	1m16.091s
6	K Räikkönen	1m16.281s
7	G Fisichella	1m16.345s
8	P de la Rosa	1m16.632s
9	D Coulthard	1m18.663s
10	M Webber	1m16.129s
11	N Heidfeld	1m16.294s
12	C Klien	1m16.433s
13	R Barrichello	1m17.027s
14	S Speed	1m17.063s
15	C Albers	1m17.105s
16	J Villeneuve	1m17.304s
17	J Button	1m17.495s
18	T Monteiro	1m17.589s
19*	N Rosberg	1m18.272s
20	F Montagny	1m18.637s
21	T Sato	1m18.845s
22*	V Liuzzi	1m17.164s

* 10-PLACE GRID PENALTY

RACE

	Driver	Car	Laps	Time	Avg. mph	Fastest	Stops
1	M Schumacher	Ferrari 248	70	1h32m07.803s	124.714	1m17.111s	3
2	F Alonso	Renault R26	70	1h32m17.934s	124.653	1m17.770s	2
3	F Massa	Ferrari 248	70	1h32m30.349s	124.374	1m17.141s	2
4	R Schumacher	Toyota TF106B	70	1h32m35.015s	124.269	1m17.809s	2
5	K Räikkönen	McLaren-Mercedes MP4-21	70	1h32m40.809s	124.140	1m17.717s	3
6	G Fisichella	Renault R26	70	1h32m53.068s	123.867	1m18.057s	2
7	P de la Rosa	McLaren-Mercedes MP4-21	70	1h32m57.210s	123.775	1m17.625s	2
8	N Heidfeld	BMW Sauber F1.06	69	1h32m20.892s	122.805	1m18.809s	2
9	D Coulthard	Red Bull-Ferrari RB2	69	1h32m24.118s	122.734	1m18.978s	2
10	S Speed	Toro Rosso-Cosworth STR01	69	1h32m41.592s	122.348	1m18.674s	2
11	J Villeneuve	BMW Sauber F1.06	69	1h32m49.908s	122.166	1m17.906s	3
12	C Klien	Red Bull-Ferrari RB2	69	1h32m50.705s	122.148	1m18.968s	3
13	V Liuzzi	Toro Rosso-Cosworth STR01	69	1h32m54.565s	122.083	1m18.241s	2
14	N Rosberg	Williams-Cosworth FW28	68	1h32m08.267s	121.301	1m18.796s	3
15	C Albers	Midland-Toyota M16	68	1h32m12.747s	121.203	1m19.356s	2
16	F Montagny	Super Aguri-Honda SA05	67	1h32m48.547s	118.651	1m20.113s	3
R	J Button	Honda RA106	61	Engine	-	1m18.510s	2
R	M Webber	Williams-Cosworth FW28	53	Wheel rim	-	1m18.859s	4
R	J Trulli	Toyota TF106B	39	Brakes	-	1m18.036s	2
R	R Barrichello	Honda RA106	18	Engine	-	1m20.094s	0
R	T Monteiro	Midland-Toyota M16	11	Accident	-	1m21.663s	0
R	T Sato	Super Aguri-Honda SA05	0	Clutch	-	-	0

CHAMPIONSHIP

	Driver	Pts
1	F Alonso	96
2	M Schumacher	79
3	G Fisichella	46
4	K Räikkönen	43
5	F Massa	42
6	JP Montoya	26
7	J Button	16
8	R Barrichello	16
9	R Schumacher	13
10	N Heidfeld	13
11	D Coulthard	10
12	J Trulli	8
13	J Villeneuve	7
14	M Webber	6
15	N Rosberg	4
16	P de la Rosa	2
17	V Liuzzi	1
	C Klien	1

Speed trap – Qualifying

1	M Schumacher	191.0mph
2	K Räikkönen	189.5mph
3	G Fisichella	189.2mph

Fastest Lap

M Schumacher 1m17.111s
(127.966mph) on lap 46

Fastest speed trap

F Alonso 190.0mph

Slowest speed trap

R Barrichello 182.4mph

Fastest pit stop

1	M Schumacher	19.423s
2	M Schumacher	19.686s
3	N Rosberg	19.951s

Constructor

	Constructor	Pts
1	Renault	142
2	Ferrari	121
3	McLaren-Mercedes	71
4	Honda	32
5	Toyota	21
6	BMW Sauber	20
7	Red Bull-Ferrari	11
8	Williams-Cosworth	10
9	Toro Rosso-Cosworth	1

David Coulthard

"That was the worst result we could get, having started from ninth on the grid. We're vultures at the moment, picking up points when other people fall out."

Mark Webber

"I'm massively disappointed as we could have scored a point. I was trying to stay with the quicker guys, but we had heat issues with the inside edge of the tyre."

Vitantonio Liuzzi

"Being at the back isn't the best way to start, especially at a track like this. I don't think having a V10 engine helped us, but the tyres and car worked well."

Tiago Monteiro

"I was trying to pass Montagny when the car suddenly snapped around at the entry to the first high-speed chicane and I flew over the kerb very violently."

Takuma Sato

"I had a clutch problem and struggled to pull away. I caught up with the group on the straight and passed a Midland into the hairpin! Then I couldn't select any gears."

Christian Klien

"I lost revs and dropped places at the start. My rear tyres were going off and I couldn't drive in the slipstream of other cars as my car's temperature went too high."

Nico Rosberg

"It was very hard, as I started from the back and then because the car was difficult to drive. We were struggling with the tyres, and I was also unlucky with the stops."

Scott Speed

"I had a good first lap battle with Rubens. After the first stop, I was in so much pain it was hard to concentrate. I went off the track at one point because of it."

Christijan Albers

"After the first pit stop, I lost first gear and was having problems shifting into others. Had this not occurred, I might have been able to overtake Rosberg."

Franck Montagny

"I had a good start and could fight with the others. I cut the chicane as I'd been passed by Monteiro and couldn't get into the chicane. I have to thank Super Aguri F1."

FORMULA 1™ GROSSER MOBIL 1
PREIS VON DEUTSCHLAND 2006
Hockenheim

RENAULT
PEGGED

The mass damper may be concealed
beneath bodywork, but it was the talk of
Germany as Renault struggled without it
and Ferrari raced to another 1–2

In Germany, it seemed for the first time that Michael
Schumacher really could beat the hitherto dominant
Fernando Alonso to the World Championship. A
crushing performance from Ferrari resulted in Michael
scoring his third win a row, while Alonso was left trailing
home in fifth place. Thus Michael gained six points, but
crucially the reduction of the gap to 11 meant that the
championship was now 'in his hands', which was an
important psychological hurdle. In other words, if he
won all six races from here on, there would be nothing
Alonso could do to stop him from snatching the title.

Renault's poor performance at Hockenheim was
perhaps not unrelated to the major story of the
weekend which concerned the banning of a previously
obscure mechanical development.

Mass dampers were introduced by Renault at the
end of 2005, and since then six other teams had run
them on race weekends. However, FIA Technical
Delegate Charlie Whiting decided after the French GP
that it was time to outlaw them, essentially on the
grounds that they affected aerodynamic performance
by controlling ride height. The inevitable conclusion of
the conspiracy theorists was that this was part of an
attempt to derail the championship leaders…

INSIDE LINE
MARK WEBBER
WILLIAMS DRIVER

"The car felt pretty good, and Bridgestone did a strong job. I think Ferrari opted for a softer tyre, and although my Q2 was about 1.3s from Michael's pace, I was confident that going heavy for a long first stint would make me competitive.

Qualifying 11th meant I was the first car with a free strategy, and I went for a 28-lap opening stint. I got a good start, passed Rubens, then made up more ground when DC and Ralf tangled at the hairpin.

Rubens was quite a bit lighter than me and I was having to work hard to keep him behind. He eventually got down the inside of me into the hairpin, around lap 16 I think, but then his engine let go a couple of laps later.

Pedro de la Rosa had dropped out early on and then Jenson and the Renaults made their first stops about 10 laps before I was due in.

I was really on it, and when Jenson came out behind me with his heavier fuel load, I was able to pull away. The harder-compound Bridgestone stood up well, and I was going quicker every lap. I was up to third by my stop and I came out ahead of Fernando, and was then able to close down and pass Fisichella, who was struggling a bit.

Kimi Räikkönen had been on the pole, but I think they'd had a problem with a sensor and hadn't got much fuel in the car, meaning that he'd run a very short first stint, about 10 laps, and was on a three-stopper. The way it panned out, it was going to be a close-run thing between Kimi, Jenson and myself and I had a chance of a podium.

After his last stop, Kimi came out alongside me and we were just inches apart, but he had the inside for Turn 2. Jenson was a couple of seconds up the road and I thought I had a realistic chance of getting him, but then, with eight laps to go, the water pump broke. It was disappointing but it had been one of our strongest races of the season.

I had told Frank earlier in the week that I was looking elsewhere for 2007. When I originally signed with Williams the circumstances were different, and they were reasonably flush with BMW money. Things had obviously changed and I had agreed to renegotiate the '07 deal. But then my management advised me to look at other options. In 2004 Flavio told me to join Renault when I wanted to drive for Frank and I've had to put up with him for the last two years! This time I thought I'd better listen…"

The judgement came in time for teams to test without the systems and attempt to optimise their cars for Hockenheim. However, having invested time and money in something that had previously been cleared, Renault decided to get the matter out in the open by leaving the system on the T-car for scrutineering here.

That duly generated a report to the stewards from Technical Delegate Jo Bauer, and in turn the stewards asked Renault to offer an explanation. Renault's Executive Director of Engineering Pat Symonds argued that mass dampers were all about mechanical grip and getting the best out of the tyres, and nothing to do with any aero benefit. He also made the obvious point that parts in conventional suspension systems also move, and they affect ride height too.

The stewards deemed that mass dampers were legal after all. Whiting wasn't happy and told the teams of the FIA's intention to appeal. Aware that an appeal couldn't be convened until after the Hungarian GP, he also informed them that if they fitted the dampers and the appeal went against the stewards' decision, they risked a retrospective penalty. Thus Renault ran for the rest of the weekend without the system.

On the surface, it appeared that we had a McLaren

resurgence in Hockenheim, in that Kimi Räikkönen claimed pole and finished on the podium behind the Ferraris, but in reality it was a difficult weekend for the team. A mess-up in qualifying led to the Finn running less fuel than planned and stopping very early in the race (although a lighter load was always on the cards).

He led the Ferraris for the first 10 laps, but in that first stop he had a problem when a nut cross-threaded, so any chance of battling with the Ferraris was gone.

Schumacher and team-mate Felipe Massa then disappeared into the distance. With due respect to the Brazilian, who was getting better by the race, the fact that he was so close to Michael suggested that both had plenty in hand. It was an awesome performance and was perfectly timed for his championship chase.

"We had a nice situation together after the first pit stop," said Michael. "I hit traffic the lap I had to go into the pit stop. He had a free lap, new tyres obviously, and he came out just behind me. I had to take the inner line into Turn 2, which meant that I didn't have a very good exit, and he was alongside on the straight. Luckily he played it safe and we kept position.

"Because we had such a margin we could really drive safely. It would have been difficult and probably you saw

ABOVE Rubens Barrichello runs ahead of Mark Webber on lap 1, but the order was soon reversed

OPPOSITE Sakon Yamamoto took over the second Super Aguri, but his debut lasted for only one lap

cars going off track as it was very dirty off-line. We were running pretty soft compounds and there's a lot of rubber next to the line, with all the dust and so on."

Even Ferrari's usually cautious Technical Director Ross Brawn admitted the race was fairly uneventful: "We didn't quite know where Kimi was in the first stint," he said, "so we had a little bit of concern about graining with the front tyres. We pushed as hard as we thought we could and, when he came in on lap 10, we had the rest of that stint with the knowledge of what was going on, so it was a little more controlled. After the first round of pit stops, everything settled down and we were just nursing the car to the end."

Brawn was also quick to praise Massa: "Felipe's done a great job and for quite a large part of the weekend he found solutions for his car more quickly than Michael did, and we saw that particularly on Friday and Saturday morning – he was much more comfortable with the car, and Michael had to catch up."

In the middle of the race, a hydraulic failure led to Räikkönen driving for a while with key systems switched off while the team sorted it out. With Pedro de la Rosa retiring early, McLaren was continuing to drop the ball. Räikkönen did at least salvage third place.

"When we were fuelling the car, we didn't get as much as we wanted," noted the Finn. "Then it turned out that we needed to get on pole as we knew that we didn't have as much fuel as planned, but it worked out pretty well, because we came in quite early though the tyres were on the limit. I blistered my second set too, so it was a bit difficult. I also had a hydraulic problem so I lost a place to Jenson earlier on. Because of that, the car was behaving really badly and I wasn't getting full power and the gearshifting was all over the place."

Button's eventual fourth place was a solid showing for Honda after a nightmare run of results, but he was flattered to some degree by Renault's problems. It wasn't all good news for Honda, though, as Rubens Barrichello suffered another engine failure.

Renault went for a tyre that had a different construction to those chosen by McLaren and Honda, but was otherwise quite similar. For some reason, though, it blistered despite having more 'blistering control' built into it. Alonso had the problem with his first set, and soon dropped way back. Team-mate Giancarlo Fisichella had the same dramas in the middle stint, which allowed Alonso to catch and eventually pass him as they raced to fifth and sixth.

"The tyres are an important part, and a very important part at the minute," said Technical Director Bob Bell, who was unable to quantify the damage done by the mass damper ban. "But it's not everything. Clearly we have a huge responsibility to develop the car and the engine not only to totally perform in their own right, but also to work in harmony with the tyres. It's a package. You can't just take a tyre and bolt it on to any car and expect it to do the same job."

Meanwhile, Alonso gave the impression that this was another routine day at the office. The clear message was 'I've done the best I could with the equipment I had today and', perhaps more to the point, 'it might have been worse'.

"Well, you always want to be on the podium and if possible fight for the victory," said the Spanish points leader. "It wasn't possible today, so at the end of the day I think we did the maximum, so I'm happy. We weren't very competitive, and then I had rear blistering with the first set of tyres and that stopped me from reaching the podium. After that, Fisichella had the same problem with the second set of tyres, so I caught up with him."

Mark Webber's good pace for Williams – he should have finished fifth but was thwarted by a water leak, possibly caused by debris damaging a pipe – emphasised how competitive Bridgestone's tyres were, as did Jarno Trulli's charge from the back of the grid

INSIDE LINE
BOB BELL
RENAULT TECHNICAL DIRECTOR

"The only thing I can think about is the mass damper issue. It was galling that we couldn't run something that we considered, and still consider, to be a perfectly legal system. It wasn't one of our strongest weekends anyhow, but certainly the mass damper situation completely overshadowed it and I just look back with a degree of bitterness.

Not using the mass damper costs us about 0.3s per lap. We maintain that it's a completely functional part of the suspension system. With a conventional damper on the suspension system, it's there to damp out the oscillatory motion that exists between the chassis and the wheels, and by doing that you maintain a more even load between the tyre and track, which buys you grip and lap time. The difference is that unlike a conventional damper connected between the wheel upright and the chassis in some way, the mass damper can actually be remote from it and mounted within the chassis. It performs exactly the same function, but if you took it off the car the wheel wouldn't fall off. Well, it wouldn't with the conventional damper either, but the conventional damper is a much more obvious kinematic part of the suspension.

What the mass damper does is reduce the variation in contact patch load. If you do that, you increase grip because the rubber that the tyre is made out of is springy and has damping inherent in it as well. So, if you compress it and then let go, it takes a certain amount of time to come back to its original form. You can imagine, pounding an F1 car up and down means there are times when the tyre is recovering when it's not pushing down on the surface as you want. So the idea of any damping is to reduce those undulating forces so that you don't suffer that effect. To us, if that's the purpose of the device, which it was, it doesn't matter whether it's a conventional damper or whether it sits like a mass damper completely within the chassis. It does the same thing.

Because we had ran it in 2005 and knew it was a good solution that worked well, we optimised the 2006 car around it, so I think the ban hurt us more than other teams [using mass dampers].

The German GP just wasn't a good weekend for Renault. The car was OK and we weren't struggling massively with balance problems, Fernando just didn't get the best out of the package. How much of that was because the car felt a bit different to him because the dampers weren't there, is extremely hard to judge."

ABOVE Kimi Räikkönen started from pole position and led the first 10 laps, but had no answer to the Ferraris

BELOW Thumbs up and celebrations as Michael leads home Massa in the second Ferrari one–two in three races

(after an engine penalty) into seventh for Toyota, but Renault also lost out to fellow Michelin users McLaren and Honda, who had opted for slightly different tyres.

Christian Klien took the final point for Red Bull in a race in which his team-mate David Coulthard was lucky to keep going after a spectacular first-lap leap over Ralf Schumacher's Toyota. Nico Rosberg also crashed out on that busy first lap.

The BMWs also contrived to collide on lap 1 and both eventually retired, Heidfeld after a damaged brake duct led to problems and Villeneuve after he

crashed at the last corner of the lap. He took a bang on the head, but at the time no one realised that this undistinguished exit marked the end of his F1 career.

It was clear that while the man himself kept a brave face, the pressure was mounting on Renault and Alonso: "It's a very interesting championship and very close, so it's up to us if we want to win. We need to improve, we need to beat Ferrari and we'll try. It's clear that the opponents make steps every time, and they are quicker and quicker. We finish all the races, but in the last two or three, not very competitively."

SNAPSHOT FROM
GERMANY

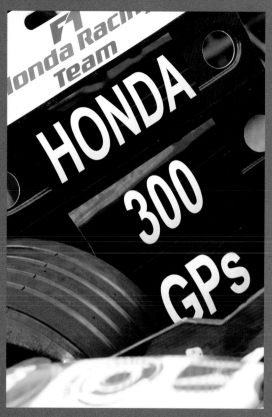

CLOCKWISE FROM RIGHT Another race, another landmark, this time Honda's 300th start; Bernie Ecclestone urges Barrichello to cheer up; German fans root for Italian success, with a German driver...; Saturday was Alonso's 25th birthday; she's not dressed in traditional German costume, but no-one is complaining; he dresses like his hero, but probably went home by train...; the Williams-Toyota deal is finally announced

WEEKEND HEADLINES

■ Williams confirmed at the German Grand Prix that it had come to an engine supply arrangement with Toyota, which was a deal that had been an open secret in the paddock for months. It wasn't enough to tempt Mark Webber to stay, though, and two days after the race the team confirmed that its test driver Alexander Wurz would race alongside Nico Rosberg in 2007.

■ Toyota finally announced at Hockenheim that Jarno Trulli had signed a new deal, which would keep him at the team until the end of 2009, when he would be 35. The length of the contract gave the Italian driver unprecedented job security, but came as something of a surprise to most observers.

■ Suggestions that Ferrari Technical Director Ross Brawn would be taking a sabbatical in 2007 created a little uncertainty as to whether Michael Schumacher would or would not be staying at the Italian team for another year, and how it might affect Kimi Räikkönen's potential transfer from McLaren. Ferrari chief Jean Todt added fuel to the fire by saying that his three favourite drivers were on the podium...

■ A meeting of the Technical Working Group on the Saturday of the event came to the conclusion that tyres should be the main method of keeping speeds in check in the short-term. As part of the package, a ban on any form of tyre-warming device was mooted by the FIA. Some parties had hoped to use the meeting to rush in an engine freeze for 2007, but the idea was outvoted.

■ GP2 star and Honda Racing protégé Adam Carroll opted to cut his ties with the team after coming to the conclusion that he wasn't gaining anything from the arrangement. Any extra testing miles available in 2006 had gone to James Rossiter, who appeared to be more in favour.

RACE RESULTS
GERMANY HOCKENHEIM

RACE DATE July 30th
CIRCUIT LENGTH 2.842 miles
NO. OF LAPS 67
RACE DISTANCE 190.432 miles
WEATHER Humid & bright, 33°C
TRACK TEMP 50°C
RACE DAY ATTENDANCE 80,000
LAP RECORD Kimi Räikkönen,
1m14.917s, 138.685mph, 2004

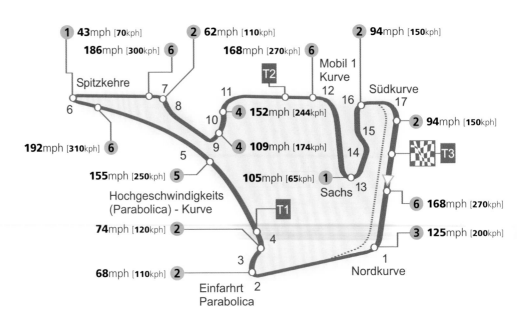

PRACTICE 1

	Driver	Time	Laps
1	A Wurz	1m16.349s	26
2	A Davidson	1m16.523s	29
3	R Kubica	1m17.343s	29
4	J Button	1m17.439s	5
5	R Doornbos	1m17.835s	25
6	R Barrichello	1m18.085s	6
7	F Alonso	1m18.328s	5
8	N Jani	1m18.539s	24
9	G Fisichella	1m18.664s	6
10	D Coulthard	1m18.795s	5
11	M Winkelhock	1m18.964s	27
12	J Villeneuve	1m18.972s	6
13	V Liuzzi	1m19.214s	5
14	N Heidfeld	1m19.507s	7
15	T Sato	1m20.102s	14
16	C Albers	1m20.132s	5
17	T Monteiro	1m20.575s	7
18	S Speed	1m20.950s	7
19	S Yamamoto	1m21.218s	21
20	N Rosberg	1m34.942s	3
21	R Schumacher	no time	4
22	J Trulli	no time	4
23	P de la Rosa	no time	1
24	C Klien	no time	1
25	K Räikkönen	no time	1
26	F Massa	no time	0
27	M Schumacher	no time	0
28	M Webber	no time	0

PRACTICE 2

	Driver	Time	Laps
1	R Kubica	1m16.225s	18
2	M Schumacher	1m16.502s	14
3	R Doornbos	1m16.549s	18
4	K Räikkönen	1m17.040s	9
5	F Massa	1m17.205s	11
6	A Davidson	1m17.294s	26
7	M Webber	1m17.344s	6
8	P de la Rosa	1m17.516s	10
9	R Barrichello	1m17.519s	13
10	J Button	1m17.542s	13
11	G Fisichella	1m17.672s	10
12	J Trulli	1m17.844s	13
13	R Schumacher	1m17.895s	14
14	M Winkelhock	1m17.962s	20
15	F Alonso	1m18.082s	8
16	A Wurz	1m18.164s	36
17	C Klien	1m18.223s	13
18	V Liuzzi	1m18.366s	13
19	N Jani	1m18.460s	19
20	D Coulthard	1m18.616s	10
21	N Heidfeld	1m18.636s	10
22	C Albers	1m18.643s	11
23	T Monteiro	1m18.991s	11
24	J Villeneuve	1m19.113s	9
25	S Speed	1m19.232s	12
26	T Sato	1m19.365s	8
27	S Yamamoto	no time	2
28	N Rosberg	no time	0

PRACTICE 3

	Driver	Time	Laps
1	C Klien	1m15.628s	14
2	J Button	1m15.651s	15
3	R Barrichello	1m15.963s	19
4	F Massa	1m15.977s	13
5	D Coulthard	1m16.080s	14
6	G Fisichella	1m16.130s	16
7	N Heidfeld	1m16.167s	14
8	K Räikkönen	1m16.218s	12
9	M Schumacher	1m16.307s	11
10	P de la Rosa	1m16.322s	12
11	F Alonso	1m16.427s	15
12	V Liuzzi	1m16.532s	18
13	S Speed	1m16.600s	17
14	N Rosberg	1m16.690s	20
15	M Webber	1m16.834s	16
16	R Schumacher	1m17.419s	17
17	J Villeneuve	1m17.740s	16
18	T Monteiro	1m17.793s	23
19	S Yamamoto	1m18.643s	19
20	T Sato	1m18.668s	21
21	C Albers	1m19.254s	15
22	J Trulli	no time	2

QUALIFYING 1

	Driver	Time
1	F Massa	1m14.412s
2	M Schumacher	1m14.904s
3	K Räikkönen	1m15.214s
4	J Trulli	1m15.430s
5	F Alonso	1m15.518s
6	P de la Rosa	1m15.655s
7	M Webber	1m15.719s
8	R Barrichello	1m15.757s
9	R Schumacher	1m15.789s
10	C Klien	1m15.816s
11	D Coulthard	1m15.836s
12	J Button	1m15.869s
13	G Fisichella	1m15.916s
14	N Rosberg	1m16.183s
15	N Heidfeld	1m16.234s
16	J Villeneuve	1m16.281s
17	V Liuzzi	1m16.399s
18	C Albers	1m17.093s
19	T Sato	1m17.185s
20	T Monteiro	1m17.836s
21	S Yamamoto	1m20.444s
22	S Speed	no time

QUALIFYING 2

	Driver	Time
1	M Schumacher	1m13.778s
2	F Massa	1m14.094s
3	J Button	1m14.378s
4	K Räikkönen	1m14.410s
5	G Fisichella	1m14.540s
6	R Barrichello	1m14.652s
7	R Schumacher	1m14.743s
8	F Alonso	1m14.746s
9	D Coulthard	1m14.826s
10	P de la Rosa	1m15.021s
11	M Webber	1m15.094s
12	C Klien	1m15.141s
13	J Trulli	1m15.150s
14	J Villeneuve	1m15.329s
15	N Rosberg	1m15.380s
16	N Heidfeld	1m15.397s

Best sectors – Practice

Sec 1	M Schumacher	16.339s
Sec 2	M Schumacher	36.008s
Sec 3	F Massa	22.926s

Speed trap – Practice

1	F Alonso	191.9mph
2	G Fisichella	191.7mph
3	P de la Rosa	190.6mph

Best sectors – Qualifying

Sec 1	M Schumacher	16.137s
Sec 2	M Schumacher	35.336s
Sec 3	M Schumacher	22.305s

Fernando Alonso
"Without the blistering, the podium was a possibility. I got a good start and passed both Hondas, but the tyres blistered. I was pushing hard in the final laps when I went off."

Michael Schumacher
"Superb! I can't find the right adjectives to describe the car-engine-tyre package and the performance of the team. The fight for both titles is now very open."

Kimi Räikkönen
"I was delayed in my first stop by a crossed wheelnut; I had blistering on my second set of tyres, and there was an issue with the hydraulics, which let Button by."

Jenson Button
"I'd a great race. To get past both Renaults at the start and then pass Kimi felt very good. The last stint was tough as I had huge amounts of graining on the front left."

Jacques Villeneuve
"The impact was quite hard. After we changed the nose at the end of lap 1, the car was very oversteery. I pushed just a little too hard and got caught out."

Jarno Trulli
"Even though I started from the back, we can be very happy. I had an incredible start and could do a lot of overtaking which made the race quite exciting for me."

Giancarlo Fisichella
"Both Renaults had the same problem with blistering, and for me it came in the second stint. After just a few laps, the car had become nearly undriveable."

Felipe Massa
"After a good start and good first pit stop I saw that I had a big gap to the following cars and from then on I concentrated on looking after the car and bringing it home."

Pedro de la Rosa
"It's a shame my race ended so soon, especially after I'd moved up two places. The car felt quick and I was catching the Renaults when I lost power and had to pull up."

Rubens Barrichello
"It's disappointing that we lost our progress with a bad start and engine failure. Soon after my first stop, the engine caught fire and oil on my tyres caused me to spin."

Nick Heidfeld
"I passed several cars at Turn 2. Although I braked very late, I got through. Then I felt a hit on the right rear. I pitted with a puncture, but the brakes were damaged."

Ralf Schumacher
"The start was quite difficult and then I had the unlucky collision with David Coulthard in the third corner. The tyres locked up and I couldn't steer away from him."

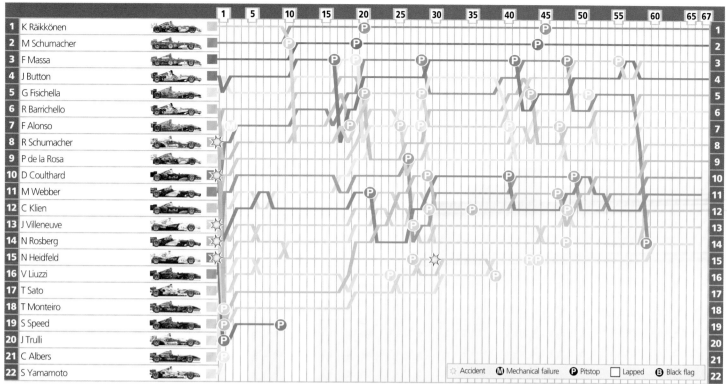

	1	5	10	15	20	25	30	35	40	45	50	55	60	65 67
1 K Räikkönen														
2 M Schumacher														
3 F Massa														
4 J Button														
5 G Fisichella														
6 R Barrichello														
7 F Alonso														
8 R Schumacher														
9 P de la Rosa														
10 D Coulthard														
11 M Webber														
12 C Klien														
13 J Villeneuve														
14 N Rosberg														
15 N Heidfeld														
16 V Liuzzi														
17 T Sato														
18 T Monteiro														
19 S Speed														
20 J Trulli														
21 C Albers														
22 S Yamamoto														

☆ Accident   Ⓜ Mechanical failure   Ⓟ Pitstop   ☐ Lapped   Ⓑ Black flag

QUALIFYING 3

	Driver	Time
1	K Räikkönen	1m14.070s
2	M Schumacher	1m14.205s
3	F Massa	1m14.569s
4	J Button	1m14.862s
5	G Fisichella	1m14.894s
6	R Barrichello	1m14.934s
7	F Alonso	1m15.282s
8	R Schumacher	1m15.923s
9	P de la Rosa	1m15.936s
10	D Coulthard	1m16.326s

GRID

	Driver	Time
1	K Räikkönen	1m14.070s
2	M Schumacher	1m14.205s
3	F Massa	1m14.569s
4	J Button	1m14.862s
5	G Fisichella	1m14.894s
6	R Barrichello	1m14.934s
7	F Alonso	1m15.282s
8	R Schumacher	1m15.923s
9	P de la Rosa	1m15.936s
10	D Coulthard	1m16.326s
11	M Webber	1m15.094s
12	C Klien	1m15.141s
13	J Villeneuve	1m15.329s
14	N Rosberg	1m15.380s
15	N Heidfeld	1m15.397s
16	V Liuzzi	1m16.399s
17	T Sato	1m17.185s
18	T Monteiro	1m17.836s
19	S Yamamoto	1m20.444s
20*	J Trulli	1m15.150s
21*	C Albers	1m17.093s
22	Scott Speed	no time

*10-PLACE GRID PENALTY

RACE

	Driver	Car	Laps	Time	Avg. mph	Fastest	Stops
1	M Schumacher	Ferrari 248	67	1h27m51.693s	130.045	1m16.357s	2
2	F Massa	Ferrari 248	67	1h27m52.413s	130.027	1m16.392s	2
3	K Räikkönen	McLaren-Mercedes MP4-21	67	1h28m04.899s	129.720	1m16.475s	3
4	J Button	Honda RA106	67	1h28m10.591s	129.581	1m16.818s	2
5	F Alonso	Renault R26	67	1h28m15.400s	129.463	1m17.256s	2
6	G Fisichella	Renault R26	67	1h28m16.507s	129.436	1m16.981s	2
7	J Trulli	Toyota TF106B	67	1h28m18.237s	129.394	1m16.807s	2
8	C Klien	Red Bull-Ferrari RB2	67	1h28m39.824s	128.868	1m17.719s	2
9	R Schumacher	Toyota TF106B	67	1h28m52.044s	128.573	1m16.763s	4
10	V Liuzzi	Toro Rosso-Cosworth STR01	66	1h27m54.567s	128.034	1m17.407s	2
11	D Coulthard	Red Bull-Ferrari RB2	66	1h27m59.119s	127.924	1m17.811s	2
12	S Speed	Toro Rosso-Cosworth STR01	66	1h28m14.038s	127.563	1m17.450s	2
D	C Albers	Midland-Toyota M16	66	1h28m25.609s	-	1m18.247s	2
D	T Monteiro	Midland-Toyota M16	65	1h27m58.453s	-	1m18.718s	3
R	M Webber	Williams-Cosworth FW28	59	Water leak	-	1m16.812s	2
R	T Sato	Super Aguri-Honda SA06	38	Gearbox	-	1m19.413s	1
R	J Villeneuve	BMW Sauber F1.06	30	Accident	-	1m18.904s	1
R	R Barrichello	Honda RA106	18	Engine	-	1m18.029s	1
R	N Heidfeld	BMW Sauber F1.06	9	Brakes	-	1m19.264s	1
R	P de la Rosa	McLaren-Mercedes MP4-21	2	Fuel pump	-	1m19.649s	0
R	S Yamamoto	Super Aguri-Honda SA06	1	Driveshaft	-	-	0
R	N Rosberg	Williams-Cosworth FW28	0	Accident	-	-	0

CHAMPIONSHIP

	Driver	Pts
1	F Alonso	100
2	M Schumacher	89
3	F Massa	50
4	G Fisichella	49
5	K Räikkönen	49
6	JP Montoya	26
7	J Button	21
8	R Barrichello	16
9	R Schumacher	13
10	N Heidfeld	13
11	D Coulthard	10
12	J Trulli	10
13	J Villeneuve	7
14	M Webber	6
15	N Rosberg	4
16	P de la Rosa	2
17	C Klien	2
18	V Liuzzi	1

	Constructor	Pts
1	Renault	149
2	Ferrari	139
3	McLaren-Mercedes	77
4	Honda	37
5	Toyota	23
6	BMW Sauber	20
7	Red Bull-Ferrari	12
8	Williams-Cosworth	10
9	Toro Rosso-Cosworth	1

Speed trap – Qualifying

1	R Schumacher	193.6mph
2	J Trulli	193.4mph
3	F Alonso	192.4mph

Fastest Lap

M Schumacher 1m16.357s
(134.005mph) on lap 17

Fastest speed trap

| J Trulli | 197.2mph |

Slowest speed trap

| N Heidfeld | 188.0mph |

Fastest pit stop

1	K Räikkönen	20.425s
2	V Liuzzi	20.442s
3	S Speed	20.675s

David Coulthard

"I started 10th and finished 11th. That was my race and I've nothing more to say."

Mark Webber

"I climbed from 11th to sixth on lap 1 then fought with Rubens. After the first stop, I passed Fisichella. After that, I lost a bit of balance and suddenly lost power."

Vitantonio Liuzzi

"On lap 1, I was on fire! It was fun out there, fighting with Jarno, Ralf and David. It was difficult to keep them behind as they were quicker. We just didn't have the power."

Tiago Monteiro

"Christijan and I were on different tyres, and it ended up being the wrong choice. I'd get only two or three good laps out of each set, though the balance was decent."

Takuma Sato

"The SA06's debut has been positive. We were expecting more in terms of race pace, but it's a step up from the SA05. It was exciting to be able to race the Midlands."

Christian Klien

"I've had a lot of bad luck, but finally we've scored again. The start was really good. I gained a position at Turn 1 and another two at the hairpin. We pushed 100%."

Nico Rosberg

"The car was good and I wanted to advance as quickly as possible. I lost the rear in the Motodrome, probably overdoing it as I wanted to get too much out of the first lap."

Scott Speed

"The mechanics did an awesome job to get my car rebuilt. Early on, I was catching David, Trulli and Tonio, but I'd too much front wing and it went to big oversteer."

Christijan Albers

"We were competitive against Toro Rosso, and it was nice to fight with Speed. It's just a shame that about nine or 10 laps from the end of the race I began to lose power."

Sakon Yamamoto

"I'm disappointed not to have raced here today as I completed only one lap before driveshaft failure. On the plus side, we've collected more data for the SA06."

FORMULA 1™
MAGYAR NAGYDÍJ 2006
Budapest

THE EYES HAVE IT...

Not only did Honda's Jenson Button race to his first grand prix victory, but he did so from 14th on the grid in a truly enthralling race made topsy-turvy by rain and incident

The Hungarian GP was the sort of race that reminded us how great Formula One can be, although, as so often in the past, it took a little rain to spice up the show. On a weekend when everything went wrong for the title contenders, Honda's nightmare season was turned on its head when Jenson Button took advantage of the opportunity created by the tricky conditions to score his first win. It was also the first under the Japanese manufacturer's name since 1967 and, by lucky chance, the company CEO was on hand to pick up the trophy and hear his country's national anthem played.

It was a fascinating event that saw form change as the conditions suited the tyres a driver was on at any given time. For a brief period, we had the rare sight of the championship contenders running wheel-to-wheel. Despite his history of wet-weather successes, Michael Schumacher didn't get the better of the confrontation. When he and Fernando Alonso crossed paths for a second time, the Ferrari ace was being lapped…

We knew from Friday that this was going to be an oddball weekend. Firstly, the weather was much cooler than the tyre companies had anticipated, and both had brought tyres tailored for the usual heatwave. Most teams struggled, but the big news of Friday was a

ABOVE Michael Schumacher rockets through the pack on lap 1, with Mark Webber, debutant Robert Kubica, Nick Heidfeld and the pair of Toyotas behind him

combined 2s qualifying penalty awarded to Fernando Alonso for overtaking when a yellow flag was being displayed and then a 'road rage' incident with Red Bull Racing's third driver Robert Doornbos.

It looked as though Michael and Ferrari would take a chunk out of Alonso's points lead, but on Saturday morning Michael received an identical penalty for passing when a red flag was being shown. Bizarrely, one of the two cars he overtook was Alonso's, and Ferrari intimated that the slowing Spaniard had duped Michael into going by him.

Neither driver had any chance of making the top 10 and they would start 11th and 15th. Michael had

gained an extra place as Button had an engine-change penalty after failure in Saturday practice that led to the troublesome red flag, dropping him from fourth to 14th.

With these three big names pushed back, it was left to Kimi Räikkönen to take his second successive pole, ahead of Felipe Massa, Rubens Barrichello and Pedro de la Rosa. Nobody knew how the tyre situation would unfold – Ferrari were concerned by graining problems – but all plans went out of the window when it poured on Sunday morning. The track was soaking when the cars went to the grid, with everyone on intermediate (officially 'standard wet') tyres bar Barrichello, who went for extreme wet Michelins.

INSIDE LINE
NICK FRY
HONDA
CHIEF EXECUTIVE OFFICER

"What a fantastic race! I'm just so thrilled for Jenson and the entire team. Everyone has worked so hard for this and it's so well-deserved.

We had a difficult start to the season, but there have been no recriminations, and everyone has stuck together and just worked harder. There

hasn't been a blame culture, it's been a case of, 'let's get on and do better.'

Two years ago we sat down with Jenson and asked him to become a real team leader as well as the superb driver that he obviously is. And he really has stepped into the role and keeps everybody motivated. He's always the one who says, 'Yes, I'll test, yes, I'll do the PR event, yes, I'll come to the factory and talk to everyone.' He really is very quick to take things on board now and he has been helped massively in that regard by his new management team.

Jenson has said many times how much he has enjoyed the last two years, which is odd, as he was more successful in 2004. I'm sure that's because he feels integrated in a way that perhaps he didn't. Today might not have been a normal race but it was

superbly won and now here we are!

It's great for the Japanese. Honda have been huge backers of the team and they have supported us all the way. They have encouraged us to make difficult decisions and to take risks. Even when things have gone wrong their view has always been that, so long as we have learned from it, then it has been worthwhile.

It was a fantastic bonus that Fukui-san, the Chief Executive of Honda, was here. Honda deserves a huge amount of credit because many companies wouldn't have given us the backing or the resources that they have.

Fukui-san came to an early season race and he had the intention of coming to Hockenheim and Budapest, but he didn't make it to Germany. We had dinner on Saturday night and, as

usual, he was encouraging and pushing everyone because he's impatient for success. He asked me where Jenson could finish in the race? I told him, 'well, in the points, maybe seventh or eighth.' But for him to win was something we couldn't dream about.

We didn't want to tempt fate but, about three laps from the end, we had a discussion about the podium. Wada-san and I run the team but we both felt that it was entirely appropriate for Fukui-san to go up there and hear the Japanese national anthem. I still went to *parc fermé* to greet Jenson. It was a great honour and a great moment, the kind of thing that stays with you."

Räikkönen set off in the lead, while the two title contenders made impressive progress. In just one lap, Michael got up to fourth and Fernando to sixth. But then their fortunes diverged. It was soon obvious that the Bridgestone intermediates were hopeless, especially when the rain returned, and Michael tumbled back down the order. Other Bridgestone runners were in dire trouble, none more so than fifth-placed qualifier Mark Webber, an early casualty of the tricky track conditions.

On lap 4, Alonso hustled his way past a frazzled Schumacher in a grandstanding, around-the-outside move, and had only the two flying McLarens in front of him. Two laps later, Michael lost another spot to Button, who was making great progress after being cautious around the opening lap.

The McLarens looked really strong, but having run in top-10 qualifying they had relatively small fuel loads. De la Rosa pitted on lap 16, and Räikkönen a lap later. Button also stopped on lap 17, as did Michael. In the Ferrari man's case, though, it wasn't planned: he'd crunched his nose on Giancarlo Fisichella after the Italian's Renault had got past. It meant Michael was unable to make use of his heavier fuel load.

Alonso, who was running very heavy and had no short-term plans to stop, thus assumed a huge lead. Räikkönen began to fade as he struggled on his second set of Michelins, a wing adjustment at the pit stop also hampering his progress. Soon, a charging de la Rosa was on his tail. The Finn was just preparing to wave his team-mate past when he misjudged his approach to the lapped Tonio Liuzzi at the final corner and ran over the Scuderia Toro Rosso car.

A safety-car period was triggered and Alonso took the opportunity to make his first stop. That guaranteed he maintained his lead, although Button, who hadn't stopped under caution, began to reel him in. He caught the Renault and then, on lap 46, had to pit to take on fuel (he also kept the same worn intermediates). That took the pressure off Alonso who had a heavy fuel load that gave him a large window for pitting.

By now, the track was drying, and Renault timed it perfectly. When he came in for a second and final time on lap 51, Alonso was able to go straight to dry tyres. But when he exited the pits the car wobbled a few times before sliding into the tyre wall after a problem with the wheel nut mechanism. That left Button with a huge lead, and he even had time to make a third stop

BELOW The outlook was gloomy for Jenson Button at the start, but he climbed 10 places in the first four laps, then kept on advancing up the order

INSIDE LINE
ROBERT KUBICA

BMW SAUBER DRIVER

"I found out that I would be racing in the Hungarian Grand Prix about half an hour before the official statement went out on Tuesday. I was quite relaxed. I knew it was a good opportunity that I hadn't been expecting.

I have a lot of confidence in myself and the car, but Friday at the

Hungaroring was unusual because, even though the track is dirty and slippery on the first day, it was especially so this year because the track temperature was about 20 degrees lower than expected. I wasn't nervous and became more relaxed with every session.

Hungaroring is not an easy track – a lot of corners and bumps – and I'd only been there once, in 2001. After just a couple of laps, though, I saw that my pace compared to Nick [team-mate Heidfeld] was not slow, and so I was confident. The last time I did a qualifying session was November 2005 in Macau, but after my first lap in Q1, which put me sixth, I knew I had what I needed for the moment! I was still a bit surprised to qualify 0.4s quicker than Nick.

People ask about my car control and maybe it's a strength. I must admit I like rallying and will probably do some

when I finish racing. It's about improvisation, whereas F1 is about different skills. Although I'm only 21, I have driven for 17 years on asphalt and you have to be really precise and smooth. I actually have quite a quick, aggressive turn-in, so an oversteering car is not good!

I made it into Q3 alright because Alonso and Schumacher had penalties, but we knew we would not be challenging at the front, so we went really heavy on fuel, then it was a big surprise when we saw the weather on Sunday!

In the first stint, I could barely stay on the track, I crashed and we changed the nose. In the second stint, I was really quick when the track was drying. When Michael lapped me, I was losing only 0.2s per lap when a lot of Michelin drivers were losing much more.

We were really heavy and knew we could go really long before the first pit stop. We thought the track would dry more quickly and so we tried some gambles on tyre pressures, which just didn't work in that first stint. Such a crazy race happens maybe once in 10 years and when it's your debut…

The result, seventh, would not have been easy in dry conditions but it was good experience. Then the car was found to be fractionally underweight, due to loss of tyre rubber, and they took it away. I wasn't worried. It meant that there were no points beside my name in the papers, but that didn't matter."

on lap 54 to go to dries. After that, it was a cruise to the chequered flag, with fingers crossed.

"It was obviously fun closing down Alonso," said Button. "We made a great choice on the tyres and also on the last pit stop. We've been a real thinking team today. We haven't just gone out there and had the best car and won the race. We've thought hard about this strategy and we've won, not just through speed but also because of our strategy.

"Normally, when you're in the lead – I suppose – it goes on forever, but I was loving it. We turned the revs down a lot, so I knew we'd get to the finish. I had a 40s lead and I didn't want the race to end. It was the best feeling, knowing that you're on the way home to taking your first grand prix win."

In the latter stages of the race, the excitement was behind him. After stopping on lap 46 and, like Button, staying on the same intermediate tyres, Michael had advanced to second place when Alonso retired. At around that time, though, his pace began to drop as the track dried, his tyres faded and rivals switched to dry tyres. Ferrari Technical Director Ross Brawn, concerned about the form of the dries he'd seen on Friday, refused to bring him in for grooved tyres.

So, Michael continued to plod around. It took several laps, but de la Rosa eventually fought his way past the German to claim second place.

Next up was BMW's Nick Heidfeld. Again Michael launched a fruitless defence, this time banging wheels, and the Ferrari was an instant retirement with broken suspension with just three laps to go. Heidfeld deserved his eventual third after a sensible if unspectacular drive.

A more cautious approach would have, at worst, earned Michael the four points for fifth place. As it was, he was classified ninth, but then later got an unexpected bonus point after BMW rookie Robert Kubica was excluded from the results.

Barrichello qualified fourth in the other Honda RA106 and ran second from the start of the race, but he was the only driver out there on extreme wets, and an early extra tyre stop helped to ensure that he could not better fourth. Usually he is a master in races like this, but he proved no match for Button.

David Coulthard showed that experience pays in tricky conditions when he put in a faultless display to finish fifth. He made a good start, although along the way managed to make contact with Kubica,

ABOVE Ralf Schumacher pits en route to sixth place for Toyota

OPPOSITE TOP LEFT Robert Kubica calls in for a new nose for his BMW after one of two *faux pas*

OPPOSITE TOP RIGHT Usually so good in the wet, Giancarlo Fisichella drops his Renault into the gravel at Turn 8 and into retirement

OPPOSITE BOTTOM Button dives inside Michael Schumacher's Ferrari for fourth early in the race

ABOVE Fernando Alonso splashes his way down the pitlane, unaware that his car is about to shed a wheel and cost him the race

BELOW McLaren stand-in Pedro de la Rosa just avoided his crashing team-mate and raced on to a career-best second place

Michael, Barrichello and Trulli, but still managed to bring the car home more or less in one piece...

Kubica had stepped up from the third driver role to replace Jacques Villeneuve, who'd taken a knock on the head in Germany. In fact, his appearance had already been planned by the team, who wanted to try him in a race environment, although the truth of what transpired with Jacques remained murky.

The Pole did a good job to make it through to top 10 qualifying, with a little help from the penalties given to his rivals. He spun on lap 2 and later hit the tyre wall, which required a stop for a new nose. He still managed seventh, only to be disqualified for having an underweight car, this a result of his tyres being comprehensively worn out.

The other driver to benefit was Michael's team-mate Massa, who'd finished eighth after a difficult race in which he'd even tried extreme wets in his quest for traction. The Brazilian eventually set the race's fastest lap when he had new dry tyres fitted near the end, but the disparity of performance underlined that Michael could still extract more from a given situation.

Toyota had a difficult weekend. Both cars qualified in the top 10, but the drivers found that the Bridgestone intermediates made life difficult when it was really wet. Both fell down the order, but picked up again after they switched to dry tyres. Jarno Trulli retired with a late engine failure, while Ralf Schumacher plugged away to an eventual sixth place.

Nico Rosberg failed to make it through the first round of qualifying and started his Williams well down the field. He didn't make much progress before an electrical problem contributed to a spin on lap 20. Christian Klien had a problem with a fuel leak just before the start of the race so had to use Red Bull's T-car from the pits. He too spun off early on. Scuderia Toro Rosso's Scott Speed was the first to change to dry tyres, but the young American was way too early for this to succeed and, after several excursions, had to switch back to intermediate tyres.

Finally, it wasn't a great weekend for Fisichella, who was running well early on but spun off shortly after overtaking (and being hit by) Schumacher. So Renault failed to score any points, and yet the team went away satisfied that Ferrari hadn't taken a major bite out of Alonso's lead. However, the bottom line was that Michael was now only 10 points behind. With just five races to go, it was still an open issue.

SNAPSHOT FROM
HUNGARY

CLOCKWISE FROM RIGHT John Button was understandably delighted with his son Jenson's breakthrough win; the weather wasn't as hot and humid as usual...; Honda Chief Executive Takeo Fukui was on hand to lift the constructors' trophy; a smile to make up for the lack of sunny weather; this statue at the circuit emphasised Hungary's lengthy motorsport history

WEEKEND HEADLINES

■ With very little fanfare, the FIA granted Scuderia Toro Rosso a 300rpm increase in revs from 16,700rpm to 17,000rpm. Oddly enough, the new limit was only available for Saturdays, and was designed to reflect the fact that the maximum qualifying revs of the V8 runners had risen since the start of the season.

■ On the Monday after the race, Grand Prix Manufacturers' Association leader Burkhard Goeschel met Max Mosley in Nice for yet another discussion of the future engine rules. This one brought a clear answer when it was announced that the freeze would be brought forward to 2007 and, in return, teams could homologate their engines in October 2006 rather than June, as had previously been the case.

■ The day after the Hungarian GP, Red Bull Racing confirmed that Mark Webber would be joining the team for 2007, alongside David Coulthard. That meant there was no place for long-time Red Bull protégé Christian Klien. It remained to be seen whether the team would also land a Renault engine deal, as it remained contracted to Ferrari.

■ On the Tuesday after the race, BMW announced that Robert Kubica would drive the second car for the remainder of the season. In essence, Jacques Villeneuve didn't take too kindly to being replaced for the Hungarian GP and decided that he didn't want to remain on board. His likely destination appeared to be NASCAR.

■ During the summer break, Honda took the opportunity to announce that erstwhile Technical Director Geoff Willis was definitely leaving the team, having been on 'gardening leave' since the British GP. Team boss Nick Fry had suggested that Willis might return, but that was clearly never going to happen.

RACE RESULTS
HUNGARY
BUDAPEST

Official Results © [2006]
Formula One Administration Limited,
6 Princes Gate, London SW7 1QJ.
No reproduction without permission.
All copyright and database rights reserved

RACE DATE August 6th
CIRCUIT LENGTH 2.722 miles
NO. OF LAPS 70
RACE DISTANCE 190.528 miles
WEATHER Wet then overcast, 21°C
TRACK TEMP 39°C
RACE DAY ATTENDANCE 50,000
LAP RECORD Michael Schumacher,
1m19.071s, 123.966mph, 2004

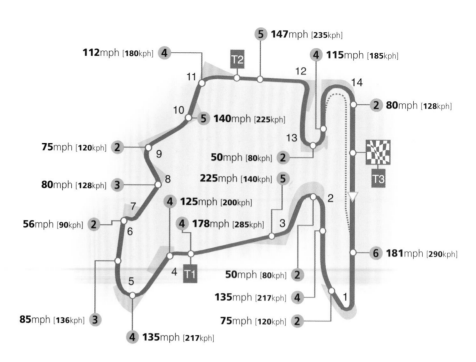

PRACTICE 1

	Driver	Time	Laps
1	K Räikkönen	1m21.624s	5
2	A Davidson	1m22.396s	28
3	M Schumacher	1m22.499s	5
4	P de la Rosa	1m22.730s	6
5	A Wurz	1m22.941s	25
6	R Barrichello	1m23.553s	6
7	J Button	1m23.659s	5
8	R Doornbos	1m23.999s	27
9	J Trulli	1m24.620s	9
10	M Winkelhock	1m25.194s	26
11	N Jani	1m25.424s	17
12	V Liuzzi	1m25.477s	6
13	S Speed	1m26.678s	7
14	C Albers	1m26.680s	5
15	T Monteiro	1m27.321s	8
16	T Sato	1m29.765s	4
17	R Schumacher	1m30.110s	5
18	S Yamamoto	1m30.353s	12
19	F Alonso	no time	1
20	D Coulthard	no time	1
21	G Fisichella	no time	1
22	C Klien	no time	1
23	F Massa	no time	0
24	N Heidfeld	no time	0
25	R Kubica	no time	0
26	N Rosberg	no time	0
27	M Webber	no time	0

PRACTICE 2

	Driver	Time	Laps
1	F Massa	1m21.778s	12
2	F Alonso	1m23.097s	15
3	G Fisichella	1m23.189s	14
4	R Doornbos	1m23.195s	30
5	A Davidson	1m23.498s	31
6	R Schumacher	1m23.747s	19
7	J Trulli	1m23.771s	18
8	M Schumacher	1m23.931s	19
9	N Heidfeld	1m23.934s	11
10	R Kubica	1m24.106s	11
11	P de la Rosa	1m24.252s	11
12	M Winkelhock	1m24.381s	28
13	R Barrichello	1m24.445s	17
14	J Button	1m24.465s	15
15	T Monteiro	1m24.508s	8
16	A Wurz	1m24.609s	31
17	T Sato	1m24.623s	23
18	N Rosberg	1m24.793s	12
19	N Jani	1m24.854s	33
20	C Albers	1m25.038s	7
21	S Speed	1m25.152s	16
22	M Webber	1m25.393s	8
23	C Klien	1m25.647s	14
24	D Coulthard	1m25.843s	12
25	K Räikkönen	1m25.968s	11
26	V Liuzzi	1m26.198s	16
27	S Yamamoto	1m26.877s	20

PRACTICE 3

	Driver	Time	Laps
1	M Schumacher	1m20.795s	11
2	F Massa	1m21.472s	11
3	R Kubica	1m21.806s	18
4	R Barrichello	1m21.833s	18
5	F Alonso	1m22.119s	25
6	G Fisichella	1m22.340s	13
7	C Klien	1m22.362s	15
8	P de la Rosa	1m22.424s	14
9	V Liuzzi	1m22.560s	13
10	K Räikkönen	1m22.599s	8
11	D Coulthard	1m22.643s	14
12	M Webber	1m22.839s	17
13	T Monteiro	1m23.819s	12
14	S Speed	1m23.858s	16
15	R Schumacher	1m23.963s	13
16	N Rosberg	1m24.381s	15
17	J Button	1m24.731s	4
18	T Sato	1m24.847s	15
19	J Trulli	1m25.373s	16
20	N Heidfeld	1m25.597s	14
21	C Albers	1m26.047s	12
22	S Yamamoto	1m26.260s	19

QUALIFYING 1

	Driver	Time
1	F Massa	1m19.742s
2	K Räikkönen	1m20.080s
3	J Button	1m20.820s
4	R Kubica	1m20.891s
5	R Schumacher	1m21.112s
6	R Barrichello	1m21.141s
7	D Coulthard	1m21.163s
8	P de la Rosa	1m21.288s
9	M Webber	1m21.335s
10	G Fisichella	1m21.370s
11	J Trulli	1m21.434s
12	N Heidfeld	1m21.437s
13	M Schumacher	1m21.440s
14	F Alonso	1m21.792s
15	T Monteiro	1m22.009s
16	C Klien	1m22.027s
17	V Liuzzi	1m22.068s
18	N Rosberg	1m22.084s
19	T Sato	1m22.967s
20	S Speed	1m23.006s
21	C Albers	1m23.146s
22	S Yamamoto	1m24.016s

QUALIFYING 2

	Driver	Time
1	F Massa	1m19.504s
2	K Räikkönen	1m19.704s
3	R Barrichello	1m19.783s
4	J Button	1m19.943s
5	P de la Rosa	1m19.991s
6	M Webber	1m20.047s
7	G Fisichella	1m20.154s
8	J Trulli	1m20.231s
9	R Schumacher	1m20.243s
10	R Kubica	1m20.256s
11	N Heidfeld	1m20.623s
12	M Schumacher	1m20.875s
13	D Coulthard	1m20.890s
14	C Klien	1m21.207s
15	F Alonso	1m21.364s
16	T Monteiro	1m23.767s

Best sectors – Practice

Sec 1	M Schumacher	29.379s
Sec 2	M Schumacher	28.628s
Sec 3	K Räikkönen	22.675s

Speed trap – Practice

1	K Räikkönen	178.3mph
2	M Schumacher	178.2mph
3	A Wurz	177.0mph

Best sectors – Qualifying

Sec 1	M Schumacher	28.602s
Sec 2	M Schumacher	27.968s
Sec 3	M Schumacher	22.125s

 Fernando Alonso

"The car felt great in the wet. After the safety car, we avoided taking too many risks and with the dry tyres. But as I came out of the pits, something broke at the rear."

 Michael Schumacher

"We had a great opportunity but didn't take it. The trackrod broke as Heidfeld went past. We touched, partly because the track was still a bit slippery. These things happen."

 **Kimi Räikkönen**

"Liuzzi slowed on the racing line and there was nowhere for me to go except into him. It's never great to end a race like that, but I appreciate him apologising."

 Jenson Button

"What a day! To win such a tough and challenging race from 14th on the grid is incredible and all the more important because I know I won on merit today."

 **Robert Kubica**

"I made a mistake in the chicane on lap 2 and spun. Then I made another and hit the barriers. Due to this, we had to change strategy and I finished on intermediates."

Jarno Trulli

"I was hit on lap 1 and lost several places. When the safety car was deployed, I pitted a lap too soon, getting stuck behind slower cars. Then the engine failed."

Giancarlo Fisichella

"I followed Michael for ages and finally got past, but went off in Turn 8. I was pushing to build a gap, lost the rear and damaged the wing. I carried on, but it came off."

Felipe Massa

"We weren't competitive on wets or extreme wets. But, as the track began to dry, we began to run strongly, even more so as soon as I fitted the dry weather tyres."

Pedro de la Rosa

"I'm extremely happy to score my first podium. We backed off as we were heavy and wanted to go as long as possible, but the conditions changed and we pitted."

Rubens Barrichello

"I'm truly happy for Jenson and the Honda Racing F1 Team. It was a shame for me that we had the wrong tyres at the start or we could have both been on the podium."

Nick Heidfeld

"This is a fantastic day. The pit crew got me ahead of Coulthard and let me reach the podium. I had a scary moment when I passed Michael and he ran into the back of me."

Ralf Schumacher

"We couldn't warm the tyres. As the track got drier, the Bridgestone standard wets worked well. The moment we changed to dry tyres was quite risky, but it worked."

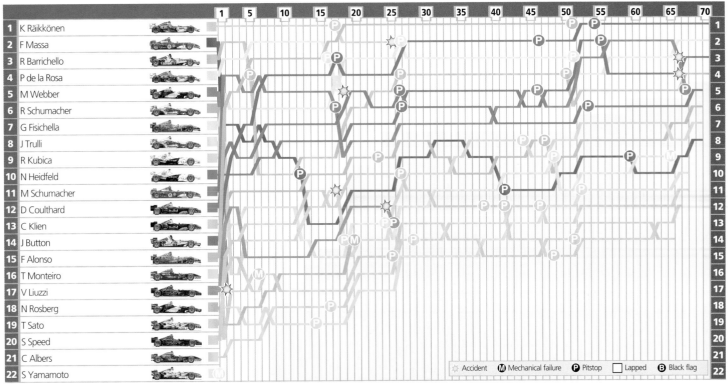

1	K Räikkönen	
2	F Massa	
3	R Barrichello	
4	P de la Rosa	
5	M Webber	
6	R Schumacher	
7	G Fisichella	
8	J Trulli	
9	R Kubica	
10	N Heidfeld	
11	M Schumacher	
12	D Coulthard	
13	C Klien	
14	J Button	
15	F Alonso	
16	T Monteiro	
17	V Liuzzi	
18	N Rosberg	
19	T Sato	
20	S Speed	
21	C Albers	
22	S Yamamoto	

☼ Accident Ⓜ Mechanical failure Ⓟ Pitstop ☐ Lapped Ⓑ Black flag

QUALIFYING 3

	Driver	Time
1	K Räikkönen	1m19.599s
2	F Massa	1m19.886s
3	R Barrichello	1m20.085s
4	J Button	1m20.092s
5	P de la Rosa	1m20.117s
6	M Webber	1m20.266s
7	R Schumacher	1m20.759s
8	G Fisichella	1m20.924s
9	J Trulli	1m21.132s
10	R Kubica	1m22.049s

GRID

	Driver	Time
1	K Räikkönen	1m19.599s
2	F Massa	1m19.886s
3	R Barrichello	1m20.085s
4	P de la Rosa	1m20.117s
5	M Webber	1m20.266s
6	R Schumacher	1m20.759s
7	G Fisichella	1m20.924s
8	J Trulli	1m21.132s
9	R Kubica	1m22.049s
10	N Heidfeld	1m20.623s
11^	M Schumacher	1m20.875s
12	D Coulthard	1m20.890s
13	C Klien	1m21.207s
14*	J Button	1m20.092s
15^	F Alonso	1m21.364s
16	T Monteiro	1m23.767s
17	V Liuzzi	1m22.068s
18	N Rosberg	1m22.084s
19	T Sato	1m22.967s
20	S Speed	1m23.006s
21	S Yamamoto	1m24.016s
22*	C Albers	1m23.146s

* 10-PLACE GRID PENALTY
^ TWO SECOND PENALTY

RACE

	Driver	Car	Laps	Time	Avg. mph	Fastest	Stops
1	J Button	Honda RA106	70	1h52m20.941s	101.769	1m25.143s	3
2	P de la Rosa	McLaren-Mercedes MP4-21	70	1h52m51.778s	101.306	1m24.315s	3
3	N Heidfeld	BMW Sauber F1.06	70	1h53m04.763s	101.112	1m25.801s	2
4	R Barrichello	Honda RA106	70	1h53m06.146s	101.091	1m24.678s	3
5	D Coulthard	Red Bull-Ferrari RB2	69	1h52m42.055s	100.002	1m25.572s	2
6	R Schumacher	Toyota TF106B	69	1h53m05.344s	99.658	1m25.247s	2
D	R Kubica	BMW Sauber F1.06	69	1h53m24.265s	-	1m28.154s	2
7	F Massa	Ferrari 248	69	1h53m24.702s	99.375	1m23.516s	3
8	M Schumacher	Ferrari 248	67	Track rod	-	1m27.834s	2
9	T Monteiro	Midland-Toyota M16	67	1h53m15.391s	96.626	1m28.178s	3
10	C Albers	Midland-Toyota M16	67	1h53m19.136s	96.574	1m26.117s	2
11	S Speed	Toro Rosso-Cosworth STR01	66	1h53m32.755s	94.942	1m26.249s	4
12	J Trulli	Toyota TF106B	65	Engine	-	1m25.779s	2
13	T Sato	Super Aguri-Honda SA06	65	1h52m23.674s	94.461	1m30.957s	2
R	F Alonso	Renault R26	51	Wheel nut	-	1m29.408s	2
R	K Räikkönen	McLaren-Mercedes MP4-21	25	Accident	-	1m33.690s	1
R	V Liuzzi	Toro Rosso-Cosworth STR01	25	Accident	-	1m38.858s	0
R	N Rosberg	Williams-Cosworth FW28	19	Spin	-	1m38.964s	0
R	G Fisichella	Renault R26	18	Crash damage	-	1m35.550s	0
R	C Klien	Red Bull-Ferrari RB2	6	-	-	1m38.702s	0
R	M Webber	Williams-Cosworth FW28	1	Spin	-	-	0
R	S Yamamoto	Super Aguri-Honda SA06	0	Spin	-	-	0

CHAMPIONSHIP

	Driver	Pts
1	F Alonso	100
2	M Schumacher	90
3	F Massa	52
4	G Fisichella	49
5	K Räikkönen	49
6	J Button	31
7	JP Montoya	26
8	R Barrichello	21
9	N Heidfeld	19
10	R Schumacher	16
11	D Coulthard	14
12	P de la Rosa	10
13	J Trulli	10
14	J Villeneuve	7
15	M Webber	6
16	N Rosberg	4
17	C Klien	2
18	V Liuzzi	1

Speed trap – Qualifying

1	F Massa	179.3mph
2	M Schumacher	179.1mph
3	K Räikkönen	177.7mph

Fastest Lap

F Massa 1m23.516s
(117.343mph) on lap 65

Fastest speed trap

M Schumacher 181.6mph

Slowest speed trap

S Yamamoto 165.7mph

Fastest pit stop

1	J Button	20.480s
2	F Massa	20.686s
3	J Button	20.869s

 **David Coulthard**

"I came together with Kubica in Turn 1 and lost some endplate, then later with Michael when he spun. Rubens banged wheels with me and then Trulli nearly hit me."

Mark Webber

"Lap 1 was unreal as I had zero grip at the rear. Going through the kink at the back of the circuit, I grazed the barrier and the wing became stuck under the tub."

Vitantonio Liuzzi

"In the incident with Kimi, I went wide, trying to let him by. Maybe he didn't expect me to slow and so he ran into the back of me. I was trying to move over to let him by."

Tiago Monteiro

"We had a great strategy, especially with the conditions. It was very difficult to drive initially and I made a lot of mistakes. Once I got settled, the balance was pretty good."

Takuma Sato

"In the first stint, I was pulling away from the Midlands. After the stop, I had a clutch problem. I solved it by changing the setting, but I later had a gearbox problem."

 Christian Klien

"I had to start from the pits as I'd a problem with my car. It was very difficult, as you couldn't see much. I passed a few cars, but then was a little bit too quick and went off."

Nico Rosberg

"It was almost impossible in the wet as the rear was so nervous. Unluckily, something went wrong with the electrics and the engine cut out on the exit of Turn 1."

Scott Speed

"My race was over when my team fuelled me to the end even though a dry line was appearing. After that, I was slow and was optimistic in going for dries too early."

Christijan Albers

"We made the wrong tyre choice. I was too slow on wets and took too long passing Tiago. The stops and traffic were always a problem and I kept having to race off-line."

 Sakon Yamamoto

"I made a reasonable start and tried to pass a few cars at Turn 1, but the engine stalled and my race was over for a disappointing end to the weekend again for me."

Constructor		Pts
1	Renault	149
2	Ferrari	142
3	McLaren-Mercedes	85
4	Honda	52
5	Toyota	26
6	BMW-Sauber	26
7	Red Bull-Ferrari	16
8	Williams-Cosworth	10
9	Toro Rosso-Cosworth	1

2006 FORMULA 1™
PETROL OFISI TURKISH GRAND PRIX
Istanbul

THE MAN
IN FRONT

There had been flashes of speed, but Felipe
Massa really came good in Turkey, and the
fact that he was ahead of his team-mate
when Liuzzi spun was what helped him win

It was a great shame that the battle for second place
took attention away from Felipe Massa's superb victory.
Indeed, what better way to score your first grand prix
win than by taking pole position and heading home a
pair of World Champions? But when Michael
Schumacher's initial second place in the Turkish Grand
Prix became third behind rival Fernando Alonso, after
confusion in the pitlane, the German in effect lost four
points rather than just a couple, for that was the real
swing represented by their change of position.

As ever, the weekend was all about tyres. It was
apparent from early in practice that Bridgestone was
back on song after something of a glitch at the
Hungarian Grand Prix (although the wet race spared
the Japanese tyre manufacturer some embarrassment),
and Ferrari had a tyre that was not only quick over one
lap but also very consistent. At the same time, Renault
soon found that its softer Michelin tyre wasn't up to the
task, so the team switched to the harder tyre for
Saturday. That worked out well, and while ultimate
pace was lacking, there was enough to secure the
second row of the grid.

The real story of Saturday was Felipe Massa's charge
to pole position for Ferrari. He did a better job than his

team-mate on the day, as in the third qualifying session Michael had to abort his first run after a mistake at Turn 1, and he also had a wobble on his second set of tyres. He still had sufficient margin to guarantee second on the timesheets, but this meant that he would start on the dirty side of the grid and, with both Renaults behind him, he was always going to have an exciting run to the first corner.

Pole man Massa couldn't exactly move over and say "after you", as the Renaults were bound to be right there, and he was probably quite surprised at how close Michael actually got to him, Michael having successfully edged out the blue and yellow cars. Meanwhile, Giancarlo Fisichella was so keen to avoid tapping his own team-mate, that he slammed on the brakes and spun. Fifth qualifier Nick Heidfeld had nowhere to go, and half the field was either involved in contact, or badly delayed. Fisichella resumed after pitting while, after a stop for repairs, Kimi Räikkönen crashed out due to damage received.

No safety car was deployed, and the Ferraris pulled away from Alonso with apparent ease. It was a surprise, though, to see Michael drop behind his team-mate, even allowing for the likely difference in

fuel loads. The gap opened up to 3.6s by lap 7, but then Michael began to reel Massa in, slowly but surely. Over successive laps, it came down to 3.4s, 3.2s, 2.8s, 2.5s, 2.2s and then, on what turned out to be an unlucky lap 13, 1.9s. Massa's pitstop was fast approaching, and Michael's was to follow it. All he had to do was have Massa in his sights and they would neatly change positions.

However, everything changed on lap 13 when Tonio Liuzzi spun at the first corner as a result of a traction-control glitch. The Toro Rosso was stranded pretty much on the racing line between the first and second turns, and a safety car was called for.

For anyone who had qualified at the sharp end of the top 10, and who had started with a compromised fuel load, a stop at this point in the race was a no-brainer. And that's where it became difficult for Ferrari. In such circumstances, a stacked double stop was the only solution, but the team was in the unexpected position of having the cars the 'wrong' way around. Alonso was a useful 10.7s behind Michael at the end of lap 13, but there still was not going to be enough time to get both Ferraris in and out of the pits before Alonso jumped Michael.

OPPOSITE **Nick Heidfeld qualified well, but a first-lap clash with Giancarlo Fisichella cost him dear...**

BELOW **...And this is how it happened, with Fisichella rotating in front of the pack and Scott Speed hitting Kimi Räikkönen's McLaren**

BOTTOM **Kimi Räikkönen limps back to the pits to retire**

INSIDE LINE
MARIO THEISSEN

**BMW SAUBER
TEAM PRINCIPAL**

"The process with Jacques Villeneuve was that after the German GP (in which the two BMW Saubers collided) we decided we wanted Robert Kubica to race in the Hungarian GP. The German GP kicked it off, so to speak, and we wanted to see Robert in a race before the end of the season. I wasn't able to guarantee Jacques that he would come back after that, which was the basis on which he said, 'OK, let's split, let's terminate the contract.'

Many people think Jacques performed much better than expected in comparison to Nick Heidfeld, but I'm not among them. I expected him to do well. He was part of the team, but we had to explore future options. Jacques could have been part of the consideration, but he didn't want to take the risk of not being brought back.

I thought Robert's debut in Hungary was very strong. A weekend as a race driver is much more complex than being a Friday third driver when you do what you are told in your two hours of practice. As a race driver, you work right through the weekend evaluating options and you do the marketing and media stuff too. With Robert,. I saw no difference in how he dealt with the weekend and that was very positive. His qualifying performance in Hungary was excellent. In the race, he made two mistakes early on and the best thing from my point-of-view was that, having finished seventh, he was extremely unhappy about his mistakes and didn't care about the position. It shows how determined he is.

We gave Robert a lot of winter testing, and his performance encouraged me to bring Sebastian Vettel through, who did a super job in Turkey, setting quickest time in each session. With Sebastian, it was an even more difficult decision. Normally, I am not the kind of person to rush a young guy, because in F1 you tend to get just one chance and, if you aren't prepared for it, it's gone.

However, we've known Sebastian for many years now. He started karting at the age of six, and at 16 he dominated Formula BMW like nobody before or since. We followed his development and I was confident he would make it and be ready to take on the Friday job. He has proved me right.

We will decide who drives our third car the rest of the season on a race-by-race basis, but Sebastian has been very impressive. He did long runs, used tyres, new tyres, low fuel, race fuel, everything, and delivered the entire package for the set-up. It was much more than just a quick lap. I was extremely impressed."

The Ferraris could not swap places on the track – that would have been passing under the safety car – but there could have been a shuffle in the pits. Instead, Massa was serviced first and Michael had to wait. By the time Michael got going, Alonso had jumped him for second place.

Ferrari technical director Ross Brawn admitted that there wasn't much else the team could do: "You're not allowed to overtake under the safety car, and I think swapping cars in the pitlane might not have been too popular. So I don't think there was, no."

There was no denying that Massa was ahead of his senior team-mate on pure performance, and to deprive him of his hard-earned advantage in such a blatant manner was not seen as acceptable.

Ferrari still had every reason to expect that Michael could recover his second place fair and square. In just 13 laps he had pulled 10s clear of Alonso. The team naturally assumed that once the safety car went away he would have the pace to sit on Alonso's tail, and possibly even find a way past. If he couldn't do it on the track, he would do it by pitting later.

What Ferrari didn't allow for was Michael's unexpected loss of form on his second set of tyres. On

the first flying lap after the safety car withdrew, Michael lost a full second to Alonso – some of that might have been down to the need to get past the lapped Nick Heidfeld – and from then on the Renault driver began to edge away by 0.3s here, 0.2s there. It soon added up to a significant margin and, as ever, tyres were the decisive factor.

It wasn't just that Michael had problems, but also that Alonso had simply got quicker, as he noted after the race: "I think the first set of tyres I put on the car had a little bit of front graining and I was a bit worried for the next stints, but I think I started with new tyres and that was the problem. Then in the stints, in the pit stops, with scrubbed tyres, it was much more consistent."

After a while, the gap stabilised, and Michael lost just the odd tenth of a second. In all but matching Alonso's times, the Ferrari ace was really on the limit. Then, on lap 28, he ran wide at Turn 8. Interestingly, that lap was also the fastest Alonso had done up to that point in the race, being faster than his previous lap by nearly half a second. Was Michael trying just a little bit too hard to maintain the gap?

"The second set of tyres blistered for some reason,

OPPOSITE **This is the move that helped Massa win: Michael Schumacher emerges from his first pit stop behind Alonso, having had to wait his turn at Ferrari**

BELOW **Rubens Barrichello and Jarno Trulli ran together until the Brazilian Honda driver pulled ahead by pitting later and raced on to claim a point by finishing eighth**

so Michael was struggling with them," said Brawn." If you look at Felipe's pace in that middle part of the race, Michael wasn't able to hold the pace. He was trying to push and he went off."

On that fateful lap, the gap went out from 3.6s to 8.3s, a differential that must have been extremely demoralising for Michael. The tide finally turned on lap 34, when he began to chip away at Alonso's advantage, before the Spaniard came in on lap 39. Michael still had another four full laps of fuel on board, but there were never going to be enough laps to make up the gap.

"I think Michael was quicker, but you've really got to be a lot quicker to do anything," said Brawn. "We obviously went longer than Fernando with the fuel, so we were hoping that Michael would get a bit of a window in the second stint. We didn't know how much longer, but we hoped he would, and he did. Unfortunately, the tyres had blistered and there was nothing left to push on, so he wasn't able to take advantage of that little gap, and he had his mistake at Turn 8."

As Michael charged out of the pits on lap 43, he could see Alonso's Renault rounding the first corner. It was so, so close. Next time around, we got the real

INSIDE LINE
FELIPE MASSA

FERRARI DRIVER

"Getting my first pole position was a fantastic moment but also a bit of a surprise. When was I last on pole? For a kart race in Brazil, last year!

Going into the race the tyres were working well, not just on qualifying runs, and I was confident, but you don't dare dream… I've been working so hard through my whole career for this moment. It's hard to take in – looking back on everything in my life to get here. I'm really happy. Very emotional. A fantastic weekend.

I made a very good start, I saw that Michael and Fernando had a big fight at the first corner, and I did a strong first lap. The car was well balanced through the whole race, and even after the safety car I was able to pull away without being too hard on it. Every set of tyres and every part of the car just responded perfectly and I was able to keep the gap throughout the whole race.

Before the safety car came out Michael was catching me but, unfortunately for him, he lost a position at the pit stop. For sure, the safety car wasn't very useful for us today…

On the slowing down lap I said on the radio, 'Sorry for Michael…' I meant I was sorry that he ended up behind Fernando. We are a team. For sure Michael is happy that I won the race, but I was also looking out for him as well. I was sorry because I had the feeling that maybe there was an opportunity to get even more points.

Seeing the chequered flag and crossing the line first is hard to describe. It's like a dream come true. Michael and Fernando know all about it and they'll know what I mean. I always dreamed of being a Ferrari driver and to win my first grand prix in a Ferrari is something very special for me.

You spend your whole career getting to F1 and when you get there and win your first race – it's just amazing. Hard to put into words, but like a release. I'm really happy to be here with this incredible team who gave me such a fantastic car. I'm going to enjoy this time a lot.

Looking at our potential, the championship is still open. There are four races still to go and you never know what can happen. Michael still has a chance to win the Drivers' Championship and the team now has a big, big chance to win the Constructors'. And I am focused on finishing my championship in third place, I think it's still possible.

I want to enjoy every minute of this. I'm not going anywhere tonight. I'm staying in Istanbul to enjoy myself!"

ABOVE David Coulthard's Red Bull looks great, but it struggled and was hit by a late-race gearbox problem

BELOW Engineer Rob Smedley joins Massa on the podium to celebrate the Brazilian's maiden victory

picture – Michael was just a second behind Alonso, with 13 laps to go. After the race, someone asked him if his moment at Turn 8 had cost him second place, and he didn't duck the issue: "I think you can say that if you want to, yeah."

The last part of the race was gripping, as the gap ebbed and flowed and Alonso ensured that the door remained firmly shut. All the while, he was playing with the rev limit, using a little more power as and when he needed to. It was a brilliant, defensive performance from a man with an ever so slightly slower package, and there was little Michael could do.

Inevitably, Massa's superb win was overshadowed by events in his wake: "It's just fantastic, I've been working so hard through my whole career to get to this moment. Just amazing, looking back to everything in my life to get to here – I'm really happy and very emotional. It's a fantastic day for me, like yesterday was. I did a very good start and first lap. The car was well balanced through the whole race, and even after the safety car I was able to pull away and wasn't too aggressive on the car. Every set of tyres and every part of the car was just responding in a fantastic way, and I was able to keep the gap through the whole race."

Jenson Button put in a faultless performance for Honda that saw him almost on the tail of the title contenders, and miles clear of the rest. From sixth on the grid, he ran very wide to avoid the first-lap chaos, and emerged in fifth place, going on to slip past Mark Webber's Williams to take fourth on the next lap, then staying there to the flag.

Pedro de la Rosa was badly delayed at the first corner, but still ended the opening lap with a one-place gain in 10th. The Spanish McLaren driver had chosen a one-stop strategy, which made life difficult with a heavy fuel load in the early laps, but it worked well enough to secure him fifth place.

Fisichella did a great job to salvage sixth place after a first-lap nose change, with the deployment of the safety car having allowed him to catch the pack. Ralf Schumacher also overcame a first-lap stop to take an eventual seventh place for Toyota. Both men had converted to one-stop race strategies following that early safety car deployment. Rubens Barrichello was well off team-mate Button's pace all weekend. He was also forced wide in the first-lap accident, and left the scene in 14th place before putting in a feisty recovery drive to take the final point for eighth place.

SNAPSHOT FROM
TURKEY

CLOCKWISE FROM RIGHT Istanbul and the River Bosphorus are a buzz of activity, and traffic jams...; Patrick Head indicates to Sam Michael where Williams is going wrong; Sebastian Vettel became the youngest driver to try F1, making a massive impression at BMW Sauber; Renault boss Flavio Briatore appears to rather like whichever young lady is in his sights; Istanbul Park's huge grandstands weren't full, but the pylons still proved attractive to some foolhardy spectators

WEEKEND HEADLINES

■ Just before the Turkish Grand Prix, an FIA Court of Appeal finally confirmed that mass dampers were no longer legal, much to the chagrin of Pat Symonds and the Renault team. The appeal was called after the FIA had refused to accept the stewards' decision at the German Grand Prix that had said the dampers were legal.

■ Euro F3 contender and Red Bull protégé Sebastian Vettel became the youngest driver to participate in a grand prix weekend when he drove the third BMW on Friday, aged just 19 years and 53 days. He carried on Robert Kubica's good work by making no serious mistakes and topping the timesheets with apparent ease.

■ Ferrari caused a stir by running the most extreme version yet of its unusual rear brake ducts, which to most people looked like the aerodynamic aids long used in oval racing to minimise drag. Ferrari denied that gaining an aerodynamic advantage was the primary aim of the devices, which were also tried by Scuderia Toro Rosso.

■ In the break between the Turkish and Italian Grands Prix, Renault announced that its test driver Heikki Kovalainen would replace Fernando Alonso in 2007, finally confirming that efforts to bring McLaren's Kimi Räikkönen on board had failed. The team also revealed that Flavio Briatore had finally extended his deal as Team Principal.

■ Nelson Piquet Jr was announced as a test driver for Renault with immediate effect, much to the disappointment of the Renault-backed youngsters who competed against him in GP2. Toyota's Ricardo Zonta was also revealed as a future Renault tester, and it was also announced that Super Aguri's Franck Montagny was destined for a testing job with Toyota.

RACE RESULTS
TURKEY
ISTANBUL

Official Results © [2006]
Formula One Administration Limited,
6 Princes Gate, London SW7 1QJ.
No reproduction without permission.
All copyright and database rights reserved

RACE DATE August 27th
CIRCUIT LENGTH 3.317 miles
NO. OF LAPS 58
RACE DISTANCE 192.388 miles
WEATHER Hot & bright, 35°C
TRACK TEMP 52°C
RACE DAY ATTENDANCE 80,000
LAP RECORD Juan Pablo Montoya,
1m24.770s, 138.056mph, 2005

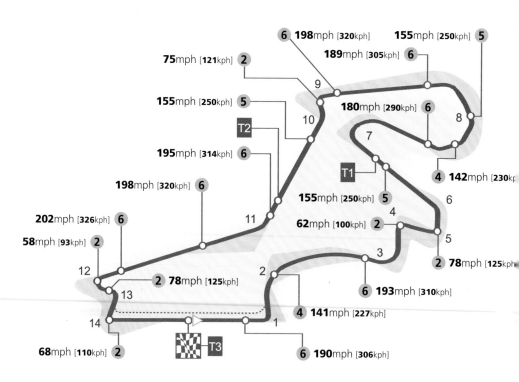

PRACTICE 1

	Driver	Time	Laps
1	K Räikkönen	1m28.315s	5
2	M Schumacher	1m28.777s	4
3	J Button	1m28.785s	5
4	A Wurz	1m28.959s	24
5	A Davidson	1m29.193s	19
6	P de la Rosa	1m29.376s	5
7	N Heidfeld	1m29.780s	6
8	S Vettel	1m29.964s	25
9	R Doornbos	1m30.391s	16
10	N Jani	1m30.576s	22
11	R Barrichello	1m30.838s	5
12	G Mondini	1m30.846s	28
13	S Speed	1m31.416s	5
14	C Albers	1m31.475s	10
15	T Monteiro	1m31.566s	10
16	F Montagny	1m31.814s	13
17	F Massa	1m31.904s	5
18	S Yamamoto	1m32.212s	11
19	V Liuzzi	1m32.497s	6
20	R Schumacher	no time	5
21	J Trulli	no time	2
22	F Alonso	no time	1
23	D Coulthard	no time	1
24	G Fisichella	no time	1
25	C Klien	no time	1
26	R Kubica	no time	1
27	T Sato	no time	1
28	N Rosberg	no time	0
29	M Webber	no time	0

PRACTICE 2

	Driver	Time	Laps
1	S Vettel	1m28.091s	29
2	F Massa	1m28.164s	18
3	J Button	1m28.506s	10
4	A Davidson	1m28.598s	31
5	R Schumacher	1m28.614s	21
6	M Schumacher	1m28.819s	13
7	R Doornbos	1m28.848s	15
8	K Räikkönen	1m29.042s	10
9	P de la Rosa	1m29.112s	10
10	R Barrichello	1m29.214s	16
11	G Mondini	1m29.719s	27
12	F Alonso	1m29.741s	16
13	N Jani	1m29.858s	30
14	S Speed	1m29.890s	20
15	J Trulli	1m30.006s	18
16	F Montagny	1m30.491s	25
17	R Kubica	1m30.502s	9
18	G Fisichella	1m30.504s	16
19	A Wurz	1m30.509s	36
20	V Liuzzi	1m30.551s	17
21	M Webber	1m30.775s	13
22	C Klien	1m30.889s	16
23	N Rosberg	1m31.015s	17
24	T Sato	1m31.091s	11
25	S Yamamoto	1m31.316s	21
26	T Monteiro	1m31.519s	15
27	N Heidfeld	1m31.526s	10
28	D Coulthard	1m31.540s	10
29	C Albers	1m32.102s	7

PRACTICE 3

	Driver	Time	Laps
1	M Schumacher	1m27.203s	12
2	F Alonso	1m27.924s	16
3	G Fisichella	1m27.963s	17
4	R Kubica	1m27.964s	15
5	N Heidfeld	1m28.151s	14
6	J Button	1m28.190s	17
7	F Massa	1m28.266s	14
8	R Barrichello	1m28.359s	15
9	K Räikkönen	1m28.368s	11
10	C Klien	1m28.830s	9
11	J Trulli	1m28.861s	17
12	S Speed	1m28.861s	14
13	P de la Rosa	1m29.034s	12
14	M Webber	1m29.069s	10
15	N Rosberg	1m29.176s	13
16	D Coulthard	1m29.357s	12
17	R Schumacher	1m29.374s	18
18	V Liuzzi	1m29.426s	19
19	C Albers	1m29.668s	19
20	S Yamamoto	1m29.881s	17
21	T Monteiro	1m29.915s	17
22	T Sato	1m30.151s	21

QUALIFYING 1

	Driver	Time
1	F Massa	1m27.306s
2	M Schumacher	1m27.385s
3	R Schumacher	1m27.668s
4	F Alonso	1m27.861s
5	G Fisichella	1m28.175s
6	N Heidfeld	1m28.200s
7	R Kubica	1m28.212s
8	J Button	1m28.222s
9	K Räikkönen	1m28.236s
10	C Klien	1m28.271s
11	M Webber	1m28.307s
12	P de la Rosa	1m28.403s
13	R Barrichello	1m28.411s
14	J Trulli	1m28.549s
15	N Rosberg	1m28.889s
16	C Albers	1m29.021s
17	D Coulthard	1m29.136s
18	S Speed	1m29.158s
19	V Liuzzi	1m29.250s
20	T Monteiro	1m29.901s
21	S Yamamoto	1m30.607s
22	T Sato	1m30.850s

QUALIFYING 2

	Driver	Time
1	M Schumacher	1m25.850s
2	J Button	1m26.872s
3	F Alonso	1m26.917s
4	F Massa	1m27.059s
5	R Schumacher	1m27.062s
6	K Räikkönen	1m27.202s
7	N Heidfeld	1m27.251s
8	G Fisichella	1m27.346s
9	R Kubica	1m27.405s
10	M Webber	1m27.608s
11	C Klien	1m27.852s
12	P de la Rosa	1m27.897s
13	J Trulli	1m27.973s
14	R Barrichello	1m28.257s
15	N Rosberg	1m28.386s
16	C Albers	1m28.639s

Best sectors – Practice

Sec 1	M Schumacher	32.438s
Sec 2	M Schumacher	30.446s
Sec 3	G Fisichella	24.064s

Speed trap – Practice

1	R Schumacher	195.7mph
2	F Alonso	195.6mph
3	G Fisichella	195.4mph

Best sectors – Qualifying

Sec 1	M Schumacher	31.964s
Sec 2	M Schumacher	30.091s
Sec 3	M Schumacher	23.795s

Fernando Alonso
"Michael only had two chances to pass, in Turn 12 and Turn 14. That meant I could get a bigger gap at those places by turning it up to max revs. It was enough to keep second."

Michael Schumacher
"For some reason, the car was nervous in the second stint and my mistake at Turn 8 on lap 28 didn't help. In the end, I tried to stick with Alonso in case he made a mistake."

Kimi Räikkönen
"I tried to avoid Fisichella, but then Speed hit my left rear causing a puncture. The team changed it, but when I re-joined, I had no grip and hit the Turn 4 tyre wall."

Jenson Button
"We didn't have the pace of the Ferraris or Alonso, but we know where we're losing out to them and the last stint was very strong for us with a lot less graining."

Robert Kubica
"I went wide when Fisichella spun, but was able to pass some drivers before the safety car came out and we changed tyres. On my last stint, the tyres were graining."

Jarno Trulli
"When I was hit from behind at Turn 1, I couldn't avoid hitting a car in front of me. The safety car came at just the wrong time, but the main problem was my tyres."

Giancarlo Fisichella
"I got a good start but Michael was weaving a lot. I braked quite late, but was close to Fernando, so braked even harder which locked the rears and put me in a spin."

Felipe Massa
"Today is a day I'll never forget. I had a very good start and, as I left the grid, I could see Michael and Alonso fighting but was able to pull away from them."

Pedro de la Rosa
"There was mayhem at Turn 1 after Fisichella's spin and I just made it through. It was a tough race with the one-stop strategy as I had to look after my rear tyres."

Rubens Barrichello
"We had a competitive car, so it's a shame someone pushed me wide at the first corner. Without that, I could have been fighting closer to the front. We had the pace and the will."

Nick Heidfeld
"I went into Turn 1 on the inside, but Fisichella hit the front of my car. On the way back to the pits, the wing got stuck beneath, leaving me with no grip and damaging the floor."

Ralf Schumacher
"It was always going to be hard starting so far back. I lost my front wing at the first corner and pitted, but at least we were able to fill up so we'd need only one more stop."

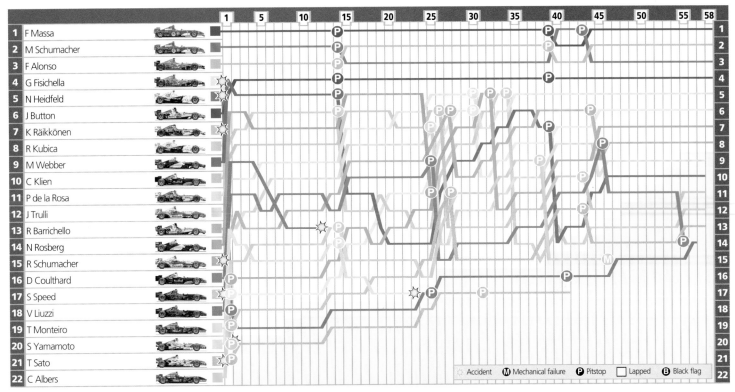

| Accident | Mechanical failure | Pitstop | Lapped | Black flag |

	1	F Massa
	2	M Schumacher
	3	F Alonso
	4	G Fisichella
	5	N Heidfeld
	6	J Button
	7	K Räikkönen
	8	R Kubica
	9	M Webber
	10	C Klien
	11	P de la Rosa
	12	J Trulli
	13	R Barrichello
	14	N Rosberg
	15	R Schumacher
	16	D Coulthard
	17	S Speed
	18	V Liuzzi
	19	T Monteiro
	20	S Yamamoto
	21	T Sato
	22	C Albers

QUALIFYING 3

	Driver	Time
1	F Massa	1m26.907s
2	M Schumacher	1m27.284s
3	F Alonso	1m27.321s
4	G Fisichella	1m27.564s
5	R Schumacher	1m27.569s
6	N Heidfeld	1m27.785s
7	J Button	1m27.790s
8	K Räikkönen	1m27.866s
9	R Kubica	1m28.167s
10	M Webber	1m29.436s

GRID

	Driver	Time
1	F Massa	1m26.907s
2	M Schumacher	1m27.284s
3	F Alonso	1m27.321s
4	G Fisichella	1m27.564s
5	N Heidfeld	1m27.785s
6	J Button	1m27.790s
7	K Räikkönen	1m27.866s
8	R Kubica	1m28.167s
9	M Webber	1m29.436s
10	C Klien	1m27.852s
11	P de la Rosa	1m27.897s
12	J Trulli	1m27.973s
13	R Barrichello	1m28.257s
14	N Rosberg	1m28.386s
15*	R Schumacher	1m27.569s
16	D Coulthard	1m29.136s
17	S Speed	1m29.158s
18	V Liuzzi	1m29.250s
19	T Monteiro	1m29.901s
20	S Yamamoto	1m30.607s
21	T Sato	1m30.850s
22*	C Albers	1m28.639s

*10-PLACE GRID PENALTY

RACE

	Driver	Car	Laps	Time	Avg. mph	Fastest	Stops
1	F Massa	Ferrari 248	58	1h28m51.082s	129.829	1m28.123s	2
2	F Alonso	Renault R26	58	1h28m56.657s	129.694	1m28.245s	2
3	M Schumacher	Ferrari 248	58	1h28m56.738s	129.692	1m28.005s	2
4	J Button	Honda RA106	58	1h29m03.416s	129.530	1m28.474s	2
5	P de la Rosa	McLaren-Mercedes MP4-21	58	1h29m36.990s	128.721	1m28.959s	1
6	G Fisichella	Renault R26	58	1h29m37.676s	128.704	1m28.546s	2
7	R Schumacher	Toyota TF106B	58	1h29m50.419s	128.401	1m29.084s	2
8	R Barrichello	Honda RA106	58	1h29m51.116s	128.384	1m28.733s	2
9	J Trulli	Toyota TF106B	57	1h28m53.202s	127.539	1m30.048s	2
10	M Webber	Williams-Cosworth FW28	57	1h28m53.683s	127.527	1m30.088s	2
11	C Klien	Red Bull-Ferrari RB2	57	1h29m01.283s	127.346	1m30.025s	2
12	R Kubica	BMW Sauber F1.06	57	1h29m09.330s	127.154	1m29.723s	2
13	S Speed	Toro Rosso-Cosworth STR01	57	1h29m09.660s	127.147	1m29.933s	3
14	N Heidfeld	BMW Sauber F1.06	56	1h29m57.326s	123.811s	1m30.335s	3
15	D Coulthard	Red Bull-Ferrari RB2	55	Gearbox	127.004	1m30.026s	2
R	C Albers	Midland-Toyota M16	46	Accident	-	1m30.403s	2
NC	T Sato	Super Aguri-Honda SA06	41	1h29m36.815s	90.970	1m31.814s	2
R	N Rosberg	Williams-Cosworth FW28	25	Water pressure	-	1m30.071s	0
R	S Yamamoto	Super Aguri-Honda SA06	23	Spun	-	1m32.337s	1
R	V Liuzzi	Toro Rosso-Cosworth STR01	12	Spun	-	1m32.148s	0
R	K Räikkönen	McLaren-Mercedes MP4-21	1	Accident	-	-	1
R	T Monteiro	Midland-Toyota M16	0	Accident	-	-	0

CHAMPIONSHIP

	Driver	Pts
1	F Alonso	108
2	M Schumacher	96
3	F Massa	62
4	G Fisichella	52
5	K Räikkönen	49
6	J Button	36
7	JP Montoya	26
8	R Barrichello	22
9	N Heidfeld	19
10	R Schumacher	18
11	P de la Rosa	14
12	D Coulthard	14
13	J Trulli	10
14	J Villeneuve	7
15	M Webber	6
16	N Rosberg	4
17	C Klien	2
18	V Liuzzi	1

Speed trap – Qualifying

1	M Schumacher	196.1mph
2	F Massa	196.1mph
3	G Fisichella	195.4mph

Fastest Lap

M Schumacher 1m28.005s
(135.689mph) on lap 55

Fastest speed trap

G Fisichella 197.5mph

Slowest speed trap

T Sato 184.2mph

Fastest pit stop

1	D Coulthard	23.194s
2	R Barrichello	23.248s
3	J Trulli	23.864s

Constructor

	Constructor	Pts
1	Renault	160
2	Ferrari	158
3	McLaren-Mercedes	89
4	Honda	58
5	Toyota	28
6	BMW Sauber	26
7	Red Bull-Ferrari	16
8	Williams-Cosworth	10
9	Toro Rosso-Cosworth	1

David Coulthard
"The car's balance improved after we adjusted the front wing and tyre pressures. Late in the race, I was catching Webber, but had to retire with a gearbox problem."

Mark Webber
"It was going fine until the safety car, given our plans to go long. The stint following the first stop was hard as I was carrying a bit of fuel. The last stint was much better."

Vitantonio Liuzzi
"My car began to go slower and slower. On lap 12, the rear axle locked as I turned into Turn 1 and I couldn't avoid the spin. That was the end, as the engine stalled."

Tiago Monteiro
"Everyone was trying to avoid a car that had spun, and someone turned into me as it was trying to avoid another car. He hit my wheel and my radiator and that was it."

Takuma Sato
"I passed two or three cars going to Turn 1, but someone ran into the back of my car. The mechanics did a fantastic job, but the car was not fully repaired, so I struggled."

Christian Klien
"That was a tough race. It was so hot and Turn 8 is so long, it's very tough on the neck. The car had understeer in the second part, but we weren't really racing here."

Nico Rosberg
"It was a good day as I claimed a few places on lap 1. Racing was fun and I was pushing without being worried, but then I was told we'd lost water pressure."

Scott Speed
"I don't know what happened. Maybe I got hit from behind. I lost the wing and pitted, but we got a lucky break as the safety car came out, but a good finish was out."

Christijan Albers
"It's a shame we made a mistake at the second stop. Then I made an error: touching the grass, which caused me to slam into the guardrail, hurting my shoulder."

Sakon Yamamoto
"I avoided the incident at Turn 1, and made up several places, then had a good fight with the Toro Rossos and Midlands. Sadly, I spun and then the engine stalled."

FORMULA 1™ GRAN PREMIO
VODAFONE D'ITALIA 2006
Monza

ONE FOR THE FANS

Michael Schumacher winning on Ferrari's home ground, then announcing his retirement, made the news, as did Alonso's penalty in qualifying and his engine failure

Michael Schumacher put his World Championship challenge back on course with a superb victory in the Italian Grand Prix. Then, as almost everyone had expected, he followed this up by announcing to millions of TV viewers that he would indeed retire from driving at the end of the season. It's safe to say that the news completely overshadowed the usual detail of Monza's race weekend.

Ferrari had revealed some weeks before the teams arrived at Monza that it would announce its 2007 driver line-up after the race, and there was fevered speculation about what Michael's final decision would be, about whether he'd stay or whether he would hang up his helmet.

However, as the deadline approached, it became increasingly clear that Michael would be stopping at the end of the year, leaving McLaren's Kimi Räikkönen to join Felipe Massa as a Ferrari driver in 2007. It was just a question of exactly how and when the announcement would be made. Ferrari hoped that by postponing the news until after the race, driver and team would somehow be able to fly under the media radar. That was an optimistic idea, at best…

In the end, the Italian GP could hardly have turned

INSIDE LINE
JEAN TODT

FERRARI GENERAL DIRECTOR

"The speculation over Michael's future was becoming more and more intense, but there is a difference between strong speculation and an announced decision. One of the reasons we wanted to make the announcement at the Italian Grand Prix at Monza was to be able to focus on the rest of the season with everyone knowing what the situation was.

The speculation is all a part of our world and you have to accept it. The day that I can't, I will go, because the only reason I'm still in this business is that I enjoy being with the team and I enjoy the people around me. As regards my own future, it has been clear in my head for a while.

I've obviously got mixed feelings about Michael stopping, but I will only be able to speak about them after Brazil. At the moment, Michael is very strong, among the strongest drivers in the history of motor racing, and there are still three races to go.

As far as Kimi is concerned, what's important is that we never had any kind of pre-contract, so sometimes I was smiling a bit when I saw people writing about private meetings to get Kimi. The important thing is that we feel Kimi is very strong and very talented. I like him as a person and he is committed to Ferrari for the next few years (to the end of 2009).

Replacing Michael was never going to be easy, and all you can do is look to see who is available and make a decision about who you would like. Of the three quickest drivers around, one was already with us and another one was our favourite – and we had him, too. So it was an easy choice and fortunately it was also a very simple discussion. Kimi wanted to join Ferrari and we wanted him to join Ferrari, so it was easy.

I will obviously have a different relationship with Kimi to the one I have had with Michael, because every person is different. I'm sure it will be a very strong relationship, just different.

People ask whether Kimi can have the same level of success as Michael and that would obviously be difficult. He's a highly competitive driver and it's up to us to try to deliver to him the best support and the best car. But it's never easy. Last year Michael accepted a given race (Indianapolis), a gift, but he didn't win a single other one and so you see the importance of a good, reliable car. If we can give Kimi one, I'm sure he will make great use of it.

Finally, people who speculate that Michael decided to retire because he did not want to compete with Kimi are simply stupid."

out any better for the Ferrari ace, who was clearly under considerable pressure. Formula One's most successful driver ever qualified only second, but he managed to get ahead of polesitter Räikkönen in the race by making a later first pit stop. After that, Michael just had to keep his focus and forget about what he had in mind for after the race. And this he did in style.

When title rival Fernando Alonso retired 10 laps from the finish, after a rare engine failure on his Renault, Michael was assured of a 10-point gain in the World Championship, and the day was even sweeter. The victory gave him the perfect stage on which to make his big announcement, which he did with some dignity.

"It was obviously pretty emotional to drive the lap back after the race," said Michael. "I informed everybody of my decision, and probably this was the most emotional moment, along with being on the podium to celebrate, and at that moment knowing it's the last opportunity I would have to finish so well with such a crowd that gave me so much in terms of their feeling. It just overwhelmed me.

"It has been such a good time for all these years and there's simply no point just to hang in there and maybe take away the future of a very young talented driver like Felipe. I was aware of this for quite a long time, but with Felipe it was around Indianapolis that his future had to be decided, and I didn't see a reason to just hang in there and maybe take away his chance."

Michael's insistence that he made an early decision to give his team-mate a chance came as a surprise. The day itself turned into a difficult one for Massa, who was bogged down in traffic for much of the race, and dropped out of the points after stopping to change a flat-spotted front tyre, caused when he locked up after Alonso's engine blew in front of him.

Indeed, Renault had a disappointing weekend in Italy that culminated in Alonso's World Championship lead shrinking from 12 points to just two.

Alonso had a puncture early in the final qualifying session, but still managed to recover to fifth place with a damaged car. However, he was then demoted to 10th, having been deemed to have blocked Massa, a controversial decision that left him well and truly wound up. Team principal Flavio Briatore made it clear to anyone who would listen that he felt Renault's championship campaign was being undermined and, in private, Alonso was distraught.

In the race, he managed to make his way forward to third place before his engine failed for what was only his second retirement of the season.

"What happened was a disappointment for sure," said the Spaniard, "but I think we have to think about the next race and the next opportunity. There are three races to go, a championship to be decided, and I think we should be very optimistic. We were very, very quick in the last three races, maybe even as quick as Ferrari or even more, so for the last three races we should be the favourite.

"You try to make a good result and not to lose too many points, but for sure you have to push the engine more starting from there, with a lot of traffic and not the same airflow into your car. It's much more difficult. But these things happen to everyone. I think we had the engine failure today and the tyre failure in Hungary not at the right moment. But maybe these things will happen to Ferrari rather than us in the last three races, and we will be happy again. So we will simply have to concentrate and do our job."

Alonso's team-mate Giancarlo Fisichella could not match his pace all meeting. Heavier in qualifying, he went for a one-stop strategy in the race, and ultimately it was good enough to get him up to fourth, earning valuable constructors' points for the team.

Räikkönen did a good job to claim his third pole in four races, albeit by just 0.002s. The race proved that he had just two laps less fuel than Schumacher, so it

OPPOSITE There's almost always trouble at the first chicane on lap 1 at Monza. This year was no different. The Spyker MF1s and Klien take to the grass, as Webber and Speed stay on the black stuff

BELOW Robert Kubica benefited from a great start to be third at the end of lap 1, a position that was still his at the finish of his third race

"It's been a very special day here at Monza, and to finish it with a win and 10 points, and looking at the World Championship as well… However, it's more about what's going to happen in the future. I'm sorry it's taken longer than some of you would have wanted, but you have to find the right moment.

This was my last Italian Grand Prix and I've decided, together with the team, that at the end of the year I am going to retire from racing. It has been a really exceptional time when I look at what motor sport has given to me in more than 30 years. I've loved every single moment, the good times and the bad.

I should thank my family, starting with my Dad, my passed-away Mum and obviously my wife and kids who, at all times, supported what I was doing. Also my mates from the Benetton time and, obviously, especially the Ferrari days when I made so many friends. But one day the moment has to come and, in terms of timing the decision, it was fair so that Felipe had a chance to decide his future because I think he's a great guy.

As to my replacement [Kimi Räikkönen], I was always pleased and I knew a long time ago. Now I just want to concentrate on the last three races and finish the season in style.

Making the decision has been difficult, but I simply knew that all the effort you need to be competitive – and that's the only reason I want to be here – I can't see that I am going to have it for further years. It was around Indianapolis that Felipe's future had to be decided and that's when I made the decision and informed the team.

The team left me every door open. Obviously, I have a lot of friends there and naturally we discussed the upsides and downsides but, in the end, it was down to my wife Corinna and myself. She gave me her point-of-view and we discussed it, but there was no point when she went in another direction. She simply helped me take my decision.

The slowing-down lap was pretty emotional. I was talking to the team and informed everybody of my decision. This was the most emotional moment, along with being on the podium and knowing it was the last opportunity I would have in front of a Monza crowd. They gave me so much feeling and it just overwhelmed me."

was quite a realistic effort. As noted, the Finn led until the first round of pit stops, but those two laps allowed the Ferrari man to get ahead. After that, Räikkönen had little choice but to follow him home in second place, and it was only appropriate that he was on the podium to share Michael's big moment.

"I was a little bit concerned about our start," explained Räikkönen, "because the previous starts haven't exactly been good. Luckily, the guys did an excellent job fixing the start system, and everything worked well. I had a good start and was just trying to go as fast as I could before the first pit stop, because I was thinking that they might stop a little bit later, so if I could pull out any gap, any chance we could have to try and fight for a win. But, as it turned out, we were not quick enough today.

"Second place was quite easy, though, so in the end I just slowed down and brought the car home and got second place. Unfortunately, that was the maximum that we could have today, but it is still a good weekend."

It was a frustrating weekend for Pedro de la Rosa in the second McLaren, however, as the Spaniard started seventh, but retired early with engine failure.

The BMWs were clearly suited to the high-speed nature of Monza, and showed impressive straightline speed. Nick Heidfeld did a good job to qualify third, while rookie team-mate Robert Kubica was not far behind in sixth. It was the Pole who shone at the start, though, quickly charging up to third place. He then showed that it wasn't a fluke by staying out and leading several laps after the frontrunners had called in for their first pit stops.

Kubica was passed in the final round of pit stops by Alonso, but recovered his third place when the Renault retired with 10 laps remaining. Any questions about the Pole's long-term prospects with the team had by now been forgotten. Heidfeld lost ground with a drive-through penalty for speeding in the pits, but still finished eighth. Nevertheless, he was left in the shade by his young team-mate.

"I could have qualified better," said Kubica, "but unfortunately I made some small mistakes at Lesmo, and for us anyway the third row was really good with the tyres that we had. We also knew we were carrying a lot of fuel compared to the others. And with the good start that we had in Hungary and then in Turkey I hoped to gain some positions. We took more positions

OPPOSITE TOP Michael runs ahead of the Renaults after emerging from his first pit stop. It was Ferrari's day

OPPOSITE BOTTOM Jenson Button headed a third straight double points score for Honda, by finishing in fifth place

ABOVE Michael Schumacher ran second behind Kimi Räikkönen, but pitted later and controlled the race thereafter, for victory number 90

ABOVE It's over and out for
Fernando Alonso as his Renault V8
blows after his climb to third

BELOW For Michael Schumacher,
winning the grand prix was the
easy part. Making it sound as
though he was 100% happy to
retire was altogether more difficult

at the start than we expected, and then I just concentrated on keeping the pace, and the pace was good.

"Before the car went to the grid, some of my team told me they wanted to see me standing on the podium. I took it like a joke, but it happened, so we are really proud of it…"

Honda had a terrible time on Friday when test driver Anthony Davidson suffered two engine failures with a brand-new specification V8. Then, because of the problems, the team kept both race drivers in the garage all day, and then gave them an older specification engine for Saturday. Fortunately, there were no problems for the remainder of the weekend. Both drivers made the top 10 in qualifying, but elected to run differing strategies for the race. Jenson Button opted for a lighter fuel load and, after starting fifth on the grid and making two pit stops, he finished in the same position. Rubens Barrichello went for just one pit stop during the 53 laps and finished a place behind in sixth.

The Italian Grand Prix was a low-key weekend for Toyota. The white and red cars never looked quick on a track where low drag and top speed is everything. In his home race, Jarno Trulli just missed making the Q3 cut, and started 11th. From there, he adopted a one-stop strategy that enabled him to move up to seventh by the flag, earning two points. Ralf Schumacher complained of handling problems throughout the weekend, starting a disappointing 13th, and struggling to make much progress through the traffic because of an overall lack of straightline speed. He eventually finished 15th.

Nico Rosberg did a better job than Williams teammate Mark Webber in qualifying, and started his first Italian GP from 12th place. He got ahead of Trulli at the start and was running in 11th when he suffered a driveshaft problem and toured back to the pits to retire after only nine laps. Webber was disappointed not to get past the first qualifying session, but he made a good start from 19th and did a lot of passing on the first lap, but it was always going to be difficult to make much progress. He crossed the line in 10th. Incredibly, Williams had not scored a point since the European GP, 10 races before Monza.

All things considered, though, the day was really all about Michael. His three-race farewell tour would commence in China…

SNAPSHOT FROM
ITALY

CLOCKWISE FROM RIGHT Circuits come and go, but entering the Parco di Monza is still magical; eleven teams turn up at Monza but, to the fans, only the one in red counts; sponsor Martini & Rossi was back on show; Spyker's take-over of Midland brought Mike Gascoyne (on left) back into the mix; Michael had more reason than ever before to feel the warmth of the reception from the tifosi as he greeted them for the final time

WEEKEND HEADLINES

■ Flavio Briatore made no secret at Monza of the fact that he felt the World Championship was being manipulated, and felt that Fernando Alonso's penalty for alleged blocking in qualifying was the last straw. His strong comments to Italian TV drew a swift reaction from the FIA, and Briatore was forced to issue an apology, claiming that he had been joking.

■ The Grand Prix Drivers' Association had strong feelings about some aspects of circuit safety at Monza, and especially the run-off at the second chicane. They were frustrated when the circuit boss changed his mind about attending their regular Friday meeting. The following week, the FIA issued a stinging rebuke to the drivers' criticisms…

■ MF1 Racing's weekend was dominated by news of their sale to the Dutch Spyker car company, after months of negotiations with entrepreneur Michiel Mol. The team also confirmed that it had hired former Jordan, Renault and Toyota man Mike Gascoyne as its new technical boss. Alas, the re-badged outfit had a disappointing weekend on the track.

■ Christian Klien ran his last race for Red Bull Racing in Italy, having told boss and erstwhile mentor Dietrich Mateschitz that he did not want to take up the offer of a Champ Car ride in 2007. Instead, he had his eyes on the new Spyker/MF1 project. RBR third driver Robert Doornbos was thus promoted to race driver for the last three races of 2006.

■ Immediately after the Italian GP, FIA Race Director Charlie Whiting informed the teams that he was henceforth going to reduce the likelihood of penalties for blocking in qualifying, by only forwarding what he felt were genuine complaints to the stewards. As the public face of the FIA, Whiting had received considerable criticism for stewards' decisions with which he did not always agree.

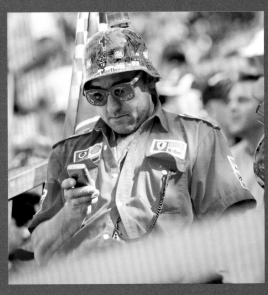

RACE RESULTS
ITALY
MONZA

RACE DATE September 10th
CIRCUIT LENGTH 3.600 miles
NO. OF LAPS 53
RACE DISTANCE 190.800 miles
WEATHER Hot & bright, 28°C
TRACK TEMP 42°C
RACE DAY ATTENDANCE 80,000
LAP RECORD Rubens Barrichello,
1m21.046s, 159.726mph, 2004

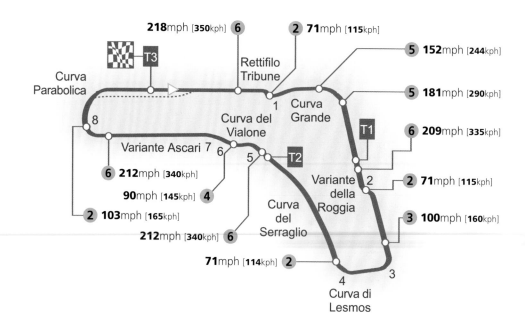

PRACTICE 1

	Driver	Time	Laps
1	S Vettel	1m23.263s	22
2	R Kubica	1m23.745s	5
3	A Wurz	1m23.868s	19
4	K Räikkönen	1m24.037s	5
5	N Jani	1m24.196s	24
6	T Monteiro	1m25.413s	7
7	R Doornbos	1m25.578s	19
8	C Albers	1m25.766s	7
9	T Sato	1m26.708s	20
10	S Yamamoto	1m27.310s	20
11	F Montagny	1m27.597s	7
12	G Mondini	1m28.444s	7
13	V Liuzzi	no time	3
14	A Davidson	no time	2
15	R Schumacher	no time	2
16	J Trulli	no time	2
17	D Coulthard	no time	1
18	P de la Rosa	no time	1
19	N Heidfeld	no time	1
20	C Klien	no time	1
21	F Massa	no time	1
22	N Rosberg	no time	1
23	S Speed	no time	1
24	M Webber	no time	1
25	F Alonso	no time	0
26	R Barrichello	no time	0
27	J Button	no time	0
28	G Fisichella	no time	0
29	M Schumacher	no time	0

PRACTICE 2

	Driver	Time	Laps
1	S Vettel	1m22.631s	29
2	M Schumacher	1m23.138s	11
3	F Massa	1m23.182s	12
4	A Wurz	1m23.414s	26
5	P de la Rosa	1m23.970s	12
6	K Räikkönen	1m24.034s	11
7	N Heidfeld	1m24.330s	9
8	F Alonso	1m24.577s	15
9	R Kubica	1m24.813s	5
10	F Montagny	1m24.943s	24
11	C Albers	1m24.985s	11
12	J Trulli	1m25.027s	12
13	N Rosberg	1m25.040s	9
14	C Klien	1m25.108s	11
15	G Fisichella	1m25.160s	14
16	T Monteiro	1m25.277s	12
17	R Schumacher	1m25.316s	22
18	D Coulthard	1m25.318s	11
19	A Davidson	1m25.356s	8
20	M Webber	1m25.500s	11
21	G Mondini	1m25.586s	29
22	V Liuzzi	1m25.707s	19
23	S Speed	1m25.755s	21
24	N Jani	1m25.878s	32
25	R Doornbos	1m26.058s	31
26	T Sato	1m26.118s	21
27	S Yamamoto	1m26.705s	14
28	R Barrichello	no time	0
29	J Button	no time	0

PRACTICE 3

	Driver	Time	Laps
1	F Massa	1m21.665s	12
2	N Heidfeld	1m22.052s	13
3	M Schumacher	1m22.257s	14
4	R Kubica	1m22.280s	12
5	F Alonso	1m22.371s	15
6	G Fisichella	1m22.412s	15
7	K Räikkönen	1m22.682s	11
8	R Barrichello	1m22.835s	18
9	P de la Rosa	1m22.915s	11
10	C Klien	1m23.081s	11
11	R Schumacher	1m23.244s	17
12	J Button	1m23.295s	15
13	N Rosberg	1m23.334s	8
14	J Trulli	1m23.467s	15
15	D Coulthard	1m23.536s	9
16	M Webber	1m23.599s	8
17	S Speed	1m23.659s	20
18	V Liuzzi	1m23.777s	20
19	C Albers	1m24.186s	17
20	T Monteiro	1m24.541s	14
21	T Sato	1m24.549s	25
22	S Yamamoto	1m24.717s	19

QUALIFYING 1

	Driver	Time
1	M Schumacher	1m21.711s
2	F Alonso	1m21.747s
3	N Heidfeld	1m21.764s
4	K Räikkönen	1m21.994s
5	F Massa	1m22.028s
6	J Trulli	1m22.093s
7	P de la Rosa	1m22.422s
8	R Kubica	1m22.437s
9	G Fisichella	1m22.486s
10	J Button	1m22.512s
11	N Rosberg	1m22.581s
12	D Coulthard	1m22.618s
13	M Schumacher	1m22.622s
14	R Barrichello	1m22.640s
15	C Klien	1m22.898s
16	S Speed	1m22.943s
17	V Liuzzi	1m23.043s
18	C Albers	1m23.116s
19	M Webber	1m23.341s
20	T Monteiro	1m23.920s
21	T Sato	1m24.289s
22	S Yamamoto	1m26.001s

QUALIFYING 2

	Driver	Time
1	F Massa	1m21.225s
2	R Kubica	1m21.270s
3	K Räikkönen	1m21.349s
4	M Schumacher	1m21.353s
5	N Heidfeld	1m21.425s
6	F Alonso	1m21.526s
7	J Button	1m21.572s
8	R Barrichello	1m21.688s
9	G Fisichella	1m21.722s
10	P de la Rosa	1m21.878s
11	J Trulli	1m21.924s
12	N Rosberg	1m22.203s
13	R Schumacher	1m22.280s
14	D Coulthard	1m22.589s
15	S Speed	1m23.165s
16	C Klien	no time

Best sectors – Practice

Sec 1	R Kubica	26.706s
Sec 2	F Massa	27.482s
Sec 3	F Massa	27.384s

Speed trap – Practice

1	N Heidfeld	213.5mph
2	R Kubica	213.0mph
3	N Rosberg	211.6mph

Best sectors – Qualifying

Sec 1	R Kubica	26.462s
Sec 2	F Massa	27.378s
Sec 3	M Schumacher	27.152s

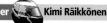

Fernando Alonso
"When you start 10th, you have to push to the limit. I was going to easily finish on the podium, and we showed that without the penalty, we had the pace to fight for the win."

Michael Schumacher
"We were hoping Kimi would pit before us and he did. The most emotional moment was the last lap. After the finish, it was difficult to keep my emotions under control."

Kimi Räikkönen
"I'm happy. We've improved our starting system and I was controlling the race, but the fact that Michael was able to stay out for one more lap decided the outcome."

Jenson Button
"The balance wasn't anywhere near as good as we'd hoped for. We made some adjustments at the first pit stop, but we were still not as quick as we needed to be."

Robert Kubica
"I locked my fronts into Turn 1 and flat-spotted. It was tough fighting Massa and Alonso. I came out of the second stop side-by-side with Alonso. Then his engine blew."

Jarno Trulli
"That was the most we could have achieved. It went well, especially considering that I had Barrichello slowing me down. Otherwise I could have gone slightly better."

Giancarlo Fisichella
"It wasn't easy, starting from ninth and running with a heavy load, but the tyres were extremely consistent, the balance was good and I managed to make up five places."

Filipe Massa
"I was always in traffic, never able to use the car's potential. When it seemed like I could finish fourth, I flat-spotted my right front when I had to brake on Alonso's oil."

Pedro de la Rosa
"I lost a place at the start. We put a lot of fuel in at my first stop to ensure a long second stint, which was aimed to get me in clean air. Then, suddenly, the engine failed."

Rubens Barrichello
"I suffered at the start as I was heavy with fuel. Sadly, we didn't have straightline speed which is why Fisichella was able to pass me. From there on, I struggled for rear grip."

Nick Heidfeld
"I was ahead of Michael into Turn 1. He came alongside me and I had to move over. I got dirt on my tyres and this slowed me for the whole lap. Later, I got a drive-through penalty."

Ralf Schumacher
"We were facing a difficult task starting so far back. I struggled for balance and found myself in traffic, and we didn't have enough speed to overtake on the straights."

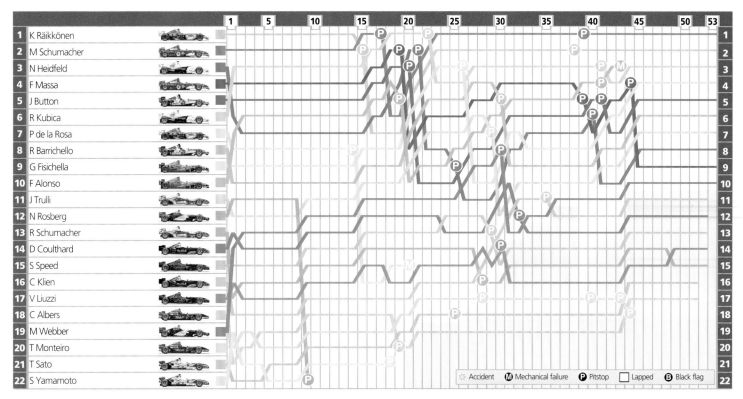

	Driver
1	K Räikkönen
2	M Schumacher
3	N Heidfeld
4	F Massa
5	J Button
6	R Kubica
7	P de la Rosa
8	R Barrichello
9	G Fisichella
10	F Alonso
11	J Trulli
12	N Rosberg
13	R Schumacher
14	D Coulthard
15	S Speed
16	C Klien
17	V Liuzzi
18	C Albers
19	M Webber
20	T Monteiro
21	T Sato
22	S Yamamoto

Legend: ☼ Accident　Ⓜ Mechanical failure　Ⓟ Pitstop　☐ Lapped　Ⓑ Black flag

QUALIFYING 3

	Driver	Time
1	K Räikkönen	1m21.484s
2	M Schumacher	1m21.486s
3	N Heidfeld	1m21.653s
4	F Massa	1m21.704s
5	J Button	1m22.011s
6	R Kubica	1m22.258s
7	P de la Rosa	1m22.280s
8	R Barrichello	1m22.787s
9	G Fisichella	1m23.175s
10*	F Alonso	1m25.688s

* BEST THREE LAPS ANNULLED

GRID

	Driver	Time
1	K Räikkönen	1m21.484s
2	M Schumacher	1m21.486s
3	N Heidfeld	1m21.653s
4	F Massa	1m21.704s
5	J Button	1m22.011s
6	R Kubica	1m22.258s
7	P de la Rosa	1m22.280s
8	R Barrichello	1m22.787s
9	G Fisichella	1m23.175s
10	F Alonso	1m25.688s
11	J Trulli	1m21.924s
12	N Rosberg	1m22.203s
13	R Schumacher	1m22.280s
14	D Coulthard	1m22.589s
15	S Speed	1m23.165s
16	C Klien	no time
17	V Liuzzi	1m23.043s
18	C Albers	1m23.116s
19	M Webber	1m23.341s
20	T Monteiro	1m23.920s
21	T Sato	1m24.289s
22	S Yamamoto	1m26.001s

RACE

	Driver	Car	Laps	Time	Avg. mph	Fastest	Stops
1	M Schumacher	Ferrari 248	53	1h14m51.975s	152.749	1m22.575s	2
2	K Räikkönen	McLaren-Mercedes MP4-21	53	1h15m00.021s	152.476	1m22.559s	2
3	R Kubica	BMW Sauber F1.06	53	1h15m18.389s	151.856	1m23.111s	2
4	G Fisichella	Renault R26	53	1h15m24.020s	151.667	1m23.617s	1
5	J Button	Honda RA106	53	1h15m24.660s	151.646	1m23.518s	2
6	R Barrichello	Honda RA106	53	1h15m34.384s	151.320	1m23.794s	1
7	J Trulli	Toyota TF106B	53	1h15m36.637s	151.245	1m23.869s	1
8	N Heidfeld	BMW Sauber F1.06	53	1h15m37.284s	151.224	1m23.294s	3
9	F Massa	Ferrari 248	53	1h15m37.930s	151.202	1m23.003s	3
10	M Webber	Williams-Cosworth FW28	53	1h16m04.577s	150.320	1m24.197s	1
11	C Klien	Red Bull-Ferrari RB2	52	1h14m55.976s	149.731	1m24.571s	1
12	D Coulthard	Red Bull-Ferrari RB2	52	1h15m00.600s	149.577	1m24.984s	1
13	S Speed	Toro Rosso-Cosworth STR01	52	1h15m01.696s	149.541	1m25.094s	1
14	V Liuzzi	Toro Rosso-Cosworth STR01	52	1h15m02.135s	149.526	1m24.764s	1
15	R Schumacher	Toyota TF106B	52	1h15m03.317s	149.486	1m24.837s	1
16	T Sato	Super Aguri-Honda SA06	51	1h15m41.343s	145.382	1m25.676s	1
17	C Albers	Spyker MF1-Toyota M16	51	1h16m02.248s	144.715	1m25.494s	1
R	T Monteiro	Spyker MF1-Toyota M16	44	Brakes	-	1m24.822s	3
R	F Alonso	Renault R26	43	Engine	-	1m23.121s	2
R	P de la Rosa	McLaren-Mercedes MP4-21	20	Engine	-	1m23.702s	1
R	S Yamamoto	Super Aguri-Honda SA06	18	Hydraulics	-	1m26.548s	0
R	N Rosberg	Williams-Cosworth FW28	9	Driveshaft	-	1m25.362s	0

CHAMPIONSHIP

	Driver	Pts
1	F Alonso	108
2	M Schumacher	106
3	F Massa	62
4	G Fisichella	57
5	K Räikkönen	57
6	J Button	40
7	JP Montoya	26
8	R Barrichello	25
9	N Heidfeld	20
10	R Schumacher	18
11	P de la Rosa	14
12	D Coulthard	14
13	J Trulli	12
14	J Villeneuve	7
15	R Kubica	6
16	M Webber	6
17	N Rosberg	4
18	C Klien	2
19	V Liuzzi	1

Speed trap – Qualifying

1	N Heidfeld	216.5mph
2	G Fisichella	215.1mph
3	F Massa	214.9mph

Fastest Lap

K Räikkönen 1m22.559s
(156.963mph) on lap 13

Fastest speed trap

F Massa 217.4mph

Slowest speed trap

S Yamamoto 207.1mph

Fastest pit stop

1	F Alonso	24.273s
2	N Heidfeld	24.406s
3	R Kubica	24.616s

David Coulthard

"It was a fitting way for Michael to announce his retirement. Whether people are believers in his race ethics or not, you must recognise that he's been a great champion."

Mark Webber

"I did some passing in the first chicane, and in the second. I passed Coulthard, then tried to stay with Trulli as I expected him to be one-stopping, but I couldn't keep up."

Vitantonio Liuzzi

"I lost ground at the start, then was on the limiter down the straight so I couldn't pass anyone. As I tried to pass DC, we made contact, after which I had a lot of understeer."

Tiago Monteiro

"I was catching the group ahead of me, so that motivated me, although we were losing out on the straights. Sadly, after my first stop, I developed a random brake problem."

Takuma Sato

"We had a hydraulic problem, so I had to take the T-car and start from the pitlane. I began to struggle with a chassis problem. We found the floor had delaminated."

Christian Klien

"I was too slow on the straights to pass anyone, but the one-stop strategy worked, as I stayed out for a long time and overtook a couple of people in their second stops."

Nico Rosberg

"A driveshaft was damaged at the second chicane. It's unlucky, as we ran through that chicane for three test days and the whole weekend and nothing untoward happened."

Scott Speed

"I was able to keep ahead of DC and Ralf, but was unlucky in the pit stop as I had to let the leaders go by as I returned, and DC made up all the ground I had over him."

Christijan Albers

"First I had a flat. Two laps later, I developed a transmission problem. We know what it is, so hopefully we'll be able to solve it. It's a shame, as the pace was there."

Sakon Yamamoto

"We had a good start. After a few laps, we realised that we had a car problem that we fixed quickly. But then we had a hydraulic problem which forced me to retire."

Constructor Pts

	Constructor	Pts
1	Ferrari	168
2	Renault	165
3	McLaren-Mercedes	97
4	Honda	65
5	BMW Sauber	33
6	Toyota	30
7	Red Bull-Ferrari	16
8	Williams-Cosworth	10
9	Toro Rosso-Cosworth	1

2006 FORMULA 1™ SINOPEC CHINESE GRAND PRIX
Shanghai

MICHAEL'S MIRACLE

This was a race that Renault ought to have won, and Fernando Alonso knew it, but victory was a masterstroke from Michael Schumacher in which tyres were key

We enjoyed some entertaining races in 2006, but the Chinese GP was in a class of its own, beating even the Hungarian GP in terms of the thrill-a-minute factor. Just consider that Fernando Alonso was so fast at the beginning that he was 11.5s ahead of sixth-placed Michael Schumacher after just three laps. And yet, an hour and a half later, when it really mattered, the Ferrari man was in front of his rival by 3.1s. And this in a race in which safety cars played no part in compromising the action. The result put the drivers equal on points as they headed to Suzuka, leaving the title battle wide open.

After the Hungarian GP, it was clear that Bridgestone was in serious trouble with its intermediate tyre when the track was wet. But during the crossover period to dries, Bridgestone was in pretty good shape, as Michael had demonstrated. The nightmare scenario for Ferrari was a wet qualifying session, with the track not drying fast enough, and that is what we got in China. The sight of the 10 Bridgestone runners in the bottom 10 places at the end of the first session said it all.

Amazingly, having fought his way through to the third session Michael nabbed sixth place on a drying track. Still, Alonso and Giancarlo Fisichella looked pretty well set for the race, having qualified on the front row.

Sunday brought more rain, and there were miserable faces in the Ferrari camp, although the rain stopped before the start. The key to Michael's race was the opening lap. Ahead of him, Kimi Räikkönen and the two Honda drivers were never going to make life easy.

In the event, Michael kept his sixth place and held it as he waited for the tyre advantage to go in his favour. Finally, it did. He passed Barrichello on lap 8, Button on lap 13 and Räikkönen when he pitted on lap 16. In fact, the Finn was well set for a good result until a throttle problem caused his demise a couple of laps later.

For Michael, the crucial thing was his gap to Alonso, and that peaked at 25.3s on lap 14, then began to drop as the stops approached. It had fallen to just over 18s when Michael pitted on lap 21, to be followed by Alonso and Fisichella over the next two laps.

"That was a fantastic drive," said Ferrari Technical Director Ross Brawn. "As we couldn't afford to drop a pit stop to Alonso, it was a crucial part of the race that he did very well. Then everything started to come to us."

That's when Alonso's nightmare began. While nearly everyone else was following the now common practice of leaving used intermediates on, and taking advantage of their gradual progress towards slicks, Alonso changed only the fronts. It was his decision.

He knew that his fronts were badly worn, especially the left, and felt that another stint on them would be too much to ask. It was a legacy of the fact that he had been pushing so hard, and perhaps also his aggressive driving style, which asks a lot of the front tyres. Team-mate Fisichella, in contrast, had no worries.

For Alonso, the unusual mixture of old rears and newer fronts didn't work, and there was nothing he could do to stop Fisichella and Michael catching up. Straight after his stop, Alonso had a 15s advantage over Michael, having lost 3s on his out lap alone. Then it came tumbling down with every lap.

The sight of the three of them circulating together,

with Fisichella in the middle and not quite sure what he should do, was an amazing one.

"It was quite tricky, as Michael was behind me and Fernando was quite slow, so I was a bit worried about that," said the Italian. "On the normal line, the circuit was dry. Just inside it was wet. Once I tried to overtake Fernando, I was on the wet and had the rears lock, so I lost the position again. The lap after that, I overtook him on the straight."

Michael chose his moment well and, having passed him for second, soon began to pull away from Alonso.

A few drivers used their scheduled first stops to change to dries, but it was way premature. The Toyotas were first, with Ralf on lap 24, and Trulli a lap later. Both were soon in serious trouble, slithering around. Kubica and Albers came in on lap 25. The Dutchman returned the next lap for more intermediates, while Kubica had several off-track adventures. Dries were not yet an issue for the top teams because of their fuel strategy, but they had to keep an eye on things.

"You saw people going out on dries mid-race, and you still couldn't use them," said Brawn. "It's peculiar because the compounds we're using now are very sensitive to temperature, and if you don't generate the temperature in them, you struggle."

For Michael, the next problem was dealing with Fisichella. The timing of the second stops was crucial. To make things even more interesting, the window for changing to dries had now opened properly. Ferrari showed that it had learned a crucial lesson at the Hungaroring – that it was worth using Massa as a guinea pig to try the dry tyres.

"We put Felipe out on slicks to see how it looked," Ross confirmed. "He was reporting back on how the tyres were doing and said it was very difficult to warm them up but, after one or two laps, they were good."

Massa changed on lap 34, only five laps after he'd made his scheduled stop following a long opening

INSIDE LINE
FERNANDO ALONSO

RENAULT DRIVER

"Things looked very good in qualifying. The performance of the car, the team and the tyres was fantastic in the conditions. I felt very comfortable and took full advantage to be quickest in Q1, Q2 and Q3.

I made a good start to the race, had a good 15 or 20 laps, but the left front intermediate was almost slick and we decided to change it at the first pit stop. It proved to be the wrong thing to do, because Michael and Giancarlo left their tyres on at their first pit stops and were much quicker and caught me really quickly. I had had a big gap, but it just disappeared.

You need to take the top off the new tyres and lose the groove. After my stop, the nine or 10 laps that I was really slow were the laps that it took to wear the rubber down. It was hard to know how long that was going to take. I thought that with Giancarlo running second it wouldn't be too big a problem and that it would take four or five laps. In fact, it took nine or 10.

In retrospect, the best option was to leave the same tyres on, but when you come in after 21 laps and you have a tyre that is almost a slick and are faced with another 20-lap stint, you change it for safety reasons.

Probably, if we had left the tyre on it would have been OK, but you're not sure. The surprise for us was the time the new tyres took to clean up.

After that, I took a risk and pitted to go onto dry tyres as soon as possible to try to find a miracle cure, but it was too late for me to make up enough ground.

Unfortunately, over the whole weekend, I think the specific race conditions were the only ones in which we weren't quickest. In wet conditions, we were much quicker and I think we were in dry conditions too. We were unfortunate: it was an opportunity lost.

I lost time at my second stop when there was a problem with the right rear wheel, but Fisi and Michael had already overtaken me by then and the race was going to be hard in any case.

What I did feel is that I had a specific problem for nine or 10 laps or whatever, and I felt alone in the team. Fisi and Michael overtook me and were gone. By the time I recovered, they were too far ahead. It's like climbing in the mountains in the Tour de France, you have a puncture, and your team goes uphill without stopping. That was a bit difficult to understand. I fought with Fisi in Turn 14, he overtook me and ran too deep and I passed him again. Risky moments and, with three races left to win the championship, not good enough, I think…"

stint. Alonso got rid of his troublesome intermediates on lap 35, but the team made its second mistake when there was 'finger trouble' over a rear wheel nut, and 12 very expensive seconds went to waste.

The Ferrari mechanics appeared to be getting ready for Michael, before going back into the garage. When Michael finally did stop on lap 40, the crew came out late. The obvious implication was that the team was trying to confuse Renault, although Brawn denied it.

"We were debating whether to anticipate the stop, as we weren't sure whether we would be quicker on new dry tyres for one or two laps, so we left it a lap. The second stop was pretty much when he was due in, but it almost went out of our hands when we made the decision at the first stop on how much fuel to put in. There was a little surprise that we had to go all the way on it, but we did, and everything worked out very well."

Perhaps the most dramatic moment of the race was Michael's opportunistic pass on Fisichella. Nearly everyone had trouble coming out of the still damp pitlane, especially when they made the move to dries. Michael himself had a wobble, and took note.

"We said to Michael, 'with Fisichella your chance is going to be on the lap when he comes out, because the Michelins struggle'," said Brawn. "We were watching Fisichella's lap time, and of course Michael took it easy on the dries when he came out, we asked him not to push too much…"

Having run 41 laps on his intermediates – Alonso's fronts only went to lap 22 – Fisichella had a good in-lap, and arrived at the pit exit in time to get out ahead. His engineer told him he'd made it, and Fisichella was sure that he was now well set. He then slid just off line and saw a flash of red on his right as Michael went for a gap that didn't really exist, with two wheels over the kerb. He would probably have been able to squeeze through in the next couple of corners in any case, but nevertheless, this was one of the great Michael moves.

"The pitlane, especially at the exit, was wet," said Fisichella. "You can't go on the left-hand side because of the white line. As soon as you go into Turn 1, you get the tyres completely cold and you are on the wet side. So I was very cautious but, even with that, I lost the car and Michael was able to get past. Alan [his engineer] told me, 'You are OK, you are in P1.' Michael had been able to do one lap and keep the tyres very warm, and there he was just quicker than me."

Fisichella began to fall back at that point, aware that his job now was to await Alonso's arrival and cede second place, although of course it wasn't made too obvious on the radio traffic with Giancarlo: "They

OPPOSITE TOP Nico Rosberg's Williams looked the business, but it was Mark Webber who scored

OPPOSITE BOTTOM Michael Schumacher holds off Pedro de la Rosa for sixth in the early laps

ABOVE Giancarlo Fisichella and Fernando Alonso ran in close company until Alonso moved ahead to chase after Michael Schumacher

INSIDE LINE
SIMON CORBYN

COSWORTH HEAD OF F1 RACE ENGINEERING

"We found out that Spyker had signed a deal for Ferrari engines on Saturday, and the guys heard the news as they were doing final checks before Q3. Professional as ever, they just got on with the job, but after 40 years in Formula One…

Bernard (Ferguson) had come to

China with two contracts in his briefcase, signed by us, in the hope of going home with counter-signatures.

We'd been talking to the team in its various guises since January or February. We'd already started an exchange of engineering information and the car design was already well underway around our engine, but when Spyker got involved it became clear that the priorities and objectives for the programme were being reconsidered.

Spyker acknowledged that we had a fabulous product with as good a support group as there is in the paddock, but they wanted a road-car relationship. Wider business issues were involved. Midland would have made the decision based on the best F1 engine they could get their hands on, which we are confident is ours.

How do you go and talk to your

workforce? How do you say, actually guys, you've done a stunning job on the lowest budget by some considerable margin. You've got the best engine on the grid, the potential customers acknowledge it, we've put a reasonable price together for 2007, even offered the naming rights, but, sorry, nobody wants it.

That's difficult to take, and don't overlook the fact that a lot of people at Cosworth have enjoyed working there a long time. For anyone who works in an industry for 10–15 years and comes on a fortnightly basis to do a specific job, it's a big shock to have to re-train. We're not closing the door on F1, but Cosworth will now be pushing hard into new markets including non-racing and non-engine-related work.

Cosworth can be extremely proud of what we have achieved this year. We

qualified with 20,000rpm in Bahrain and we'll finish the season potentially doing a complete race distance in Brazil with 20,000rpm.

The interesting thing is that looking at next year, re-tuning to 19,000rpm is quite a reduction of loadings and we'd be confident our engine would be extremely reliable. If it runs all day at 19,500rpm, as it does now, it's going to be fine at 19,000rpm. We've actually only experienced one failure so far in 2006, which was Nico's engine in the Malaysian GP. We would be very competitive in 2007 as we're already very competitive and the scope for changing things is relatively small. We would probably have 750bhp available all race, some 20bhp-plus more than some of the other engines on the grid. You'd have thought someone would be interested in that…"

ABOVE Jenson Button's Honda had a new livery, but went as well as ever and he finished fourth

BELOW Nick Heidfeld was heading for fourth place until a little contretemps on the final lap

BELOW RIGHT Bridgestone provided the tyres, the Ferrari team provided the car and Michael Schumacher provided the bubbly

called me and said go down with the revs, and just go to the end of the race, which is the important thing."

So Alonso closed in on Michael as his dry tyres began working well, while Michael was going just as fast as he needed to.

Rain in the final few laps added to the fun. In general, the Michelins seemed to suffer a little more and Alonso couldn't afford to make a mistake, so his charge wasn't as spectacular as it might have been. Michael had the race under control, but a couple of more laps would have been very interesting.

What happened behind the top three was almost irrelevant until the last couple of laps when there was a fantastic scrap for fourth place involving Heidfeld, Barrichello, Button and de la Rosa. The BMW driver was wrongfooted by backmarkers Albers and Sato (both of whom were later penalised), and then hit under braking by Barrichello with two corners to run. Button took advantage of the chaos to claim fourth ahead of de la Rosa, Barrichello (without a front wing) and a furious Heidfeld, who crossed the finish line with his right rear at a drunken angle. The final point, and the first for Williams in an age, went to Webber, despite a couple of spins.

It was a truly remarkable afternoon, and the momentum seemed now to be with Michael.

SNAPSHOT FROM
CHINA

CLOCKWISE FROM RIGHT New ownership by Spyker led to a more orange livery for the newly retitled Spyker MF1 team; well, the girls have spotted something amusing...; ...but Ferrari's Jean Todt and Ross Brawn aren't quite so sure; with the title race in the balance, work always goes on into the night at Shanghai; the Chinese fans, passionate as ever, show their respect for Michael Schumacher; these two are lost in translation...

WEEKEND HEADLINES

■ To nobody's great surprise, Spyker MF1 confirmed that Christijan Albers would stay on for 2007. Less predictable was the winner of a shoot-out for the team's engine deal, as Ferrari got a last-minute nod over Cosworth. The news meant that the British company would be frozen out of F1 for the first time since 1967.

■ The Grand Prix Drivers' Association held an election on the Friday at Shanghai to find three new directors to replace the retiring Michael Schumacher and other incumbents David Coulthard and Jarno Trulli. Longtime renegade Fernando Alonso was persuaded to return to the fold and take the job, while the other successful candidates were Mark Webber and Ralf Schumacher.

■ Hockenheim and the Nürburgring successfully reached an agreement to share the German Grand Prix in forthcoming years, with the latter to hold the race in 2007 and then again in subsequent odd-numbered years. Both venues had struggled in recent years to make their races financially viable. Meanwhile, the European Grand Prix title would presumably be kept in reserve in case needed.

■ Plans for a Korean Grand Prix were confirmed formally, with a race to be held in the south of the country from 2010 onwards. Inevitably, the deal to design the new venue went to Hermann Tilke, the man responsible for the circuits in Malaysia, Bahrain, Turkey and China. Bernie Ecclestone had tried to take Formula One to the country as long ago as 1998, but that deal subsequently collapsed.

■ After the unfortunate end to his race, when fourth place was wrested from him, Nick Heidfeld launched a verbal assault on Sakon Yamamoto in the scrutineering bay, not realising that the Super Aguri he had got caught up with in the closing laps was driven by Takuma Sato... A bewildered Yamamoto took the punishment without complaint. A sheepish Heidfeld eventually made his apologies at Suzuka...

RACE RESULTS
CHINA SHANGHAI

Official Results © [2006]
Formula One Administration Limited,
6 Princes Gate, London SW7 1QJ.
No reproduction without permission.
All copyright and database rights reserved

RACE DATE 1 October
CIRCUIT LENGTH 3.390 miles
NO. OF LAPS 56
RACE DISTANCE 189.680 miles
WEATHER Overcast and wet, 22°C
TRACK TEMP 23°C
RACE DAY ATTENDANCE 140,000
LAP RECORD Michael Schumacher, 1m32.238s, 132.202mph, 2004

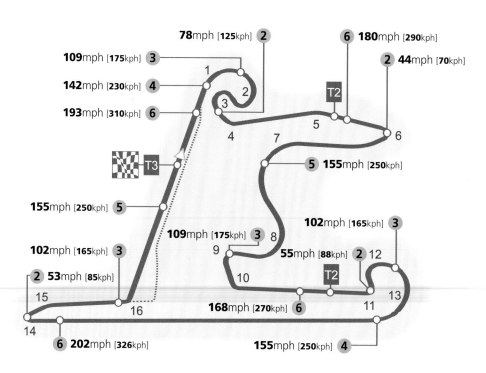

	PRACTICE 1 Driver	Time	Laps
1	A Wurz	1m35.574s	21
2	A Davidson	1m35.591s	26
3	J Button	1m37.291s	4
4	M Schumacher	1m37.712s	4
5	N Jani	1m37.734s	21
6	A Prémat	1m37.787s	24
7	S Vettel	1m37.913s	24
8	R Kubica	1m38.062s	6
9	M Ammermüller	1m38.460s	18
10	F Montagny	1m38.464s	19
11	V Liuzzi	1m39.000s	6
12	R Barrichello	1m39.217s	4
13	S Speed	1m39.428s	7
14	C Albers	1m39.494s	6
15	T Sato	1m39.887s	8
16	T Monteiro	1m39.947s	7
17	S Yamamoto	1m41.415s	10
18	K Räikkönen	1m45.890s	4
19	R Doornbos	no time	2
20	R Schumacher	no time	2
21	J Trulli	no time	2
22	D Coulthard	no time	1
23	N Heidfeld	no time	1
24	F Alonso	no time	0
25	P de la Rosa	no time	0
26	G Fisichella	no time	0
27	F Massa	no time	0
28	N Rosberg	no time	0
29	M Webber	no time	0

	PRACTICE 2 Driver	Time	Laps
1	A Wurz	1m35.539s	26
2	S Vettel	1m35.579s	23
3	A Davidson	1m35.714s	30
4	F Massa	1m36.599s	8
5	M Schumacher	1m36.641s	12
6	F Alonso	1m36.739s	10
7	F Montagny	1m37.278s	26
8	M Ammermüller	1m37.678s	26
9	T Monteiro	1m37.698s	13
10	G Fisichella	1m37.718s	12
11	J Button	1m37.861s	10
12	P de la Rosa	1m38.022s	9
13	M Webber	1m38.045s	6
14	N Heidfeld	1m38.062s	11
15	A Prémat	1m38.098s	26
16	R Barrichello	1m38.276s	16
17	R Schumacher	1m38.888s	14
18	J Trulli	1m38.959s	11
19	S Speed	1m39.080s	18
20	N Jani	1m39.118s	28
21	K Räikkönen	1m39.179s	4
22	R Kubica	1m39.217s	5
23	N Rosberg	1m39.522s	15
24	V Liuzzi	1m39.570s	20
25	S Yamamoto	1m39.636s	22
26	D Coulthard	1m40.155s	15
27	R Doornbos	1m40.214s	15
28	C Albers	1m40.319s	14
29	T Sato	1m41.315s	15

	PRACTICE 3 Driver	Time	Laps
1	M Schumacher	1m40.193s	8
2	F Alonso	1m40.365s	7
3	J Button	1m40.590s	12
4	V Liuzzi	1m40.795s	9
5	S Speed	1m41.150s	11
6	M Webber	1m41.287s	10
7	C Albers	1m41.463s	11
8	G Fisichella	1m41.691s	6
9	P de la Rosa	1m41.823s	7
10	D Coulthard	1m41.836s	18
11	N Rosberg	1m42.588s	11
12	T Monteiro	1m42.612s	14
13	N Heidfeld	1m43.216s	5
14	R Barrichello	1m43.448s	9
15	F Massa	1m43.500s	10
16	T Sato	1m43.722s	12
17	J Trulli	1m44.027s	14
18	R Doornbos	1m45.434s	12
19	R Schumacher	1m46.023s	12
20	S Yamamoto	1m46.850s	10
21	K Räikkönen	no time	2
22	R Kubica	no time	1

	QUALIFYING 1 Driver	Time
1	F Alonso	1m44.128s
2	G Fisichella	1m44.378s
3	P de la Rosa	1m44.808s
4	K Räikkönen	1m44.909s
5	V Liuzzi	1m45.564s
6	J Button	1m45.809s
7	D Coulthard	1m45.931s
8	R Kubica	1m46.049s
9	S Speed	1m46.222s
10	N Heidfeld	1m46.249s
11	R Doornbos	1m46.387s
12	R Barrichello	1m47.072s
13	F Massa	1m47.231s
14	M Schumacher	1m47.366s
15	N Rosberg	1m47.535s
16	M Webber	1m48.560s
17	R Schumacher	1m48.894s
18	J Trulli	1m49.098s
19	C Albers	1m49.542s
20	T Monteiro	1m49.903s
21	T Sato	1m50.326s
22	S Yamamoto	1m55.560s

	QUALIFYING 2 Driver	Time
1	F Alonso	1m43.951s
2	G Fisichella	1m44.336s
3	J Button	1m44.662s
4	N Heidfeld	1m45.055s
5	P de la Rosa	1m45.095s
6	R Barrichello	1m45.288s
7	R Kubica	1m45.576s
8	K Räikkönen	1m45.622s
9	M Schumacher	1m45.660s
10	R Doornbos	1m45.747s
11	S Speed	1m45.851s
12	D Coulthard	1m45.968s
13	F Massa	1m45.970s
14	V Liuzzi	1m46.172s
15	M Webber	1m46.413s
16	N Rosberg	1m47.419s

Best sectors – Practice		Speed trap – Practice		Best sectors – Qualifying	
Sec 1 A Davidson	25.219s	1 G Fisichella	195.5mph	Sec 1 F Alonso	27.312s
Sec 2 A Wurz	27.910s	2 F Alonso	194.2mph	Sec 2 G Fisichella	31.212s
Sec 3 S Vettel	41.975s	3 F Massa	193.9mph	Sec 3 G Fisichella	44.935s

Fernando Alonso
"I built up a good lead, then we changed the fronts, but it was wrong, as Fisi and Michael kept all four and were quicker. Our only hope was go to dry tyres."

Michael Schumacher
"I thought that if I could pass Fisi I'd only lose two points to Alonso. The crucial moment came with the switch to dry tyres. In the final laps, I drove extremely carefully."

Kimi Räikkönen
"I gained a couple of places and it looked as if we could win, but suddenly the throttle didn't react correctly and the engine went into safety mode and selected neutral."

Jenson Button
"Into the last corner, I was in front of Rubens and de La Rosa. I came down the inside of Heidfeld and turned in. When I looked into my mirrors, those behind me were crashing."

Robert Kubica
"At Turn 1 I was hit, by Doornbos. Then I put on grooved tyres too soon. It was impossible to drive, and I went off twice on one lap, then changed back to intermediates."

Jarno Trulli
"The pit stops came before the ideal time to switch to dries, but it didn't pay off. It was hard to stay on the road. Then I had a problem with the pneumatic pressure."

Giancarlo Fisichella
"I started with a heavy fuel load, so it was tough, but the conditions came to me as it dried. I was able to pull away from Michael, but when I came out on dries, I slid wide."

Felipe Massa
"I was very quick on the wet track and when it was drying. Maybe it was a risk fitting dries early. It's a shame what happened with DC, as I damaged my suspension."

Pedro de la Rosa
"I made a wrong call when I asked for a set of intermediates. I should have stayed on the tyes I had. On the final lap, I was lucky to stay out of trouble and gained two places."

Rubens Barrichello
"On the last lap, Heidfeld made an avoiding manoeuvre in Turn 2, but I was there and he hit my front wing. There was more confusion at the hairpin and I clashed with Heidfeld."

Nick Heidfeld
"I was certain I would be fourth, but Albers stayed on the dry line, then Sato blocked me for a lap. Because of this, the Hondas caught up and Barrichello crashed into me."

Ralf Schumacher
"I spent much of the early laps in traffic. So the team took the risk to change to dries before the track was really ready. Later, we then had an oil pressure spike."

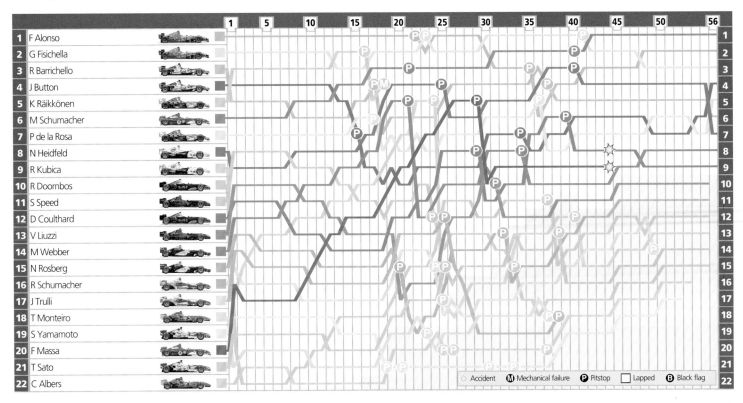

											1	5	10	15	20	25	30	35	40	45	50	56

1	F Alonso
2	G Fisichella
3	R Barrichello
4	J Button
5	K Räikkönen
6	M Schumacher
7	P de la Rosa
8	N Heidfeld
9	R Kubica
10	R Doornbos
11	S Speed
12	D Coulthard
13	V Liuzzi
14	M Webber
15	N Rosberg
16	R Schumacher
17	J Trulli
18	T Monteiro
19	S Yamamoto
20	F Massa
21	T Sato
22	C Albers

☼ Accident Ⓜ Mechanical failure Ⓟ Pitstop ☐ Lapped Ⓑ Black flag

QUALIFYING 3

	Driver	Time
1	F Alonso	1m44.360s
2	G Fisichella	1m44.992s
3	R Barrichello	1m45.503s
4	J Button	1m45.503s
5	K Räikkönen	1m45.754s
6	M Schumacher	1m45.775s
7	P de la Rosa	1m45.877s
8	N Heidfeld	1m46.053s
9	R Kubica	1m46.632s
10	R Doornbos	1m48.021s

GRID

	Driver	Time
1	F Alonso	1m44.360s
2	G Fisichella	1m44.992s
3	R Barrichello	1m45.503s
4	J Button	1m45.503s
5	K Räikkönen	1m45.754s
6	M Schumacher	1m45.775s
7	P de la Rosa	1m45.877s
8	N Heidfeld	1m46.053s
9	R Kubica	1m46.632s
10	R Doornbos	1m48.021s
11	S Speed	1m45.851s
12	D Coulthard	1m45.968s
13	V Liuzzi	1m46.172s
14	M Webber	1m46.413s
15	N Rosberg	1m47.419s
16	R Schumacher	1m48.894s
17	J Trulli	1m49.098s
18	T Monteiro	1m49.903s
19	S Yamamoto	1m55.560s
20*	F Massa	1m45.970s
21*	T Sato	1m50.326s
22*	C Albers	1m49.542s

* 10-PLACE GRID PENALTY

RACE

	Driver	Car	Laps	Time	Avg.mph	Fastest	Stops
1	M Schumacher	Ferrari 248	56	1h37m32.747s	116.603	1m38.553s	2
2	F Alonso	Renault R26	56	1h37m35.868s	116.540	1m37.586s	2
3	G Fisichella	Renault R26	56	1h38m16.944s	115.728	1m39.149s	2
4	J Button	Honda RA106	56	1h38m44.803s	115.185	1m39.206s	2
5	P de la Rosa	McLaren-Mercedes MP4-21	56	1h38m49.884s	115.086	1m39.149s	2
6	R Barrichello	Honda RA106	56	1h38m51.878s	115.047	1m39.749s	2
7	N Heidfeld	BMW Sauber F1.06	56	1h39m04.726s	114.799	1m39.164s	2
8	M Webber	Williams-Cosworth FW28	56	1h39m16.335s	114.574	1m39.907s	2
9	D Coulthard	Red Bull-Ferrari RB2	56	1h39m16.543s	114.571	1m40.549s	2
10	V Liuzzi	Toro Rosso-Cosworth STR01	55	1h38m12.368s	113.749	1m41.710s	1
11	N Rosberg	Williams-Cosworth FW28	55	1h38m13.489s	113.727	1m40.471s	2
12	R Doornbos	Red Bull-Ferrari RB2	55	1h38m24.465s	113.516	1m39.801s	3
13	R Kubica	BMW Sauber F1.06	55	1h38m38.210s	113.252	1m40.193s	3
14	T Sato	Super Aguri-Honda SA06	55	1h38m45.333s	113.116	1m40.856s	2
15	S Speed	Toro Rosso-Cosworth STR01	55	1h39m13.358s	112.583	1m39.681s	2
16	C Albers	Spyker MF1-Toyota M16	53	1h38m50.058s	108.913	1m41.483s	3
17	S Yamamoto	Super Aguri-Honda SA06	52	1h37m38.996s	108.153	1m41.847s	4
R	R Schumacher	Toyota TF106B	49	Engine	-	1m39.823s	1
R	F Massa	Ferrari 248	44	Crash damage	-	1m39.397s	2
R	J Trulli	Toyota TF106B	38	Engine	-	1m44.787s	1
R	T Monteiro	Spyker MF1-Toyota M16	37	Spun off	-	1m45.356s	2
R	K Räikkönen	McLaren-Mercedes MP4-21	18	Throttle	-	1m44.094s	1

CHAMPIONSHIP

	Driver	Pts
1	M Schumacher	116
2	F Alonso	116
3	G Fisichella	63
4	F Massa	62
5	K Räikkönen	57
6	J Button	45
7	R Barrichello	28
8	JP Montoya	26
9	N Heidfeld	22
10	P de la Rosa	18
11	R Schumacher	18
12	D Coulthard	14
13	J Trulli	12
14	M Webber	7
15	J Villeneuve	7
16	R Kubica	6
17	N Rosberg	4
18	C Klien	2
19	V Liuzzi	1

Speed trap – Qualifying
1	G Fisichella	193.8mph
2	F Alonso	193.7mph
3	P de la Rosa	192.4mph

Fastest Lap
F Alonso 1m37.586s
(124.957mph) on lap 49

Fastest speed trap
F Massa 201.6mph
Slowest speed trap
M Webber 189.8mph

Fastest pit stop
1	G Fisichella	23.403s
2	R Kubica	23.625s
3	R Doornbos	23.975s

David Coulthard
"As the track dried, it came good. Unluckily, I had an incident with Massa, leaving my car pulling left. I had difficulty braking at the hairpin, allowing Mark to pass."

Mark Webber
"After passing David, I thought about when to change to dry tyres, but we decided to leave the same tyres on. However, I spun. I then pushed to keep David behind me."

Vitantonio Liuzzi
"The fact the track dried did not suit us. I had problems with my rears as I was on a one-stopper and so had a heavy fuel load. But we called the pit stop just right."

Tiago Monteiro
"It's always frustrating to drop out of a race, but it's the first time in 35 starts that I made an unforced error. After changing to dries, I aquaplaned, spun and stalled."

Takuma Sato
"It was a fantastic result for us and a truly exciting race in difficult conditions. I communicated with my engineer and I think that we chose the right tyre at the right time."

Robert Doornbos
"I touched Kubica's car into Turn 1 and lost time when I had to pit to change the front wing. I then passed 11 people, a good performance on used intermediate tyres."

Nico Rosberg
"What messed up my race was not being able to pass Coulthard. I didn't want to risk too much. It improved when we switched to dries, but later it became difficult."

Scott Speed
"I passed a few cars, then picked up some understeer, but it was looking good as I was on a two-stopper, but when I took on intermediates the car felt horrible."

Christijan Albers
"During the weekend, there were some great developments for the team off the track and I just wish I could have achieved something to compliment these."

Sakon Yamamoto
"It was a really tough race as the conditions were ever changing. We changed to dries too early and the car was difficult, but this was my first F1 finish and it feels brilliant."

	Constructor	Pts
1	Renault	179
2	Ferrari	178
3	McLaren-Mercedes	101
4	Honda	73
5	BMW Sauber	35
6	Toyota	30
7	Red Bull-Ferrari	16
8	Williams-Cosworth	11
9	Toro Rosso-Cosworth	1

2006 FORMULA 1™ FUJI TELEVISION JAPANESE GRAND PRIX
Suzuka

OVER AND OUT?

Michael Schumacher was set for victory, but then his Ferrari's engine blew and Fernando Alonso accepted all 10 points with open arms to all but be crowned champion again

There had been many twists and turns in the World Championship since Michael Schumacher's resurgence began at the United States Grand Prix at Indianapolis at the start of July, but no single moment was quite as dramatic as that which befell the German at Suzuka, and flipped the odds in favour of Renault.

Everything was going to plan when on lap 37 Schumacher's Ferrari came to a halt with smoke billowing from the its rear and Fernando Alonso swept by into the lead. It was a devastating blow to the German's title hopes. Alonso may have had his own engine failure at Monza, but thanks to his grid penalty, at the time he was heading only for third place, thus losing a potential six points rather than 10. Furthermore, after that setback, he had three races left in which he could recover.

On this occasion, Michael was leading the race, and so his retirement created a 10-point deficit to his rival who had been running second. To make matters more intense, this left him with just one race in which to sort things out. Michael now not only had to win the Brazilian Grand Prix, but also had to rely on Alonso failing to score any points. Although that very outcome had recently occurred at Monza, nobody in

"With the season at a critical stage, we tested at Silverstone and Mugello prior to the Chinese Grand Prix, and that's when we made the selection for Japan as well.

We were very pleased with qualifying when we took the top four grid positions. The performances we saw on Saturday were down to the drivers and the fact that maybe we were a little bit on the softer side than our rivals. I think they took harder compounds and that gave us the lap-time gap.

When choosing the Suzuka specification, we took account of the roughness of the track and all the other factors you include in the analysis to point the way to the most suitable compound. The tyres we took were perhaps a little bit marginal but actually worked quite well.

From talking to the teams and drivers after the race, the initial grip was very good. However, as the laps went by, it faded. As we saw, though, Michael [Schumacher] was able to keep the lead and I believe that with 16 laps to go he had a big enough margin to win the race. Michael could feel some grip drop-off, but he just adjusted his way of driving to try to maintain his gap. I firmly believe that he would have won. Even if Fernando [Alonso] had caught him, it is very hard to overtake at Suzuka.

To be honest, after we saw the performance in qualifying, I also expected consistent race performance, but I'd say there was perhaps a bit of underestimation in our consistency predictions.

At the beginning of his second stint, it appeared that Jarno Trulli was quite slow and that he was suffering a little bit of graining, but when the tyre cleaned up, his lap times were back to normal pace.

Toyota had some graining problems, but Ferrari didn't have much problem with that. Their main problem was degradation. With Mark Webber, the rear tyres were degrading, and the car tended to oversteer towards the end of the stint. When they put new tyres on, they picked up a lot of understeer and it seems that contributed to him crashing out of the race.

When I saw the white smoke from a Ferrari, sorry to say, but I was hoping it was Felipe! Then I saw the red helmet colour and thought, 'Oh my God!' We were really disappointed because we'd done a very good job over the previous few races and Ferrari had caught up with Renault. The retirement was just so disappointing, but that's racing. You have to recognise that the same thing happened to Fernando in Monza. All we can do now is provide our best spec' in Brazil and hope for a miracle…"

the Maranello camp was putting too much faith in it happening again.

Rain on Friday meant that the real story of how Bridgestone and Michelin stacked up at Suzuka wasn't apparent until the end of the Saturday morning session, when the presence of the Ferraris and Ralf Schumacher's Toyota at the top of the timesheets told the story. Clearly, the Bridgestone tyre was good over one lap, and both teams took full advantage.

As at the Turkish Grand Prix, Michael was ultimately outqualified by his team-mate Felipe Massa. In reality, the Brazilian's fuel load was some two laps or 6kg lighter. In addition, Michael had to leave himself some margin in qualifying, however small it might be, because he couldn't afford a mistake – like the one he made in Turkey. Ralf and Jarno Trulli would line up behind the Ferraris, again emphasising Bridgestone's strength. Alonso, his Renault shod of course with Michelins, had to make do with fifth.

The early part of the race went to plan, and Ferrari showed that it learns lessons well. In Turkey, the team allowed Massa to scoot off in the lead and assumed that Michael would ease in front at the first round of pit stops. Then a safety car came out, and by being trapped behind his team-mate in the pits Michael lost

both the potential win and second place – creating an expensive six-point swing to Alonso. This time, nothing was left to chance, and Massa let Michael by at the first opportunity. Then, as Michael edged away in front, it looked as though all was going well.

Alonso, meanwhile, had made a good start and swept inside Trulli to claim fourth, but had got stuck behind Ralf, and didn't appear to be a threat.

The first hint of trouble for Ferrari was a slow puncture in Massa's right rear, caused by a cut. By lap 13, the telemetry showed that the pressure drop had reached a crisis point and there was a serious chance of a failure. So, having left it as long as possible, the team brought Massa in three laps ahead of schedule. There was no time to worry about where he would come out in traffic, and he emerged behind Nick Heidfeld – just one more lap would have made the difference, but the team couldn't take the risk.

The heavier Massa was stuck behind the BMW for five laps before Heidfeld pitted, and that cost him a great deal of time. Having earlier passed Ralf for third in another bold move at Turn 1, Alonso duly jumped Massa for second at the first stops, and that was not a situation that the men in red had planned on.

"We were competitive, as good as Ferrari's pace

OPPOSITE TOP Ferrari pole-sitter Felipe Massa leads the way from Michael Schumacher, Ralf Schumacher and Fernando Alonso in the opening laps

OPPOSITE BOTTOM Rubens Barrichello's Honda appears to be receiving synchronised attention

ABOVE Kimi Räikkönen drove an impeccable race, working his way forward from 11th to fifth place

INSIDE LINE
CHRISTIJAN ALBERS

SPYKER MF1 DRIVER

"My problems started at the beginning of the race when the exhaust broke. That's why we also lost some power. The lambda sensor was giving a different figure because we were losing exhaust air where the sensor was. That meant that I was losing performance on the straight, which is why Robert Doornbos overtook me.

I then got some information on the radio to go to another mix to get rid of the problem, and we went quicker again and I caught the Red Bulls. I was getting closer to Doornbos, Coulthard and Speed, and driving away from Liuzzi before the pit stop. But, the biggest problem was that because the exhaust was broken, everything became really hot, which caused the right-rear failure. The wishbones, driveshaft, everything was overheating, and when I arrived into the chicane braking area at 200mph with maximum downforce and load, it just blew apart.

It was a shame because we were quite competitive and we were going to pass Coulthard at the pit stop.

Looking back, I think if we'd had the car as it is now at the beginning of the season we would have been quite strong. The team pushed hard and closed the gap. But, if you look at the top speeds, you can see that we were missing power. There was too big a gap between the top teams and us.

I think the Spyker and Ferrari deals have really motivated everyone. It's great. For a long time, everyone was just waiting for a new buyer. I knew that there was a lot of talking going on and I was always confident something would happen, but I didn't know when.

Myself and the team were pushing for Mike Gascoyne, and hopefully he will feel at home with the ex-Jordan guys in the team. I'm looking forward to meeting him, going through all the information from this year and hopefully helping to put something together to be competitive from the beginning of next season.

There were some paddock rumours that we let Cosworth down, which I'm not happy with because there was always only an option. The money mentioned was almost the same as Ferrari and Ferrari was logical for us. We are a little team fighting to be a big team and fighting for the budget. The budget is coming, but we still don't have the money to help Cosworth develop the engine, so we had to find an engine with its own development budget, which is why we chose Ferrari. There's also the name, which makes it easier for the whole package, and nobody can deny it's a strong engine."

maybe and better than Toyota," said Alonso. "Anyway, I took the risk overtaking Jarno, because I thought that was the only opportunity, and then when I saw Ralf with some traction problems I tried to pass him as well. It worked fine, and at that point I was quite happy with third place."

Michael now had nobody riding shotgun, and so he had to use more of his allowance of high-rev laps than he might otherwise have done, although he was still within the permitted limits.

"The race was tougher than I think a lot of people thought," admitted Ferrari Technical Director Ross Brawn. "However, we know from past experience that even when it looks very strong in qualifying it can move back in the race, and that really was the case. We didn't have a completely comfortable race, but Michael was controlling the gap quite well, and when he needed to push he was able to push.

"However, we didn't have the comfort of Felipe there because he had that puncture, and we had to call him in because we saw the tyre pressure dropping. His whole race was compromised from then, because he went back out in traffic and got stuck. So that was really a bit unfortunate."

For obvious reasons, drivers tend to use up their higher-rev laps before and after pit stops. Michael pitted for a second time on lap 36, and barely half a lap later smoke began billowing from the back of the car. Was it a coincidence that he had been gunning the engine at that time?

The sight of Michael walking back to the pits was an unusual one. It happened an awful lot in his first year with Ferrari in 1996, but since he began collecting titles, mechanical reliability has been near bullet-proof as far as his car had been concerned, and that finishing record has made a massive contribution to his assault on the record books. His luck finally gave out at the worst possible moment.

"Everything was going fine with Michael until we had a mechanical failure, but those things happen," said Brawn. "You try and keep them as infrequent as possible, but they happen occasionally.

"We've had a lot of engines with those components and those designs, and they've gone race distances with no trouble at all, including some in Red Bull cars, some in Ferraris, but it's hard to correlate at this stage. You always try and keep the use of your engine down as best as you can, so it is something we'll have to understand.

"Michael was able to increase his pace if he needed to, so as we started approaching the rounds of pit stops we asked him to keep the gap in case anything went wrong in the stop or we had some other glitch, and he was certainly able to respond."

The initial fear was that the failure was related to the failure Massa had in practice in China, and thus it could have been foreseen. In fact, analysis back in Maranello was to prove that the problem was new.

Renault's Executive Director of Engineering Pat Symonds admitted readily that Alonso would not have beaten Michael: "On our projections, we were going to catch Michael, but I absolutely don't think we would have gone past him. The line was showing that we were going to catch him, and the trend was very, very steady. But the slope wasn't steep enough to make me think we'd get past."

The rest of the race was easy for Alonso, and he did just enough to bring the car safely home ahead of Massa. With Fisichella finishing in third place, Renault established a nine-point advantage in the constructors' table to make Ferrari's day even worse.

"Victory means a lot," said the Spaniard. "Not only for me, but for the team as well, getting their confidence back. We deserved this victory a long time ago, I think. Before the Hungarian GP we were ready to win and we never finished the job. It's a complete

OPPOSITE Toyota's Jarno Trulli struggled for grip, but kept team-mate Ralf Schumacher behind him as he raced to sixth place

BELOW Christijan Albers and Spyker MF1 continued to make good progress, but a broken exhaust put an end to that...

Michael Schumacher's Ferrari sits abandoned at the side of the track as Fernando Alonso's Renault flashes by to victory

Alonso felt avenged for his Monza failure and was more than happy to take all 10 points

surprise, so the taste of the victory is even better because in China we were the complete favourites, and everything seemed easy for us, yet we lost the race.

"It was the same thing here for Ferrari. You never know. You have to finish the races, and looking at the championship these 10 points are very important but, as we all thought, the championship will be decided in Brazil. You never know what is going to happen there. The same thing can happen [to us], so we need to be safe and not take too many risks there. I think we have an advantage, so let's try to win the championship."

For the second successive race, Jenson Button put in a solid performance to gain fourth place, and crucially Honda beat Toyota to local honours. Team-mate Rubens Barrichello damaged his front wing on the first lap, and never recovered after an extra early pit stop, finishing in 12th place.

"Off the line, we were really good," said Button. "It was the best start I've made all year. I actually overtook a Renault off the line, which was a bit surprising. The race was good and the tyres came good after about 15 laps, then we were able to get past both of the Toyotas, which was nice for the team. We were the best of the rest really, with the Ferraris and Renaults that step ahead. The Bridgestones didn't have the advantage in the race that they had in qualifying."

McLaren admitted that the choice of Michelin's softer tyre was the wrong one, and it handicapped the team both in qualifying and the race. Nevertheless, Kimi Räikkönen plugged away and from a disastrous 11th on the grid managed to salvage fifth.

In so doing, he beat the Toyotas that had looked so good in qualifying. Their biggest problem was a tyre issue suffered by Trulli that led to the Italian falling off the pace. He refused to let his frustrated team-mate past, costing him a couple of places, and the pair finished sixth and seventh. The final point went to Heidfeld, another to suffer with the softer Michelin.

Of the rest, Mark Webber had a big shunt coming onto the pit straight, while the luckiest man of the day was Christijan Albers whose Spyker had a spectacular failure at the chicane (see sidebar), but he managed to drive his three-wheeled car back to the pits.

After the race, realist Michael insisted that his title hopes were gone, but he still hoped to help Ferrari regain the constructors' title.

"I think all I would say is we've got the statistical advantage," said Symonds. "Forget the psychology and all that sort of stuff. It's a statistical advantage, and it's nothing more than that. What that says is that life is looking up for us…"

SNAPSHOT FROM
JAPAN

CLOCKWISE FROM RIGHT Suzuka looks even more spectacular at night than it does by day; don't ask...; the Renault team turned heads in the pits as well as on the track; 'Fernando' and 'Michael' seem happy enough sparring in the pits, but it was on the track that matters became really serious; now, where did I park my bicycle?; for the Honda and Honda-powered Super Aguri teams, there was simply no time to enjoy the funfair

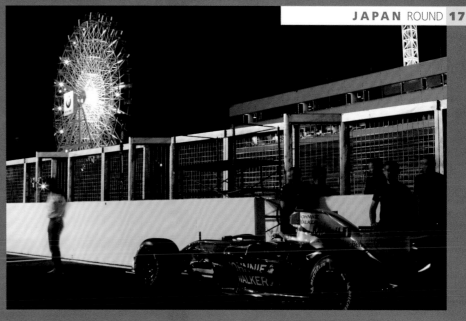

WEEKEND HEADLINES

■ McLaren team manager Dave Ryan was the driving force behind a push to get a 2007 test agreement among the teams signed off in Suzuka, and the job was completed on Sunday. The deal restricts teams to 300 sets of tyres and 30,000km of testing, and ensures that they participate in group tests at nominated circuits, and with just one car apiece.

■ After the race, the FIA sealed the first batch of engines for homologation for 2007 and beyond. Among those to hand over a V8 at the end of its second race were Ferrari (Massa) and Mercedes (de la Rosa), while their respective schedules meant that Honda and BMW could wait until Brazil before submitting engines that began their lives in Japan.

■ Michael Schumacher had been expected to take time off between the Japanese and Brazilian races, but the ongoing quest for the championship titles meant that he insisted on going to Jerez after Suzuka for what was in effect his final test outing for Ferrari. Sorting out the Bridgestone tyre choice for Brazil was a priority for Formula One's most garlanded driver.

■ A row over the use of shared car designs began to brew after it became apparent that Adrian Newey's 2007 design could accommodate either the Ferrari or Renault V8 engines, and that examples would be split between Red Bull Racing and Scuderia Toro Rosso depending on which team ended up using which engine. Rivals who put up with STR using a year-old RBR design in '06 thought the latest scheme a little bit over the top.

■ The final F1 race at Suzuka (for the time being) was marked by a demonstration run on Sunday morning that celebrated the race's 20-year history. Gerhard Berger (McLaren), Ivan Capelli (Leyton House) and Aguri Suzuki (Larrousse) all donned their original overalls for a demo run. Alas Suzuki failed to finish the lap after the car failed on him...

RACE RESULTS

JAPAN
SUZUKA

Official Results © [2006]
Formula One Administration Limited,
6 Princes Gate, London SW7 1QJ.
No reproduction without permission.
All copyright and database rights reserved

RACE DATE 8th October
CIRCUIT LENGTH 3.608 miles
NO. OF LAPS 53
RACE DISTANCE 191.126 miles
WEATHER Warm and bright, 23°C
TRACK TEMP 25°C
RACE DAY ATTENDANCE 160,000
LAP RECORD Kimi Räikkönen,
1m31.540s, 141.892mph, 2005

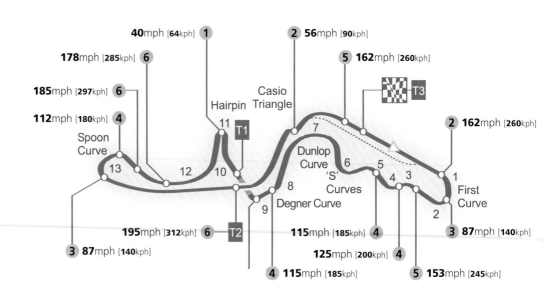

	40mph [64kph]	①
	56mph [90kph]	②
	178mph [285kph]	⑥
	162mph [260kph]	⑤

Hairpin — Casio Triangle
185mph [297kph] ⑥
112mph [180kph] ④
Spoon Curve
Dunlop Curve
162mph [260kph] ②
'S' Curves
First Curve
195mph [312kph] ⑥ — T2
115mph [185kph] ④
87mph [140kph] ③
Degner Curve
125mph [200kph] ④
87mph [140kph] ③
115mph [185kph] ④
153mph [245kph] ⑤

PRACTICE 1

	Driver	Time	Laps
1	A Davidson	1m45.349s	18
2	N Jani	1m46.138s	21
3	S Vettel	1m46.585s	20
4	M Ammermuller	1m47.162s	21
5	A Sutil	1m47.773s	21
6	S Speed	1m47.814s	7
7	C Albers	1m47.838s	6
8	F Montagny	1m47.918s	13
9	A Wurz	1m47.919s	19
10	T Sato	1m48.042s	11
11	S Yamamoto	1m50.479s	9
12	T Monteiro	no time	4
13	V Liuzzi	no time	2
14	F Alonso	no time	1
15	R Barrichello	no time	1
16	J Button	no time	1
17	D Coulthard	no time	1
18	P de la Rosa	no time	1
19	G Fisichella	no time	1
20	N Heidfeld	no time	1
21	R Kubica	no time	1
22	T Monteiro	no time	1
23	K Räikkönen	no time	1
24	N Rosberg	no time	1
25	R Schumacher	no time	1
26	J Trulli	no time	1
27	M Webber	no time	1
28	F Massa	no time	0
29	M Schumacher	no time	0

PRACTICE 2

	Driver	Time	Laps
1	G Fisichella	1m34.337s	8
2	F Massa	1m34.408s	10
3	M Schumacher	1m34.565s	10
4	F Alonso	1m34.863s	5
5	A Davidson	1m34.906s	23
6	S Vettel	1m34.912s	30
7	J Button	1m35.002s	6
8	P de la Rosa	1m35.064s	6
9	J Trulli	1m35.343s	12
10	K Räikkönen	1m35.367s	5
11	R Schumacher	1m35.375s	12
12	M Ammermüller	1m35.433s	25
13	R Barrichello	1m35.528s	10
14	M Webber	1m35.866s	5
15	N Rosberg	1m36.176s	10
16	C Albers	1m36.180s	4
17	A Wurz	1m36.234s	25
18	R Kubica	1m36.299s	5
19	F Montagny	1m37.354s	20
20	V Liuzzi	1m37.441s	15
21	S Speed	1m37.501s	16
22	D Coulthard	1m37.596s	6
23	T Monteiro	1m37.702s	9
24	N Jani	1m37.741s	26
25	R Doornbos	1m37.788s	9
26	T Sato	1m38.533s	18
27	N Heidfeld	1m38.779s	5
28	S Yamamoto	1m38.955s	14
29	A Sutil	1m43.914s	14

PRACTICE 3

	Driver	Time	Laps
1	M Schumacher	1m30.653s	13
2	R Schumacher	1m31.863s	15
3	J Button	1m32.310s	12
4	G Fisichella	1m32.527s	13
5	F Alonso	1m32.555s	14
6	N Heidfeld	1m32.590s	15
7	N Rosberg	1m32.730s	18
8	K Räikkönen	1m32.730s	12
9	R Kubica	1m32.787s	17
10	F Massa	1m32.790s	15
11	V Liuzzi	1m32.977s	20
12	P de la Rosa	1m33.163s	12
13	S Speed	1m33.213s	20
14	C Albers	1m33.270s	23
15	M Webber	1m33.339s	17
16	D Coulthard	1m33.451s	16
17	R Doornbos	1m33.663s	12
18	R Barrichello	1m33.748s	16
19	T Monteiro	1m33.824s	19
20	J Trulli	1m34.118s	15
21	S Yamamoto	1m34.646s	10
22	T Sato	1m34.727s	20

QUALIFYING 1

	Driver	Time
1	F Massa	1m30.112s
2	J Trulli	1m30.420s
3	N Rosberg	1m30.585s
4	R Schumacher	1m30.595s
5	J Button	1m30.847s
6	F Alonso	1m30.976s
7	R Kubica	1m31.204s
8	M Schumacher	1m31.279s
9	P de la Rosa	1m31.581s
10	M Webber	1m31.647s
11	G Fisichella	1m31.696s
12	V Liuzzi	1m31.741s
13	N Heidfeld	1m31.811s
14	R Barrichello	1m31.972s
15	K Räikkönen	1m32.080s
16	C Albers	1m32.221s
17	D Coulthard	1m32.252s
18	R Doornbos	1m32.402s
19	S Speed	1m32.867s
20	T Sato	1m33.666s
21	T Monteiro	1m33.709s
22	S Yamamoto	no time

QUALIFYING 2

	Driver	Time
1	M Schumacher	1m28.954s
2	F Massa	1m29.830s
3	J Trulli	1m30.204s
4	J Button	1m30.268s
5	R Schumacher	1m30.299s
6	G Fisichella	1m30.306s
7	N Rosberg	1m30.321s
8	F Alonso	1m30.357s
9	N Heidfeld	1m30.470s
10	R Barrichello	1m30.598s
11	K Räikkönen	1m30.827s
12	R Kubica	1m31.094s
13	P de la Rosa	1m31.254s
14	M Webber	1m31.276s
15	V Liuzzi	1m31.943s
16	C Albers	1m33.750s

Best sectors – Practice
Sec 1 M Schumacher 30.673s
Sec 2 M Schumacher 40.962s
Sec 3 M Schumacher 19.018s

Speed trap – Practice
1 M Schumacher 192.4mph
2 F Alonso 192.0mph
3 F Massa 191.4mph

Best sectors – Qualifying
Sec 1 M Schumacher 30.032s
Sec 2 M Schumacher 40.221s
Sec 3 M Schumacher 18.701s

Fernando Alonso
"After the second stops, the gap to Michael was only 5s. Then I saw the smoke coming into Turn 8. I thought it was a Spyker, and only when I went past did I see it was Michael."

Michael Schumacher
"I was leading and then my engine broke, but we can be proud of what we have achieved since Canada when we were 25 points behind. However, it's now lost."

Kimi Räikkönen
"Fifth was a good result for where we started, but it is not what we wanted. The car felt a lot better today especially in the long runs, but our race was lost in qualifying."

Jenson Button
"I overtook a Renault off the line then the tyres came good and I was able to overtake the Toyotas. Again, the team did an amazing job in the pit stops."

Robert Kubica
"I struggled with grip and also made a mistake, which lost me 10s, as following cars here is not easy. I perhaps risked too much, but I was able to come back."

Jarno Trulli
"I was boxed in Turn 1, so I tried to go around the outside and lost a place. I gained a place after my first pit stop, but later struggled with my last set of tyres."

Giancarlo Fisichella
"The car was not bad and we had a good strategy, as I was able to pass the Toyotas at the stops. The Michelins worked perfectly. We had the pace all through the race."

Felipe Massa
"I had a slow right-rear puncture so had my pit stop three laps early. I went out behind a slower car and that cost me my chance of staying ahead of Alonso and of winning."

Pedro de la Rosa
"Starting from 13th, it was always going to be tough to advance, as those around me were on similar strategies. I struggled to get any pace as my tyres had no grip."

Rubens Barrichello
"Heidfeld closed the door and I had nowhere to go and locked up and tapped him, damaging my front wing. After that, I was very fast but it's very difficult to overtake here."

Nick Heidfeld
"I gained one position at the start and moved to eighth, but I had trouble with the tyres. In all three stints, I suffered from graining on both the front and rear tyres."

Ralf Schumacher
"We could have achieved more. I made a strong start and held third into Turn 1. Jarno got ahead of me on his new tyres and from then on I spent the race following him."

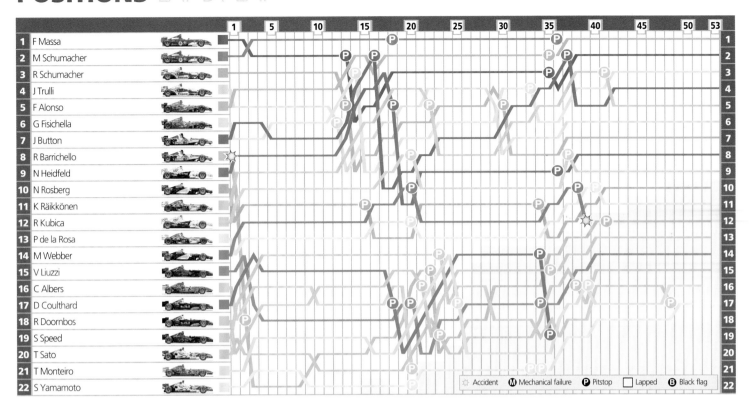

	Driver	
1	F Massa	
2	M Schumacher	
3	R Schumacher	
4	J Trulli	
5	F Alonso	
6	G Fisichella	
7	J Button	
8	R Barrichello	
9	N Heidfeld	
10	N Rosberg	
11	K Räikkönen	
12	R Kubica	
13	P de la Rosa	
14	M Webber	
15	V Liuzzi	
16	C Albers	
17	D Coulthard	
18	R Doornbos	
19	S Speed	
20	T Sato	
21	T Monteiro	
22	S Yamamoto	

Legend: ☼ Accident Ⓜ Mechanical failure Ⓟ Pitstop ☐ Lapped Ⓑ Black flag

QUALIFYING 3

	Driver	Time
1	F Massa	1m29.599s
2	M Schumacher	1m29.711s
3	R Schumacher	1m29.989s
4	J Trulli	1m30.039s
5	F Alonso	1m30.371s
6	G Fisichella	1m30.599s
7	J Button	1m30.992s
8	R Barrichello	1m31.478s
9	N Heidfeld	1m31.513s
10	N Rosberg	1m31.856s

GRID

	Driver	Time
1	F Massa	1m29.599s
2	M Schumacher	1m29.711s
3	R Schumacher	1m29.989s
4	J Trulli	1m30.039s
5	F Alonso	1m30.371s
6	G Fisichella	1m30.599s
7	J Button	1m30.992s
8	R Barrichello	1m31.478s
9	N Heidfeld	1m31.513s
10	N Rosberg	1m31.856s
11	K Räikkönen	1m30.827s
12	R Kubica	1m31.094s
13	P de la Rosa	1m31.254s
14	M Webber	1m31.276s
15	V Liuzzi	1m31.943s
16	C Albers	1m33.750s
17	D Coulthard	1m32.252s
18	R Doornbos	1m32.402s
19	S Speed	1m32.867s
20	T Sato	1m33.666s
21	T Monteiro	1m33.709s
22	S Yamamoto	no time

RACE

	Driver	Car	Laps	Time	Avg. mph	Fastest	Stops
1	F Alonso	Renault R26	53	1h23m53.413s	136.697	1m32.676s	2
2	F Massa	Ferrari 248	53	1h24m09.564s	136.260	1m33.296s	2
3	G Fisichella	Renault R26	53	1h24m17.366s	136.050	1m33.564s	2
4	J Button	Honda RA106	53	1h24m27.514s	135.778	1m33.451s	2
5	K Räikkönen	McLaren-Mercedes MP4-21	53	1h24m37.009s	135.524	1m33.344s	2
6	J Trulli	Toyota TF106B	53	1h24m40.130s	135.440	1m33.866s	2
7	R Schumacher	Toyota TF106B	53	1h24m42.282s	135.383	1m33.607s	2
8	N Heidfeld	BMW Sauber F1.06	53	1h25m09.508s	134.661	1m34.525s	2
9	R Kubica	BMW Sauber F1.06	53	1h25m10.345s	134.639	1m33.509s	2
10	N Rosberg	Williams-Cosworth FW28	52	1h24m01.311s	133.906	1m34.802s	2
11	P de la Rosa	McLaren-Mercedes MP4-21	52	1h24m06.083s	133.779	1m34.120s	2
12	R Barrichello	Honda RA106	52	1h24m31.585s	133.728	1m34.071s	3
13	R Doornbos	Red Bull-Ferrari RB2	52	1h24m53.750s	132.528	1m35.099s	2
14	V Liuzzi	Toro Rosso-Cosworth STR01	52	1h25m07.938s	132.271	1m34.131s	2
15	T Sato	Super Aguri-Honda SA06	52	1h25m19.208s	131.869	1m35.082s	2
16	T Monteiro	Spyker MF1-Toyota M16	51	1h24m01.977s	131.312	1m35.260s	2
17	S Yamamoto	Super Aguri-Honda SA06	50	1h24m19.816s	128.282	1m35.594s	3
18	S Speed	Toro Rosso-Cosworth STR01	48	Power steering	131.102	1m34.560s	2
R	M Webber	Williams-Cosworth FW28	39	Accident	-	1m35.092s	2
R	M Schumacher	Ferrari 248	36	Engine	-	1m32.792s	2
R	D Coulthard	Red Bull-Ferrari RB2	35	Gearbox	-	1m35.052s	1
R	C Albers	Spyker MF1-Toyota M16	20	Suspension	-	1m36.036s	0

CHAMPIONSHIP

	Driver	Pts
1	F Alonso	126
2	M Schumacher	116
3	F Massa	70
4	G Fisichella	69
5	K Räikkönen	61
6	J Button	50
7	R Barrichello	28
8	JP Montoya	26
9	N Heidfeld	23
10	R Schumacher	20
11	P de la Rosa	18
12	J Trulli	15
13	D Coulthard	14
14	M Webber	7
15	J Villeneuve	7
16	R Kubica	6
17	N Rosberg	4
18	C Klien	2
19	V Liuzzi	1

Speed trap – Qualifying

1	M Schumacher	194.3mph
2	F Massa	192.6mph
3	F Alonso	192.5mph

Fastest Lap

F Alonso 1m32.676s
(140.170mph) on lap 14

Fastest speed trap

M Schumacher 193.2mph

Slowest speed trap

M Webber 183.6mph

Fastest pit stop

1	K Räikkönen	19.897s
2	R Doornbos	20.754s
3	P de la Rosa	21.161s

Constructor

	Constructor	Pts
1	Renault	195
2	Ferrari	186
3	McLaren-Mercedes	105
4	Honda	78
5	BMW Sauber	36
6	Toyota	35
7	Red Bull-Ferrari	16
8	Williams-Cosworth	11
9	Toro Rosso-Cosworth	1

David Coulthard

"I had to retire when my car lost fourth. We were racing the Spykers and were quicker in some areas, but slower in others. After Tonio spun, I got stuck behind Speed."

Mark Webber

"I was struggling for balance at the chicane. After the first stop, I had no front grip and the car went just two inches onto the grass and I couldn't bring it back."

Vitantonio Liuzzi

"My race started with a clash with Mark which affected the handling until I got used to it. I also had some tyre graining early in the race, which caused me to spin."

Tiago Monteiro

"We were carrying a lot of fuel, but I was able to fight with the Toro Rossos and Red Bulls after passing Sato and Yamamoto. But during the second stint we had tyre issues."

Takuma Sato

"I overtook a few cars into Turn 1, but got held up and repassed. Then, at the Esses, I repassed Speed. Sadly, my pace was not enough and he got me back."

Robert Doornbos

"I had a poor start, but after that it was good to get the positions back. I was then behind Tonio and David for quite a while before Tonio lost a little time and David stopped."

Nico Rosberg

"I lost a place in the first couple of laps. Then I had to go around the outside of Barrichello and I made a mistake and lost another place to Kubica who I had just passed."

Scott Speed

"I had a strong first stint to keep David behind me, but we lost out to them in the stops. Then I spun trying to pass Doornbos. I pulled off with a power steering failure."

Christijan Albers

"The Red Bull cars were holding me up in the corners, but their top speed meant they were able to pull away down the straights. Then, sadly, I had driveshaft failure."

Sakon Yamamoto

"I really appreciate the support from everyone who attended this weekend. Their support helped me finish the race. It's a fantastic feeling to finish my home grand prix."

FORMULA 1™ GRANDE PRÊMIO
DO BRASIL 2006
São Paulo

MASSA AT HOME

Michael Schumacher made the headlines as he brought his career to a close, but team-mate Felipe Massa took the race win and Fernando Alonso the drivers' championship

The 2006 World Championship had plenty of twists and turns, and the Brazilian GP provided a fitting climax both to a magnificent season and to the stellar career of Michael Schumacher. He didn't win the race, but he walked away after a wonderful performance that left everyone – including his rivals – in no doubt that he was still at the very top of his game.

The drama that surrounded Michael's weekend overshadowed a championship conclusion that resulted in Fernando Alonso and Renault retaining both world titles, despite a few wobbles in the latter part of the season. Perhaps a constructors' crown for Ferrari would have been a more fitting conclusion, but in the end the Anglo-French team took the prizes.

Rain greeted arrivals to Interlagos on Thursday. Fortunately, it stayed away for the remainder of the weekend. Friday was unusually cool, though, and that's what Renault was banking on when it chose tyres that were designed to work in lower temperatures. Unluckily for them, it had already begun to warm up by Saturday, and that played into the hands of the teams using Bridgestone tyres.

It was soon obvious that the Ferraris were spectacularly fast, and after the first two stages of

INSIDE LINE
ROSS BRAWN

FERRARI TECHNICAL DIRECTOR

"Michael has been such a great example of commitment and team spirit. He was not a guy who came to the factory and said you must do this or that. He came and thanked people for what they'd done. He came and tried to explain what the car was doing. He demonstrated his commitment and expected people to do the same.

He has been an inspirational figure. For him to come to the factory and talk to people like that meant a huge amount to them. He loved being part of the team, which was important as well.

I've seen drivers come and go, and most of them are looking after Number One. I think Michael was unusual in that he's just as concerned about the wellbeing of the team. That's been one of his strengths over the years.

Michael's composure was exceptional. He never lost control with the team and the people he worked with; he never lost his temper. He is quite a firm character, as he had to be, but he always had composure, in and out of the car, that was quite exceptional. On top of that, the sheer speed. All the attributes in the world mean nothing if you don't have that…

I think Michael should take a little time away from the business to reflect on what his ambitions are. He has had a very clear programme with racing. We all have to be self-motivated, but we all know that we have to go to the next race and we have to be ready for it, and your programme is mapped out for you pretty clearly each season.

I think Michael now has to reflect on what his ambitions are for the next period of his life and how that can fit into Ferrari.

Michael certainly has a huge amount to give Ferrari still, but I am not sure whether it will be in any kind of driving role. These cars are very difficult to drive, and even with the fitness regimes they have, drivers start the season with the first test and their necks are aching and their heads are falling off. You can't just pop in, have a go in a car, give a diagnosis and then go again. I don't think that's very practical, so I don't think there will be any role of that sort for Michael.

However, Michael works so well with the engineers and understands the way things work that there could be a technical benefit.

Commercially, there is also huge potential on both the racing and the road car side. Michael needs to reflect on the end of his career and see what he wants to do next. I don't think it's clear to him. He needs some time away to arrive at that conclusion."

qualifying, it seemed clear that Michael and Felipe Massa were the only contenders for pole position.

But then it all went wrong for Ferrari. After waiting at the end of the pitlane for a couple of minutes in order to be first out for the fuel-burning laps in the third qualifying session, Michael headed out and then almost immediately slowed to a crawl. He had been hit by a loss of fuel pressure, traced later to a pump failure that the team insisted was not related to any heat build-up while he was waiting to go out. He limped back to the pits, but there was no time to fix the car. He was thus consigned to start 10th – and his championship challenge seemed to be all but over.

Massa saved Ferrari's day by taking pole, ahead of Kimi Räikkönen and Jarno Trulli. Alonso settled for fourth but, given the tyre situation, that was more than adequate, as all he needed was a point. Michael had to win and hope that Alonso failed to finish.

Temperatures rose further on Sunday, and it was clear that this would be a Bridgestone day. As the grandstands filled and expectations built up, people began to wonder if Michael really could make it to the front. All he really had to do was get to second – even if that meant jumping both Renaults – and then Massa would do his duty and fall back.

After receiving a special trophy from Pelé on the grid, Michael was finally able to get into his car and leave all the fuss about his last race behind him. Both title contenders were under enormous pressure to get around the first corner intact at a track that has produced more than its share of opening-lap incidents.

Fortunately they did, and Michael made his life easier in the course of the lap by jumping both BMWs and his brother Ralf's Toyota to come around in seventh.

Behind, there was drama half-way around the lap when Nico Rosberg assaulted his Williams team-mate Mark Webber. Both drivers tried to drive their damaged cars back to the pits, but Rosberg lost it

coming onto the pit straight and had a huge shunt, from which he was fortunate to escape unharmed. This brought out the safety car.

By now, Michael was up to sixth, having passed Rubens Barrichello. Ahead were Massa, Räikkönen, Jarno Trulli, Alonso and Fisichella, so his two most difficult targets were the next in line. At the end of the fifth lap, the safety car finally peeled in, and Michael set his sights on Fisichella. At the start of the eighth lap, he went around the outside at Turn 1.

It looked to be a good, clean pass, but as he came out of the corner he got into a huge slide, which he managed to correct. Then he slowed down in precisely

OPPOSITE It's safe to say that all attention was on Michael Schumacher before his final race

ABOVE Nico Rosberg pauses for breath after his violent exit on lap 1

BELOW This was the last race for British American Tobacco with the team now known as Honda Racing, and Jenson Button did them proud by finishing in a fighting third place

the same place where he had suffered his problem the day before. The answer was soon obvious: his Ferrari had a punctured left rear tyre. TV pictures were inconclusive, but after the race, damage on Fisichella's front wing indicated that he had clipped the Ferrari, although neither driver had felt the bump.

Michael crawled back to the pits as the rest of the field steamed past. To make matters worse, it was something of a messy pit stop, and more time was lost because the mechanics hadn't readied the tyres, despite the obvious clues on the TV monitor.

Michael blasted out of the pits stone last, some 70 seconds – and nearly one full lap – behind leader Massa. It was literally a deflating moment; it seemed that any chance for excitement in the race had gone.

But that was far from the case. Michael circulated on his own for a few laps, gradually catching the tardy tailenders and gaining places here and there. He now had a lot of fuel on board and, after the frontrunners made their scheduled stops, his pace indicated that it wouldn't be long before he began to catch them.

By the lap 30 mark, Massa was long gone in front. For a while, Pedro de la Rosa ran in an artificial second place, thanks to being on a one-stop strategy while all others were planning to pit twice, but in the real race Alonso had got up to second ahead of Button, Räikkönen and Fisichella. It was a great performance by Button, who started 14th after a traction control failure hit his Honda. Come the race, he was flying.

Alonso was well set and just had to make sure that he kept out of trouble. With the revs of his Renault V8 turned down, nothing was being left to chance. The constructors' title was also within Renault's grasp – they had a nine-point advantage before the start – and a victory for Massa wouldn't affect that.

But Michael was looming large in the mirrors of the points scorers as he set fastest lap after fastest lap. There were a couple of glitches when he overcooked

it, got on the marbles and ran wide, but otherwise his progress was simply astonishing, as he caught and passed car after car. Michael's second and final pit stop came on lap 48, shortly before the second scheduled stops of those ahead. Alonso was the last of the group to come in, on lap 54. By then, Michael had risen to sixth and was back on the tail of Fisichella, the man who had caused all his problems.

The Italian was a hard nut to crack and did his job of keeping the Ferrari at bay for a few critical laps. Finally, Michael pushed Fisichella so hard that he locked up and went straight on at Turn 1 on lap 62, before rejoining at the foot of the hill.

Next in line was Räikkönen, who proved surprisingly aggressive in his defence, to the extent that the FIA sent the team a warning by radio about his line-changing. Michael finally squeezed through on lap 68 to take fourth. There were just three laps to go.

A podium would have been some reward, but Button lay just beyond his reach and Michael crossed the line some 4.4s behind the Brit. It was a staggering performance, but one for which Bridgestone could claim considerable credit. It was hard to judge Michael against Massa, because the Brazilian was to a large degree in cruise mode, but the real clue was the pace of usual tailenders Super Aguri, with Sakon Yamamoto setting the seventh-fastest lap of the race, just 1.2s behind the seven-times World Champion…

Massa's great, crowd-pleasing performance was inevitably overshadowed, but he laid down a marker for 2007 when Räikkönen joins him at Ferrari. His second win could not have come at a more appropriate time or place.

"It's not for 13 years that a Brazilian driver has won the Brazilian Grand Prix, and for me it's just amazing: to be here, in front of my people, in my first year that I have a good car – I mean a fantastic car, because after the race today, I think it was maybe the easiest race of

BELOW Michael Schumacher goes around the outside of Giancarlo Fisichella into Turn 1, just before his left rear tyre punctured

OPPOSITE TOP Helped considerably by its Bridgestone tyres, Takuma Sato raced to a strong 10th place, a result that team owner Aguri Suzuki couldn't have predicted

OPPOSITE BOTTOM Fernando Alonso had to score a point to be champion again. He scored eight…

INSIDE LINE
MICHAEL SCHUMACHER

FERRARI DRIVER

"Interlagos was a good place to finish – a challenge, good overtaking possibilities and great from the driver's point-of-view. I'm really happy for Felipe that he could be the next Brazilian after [Ayrton] Senna to win here, and naturally I congratulate Fernando as well.

For me, it was business as usual. I was trying not to think about it being my last race. Occasionally it came to me and I felt a bit strange, but in general I was pretty relaxed. The focus was on trying to win the constructors' title. Mentally, after Suzuka, the drivers' championship was lost. I didn't want to win it on a retirement, but we knew we would require a 1–2 finish for the constructors' title.

There wasn't really much time to think about anything else. I would have liked to have finished up on the podium, but this weekend didn't run for me. There was the problem in qualifying and then my race was compromised by the puncture I picked up when I had just passed Fisichella.

I'm going to miss all the moments – good and bad – that we have had in the past 16 years. The support the fans gave me was fantastic and restored my self-confidence when things weren't going so well. That was immensely important over such a long sporting career. I'd like to say a huge thanks to them all. I know that's not nearly enough, but I'm afraid I can't do more. There may be some regrets and some things I might change, but it would get too intense to talk about that now. You know the song 'My Way?' It fits the way I feel...

This has been an amazing season. Things didn't work out so well at first, then it turned for us at Imola and, mid-season on, we became very strong. The ending was a shame but, looking back, I can't complain. I think my favourite title will remain my one from 2000, my first with Ferrari.

My retirement decision is final. I don't make a decision if I don't think I need to. It has been taken and expressed, so there is no reason to change it. What is going to be my life afterwards? I don't know. And I don't feel like I should know.

I am in the fortunate position that I can retire and not have a vision for my life afterwards. I have plenty of time to make that vision, to live a life where something will come up that interests me. I am completely relaxed and sure about this. What that will be, I don't know. But life offers plenty of opportunities and I look forward to those. As for racing in other series, I have no view and no interest in that just now."

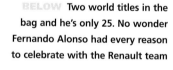

ABOVE Felipe Massa scored a result he'd been dreaming of all his life, and said that he found it all surprisingly easy as his Ferrari really flew on its Bridgestone tyres

BELOW Two world titles in the bag and he's only 25. No wonder Fernando Alonso had every reason to celebrate with the Renault team

my life, because I could control everything. I wasn't pushing a lot and you know, I'm really happy to have that moment, and I'm sure… it's difficult to explain, it's just very, very special for me."

Meanwhile, there was a collective sigh of relief from Alonso and all in the Renault camp.

"It's been a fantastic weekend," said Alonso. "And especially the race, a very long race, obviously, for us because we only needed one point to become champion, and for sure, if I could help the team become Constructors' Champions as well, I was ready to do it, and you know everything was as planned. Ferrari were too quick, but we managed to overtake Kimi in the first pit stop, and then there was a lot of pressure from Jenson, but we were able to finish second. The important thing today was to become champion again for the second consecutive time and we did it. I've nothing more to say, it's an unbelievable feeling. We did the job because we have a great team. It was very difficult after Budapest, it was very difficult after China, but we arrived in Japan, we tried to put things together, and the team was there. After that, no mistakes. In the end, Renault made less mistakes."

Button did a great job to take third after starting 14th, while Räikkönen struggled for grip on his way to fifth, one position behind the man he replaces for 2007. Fisichella did his bit for Renault by finishing sixth, ahead of Barrichello and one-stopper de la Rosa. Astonishingly, Takuma Sato finished 10th of the 16 runners, as the first of the lapped runners.

Not around at the end of the race were the two Toyotas, victims of similar suspension breakages, while Nick Heidfeld had a big shunt after earlier contact with Tonio Liuzzi led to a failure under braking for Turn 1.

Of course, all that was a sideshow because, despite Alonso's achievement, the day – the season, in fact – was all about Michael.

"I would have preferred to have been on the podium, no doubt," he said after the flag. "But seeing the circumstances of today, I guess I have reasons to be happy. Felipe did a great race, after Senna the first Brazilian to win on home ground, which is fantastic for him. It takes away a lot of pressure and gives a lot of confidence for him, which I'm happy to see. Then a great result for Fernando, and I'm happy for him too. It was a great car performance we had today. We at Ferrari finished the season on a high. We had a fantastic car and Felipe transformed it into a victory."

It was a remarkable end to a truly remarkable career. Life after Michael will be very different for Ferrari – and for the sport as a whole…

SNAPSHOT FROM
BRAZIL

CLOCKWISE FROM RIGHT The glitz and glamour of the championship shoot-out reached all corners of São Paulo, from smart to rather less so; engine experts Cosworth signed out after 37 years in Formula One; while the entire Ferrari hierarchy led the way in bidding farewell to Michael Schumacher; others just smiled and put on a very bold front...; Rubens Barrichello's helmet livery turned all patriotic for his home grand prix

WEEKEND HEADLINES

■ A World Motor Sport Council meeting earlier in the week confirmed a 17-race calendar for 2007, with no sign of Imola in the gap that Bernie Ecclestone had handily left in April. The FIA also formally confirmed that the German GP would alternate between Hockenheim and the Nürburgring, with the latter hosting the race in 2007.

■ The FIA also revealed a new safety-car procedure for 2007. In order to prevent drivers from racing back to the pits, the pit entry would be closed until the cars were running in formation behind the safety car. In addition, any backmarkers in the way of the leading group before the restart would be waved past the safety car and allowed to join the back of the queue.

■ As the teams set up at Interlagos on the Thursday morning, BMW confirmed the not entirely surprising news that Robert Kubica would continue to drive their second car in 2007, while Sebastian Vettel was signed for a full season as their third driver. Team boss Mario Theissen insisted that Vettel would be given a chance in free practice on Fridays, which meant that either Kubica or Nick Heidfeld would have to stand aside and watch.

■ Williams revealed in Brazil that American telecom giant AT&T had signed up as title sponsor for 2007, having previously been seen at Jaguar Racing. The team also announced some key appointments to its technical team as part of its ongoing effort to regain lost ground.

■ While Michael Schumacher's final race inevitably captured most of the headlines, several other big players in the sport also disappeared after Brazil, including Michelin, Mild Seven and Lucky Strike. The departure of the last two names left Marlboro as the only tobacco brand still involved in Formula One for 2007.

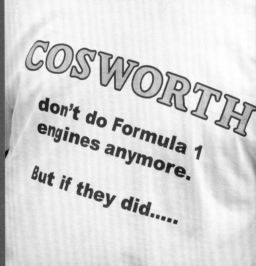

COSWORTH don't do Formula 1 engines anymore. But if they did.....

GRAZIE MICHAEL

RACE RESULTS
BRAZIL
INTERLAGOS

Official Results © [2006]
Formula One Administration Limited,
6 Princes Gate, London SW7 1QJ.
No reproduction without permission.
All copyright and database rights reserved

RACE DATE October 22nd
CIRCUIT LENGTH 2.677 miles
NO. OF LAPS 71
RACE DISTANCE 190.067 miles
WEATHER Sunny and dry, 23°C
TRACK TEMP 30-46°C
RACE DAY ATTENDANCE 64,000
LAP RECORD Juan Pablo Montoya,
1m11.473s, 134.837mph, 2004

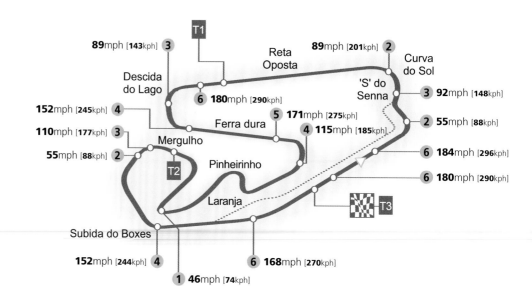

PRACTICE 1

	Driver	Time	Laps
1	K Räikkönen	1m13.764s	5
2	A Davidson	1m13.902s	32
3	A Wurz	1m13.922s	25
4	S Vettel	1m14.204s	29
5	P de la Rosa	1m14.237s	5
6	J Button	1m14.487s	4
7	J Trulli	1m14.888s	8
8	N Jani	1m15.159s	25
9	R Barrichello	1m15.661s	6
10	M Ammermüller	1m15.711s	22
11	R Schumacher	1m16.168s	6
12	T Sato	1m16.534s	16
13	E Viso	1m16.737s	32
14	S Speed	1m17.047s	14
15	V Liuzzi	1m17.311s	8
16	S Yamamoto	1m17.388s	14
17	F Montagny	1m17.744s	6
18	C Albers	no time	1
19	F Alonso	no time	1
20	D Coulthard	no time	1
21	R Doornbos	no time	1
22	G Fisichella	no time	1
23	N Heidfeld	no time	1
24	R Kubica	no time	1
25	T Monteiro	no time	1
26	F Massa	no time	0
27	N Rosberg	no time	0
28	M Schumacher	no time	0
29	M Webber	no time	0

PRACTICE 2

	Driver	Time	Laps
1	A Wurz	1m12.547s	33
2	A Davidson	1m12.653s	37
3	S Vettel	1m12.870s	33
4	J Trulli	1m13.483s	21
5	J Button	1m13.485s	13
6	M Schumacher	1m13.713s	15
7	R Schumacher	1m13.765s	22
8	F Montagny	1m13.792s	20
9	K Räikkönen	1m13.803s	8
10	F Alonso	1m13.820s	16
11	P de la Rosa	1m13.926s	16
12	G Fisichella	1m14.053s	17
13	R Barrichello	1m14.434s	17
14	M Ammermüller	1m14.436s	31
15	T Monteiro	1m14.468s	18
16	R Kubica	1m14.510s	15
17	F Massa	1m14.561s	15
18	N Heidfeld	1m14.793s	13
19	M Webber	1m14.839s	15
20	E Viso	1m14.972s	26
21	T Sato	1m15.023s	27
22	C Albers	1m15.086s	21
23	N Rosberg	1m15.124s	14
24	D Coulthard	1m15.214s	21
25	V Liuzzi	1m15.737s	22
26	S Speed	1m15.855s	28
27	N Jani	1m15.868s	22
28	R Doornbos	1m16.251s	8
29	S Yamamoto	1m18.321s	9

PRACTICE 3

	Driver	Time	Laps
1	F Massa	1m11.443s	17
2	M Schumacher	1m11.631s	15
3	J Button	1m12.306s	15
4	R Kubica	1m12.535s	20
5	G Fisichella	1m12.567s	15
6	R Barrichello	1m12.697s	18
7	F Alonso	1m12.721s	14
8	K Räikkönen	1m12.723s	12
9	P de la Rosa	1m12.780s	15
10	N Heidfeld	1m13.037s	15
11	M Webber	1m13.205s	16
12	N Rosberg	1m13.380s	13
13	S Speed	1m13.455s	18
14	V Liuzzi	1m13.530s	20
15	R Doornbos	1m13.564s	21
16	R Schumacher	1m13.642s	20
17	T Sato	1m13.814s	21
18	T Monteiro	1m13.832s	15
19	D Coulthard	1m13.944s	20
20	J Trulli	1m14.051s	19
21	C Albers	1m14.108s	19
22	S Yamamoto	1m14.875s	21

QUALIFYING 1

	Driver	Time
1	F Massa	1m10.643s
2	M Schumacher	1m11.565s
3	R Schumacher	1m11.713s
4	F Alonso	1m11.791s
5	P de la Rosa	1m11.825s
6	J Trulli	1m11.885s
7	M Webber	1m11.973s
8	N Rosberg	1m11.974s
9	R Barrichello	1m12.017s
10	K Räikkönen	1m12.035s
11	R Kubica	1m12.040s
12	G Fisichella	1m12.042s
13	J Button	1m12.085s
14	N Heidfeld	1m12.307s
15	R Doornbos	1m12.530s
16	V Liuzzi	1m12.855s
17	S Speed	1m12.856s
18	C Albers	1m13.138s
19	D Coulthard	1m13.249s
20	T Sato	1m13.269s
21	S Yamamoto	1m13.357s
22	T Monteiro	no time

QUALIFYING 2

	Driver	Time
1	M Schumacher	1m10.313s
2	F Massa	1m10.775s
3	F Alonso	1m11.148s
4	J Trulli	1m11.343s
5	K Räikkönen	1m11.386s
6	G Fisichella	1m11.461s
7	R Schumacher	1m11.550s
8	R Barrichello	1m11.578s
9	R Kubica	1m11.589s
10	N Heidfeld	1m11.648s
11	M Webber	1m11.650s
12	P de la Rosa	1m11.658s
13	N Rosberg	1m11.679s
14	J Button	1m11.742s
15	R Doornbos	1m12.591s
16	V Liuzzi	1m12.861s

Best sectors – Practice

Sec 1	M Schumacher	18.173s
Sec 2	F Massa	35.811s
Sec 3	M Schumacher	17.238s

Speed trap – Practice

1	M Schumacher	191.6mph
2	G Fisichella	191.4mph
3	P de la Rosa	191.1mph

Best sectors – Qualifying

Sec 1	M Schumacher	17.934s
Sec 2	M Schumacher	35.268s
Sec 3	M Schumacher	17.111s

Fernando Alonso
"We've scored 26 points out of 30, and that was enough to make us double champions. The atmosphere in the team is unbelievable right now. I have to thank everybody."

Michael Schumacher
"Felipe drove an amazing race. My race was compromised after the puncture I got when I had just passed Fisichella. I was unaware of it until the team told me about it."

Kimi Räikkönen
"I didn't have much grip. The straightline speed could have been better. I ran wide late on which let Michael close in, and despite my efforts I couldn't keep him back."

Jenson Button
"I'm thrilled to end the year on the podium, especially coming from 14th on the grid. This result came out of a genuine fight, with the car showing great competitiveness."

Robert Kubica
"The race started OK and I passed Nick on lap 1, but after 10 laps we didn't have any more speed. I was driving as hard as I could and pushing, but we were too slow."

Jarno Trulli
"There was a problem with the rear suspension's central element. The car was jumping around and I was not fully in control – the bumps probably made it worse."

Giancarlo Fisichella
"The first time Michael passed me, we were side-by-side, then I saw him have oversteer in Turn 2 and got back past. Late on, I braked late, locked the fronts and he got by."

Felipe Massa
"My dream has become a reality. The car was perfect, the tyres were perfect, I had it under control. Over the last few laps, I couldn't stop watching the fans celebrate!"

Pedro de la Rosa
"A very tough race. I was on a one-stop strategy and this was a little too hard for the tyres. As a result I couldn't really attack, but at least I scored one point for the team."

Rubens Barrichello
"I couldn't get a rhythm in the car and I was having some difficulties with the handling, but still we got two cars in the points once again. I'd also like to congratulate Felipe."

Nick Heidfeld
"After my first stop, I tried to pass Liuzzi, but we touched. Later, I went straight on at Turn 1 and slid off when I let Massa pass. At the end, something broke and I crashed."

Ralf Schumacher
"We made a reasonable start and were initially in good shape. Then, immediately after the safety-car period, we developed a problem at the rear of the car."

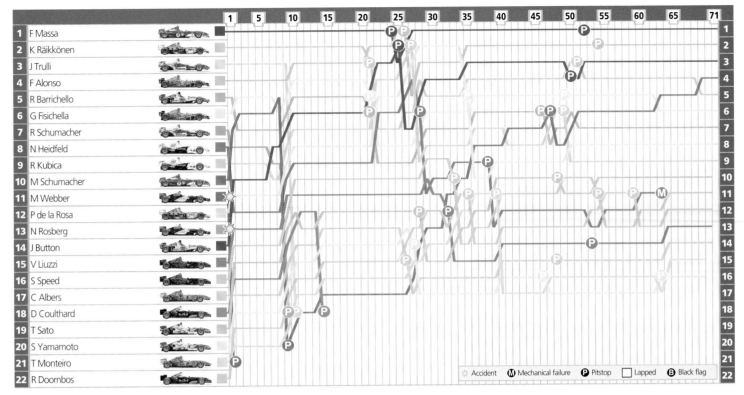

	Driver	
1	F Massa	
2	K Räikkönen	
3	J Trulli	
4	F Alonso	
5	R Barrichello	
6	G Fisichella	
7	R Schumacher	
8	N Heidfeld	
9	R Kubica	
10	M Schumacher	
11	M Webber	
12	P de la Rosa	
13	N Rosberg	
14	J Button	
15	V Liuzzi	
16	S Speed	
17	C Albers	
18	D Coulthard	
19	T Sato	
20	S Yamamoto	
21	T Monteiro	
22	R Doornbos	

☼ Accident　Ⓜ Mechanical failure　Ⓟ Pitstop　☐ Lapped　Ⓑ Black flag

QUALIFYING 3

	Driver	Time
1	F Massa	1m10.680s
2	K Räikkönen	1m11.299s
3	J Trulli	1m11.328s
4	F Alonso	1m11.567s
5	R Barrichello	1m11.619s
6	G Fisichella	1m11.629s
7	R Schumacher	1m11.695s
8	N Heidfeld	1m11.882s
9	R Kubica	1m12.131s
10	M Schumacher	no time

GRID

	Driver	Time
1	F Massa	1m10.680s
2	K Räikkönen	1m11.299s
3	J Trulli	1m11.328s
4	F Alonso	1m11.567s
5	R Barrichello	1m11.619s
6	G Fisichella	1m11.629s
7	R Schumacher	1m11.695s
8	N Heidfeld	1m11.882s
9	R Kubica	1m12.131s
10	M Schumacher	no time
11	M Webber	1m11.650s
12	P de la Rosa	1m11.658s
13	N Rosberg	1m11.679s
14	J Button	1m11.742s
15	V Liuzzi	1m12.861s
16	S Speed	1m12.856s
17	C Albers	1m13.138s
18	D Coulthard	1m13.249s
19	T Sato	1m13.269s
20	S Yamamoto	1m13.357s
21	T Monteiro	no time
22*	R Doornbos	1m12.591s

* DENOTES 10-PLACE GRID PENALTY

RACE

	Driver	Car	Laps	Time	Avg. mph	Fastest	Stops
1	F Massa	Ferrari 248	71	1h31m53.751s	124.139	1m12.877s	2
2	F Alonso	Renault R26	71	1h32m12.409s	123.695	1m12.961s	2
3	J Button	Honda RA106	71	1h32m13.145s	123.678	1m13.053s	2
4	M Schumacher	Ferrari 248	71	1h32m17.845s	123.573	1m12.162s	2
5	K Räikkönen	McLaren-Mercedes MP4-21	71	1h32m22.254s	123.475	1m13.281s	2
6	G Fisichella	Renault R26	71	1h32m24.038s	123.436	1m13.121s	2
7	R Barrichello	Honda RA106	71	1h32m34.045s	123.213	1m13.391s	2
8	P de la Rosa	McLaren-Mercedes MP4-21	71	1h32m45.819s	122.952	1m13.817s	1
9	R Kubica	BMW Sauber F1.06	71	1h33m01.393s	122.609	1m14.117s	2
10	T Sato	Super Aguri-Honda SA06	70	1h31m54.723s	122.344	1m13.401s	2
11	S Speed	Toro Rosso-Cosworth STR01	70	1h32m17.656s	121.837	1m13.862s	2
12	R Doornbos	Red Bull-Ferrari RB2	70	1h32m20.086s	121.784	1m13.700s	2
13	V Liuzzi	Toro Rosso-Cosworth STR01	70	1h32m31.287s	121.538	1m13.687s	2
14	C Albers	Spyker MF1-Toyota M16	70	1h32m47.855s	121.176	1m14.591s	2
15	T Monteiro	Spyker MF1-Toyota M16	69	1h31m56.646s	120.554	1m14.410s	1
16	S Yamamoto	Super Aguri-Honda SA06	69	1h32m02.861s	120.418	1m13.379s	3
17	N Heidfeld	BMW Sauber F1.06	63	Accident	-	1m14.163s	2
R	D Coulthard	Red Bull-Ferrari RB2	14	Gearbox	-	1m16.045s	0
R	J Trulli	Toyota TF106B	10	Suspension	-	1m14.882s	0
R	R Schumacher	Toyota TF106B	9	Suspension	-	1m16.835s	0
R	M Webber	Williams-Cosworth FW28	1	Crash damage	-	-	0
R	N Rosberg	Williams-Cosworth FW28	0	Accident	-	-	0

CHAMPIONSHIP

	Driver	Pts
1	F Alonso	134
2	M Schumacher	121
3	F Massa	80
4	G Fisichella	72
5	K Räikkönen	65
6	J Button	56
7	R Barrichello	30
8	JP Montoya	26
9	N Heidfeld	23
10	R Schumacher	20
11	P de la Rosa	19
12	J Trulli	15
13	D Coulthard	14
14	M Webber	7
15	J Villeneuve	7
16	R Kubica	6
17	N Rosberg	4
18	C Klien	2
19	V Liuzzi	1

Speed trap – Qualifying

1	G Fisichella	192.3mph
2	F Alonso	192.1mph
3	M Schumacher	191.6mph

Fastest Lap

M Schumacher 1m12.162s
(133.550mph) on lap 70

Fastest speed trap

M Schumacher 197.6mph

Slowest speed trap

T Monteiro 185.0mph

Fastest pit stop

1	S Yamamoto	22.886s
2	R Doornbos	23.266s
3	N Heidfeld	23.763s

David Coulthard

"I had a gearbox problem. At first, I thought it was the clutch, as it started to slip out of Turn 3, but I think fourth gear was broken. It was a disappointing weekend."

Mark Webber

"I was fighting with Jenson and Pedro going into Turn 1. It was shaping up to be quite fun, but I braked a bit late going into Turn 4 and then I was hit from behind."

Vitantonio Liuzzi

"After the start, I was held up by the Toyotas and BMWs. Then I collided with Heidfeld who missed his braking. The contact damaged my left front suspension."

Tiago Monteiro

"I started with a heavy fuel load. I pitted from 11th, then twice hit blue flags and lost 7s which was a shame, as without that I could have been faster than the Toro Rossos."

Takuma Sato

"This is a fantastic result. At the start, I overtook the Red Bulls and Spykers. After the safety car went in we were able to push and take it to the two Toro Rossos."

Robert Doornbos

"Today was a disaster. The car felt very bad to drive and we struggled big time. I had some battles with the Toro Rossos, but there were no real highlights during the race."

Nico Rosberg

"After the start, I was trying to get out of traffic and get back the place I had just lost to Jenson so I was close behind Mark. I think he braked an extra metre early, and I hit him."

Scott Speed

"We were a lot more competitive than we thought we were going to be, but I was surprised at the pace of the Aguris. I have learnt so much this season with every race."

Christijan Albers

"It was good for the team to see both cars finish. We didn't expect to be very strong here, as our top speed is not high enough, so we can be satisfied with our result."

Sakon Yamamoto

"I was able to push from start to finish, pushing as fast as in qualifying and battling with Spyker all the race. I want to thank the whole team for their hard work."

Constructor

	Constructor	Pts
1	Renault	206
2	Ferrari	201
3	McLaren-Mercedes	110
4	Honda	86
5	BMW Sauber	36
6	Toyota	35
7	Red Bull-Ferrari	16
8	Williams-Cosworth	11
9	Toro Rosso-Cosworth	1

DRIVER RESULTS

	Driver	Nationality	Car	ROUND 1 BAHRAIN GP March 12	ROUND 2 MALAYSIAN GP March 19	ROUND 3 AUSTRALIAN GP April 2	ROUND 4 SAN MARINO GP April 23	ROUND 5 EUROPEAN GP May 7	ROUND 6 SPANISH GP May 14
1	Fernando Alonso	SPA	Renault R26	1	2F	1	1F	2P	1P
2	Michael Schumacher	GER	Ferrari 248	2P	6	R	1P	1F	2
3	Felipe Massa	BRA	Ferrari 248	9	5	R	4	3	4F
4	Giancarlo Fisichella	ITA	Renault R26	R	1P	5	8	6	3
5	Kimi Räikkönen	FIN	McLaren-Mercedes MP4-21	3	R	2F	5	4	5
6	Jenson Button	GBR	Honda RA106	4	3	9P	7	R	6
7	Rubens Barrichello	BRA	Honda RA106	15	10	7	10	5	7
8	Juan Pablo Montoya	COL	McLaren-Mercedes MP4-21	5	4	R	3	R	R
9	Nick Heidfeld	GER	BMW Sauber F1.06	12	R	4	13	10	8
10	Ralf Schumacher	GER	Toyota TF106	14	8	3	9	R	R
			Toyota TF106B						
11	Pedro de la Rosa	SPA	McLaren-Mercedes MP4-21						
12	Jarno Trulli	ITA	Toyota TF106	16	9	R	R	9	10
			Toyota TF106B						
13	David Coulthard	GBR	Red Bull-Ferrari RB2	10	R	8	R	R	14
14	Mark Webber	AUS	Williams-Cosworth FW28	6	R	R	6	R	9
15	Jacques Villeneuve	CDN	BMW Sauber F1.06	R	7	6	12	8	12
16	Robert Kubica	POL	BMW Sauber F1.06						
17	Nico Rosberg	GER	Williams-Cosworth FW28	7F	R	R	11	7	11
18	Christian Klien	AUT	Red Bull-Ferrari RB2	8	R	R	R	R	13
19	Vitantonio Liuzzi	ITA	Toro Rosso-Cosworth STR01	11	11	R	14	R	15
	Scott Speed	USA	Toro Rosso-Cosworth STR01	13	R	11	15	11	R
	Tiago Monteiro	POR	Spyker (Midland) MF1-Toyota M16	17	13	R	16	12	16
	Christijan Albers	NED	Spyker (Midland) MF1-Toyota M16	R	12	10	R	13	R
	Takuma Sato	JAP	Super Aguri-Honda SA05	18	14	12	R	R	17
			Super Aguri-Honda SA06						
	Robert Doornbos	NED	Red Bull-Ferrari RB2						
	Yuji Ide	JAP	Super Aguri-Honda SA05	R	R	13	R		
	Franck Montagny	FRA	Super Aguri-Honda SA05					R	R
	Sakon Yamamoto	JAP	Super Aguri-Honda SA06						

RACE SCORING

1st	10	POINTS
2nd	8	POINTS
3rd	6	POINTS
4th	5	POINTS
5th	4	POINTS
6th	3	POINTS
7th	2	POINTS
8th	1	POINT

DATA KEY

D	DISQUALIFIED
F	FASTEST LAP
NC	NON-CLASSIFIED
NQ	NON-QUALIFIER
NS	NON-STARTER
P	POLE POSITION
R	RETIRED
W	WITHDRAWN

QUALIFYING HEAD-TO-HEAD

Renault
Alonso–Fisichella **12–6**

Ferrari
M Schumacher–Massa **13–5**

McLaren-Mercedes
Räikkönen–Montoya **7–3**
Räikkönen–De La Rosa **8–0**

Honda
Button–Barrichello **9–9**

BMW Sauber
Villeneuve–Heidfeld **7–5**
Heidfeld–Kubica **5–1**

Toyota
R Schumacher–Trulli **10–8**

Red Bull-Ferrari
Coulthard–Klien **9–6**
Coulthard–Doornbos **2–1**

Williams-Cosworth
Webber–Rosberg **12–6**

Toro Rosso-Cosworth
Liuzzi–Speed **12–6**

Spyker MF1-Toyota
Albers–Monteiro **13–5**

Super Aguri-Honda
Sato–Ide **4–0**
Sato–Montagny **5–2**
Sato–Yamamoto **5–2**

Race results for both drivers, ie. first and second listed as 1/2 with team's best result listed first

CONSTRUCTOR RESULTS

1	Renault
2	Ferrari
3	McLaren-Mercedes
4	Honda
5	BMW Sauber
6	Toyota
7	Red Bull-Ferrari
8	Williams-Cosworth
9	Toro Rosso-Cosworth
10	Spyker MF1-Toyota
11	Super Aguri-Honda

ROUND 7 MONACO GP May 28	ROUND 8 BRITISH GP June 11	ROUND 9 CANADIAN GP June 25	ROUND 10 UNITED STATES GP July 2	ROUND 11 FRENCH GP July 16	ROUND 12 GERMAN GP July 30	ROUND 13 HUNGARIAN GP August 6	ROUND 14 TURKISH GP August 27	ROUND 15 ITALIAN GP September 10	ROUND 16 CHINESE GP October 1	ROUND 17 JAPANESE GP October 8	ROUND 18 BRAZILIAN GP October 22	TOTAL POINTS
1	1PF	1P	5	2	5	R	2	R	2PF	1F	2	134
5F	2	2	1PF	1PF	1F	8	3F	1	1	R	4F	121
9	5	5	2	3	2	7F	1P	9	R	2P	1P	80
6	4	4	3	6	6	R	6	4	3	3	6	72
R	3	3F	R	5	3P	RP	R	2P	R	5	4	65
11	R	9	R	R	4	1	4	5	4	4	3	56
4	10	R	6	R	R	4	8	6	6	12	7	30
2	6	R	R									26
7	7	7	R	8	R	3	14	8	7	8	17	23
8	R	R	R	4	9	6	7	15	R	7	R	20
				7	R	2	5	R	5	11	8	19
17	11	6	4	R	7	12	9	7	R	6	R	15
3	12	8	7	9	11	5	15	12	9	R	R	14
R	R	12	R	R	R	R	10	10	8	R	R	7
14	8	R	R	11	R							7
						D	12	3	13	9	9	6
R	9	R	9	14	R	R	R	R	11	10	R	4
R	14	11	R	12	8	R	11	11				2
10	13	13	8	13	10	R	R	14	10	14	13	1
13	R	10	R	10	12	11	13	13	15	18	11	
15	16	14	R	R	D	9	R	R	R	16	15	
12	15	R	R	15	D	10	R	17	16	R	14	
R	17	15	R	R								
						R	13	NC	16	14	15	10
										12	13	12
16	18	R	R	16								
						R	R	R	R	17	17	16

ROUND 1 BAHRAIN GP March 12	ROUND 2 MALAYSIAN GP March 19	ROUND 3 AUSTRALIAN GP April 2	ROUND 4 SAN MARINO GP April 23	ROUND 5 EUROPEAN GP May 7	ROUND 6 SPANISH GP May 14	ROUND 7 MONACO GP May 28	ROUND 8 BRITISH GP June 11	ROUND 9 CANADIAN GP June 25	ROUND 10 UNITED STATES GP July 2	ROUND 11 FRENCH GP July 16	ROUND 12 GERMAN GP July 30	ROUND 13 HUNGARIAN GP August 6	ROUND 14 TURKISH GP August 27	ROUND 15 ITALIAN GP September 10	ROUND 16 CHINESE GP October 1	ROUND 17 JAPANESE GP October 8	ROUND 18 BRAZILIAN GP October 22	TOTAL POINTS
1/R	1/2	1/5	2/8	2/6	1/3	1/6	1/4	1/4	3/5	2/6	5/6	R/R	2/6	4/R	2/3	1/3	2/6	206
2/9	5/6	R/R	1/4	1/3	2/4	5/9	2/5	2/5	1/2	1/3	1/2	7/8	1/3	1/9	1/R	2/R	1/4	201
3/5	4/R	2/R	3/5	4/R	5/R	2/R	3/6	3/R	R/R	5/7	3/R	2/R	5/R	2/R	5/R	5/11	5/8	110
4/15	3/10	7/9	7/10	5/R	6/7	4/11	10/R	9/R	6/R	R/R	4/R	1/4	4/8	5/6	4/6	4/12	3/7	86
12/R	7/R	4/6	12/13	8/10	8/12	7/14	7/8	7/R	R/R	8/11	R/R	3/D	12/14	3/8	7/13	8/9	9/17	36
14/16	8/9	3/R	9/R	9/R	10/R	8/17	11/R	6/R	4/R	4/R	7/9	6/12	7/9	7/15	R/R	7/6	R/R	35
8/10	R/R	8/R	R/R	R/R	13/14	3/R	12/14	8/11	7/R	9/12	8/11	5/R	11/15	11/12	9/12	13/R	12/R	16
6/7	R/R	R/R	6/11	7/R	9/11	R/R	9/R	12/R	9/R	14/R	R/R	R/R	10/R	10/R	8/11	10/R	R/R	11
11/13	11/R	11/R	14/15	11/R	15/R	10/13	13/R	10/13	8/R	10/13	10/12	11/R	13/R	13/14	10/15	14/18	11/13	1
17/R	12/13	10/R	16/R	12/13	16/R	12/15	15/16	14/R	R/R	15/R	D/D	9/10	R/R	17/R	16/R	16/R	14/15	0
18/R	14/R	12/13	R/R	R/R	17/R	16/R	17/18	15/R	R/R	16/R	R/R	13/R	NC/R	16/R	14/17	15/17	10/16	0

FORMULA ONE STATISTICS

STARTS

256	Riccardo Patrese
250	Michael Schumacher
235	Rubens Barrichello
212	David Coulthard
210	Gerhard Berger
208	Andrea de Cesaris
204	Nelson Piquet
201	Jean Alesi
199	Alain Prost
194	Michele Alboreto
187	Nigel Mansell
179	Giancarlo Fisichella
176	Graham Hill
175	Jacques Laffite
171	Niki Lauda
167	Jarno Trulli
165	Jacques Villeneuve
164	Thierry Boutsen
163	Ralf Schumacher
162	Mika Häkkinen
	Johnny Herbert
161	Ayrton Senna
159	Heinz-Harald Frentzen
158	Martin Brundle
	Olivier Panis
152	John Watson
149	René Arnoux
147	Eddie Irvine
	Derek Warwick
146	Carlos Reutemann
144	Emerson Fittipaldi
135	Jean-Pierre Jarier
132	Eddie Cheever
	Clay Regazzoni
128	Mario Andretti
126	Jack Brabham
123	Ronnie Peterson
119	Jenson Button
	Pierluigi Martini
117	Nick Heidfeld
116	Damon Hill
	Jacky Ickx
	Alan Jones
114	Keke Rosberg
	Patrick Tambay

OTHERS

105	Kimi Räikkönen
97	Juan Pablo Montoya
88	Fernando Alonso
87	Mark Webber
72	Takuma Sato
71	Pedro de la Rosa
	Felipe Massa
48	Christian Klien
37	Christijan Albers
	Tiago Monteiro
22	Vitantonio Liuzzi
18	Nico Rosberg
	Scott Speed
11	Robert Doornbos
7	Franck Montagny
	Sakon Yamamoto
6	Robert Kubica
4	Yuji Ide

CONSTRUCTORS

741	Ferrari
614	McLaren
533	Williams
490	Lotus
418	Tyrrell
409	Prost
394	Brabham
383	Arrows
359	Toro Rosso (formerly Minardi)
317	Benetton
268	Spyker MF1 (formerly Jordan)
235	BMW Sauber
230	March
211	Renault
197	BRM
171	Red Bull (formerly Stewart then Jaguar)
136	Honda Racing (formerly BAR)

OTHERS

88	Toyota
18	Super Aguri

WINS

91	Michael Schumacher
51	Alain Prost
41	Ayrton Senna
31	Nigel Mansell
27	Jackie Stewart
25	Jim Clark
	Niki Lauda
24	Juan Manuel Fangio
23	Nelson Piquet
22	Damon Hill
20	Mika Häkkinen
16	Stirling Moss
15	Fernando Alonso
14	Jack Brabham
	Emerson Fittipaldi
	Graham Hill
13	Alberto Ascari
	David Coulthard
12	Mario Andretti
	Alan Jones
	Carlos Reutemann
11	Jacques Villeneuve
10	Gerhard Berger
	James Hunt
	Ronnie Peterson
	Jody Scheckter
9	Rubens Barrichello
	Kimi Räikkönen
8	Denny Hulme
	Jacky Ickx
7	Rene Arnoux
	Juan Pablo Montoya

OTHERS

6	Ralf Schumacher
3	Giancarlo Fisichella
2	Felipe Massa
1	Jenson Button
	Jarno Trulli

CONSTRUCTORS

192	Ferrari
148	McLaren
113	Williams
79	Lotus
35	Brabham
33	Renault
27	Benetton
23	Tyrrell
17	BRM
16	Cooper
10	Alfa Romeo

OTHERS

4	Spyker MF1 (formerly Jordan)
1	Honda Racing (formerly BAR)
	Red Bull (formerly Stewart then Jaguar)

IN 2006

7	Fernando Alonso
	Michael Schumacher
2	Felipe Massa
1	Jenson Button
	Giancarlo Fisichella

CONSTRUCTORS

9	Ferrari
8	Renault
1	Honda Racing (formerly BAR)

WINS IN ONE SEASON

13	Michael Schumacher	2004
11	Michael Schumacher	2002
9	Nigel Mansell	1992
	Michael Schumacher	1995
	Michael Schumacher	2000
	Michael Schumacher	2001
8	Mika Häkkinen	1998
	Damon Hill	1996
	Michael Schumacher	1994
	Ayrton Senna	1988
7	Fernando Alonso	2005
	Fernando Alonso	2006
	Jim Clark	1963
	Alain Prost	1984
	Alain Prost	1988
	Alain Prost	1993
	Kimi Räikkönen	2005
	Michael Schumacher	2006
	Ayrton Senna	1991
	Jacques Villeneuve	1997

CONSTRUCTORS

15	Ferrari	2002
	Ferrari	2004
	McLaren	1988
12	McLaren	1984
	Williams	1986
11	Benetton	1995
10	Ferrari	2000
	McLaren	1989
	McLaren	2005
	Williams	1992
	Williams	1993

POLE POSITIONS

68	Michael Schumacher
65	Ayrton Senna
33	Jim Clark
	Alain Prost
32	Nigel Mansell
29	Juan Manuel Fangio
26	Mika Häkkinen
24	Niki Lauda
	Nelson Piquet
20	Damon Hill
18	Mario Andretti
	René Arnoux
17	Jackie Stewart
16	Stirling Moss
14	Fernando Alonso
	Alberto Ascari
	James Hunt
	Ronnie Peterson

OTHERS

13	Rubens Barrichello
	Juan Pablo Montoya
12	David Coulthard
11	Kimi Räikkönen
6	Ralf Schumacher
3	Jenson Button
	Giancarlo Fisichella
	Felipe Massa
	Jarno Trulli
1	Nick Heidfeld

CONSTRUCTORS

186	Ferrari
125	McLaren
	Williams
107	Lotus
50	Renault
39	Brabham
16	Benetton
14	Tyrrell
12	Alfa Romeo

OTHERS

3	Honda Racing (formerly BAR)
2	Spyker MF1 (formerly Jordan)
1	Red Bull (formerly Stewart then Jaguar)

IN 2006

6	Fernando Alonso
4	Michael Schumacher
3	Felipe Massa
	Kimi Räikkönen
1	Jenson Button
	Giancarlo Fisichella

CONSTRUCTORS

7	Ferrari
	Renault
3	McLaren
1	Honda Racing (formerly BAR)

FASTEST LAPS

75	Michael Schumacher
41	Alain Prost
30	Nigel Mansell
28	Jim Clark
25	Mika Häkkinen
24	Niki Lauda
23	Juan Manuel Fangio
	Nelson Piquet
21	Gerhard Berger
19	Damon Hill
	Stirling Moss
	Kimi Räikkönen
	Ayrton Senna
18	David Coulthard
15	Rubens Barrichello

	Clay Regazzoni
	Jackie Stewart
14	Jacky Ickx
13	Alberto Ascari
	Alan Jones
	Riccardo Patrese
12	René Arnoux
	Jack Brabham
	Juan Pablo Montoya
11	John Surtees
	OTHERS
9	Jacques Villeneuve
8	Fernando Alonso
	Ralf Schumacher
2	Giancarlo Fisichella
	Felipe Massa
1	Nico Rosberg
	CONSTRUCTORS
192	Ferrari
129	McLaren
	Williams
71	Lotus
40	Brabham
38	Benetton
27	Renault
20	Tyrrell
15	BRM
	Maserati
	OTHERS
2	Honda Racing (formerly BAR)
1	Toyota
	IN 2006
7	Michael Schumacher
5	Fernando Alonso
3	Kimi Räikkönen
2	Felipe Massa
1	Nico Rosberg
	CONSTRUCTORS
9	Ferrari
5	Renault
3	McLaren
1	Williams

POINTS

1369	Michael Schumacher
798.5	Alain Prost
614	Ayrton Senna
519	Rubens Barrichello
513	David Coulthard
485.5	Nelson Piquet
482	Nigel Mansell
420.5	Niki Lauda
420	Mika Häkkinen
386	Gerhard Berger
371	Fernando Alonso
360	Damon Hill
	Jackie Stewart
346	Kimi Räikkönen
324	Ralf Schumacher
310	Carlos Reutemann
307	Juan Pablo Montoya
289	Graham Hill
281	Emerson Fittipaldi
	Riccardo Patrese
277.5	Juan Manuel Fangio

274	Jim Clark
261	Jack Brabham
255	Jody Scheckter
248	Denny Hulme
246	Giancarlo Fisichella
242	Jean Alesi
	OTHERS
235	Jacques Villeneuve
223	Jenson Button
174	Jarno Trulli
107	Felipe Massa
79	Nick Heidfeld
69	Mark Webber
40	Takuma Sato
29	Pedro de la Rosa
14	Christian Klien
7	Tiago Monteiro
6	Robert Kubica
4	Christijan Albers
	Nico Rosberg
2	Vitantonio Liuzzi
	CONSTRUCTORS
3645.5	Ferrari
3145.5	McLaren
2512.5	Williams
1352	Lotus
925	Renault
887.5	Benetton
854	Brabham
617	Tyrrell
439	BRM
424	Prost
333	Cooper
306	Honda Racing (formerly BAR)
287	Spyker MF1 (formerly Jordan)
232	BMW Sauber
	OTHERS
150	Toyota
138	Red Bull (formerly Stewart then Jaguar)
39	Toro Rosso (formerly Minardi)

LAPS LED

5108	Michael Schumacher
2931	Ayrton Senna
2683	Alain Prost
2058	Nigel Mansell
1940	Jim Clark
1918	Jackie Stewart
1633	Nelson Piquet
1590	Niki Lauda
1490	Mika Häkkinen
1363	Damon Hill
1347	Juan Manuel Fangio
1164	Stirling Moss
1106	Graham Hill
957	Fernando Alonso
926	Alberto Ascari
895	David Coulthard
	OTHERS
722	Rubens Barrichello
638	Kimi Räikkönen
634	Jacques Villeneuve
605	Juan Pablo Montoya
401	Ralf Schumacher
208	Giancarlo Fisichella

156	Felipe Massa
147	Jarno Trulli
104	Jenson Button
5	Robert Kubica
	Mark Webber
	IN 2006
464	Fernando Alonso
366	Michael Schumacher
154	Felipe Massa
56	Giancarlo Fisichella
54	Kimi Räikkönen
25	Jenson Button
6	Juan Pablo Montoya
5	Robert Kubica
3	Mark Webber
2	Ralf Schumacher
	Jarno Trulli
	CONSTRUCTORS
520	Ferrari
	Renault
60	McLaren
25	Honda Racing (formerly BAR)
5	BMW Sauber
4	Toyota
3	Williams

MILES LED

14992	Michael Schumacher
8345	Ayrton Senna
7751	Alain Prost
6282	Jim Clark
5905	Nigel Mansell
5789	Juan Manuel Fangio
5692	Jackie Stewart
4820	Nelson Piquet
4475	Mika Häkkinen
4386	Niki Lauda
3939	Damon Hill
2962	Graham Hill
2851	Fernando Alonso
2821	Jack Brabham
2611	David Coulthard
	OTHERS
2167	Rubens Barrichello
1901	Kimi Räikkönen
1846	Jacques Villeneuve
1843	Juan Pablo Montoya
1202	Ralf Schumacher
673	Giancarlo Fisichella
452	Felipe Massa
375	Jarno Trulli
324	Jenson Button
18	Robert Kubica
14	Mark Webber
6	Takuma Sato
4	Nick Heidfeld
	IN 2006
1353	Fernando Alonso
1120	Michael Schumacher
447	Felipe Massa
191	Giancarlo Fisichella
165	Kimi Räikkönen
72	Jenson Button
20	Juan Pablo Montoya
18	Robert Kubica

9	Mark Webber
5	Ralf Schumacher
	Jarno Trulli
	CONSTRUCTORS
1799	Renault
1382	Ferrari
184	McLaren
72	Honda Racing (formerly BAR)
18	BMW Sauber
11	Toyota
9	Williams

DRIVERS' TITLES

7	Michael Schumacher
5	Juan Manuel Fangio
4	Alain Prost
3	Jack Brabham
	Niki Lauda
	Nelson Piquet
	Ayrton Senna
	Jackie Stewart
2	Fernando Alonso
	Alberto Ascari
	Jim Clark
	Emerson Fittipaldi
	Mika Häkkinen
	Graham Hill
1	Mario Andretti
	Giuseppe Farina
	Mike Hawthorn
	Damon Hill
	Phil Hill
	Denny Hulme
	James Hunt
	Alan Jones
	Nigel Mansell
	Jochen Rindt
	Keke Rosberg
	Jody Scheckter
	John Surtees
	Jacques Villeneuve

CONSTRUCTORS' TITLES

14	Ferrari
9	Williams
8	McLaren
7	Lotus
2	Brabham
	Cooper
	Renault
1	Benetton
	BRM
	Matra
	Tyrrell
	Vanwall

NB. To avoid confusion, the Renault stats listed are based on the team that evolved from Benetton in 2002 and include those stats that have happened since plus those from Renault's first spell in F1 between 1977 and 1985. The figures for Benetton and the Toleman team from which it metamorphosed in 1986 are listed as Benetton. Conversely, the stats for Jaguar include those of the Stewart team from which it evolved in 2000.